FAMILY OF GOD

Revised Edition

Essays on the Christian Trinity and the Scripture that presents God to mankind

Arthur Perkins

Family of God
Essays on the Christian Trinity and the Scripture
that presents God to mankind
Revised Edition

by Arthur Perkins

Signalman Publishing
www.signalmanpublishing.com
email: info@signalmanpublishing.com
Tampa, Florida

Scripture verses are taken from the King James Version of the Bible with straightforward updates made to the more archaic words and phrases, but only where the word or phrase and its replacement was obvious.

ISBN: 978-1-940145-83-9 (paperback)
978-1-940145-84-6 (ebook)

Signalman
Publishing

Printed in the United States of America

Also by Arthur Perkins

Buddy: Encounters with the Holy Spirit

Cathy: Encounters with the Holy Spirit

Jacob: Encounters with the Holy Spirit

Home, Sweet Heaven: Joining the Family of God

Marching to a Worthy Drummer: A Christian Layperson Speaks Out About the Holy Spirit

Uncle Art's Bible Favorites: A Study Guide to the Bible

Dedication

As in my Christian novels *Buddy, Cathy, Jacob,* and *Home, Sweet Heaven,* and in my nonfiction work *Marching to a Worthy Drummer,* I dedicate this work to my wife Carolyn, the joy of my life. We both dedicate this work, above all, to our God, and to our four daughters and their families.

Acknowledgements

I wish to extend a grateful, heartfelt thank-you to the following people who have been instrumental in the production of my books. First, to my God, whose loving character elicits my devotion and the thrill of learning and writing of His beautiful nature. Second, to my wonderful wife Carolyn, whose loving support in all matters of our happy marriage have given me added incentive and the freedom to pursue my writing endeavors. Third, to my brother Jon, whose support has been extremely helpful. Fourth, to my friend and publisher, John McClure of Signalman Publishing, for his enthusiasm and professionalism. I'm truly fortunate to be associated with him. I also wish to thank our pastor, F. David Lambert, ThD. While we don't always agree on every theological matter, we do agree on much, particularly on the divine inspiration and inerrancy of Scripture. I have learned much about God and the Church through his very thorough exposition of Scripture and Church doctrine.

Contents

Introduction

What does it mean to worship God? Should it mean to give lip service to God's majestic greatness, or should it run deeper than that? Church leaders for centuries have self-righteously presented to their flocks a God who resides in purity above gender while many secretly indulge in depraved sexual practices of their own. Does such disrespect toward God have anything whatever to do with worship, or rather does it not replace honor with dishonor? Does their lip service to God represent true worship, or is it another symptom of disrespect?

Despite thoughts to the contrary by those who neglect the most basic, essential notion of God, the Word of God in Judeo-Christian Scripture depicts a God who is the essence of love. That being the case, there is a profound disconnect between the pattern of formal worship and the personal intimacy desired by God within too many Churches.

That disconnect may exist to some degree even within those charismatic and Pentecostal Churches that view God in a manner similar to the mainstream Churches, for how can a person approach with the possessive intimacy of romantic love a God who is limited in His interaction with us by His lack of gender to nothing more than a benign but passionless approbation?

The good news is that our worship can be greater than it now is and can be far more meaningful to us, because God Himself does possess passion. He is fully capable of a romantic interaction with us, because He is indeed capable of experiencing the same within the Godhead Itself.

The bad news is that the current leaders of the Church, from the top on down to the pastoral level, appear unwilling to countenance any deviation from their understanding of who God is, an understanding that excludes gender or its associated passion from His attributes.

There is a reason for this intractability. The Church knows that it is proper to perceive Scripture as the inspired Word of God and the only reliable means of understanding who God really is. This assessment, of course, is accurate. Scripture is indeed the inspired Word of God and the only reliable means of understanding our Lord. But there's a caveat in that assessment, one that is shared by a good many Church authorities but not by others who tend to ignore the equally accurate understanding that the inspiration applies only to the original texts and not necessarily to the various versions and translations. That fact can be readily demonstrated through a quick review of the obvious differences between the original writings and their later translations as well as the divergence of thought among Christian sects and their leaders.

One such deviation from the original Scripture that remains with us today with a profound impact is the characterization of the Holy Spirit as weakly masculine with respect to the secondary attributes of gender, and genderless with respect to gender's primary attribute. This characterization is compatible with the versions and translations common to the Western Church, but evidence derived from current research strongly suggests that it does not represent the original Scriptural depiction of the Holy Spirit, which is of the feminine gender in original Old Testament and New Testament documents. There is additional evidence that this misrepresentation was deliberately introduced under a misguided attempt to purify the Church.

A primary purpose of this book is to promote an accurate understanding of God, and in particular the Holy Spirit, to the end that a more heartfelt pattern of worship will emerge within our Churches.

Additionally, while many Churches pay lip-service to the inerrancy of Scripture, a significant portion of their congregants deny it in their minds and hearts. They accept instead the seductive myths and lies embraced by secular society. Unquestioning adherence is given to Darwinian or post-Darwinian evolutionary theory, which is so contradictory to the creation account in Genesis. The understanding of biology is sufficiently mature to negate, on the basis of science alone, the viability of evolutionary theory and its partner, uniformitarianism with its associated enormous time intervals.

Another mythical secular contender with Genesis is the notion that Noah's Flood was of a local nature and probably rather gentle. It was not. Rather, as the Bible inferred and was confirmed by modern research, the Great Flood was an enormously violent event of planetary scale that came perilously close to destroying all life on earth.

Another purpose of this book is to confront these secular myths head-on with the objective of promoting a realistic understanding of God's Word in Scripture to the ultimate end that it receives the respect that it deserves.

PART ONE

The Nature of the Godhead

Contents to Part One

PREFACE TO PART ONE

The failure of Christian theologians to provide an *intuitively reasonable* answer to the question of why God should have a triune rather than a dual, quadrune, or singular nature has led to much misunderstanding, cultism and even hatred. Those who read in Deuteronomy 6:4 and 5 of the One God without a full understanding of what is meant by that must perform an unnatural mental exercise to include the persona of Jesus Christ as fully God along with the Father. Within the larger Christian community, the *Jesus only* movement rejects such an exercise altogether, insisting upon Jesus alone as God. Other branches of Christianity hold to similar forms of modalism, in which the form and function of a single God, at least as perceived by man, is situation-dependent. The Muslim faith also insists upon the Godhood of the Father alone. To the members of that religion, along with the Christian modalists, the alternative is polytheism. Given the standard Christian explanation of the Trinity, their rejection of the Trinitarian nature of God is difficult to fault.

Surely by noting this issue we have placed ourselves in the midst of a basic conflict that has failed to be settled in Christianity's two millenia. This is a human problem, not God's. As would be expected, a careful reading of Scripture reveals that God has furnished man with His own straightforward answer to the paradox of His triune nature. It is profound in its simplicity and astonishingly beautiful in form. In the second chapter of Genesis, Adam speaks thus:

> *And Adam said, This is now bone of my bones, and flesh of my flesh: she shall be called Woman, because she was taken out of man. Therefore shall a man leave his father and his mother, and shall cleave unto his wife: and they shall be one flesh.*

This passage was repeated by Jesus and later by Paul. In the contexts in which it was presented, it is obviously of importance to God. Could there be a significant relation between the unity of flesh in marriage and the unity of spirit, as was often claimed by Jesus, between The Father and Him, and, in fact, among the three Members of the Holy Trinity?

After almost two millennia, controversial issues remain within Christian theology and Church practice. Several councils have convened throughout the centuries to reconcile some of the more important of these concerns. To date they have failed in the most central issue of all: to develop a unified Christian-wide understanding of the Judeo-Christian God with respect to His basic character and attributes, one that is compatible with Scripture and which would be satisfactory to more than half of those believers who wished to search out His essential nature.

Ironically, one significant reason for this failure of consensus is the success of the early Church's attempt to reject all association of functional sexuality with God and the worship of Him. This endeavor went so far as to remove gender from the Godhead. The result, having been accepted within Christian thought and practice long since any understanding remained of why and how that came to be, continues inviolate for the vast majority of Christian sects. The difficulty with this extra-Scriptural tradition is that it is inherently contradictory to both Scripture and logic. Consequently, it is a recurring source of confusion of mind that encourages an indifference toward God.

The misguided attempt to purify the Church through the imposition of chastity upon God also has established a precedent for a rigidity of worship and an unthinking abhorrence of any deviation from the standard rote repetitions associated with the worship of God. Some sects actively attempt to counter that trend but even they, caught up as they are in that same early tradition, have been only partially successful at it.

The following chapters address the very real and immensely important issue of gender within the Godhead.

1
Something is Kind of Wrong Here

There's a story going around about a pest problem. It started when an elderly lady, kindly but misguided, began to bring a baggy with her to Church. The baggy was filled with nuts. The first week before services began she sat on a bench beneath an oak tree and fed the squirrels. By the fourth week, the cute little creatures, emboldened by her continuing largesse, started coming into the Church itself. They brought the entire squirrel neighborhood with them. By the sixth week the Church began to be overrun with them, and the pastor was distracted by the sight of them standing on their hind legs begging for nuts as he attempted to preach the sermon.

That week the pastor convened an evening meeting of the Church staff for the purpose of arriving at a means of getting rid of the problem. The discussion quickly reached an impasse, for nobody wanted to harm the innocent little animals.

Until one elder spoke up with a sure-fire solution. He was a genius, really. "Let's baptize them all!" he said.

They did so forthwith. After that the squirrels only showed up on Christmas and Easter.

The joke would be funnier if it didn't point out such a sad truth. The apathy of Church attendees in the Western nations is dreadful and getting worse so rapidly that one hesitates to call them Christians. In fact, many societies in which they are so comfortably embedded are being labeled post-Christian, and that trend is accelerating. But it's not their fault as much as it reflects the failures of their pastors, and of the seminaries from which the pastors emerged in such a feckless state that they have been unable to effectively counter a descent into depravity and a godless society. In societies where the population has grown soft and has become used to constant gratification in a multitude of ways, many Churches continue to attempt to supply their congregants with a variety of indulgences in the form of quick and easy enjoyment, providing entertainment in the form of contemporary music, secular-oriented lectures, and gratification of appetites in the form of sticky buns and lattes. Other Churches have followed suit by attempting to furnish a God who eschews guilt, offering heaven to everybody on the basis of their humanity. Yet other Churches have gone even farther than that, promising to their congregants a God of limitless benevolence, including health and riches beyond measure.

But most Church attendees possess enough common sense to realize that they've been duped when things don't measure up to the promises. Sooner or later, they leave the quick-appeal Church behind, refusing to play along with the mythical God they've been handed. According to polls, they've been leaving in droves.

The more noble among the Christian population are leaving their Churches for a different reason. Between the first rush of joy at recognizing the beauty of the salvation story and the call to baptism, the sincere neophyte Christian has absorbed several sermons and learned a bit about Church doctrine. His take-home from this information often will tamp down his enthusiasm, as its typical dryness and lack of joy and, especially, the absence of any meaningful demonstration of the love of God toward man, may not be anything like what he first thought that God represented. By the time he gets baptized, he may well be on that bleak path toward apathy, for the typical pastor describes nothing about the nature of God that would evoke the love toward Him that He deserves as a divine Parent and a future romantic Partner.

God is great. We get that. He's so very much bigger than we are that he could treat us any way He pleases, wherever and whenever and however He wanted to. Some people think that God acts upon that largeness in capricious ways. In reading Richard Dawkins' book *The God Delusion*, we certainly get the impression that God is cruel, a terrible thought from which Dawkins seeks comfort in the notion that God doesn't exist.

In the Second World War the Marines weren't done after securing Guadalcanal, Peleliu and Tarawa. Despite the immense casualty rate in those battles and the horrors of protracted, in-your-face conflict against a rabid enemy, they weren't given a pass back into civilian life after the completion of their courageous stands on those fields of battle. Instead, they were called upon afterwards to go onto other killing grounds. Iwo Jima, Guam, Saipan and Okinawa lay ahead, waiting to claim yet more lives. The famous Eighth Air Force in Europe faced the same terrible, unending repetition of danger. They were first told that they could leave combat behind after twenty-five missions into Germany with their B-17 bombers. But as the attrition increased, that number went up, first to thirty, then thirty-five, and after that, fifty missions, in each of which they faced increasingly unpleasant odds against survival.

Some people think that God operates in the same way. In a college English class one of our books portrayed God as taking delight in persecuting a poor, miserable soul who was given the task of mowing a lawn, after which he could do whatever he wanted. The catch was that the lawn was so enormous that by the time he finished, the lawn needed to be mowed again. As the poor fellow realized his plight, "God" clapped His hands in glee and said "Let's do that again!"

Perhaps, as such people think, we could be nothing but toys in His hand that He likes to step on and break. But we're not, because He has an attribute that eclipses that size difference, and permits us to trust that He's altogether good rather than bad. That attribute is His most essential quality, love. God *is* love, according to 1 John 4:16:

> *And we have known and believed the love that God hath*
> *to us. God is love, and he that dwelleth in love dwelleth*
> *in God, and God in him.*

How can we know that? Are we just whistling in the wind, hoping in fear without any certainty that this quality of God is true, and in abundant measure?

No. We have proof to the contrary of the most amazingly generous sort: Jesus died a painful death on the cross for our sakes. We also know from Paul's description in Ephesians 5 of Christ's possessive, tender, romantic love toward His Church that He'll be treating His wife quite kindly.

Not that He won't use pain or misfortune here in this material
world to keep us on the right track. He's done it to me. In fact, at
times He takes every Christian to the woodshed. The Bible tells us
that. But He does it for a purpose, and that purpose has a lot to do
with love. Excerpts from Hebrews Chapters 11 and 12 clearly point
us to the loving reason for our own sacrifices of pain and tears.

> *By faith Moses, when he was come to years, refused to be
> called the son of Pharaoh's daughter, choosing rather to
> suffer affliction with the people of God than to enjoy the
> pleasures of sin for a season, esteeming the reproach of
> Christ greater riches than the treasures in Egypt, for he
> had respect unto the recompense of the reward. By faith
> he forsook Egypt, not fearing the wrath of the king; for
> he endured, as seeing him who is invisible. Through faith
> he kept the Passover, and the sprinkling of blood, lest he
> that destroyed the first-born should touch them. By faith
> they passed through the Red Sea as by dry land, which
> the Egyptians, attempting to do, drowned.*

> *By faith, the walls of Jericho fell down, after they were
> compassed about seven days. By faith the harlot, Rahab,
> perished not with them that believed not, when she had
> received the spies with peace.*

> *And what more shall I say? For the time would fail
> me to tell of Gideon, and of Barak, and of Samson,
> and of Jephthah, of David also, and Samuel, and of
> the prophets, who, through faith, subdued kingdoms,
> wrought righteousness, obtained promises, stopped the
> mouths of lions, quenched the violence of fire, escaped
> the edge of the sword, out of weakness were made strong,
> became valiant in fight, turned to flight the armies of the
> aliens. Women received their dead raised to life again,
> and others were tortured, not accepting deliverance, that
> they might obtain a better resurrection: and others had
> trial of cruel mockings and scourgings, yea, moreover,
> of bonds and imprisonment; they were stoned, they were
> sawn asunder, were tested, were slain with the sword;
> they wandered about in sheepskins and goatskins; being
> destitute, afflicted, tormented (of whom the world was
> not worthy); they wandered in deserts, and in mountains,
> and in dens and caves of the earth. And these all, having
> received witness through faith, received not the promise,*

God having provided some better thing for us, that they without us should not be made perfect.

Wherefore, seeing we also are compassed about with so great a cloud of witnesses, let us lay aside every weight, and the sin which doth so easily beset us, and let us run with patience the race that is set before us, looking unto Jesus, the author and finisher of our faith, who for the joy that was set before him endured the cross, despising the shame, and is set down at the right hand of the throne of God. For consider him that endured such contradiction of sinners against himself, lest ye be wearied and faint in your minds.

Ye have not yet resisted unto blood, striving against sin. And ye have forgotten the exhortation which speaketh unto you as unto children, My son, despise not thou the chastening of the Lord, nor faint when thou art rebuked of him; for whom the Lord loveth he chasteneth, and scourgeth every son whom he receiveth. If ye endure chastening, God dealeth with you as with sons; for what son is he whom the father chasteneth not? But if ye be without chastisement, of which all are partakers, then are ye bastards, and not sons. Furthermore, we have had fathers of our flesh who corrected us, and we gave them reverence. Shall we not much rather be in subjection unto the Father of spirits, and live? For they verily for a few days chastened us after their own pleasure, but he for our profit, that we might be partakers of his holiness. Now no chastening for the present seemeth to be joyous, but grievous; nevertheless, afterward it yieldeth the peaceable fruit of righteousness unto them who are exercised by it.

Wherefore, lift up the hands which hang down, and the feeble knees; and make straight paths for your feet, lest that which is lame be turned out of the way; but let it rather be healed.

In today's lingo, God tells us that discipline, while sometimes painful, is for our own good, particularly in our future relationship with Jesus – so we need to suck it up and deal with it.

But we are not without help in that endeavor. Here, as I noted in *Marching to a Worthy Drummer,* is where the beautiful nature of the Holy Spirit comes into play, by indwelling the believer to comfort him as would a mother to reconcile the loving nature of God with the suffering that the believer must face to strip him of his selfishness and thus render him capable of the love necessary for him to enjoy full communication and companionship with God. God is noble, and He wishes to extend that nobility to us as His companions in marriage. Converting the selfishness of our fallen natures into nobility takes some doing. Much of it isn't pleasant, but according to Romans 8:28 the end will be worth it.

It's probable that the typical understanding of the Church's initial meeting with Jesus Christ in the spiritual realm will include our individual possession of handsome bodies and clean, white clothing. Given some key passages of Scripture, the actuality may be quite different. We might approach Him instead with dirty, tattered clothing and bleeding bodies disfigured from abuse, evoking from Him an outpouring of compassion and a rush to heal us and clothe us in pure white linen.

And, of course, if our spiritual Husband Jesus is of such a noble, loving nature, should He not deserve a wife having those same qualities? If our spiritual Mother-in-Law possesses that same quality of selfless nobility to the delight of the Father, should we not take joy in emulating Her?

Yet, some people stick with the false Churches, not realizing that the far better God described in Scripture even exists. Earnestly wishing to understand God in some meaningful way, they fail to appreciate that no amount of music or droll pulpit wit can begin to compensate for messages so profoundly lacking regarding the true nature of God as way too many Church attendees are fed each week by their misinformed pastors.

Whether our understanding is informed or misinformed, we love to put the little we do know about God into a box of generalities and close the lid, opening it only to answer confrontational issues, and then very reluctantly. If we encounter something that doesn't seem to fit what's already in the box, well, we don't even have to lift the lid. We just toss the offensive idea out altogether. Like the scientist who, early in the twentieth century, proclaimed that the era of scientific discoveries was past, that now all science had to occupy itself with was cleanup work, we Christians are prone to thinking that everything about God that is knowable is already known.

I had a good friend, Bill, who was given some venison sausage by another friend one year and enjoyed it so much that the next year he planned to bag his own deer. He bought a beautiful, expensive rifle to do that job, and paid plenty to the government for the necessary tags. He lived in a rural area, so he didn't have to travel far to get into the forest. I went along with him on some of his treks, but I had a hunch that his lack of experience would hinder his productivity as a hunter. Unfortunately, I was right. He lost some weight tramping out in the woods, but by the time the season ended he had nothing else to show for it. Grumbling and out of sorts for his miserable performance, he put away his rifle to address other pursuits. Coming home at night the very next week, he pulled into the driveway and saw a deer. He couldn't stop fast enough to avoid hitting it.

The week after that I was on a ladder underneath the roof of our patio, touching up the paint on the bracing upon which the clear plastic sheets of the roof rested. As I applied the brush to the wood, it moved. The entire structure was shaking, which, of course, triggered in my mind the dreaded word *earthquake!* Spurred by the loud, chaotic crashing noise that accompanied the shaking, I jumped off the ladder and grabbed Carolyn, who also was underneath the patio roof, and together we fled from underneath the structure to open ground. But while the noise continued, the ground wasn't shaking. We looked up to see a young deer, just out of the fawn stage, slip again and fall crashing onto the plastic, after which it got to the edge of the roof and jumped down to the ground below. There it stood, stunned from the fall. A minute later it shook itself and bounded away. Apparently, the animal had walked into our garage and out the back door, jumping over the railing of our outside walkway and onto the roof, which still carries the imprints of its hoofs.

Life's unpredictable like that, but I don't think God is that way. The problem is with our understanding of Him. I seriously doubt that He likes being stuck in the boxes our shallow treatment of His Word often places Him. There's one box in particular that I suspect He may find odious – the mainstream Church's concept of His lack of gender. It is this issue, more than any other, that makes loving Him so difficult to many Christians.

How did that come to happen? Because we have been misled *en masse* by our Churches, both Catholic and Protestant. In our shallow acceptance of the basically genderless God that the Church has handed us, we are bereft of the kind of understanding of Him that can lead to a fervent love. How can we love Him if we can't even understand how a Trinitarian God can also be one, or what ways one Member of the Godhead may differ from the others?

Looking at Christianity's working relationship with God, it becomes obvious that the Church's treatment of gender represents a broken link between ourselves and God, fracturing our ability to know Him in the terms that He Himself has given us with the kind of intuition that promotes love – love with the fervor that He commands us to offer Him.

I'm going to get down into the weeds on this issue – it's that important. The kind of love that Jesus spoke of in Matthew 22 cannot, repeat *cannot*, be obtained by the exercise of will. Try as you might, you are simply unable to evoke heartfelt love through intellectual pressure. God through Jesus calls us to love him as a spouse, not a mere friend. *Agape* love just doesn't cut it. Our love of God must be intuitive, of the same substance as our love toward our own human spouses. That kind of love involves a possessive imprinting, obtainable only through the God-given gift of *eros*. I suppose some marriages are made on the basis of intellectual will, but I wouldn't give a nickel for the happiness they bring to their partners in, at most, an *agape* setting. Most of us expect much more than that out of marriage, and God does too.

I believe that the primitive Christians did indeed love God in the manner that He commanded. So did the eighteenth-century Moravian Church that established and so successfully developed the city of Bethlehem, Pennsylvania and sent equally successful missionaries throughout the world in the love of God. But other examples are few and far between, if any exist at all, because the Church has deliberately excluded that kind of love from our relationship with God.

Tradition and creeds, unfortunately, often misrepresent God to such an extent that they place stumbling blocks on our pathway to understating Him. There is only one reliable source of information regarding God, and that is His Word to us, Scripture, contained in the Old and New Testaments. Scripture has been acknowledged by both Paul in 2 Timothy 3:16 and 17, and by Peter in 2 Peter 1:20 and 21, to have been inspired by God:

All scripture is given by inspiration of God, and is profitable for doctrine, for instruction in righteousness, that the man of God may be perfect, thoroughly furnished unto all good works.

Knowing this first, that no prophecy of the scripture is of any private interpretation. For the prophecy came not at any time by the will of man, but holy men of God spoke as they were moved by the Holy Spirit.

While it is naturally true that the indwelling Holy Spirit seeks to bring open-minded, earnestly-seeking Christians to a proper interpretation of Scripture, it is Scripture and Scripture alone that gives us the capability through understanding to love God. In fact, Jesus commanded us to do just that, and with fervor. Having been asked which is the greatest commandment in the law, He echoed in Matthew 22:37 and 38 Moses' words in Deuteronomy 6:5:

You shall love the Lord, your God, with all your heart, and with all your soul, and with all your mind.

The Holy Spirit will never place an understanding of God at odds with Scripture. Paul demonstrated that in his approval, in Acts 17:10-12, of the Bereans verifying in Scripture the truth of his exhortations:

And the brethren immediately sent away Paul and Silas by night unto Berea, who, coming there, went into the synagogue of the Jews. These were more noble than those in Thessalonica, in that they received the word with all readiness of mind, and searched the scriptures daily, whether these things were so. Therefore, many of them believed; also of honorable women who were Greeks, and of men, not a few.

While it is accepted truth, as Peter claimed, that the messages of those who were moved by the Holy Spirit to contribute to the Word of God through the pen are considered to be infallible, we have found that the various translations of the original words do not enjoy the same status. The infallibility of the original message is demonstrable through a number of features of the Bible. One such item is Scripture's remarkable internal consistency. Another is the amazing accuracy of ancient prophecies that have come to pass. My favorite among these prophecies is Ezekiel's forecast a half-millennium before Christ of the date of Israel's return from the Diaspora to nationhood in 1948. To the very day, as asserted by the late Grant Jeffrey, the scholar who uncovered this astonishing fact.

Just as the accuracy of the originals demonstrates infallibility, so the demonstrable errors of the versions and translations point to their fallibility. Recently a new version of Scripture called the Pure Bible has come out with the claim that its translation from Hebrew to English is superior to its predecessors. One Bible scholar is said to have wept at the difference in interpretation, having been terribly misled by the earlier versions.

Most theologians don't go that far. While they generally acknowledge the multitude of errors in translation, they downplay their importance, claiming them all to be trivial as to substance.

Unfortunately, as we have seen, not all of the misrepresentations of God are trivial, and some of these misunderstandings had preceded the birth of the Church. Had the pre-Christian Jews been given an accurate understanding of Old Testament Scripture by their religious leaders, they would have recognized Jesus as their Messiah without thought or controversy. Jesus Himself implied as much.

The sincere follower of Jesus must keep in mind that important caveat to the digestion of Scripture toward a useful understanding of God: in a few very important areas the Word must be the original autograph to possess the guarantee of truth. The various versions and translations are known to have errors, even some that have been deliberately introduced by those who thought they were doing God a favor.

2
A Brief History Lesson

Say what? Errors deliberately introduced into Scripture? By Christians? Christians who supposedly have been endowed with the wisdom of the indwelling Holy Spirit? How can such a claim be possible?

It's even worse than that. The Judeo-Christian God who has been handed down to us through our Churches is distressingly different than a thorough understanding of Scripture reveals to us about Him. To understand how that disconnect came about, we need to learn a bit about the Church's history.

The earliest Church, upon its birth on the first Pentecost after Jesus' resurrection, seems to have had it all together. Its members, manifesting the gifts with which they were endowed with the indwelling Holy Spirit, lived a communal life of sharing in their love of God and each other. These first Christians were Jewish, like the Jesus whom they followed. Soon, however, through the leading of God they came to accept the addition of Gentiles into their group. They understood through the indwelling Spirit, as Paul was to tell them later in the third chapter of his letter to the Galatians, that spiritually there was no distinction between Jew and Greek.

It didn't take long for satan to hurl a wrench into the works. It is common knowledge among committed Christians that the Bible, as the Word of God, was inerrant in the original. Those who were driven by God to contribute to Scripture spoke not from themselves, but by the Holy Spirit. But almost from the beginning of the Church, other people spoke on behalf of a God whom they misunderstood, speaking not from God, but from themselves. Many of these misinformed individuals are revered as Church Fathers to this day. One of the worst anti-semites was Martin Luther, to whom Hitler on occasion referred for justification of his genocide of the Jews. Although in fairness to Luther, it should be noted that his anti-Semitism emerged after his physical and mental health had deteriorated significantly with age.

Following the Bar Kochba revolt in the early second century, the Jews and the Gentiles had a falling-out, after which the Church came to be dominated by Gentiles. Claiming to cherish Scripture, they turned away from it in ignorance. Despite Paul's clear assertion in Romans 11 that God would not forsake the Jews, a long succession of Church Fathers taught that God had rejected the Jews, replacing them with the Church in His benevolent promises. In many so-called mainstream Churches, the same is still taught today in the name of "replacement theology."

Not very long after that, these same "saints," not having read important passages of Scripture like Daniel 12, in which God explicitly states that not everything in Scripture could be understood by all generations of Christians, arrogantly decided that they could somehow understand the Book of Revelation regardless of the time in which they found themselves. Consequently, they took it upon themselves to allegorize the words of Revelation, overgeneralizing the plain text into passages of "higher moral meaning". Augustine, a highly-revered saint of the Church, was one of the worst offenders in this matter. Our own generation, finally possessing the technology so recently acquired to interpret Revelation as readily-understandable plain text, scoffs at the haughty, self-serving naivete of their theological predecessors. Or at least they should.

Scripture is inerrant in the original, although it is not necessarily inerrant in the numerous copies and versions. Where these various versions err, the inaccuracy is not necessarily trivial. In at least one case, the gender of the Holy Spirit, the misunderstanding is grave.

The femininity of the Holy Spirit was a common feature of early Christian belief. Examples of this include the Sinaitic Palimpsest, and the Book of Wisdom, in both of which the Holy Spirit is overtly identified as feminine. The Gospel of the Hebrews, also in use among early Christians and since lost, also recognized the Holy Spirit as feminine according to early Christian writers who quoted this work. In addition, language scholar and theologian Dr. Nettelhorst has found that in the Old Testament the Holy Spirit was treated as feminine in the original Hebrew, a fact that probably was understood by the early Christians. Dr. Johannes Van Oort, another language scholar and theologian, has uncovered evidence as well that the early Christians understood the Holy Spirit to be feminine.

The early Church, however, was strongly influenced by the surrounding secular society. This distancing of Christians from society, together with other more personal factors, eventually led to the abandonment of the notion of femininity within the Judeo-Christian Godhead.

Historically, we know much about the interaction of Christianity with secular society throughout the centuries since that first Pentecost following Jesus' resurrection. Of particular importance to the early Church was the off-and-on persecutions of Christians, initially by the Jewish religious authorities of the Sanhedrin against Christians of their own Jewish origins who were based in Jerusalem. This threat largely ceased with the sacking of Jerusalem by the Roman Fifteenth Legion in 70 A.D. With the removal of organized Jewish adversaries, the Roman government, supported by the secular society, became the primary persecutor of Christians.

To make matters worse, the alienation of Christians from secular society due to their persecution was amplified out of all proportion by the legendary debauchery of the Roman society with which they were surrounded. The secular community of that time had abandoned propriety, much like we in the Western world are in the process of doing after having largely cast off our God.

Prior to the legitimizing of Christianity in the fourth century, the suffering of the early Christians under persecution and their alienation from Roman society may have forged in their minds a repudiation of everything that the secular world stood for. Like fundamentalist Christians of today, they saw their religion as standing above the moral filth of Roman society, of which they had much to frown upon. The various Roman religions worshiped Gods of far lesser character than the Christian Godhead, and their services were marked by sexual indulgences of unspeakable coarseness. Roman society itself was characterized by a large measure of depravity.

Out of this disgust with society at large, the Christian community, led by highly-committed (but not altogether Bible-savvy) leaders, acted to expand further upon the distance between itself and the secular world. Christians perceived their religion as uniquely noble, an attribute of character that they found profoundly lacking in their secular contemporaries. Over-reacting to the rampant abuse of sexuality taking place around them, they began to consider all sexuality with contempt. They went overboard to the extent of equating purity with chastity.

The Church suffered under intermittent Roman persecutions up to 313 A.D., the ten-year period from 303 to 313 under Emperor Diocletian being particularly harsh. The lot of the Christians improved rather abruptly after that persecution. In 313, Roman tolerance of Christianity was declared by Emperor Constantine 1 through his Edict of Milan. The Church increased as a formal, state-approved institution following that momentous event, becoming the preeminent faith under Emperor Theodosius 1, who formally established Christianity as the state religion through the Edict of Thessalonica in 380 A.D.

A fundamental objective of Christianity as it became the new state religion under Constantine was to cleanse itself of all connotations of sexuality. In this goal, the movement to purify the Church was helped along by the increasingly odd, offbeat direction that Gnostic theology was taking, causing the more mainstream Church to distance herself from this sect. Among the beliefs attributed to Christian Gnosticism was the platonic notion of salvation through knowledge, or gnosis. Another was the notion of dualism, asserting that the spiritual world was basically good, while the material world was basically evil. Along with those beliefs was a complex, twisted and illogical description of the nature of God and His creation. The mainstream rejection of Gnosticism, along with its understanding of the femininity of the Holy Spirit, helped lay the groundwork for the later influence of Augustine in the fourth century and Jerome Zanchius in the sixteenth century toward maintaining the removal of gender from God.

The Gnostic sect was prominent during the early years of the formation of Christianity and enjoyed a large following, particularly in Alexandria. In those early years prior to Constantine the Gnostic community, in which its inclusivity allowed women to be active participants, conformed to most basic Christian beliefs, which included the original Jewish understanding of the Holy Spirit as feminine according to early Hebrew versions of Genesis, Job and Judges as well as a variety of Old Testament passages.

But then the Christian Gnostic sect, disgusted with the tampering of sacred Scripture that replaced a feminine Holy Spirit with a weakly masculine one, went overboard in their rejection of it. They responded by distancing themselves from the mainstream New Testament documentation, which itself, while remaining in a variety of differing and sometimes contradictory forms regarding some issues, was becoming increasingly accepted as canonical. In the process, this sect also distanced itself from major elements of Christian doctrine and reverted to its pagan roots, embracing some very complex and illogical doctrines. Irenaeus' witty discussions of Gnostic doctrine are sometimes hilarious, as can be seen from the following example, in which Irenaeus (130-202 A.D.) discusses Marcion's account of the creation of the earth's waters:

> Now what follows from all this? No light tragedy comes out of it, as the fancy of every man among them pompously explains, one in one way, and another in another, from what kind of passion and from what element being derived its origin. They have good reason, it seems to me, why they should not feel inclined to teach these things to all in public, but only to such as are able to pay a high price for an acquaintance with such profound mysteries. For these doctrines are not at all similar to those of which our Lord said, 'Freely ye have received, freely give.' They are, on the contrary, abstruse, and portentous, and profound mysteries, to be got at only with great labour by such as are in love with falsehood. For who would not expend [all] that he possessed, if only he might learn in return, that from the tears of the enthymesis of the Æon involved in passion, seas, and fountains, and rivers, and every liquid substance derived its origin; that light burst forth from her smile; and that from her perplexity and consternation the corporeal elements of the world had their formation?

> I feel somewhat inclined myself to contribute a few hints towards the development of their system. For when I

perceive that waters are in part fresh, such as fountains,
rivers, showers, and so on, and in part salt; such as those
in the sea, I reflect with myself that all such waters cannot
be derived from her tears, inasmuch as these are of a
saline quality only. It is clear, therefore, that the waters
which are salt are alone those which are derived from her
tears. But it is probable that she, in her intense agony and
perplexity, was covered with perspiration. And hence,
following our notion, we may conceive that fountains
and rivers, and all the fresh water in the world, are due
to this source. For it is difficult, since we know that all
tears are of the same quality, to believe that waters both
salt and fresh proceeded from them. The more plausible
supposition is, that some are from her tears, and some
from her perspiration. And since there are also in the
world certain waters which are hot and acrid in their
nature, thou must be left to guess their origin, how and
whence. Such are some of the results of their hypothesis.

Scripture as we know it was largely established by the middle
of the third century, and was formally adopted as canon soon after
Christianity became the state religion in 380 A.D. Interestingly, the
scholar Jerome, who translated Hebrew Scripture into Latin and
completed the Vulgate Bible in 405 A.D., often lamented over the
number of various Christian documents used in the Churches that
differed with respect to content.

At some point between the second and fourth centuries A.D., in a
possibly gradual manner, the mainstream Church of the time began
to refer to the Holy Spirit with the now-ubiquitous pronoun "He"
rather than "She." The motivation probably was an outgrowth of
the desire to remove sexuality from God in an attempt to elevate
the new Christian religion above the sexual filth of the prevailing
worship of pagan gods and goddesses.

The formulation of Church doctrine at the Council of Nicaea remains
among the most important regarding the issue of the Holy Spirit's
gender. It was here that seriously-conflicting views of the Godhead
came into play. The Church leadership had at that time attained to the
newfound status of acceptability. But as they attempted to establish
a unified Church doctrine they had to contend with the controversies
associated with the Arian and Gnostic positions, the pressure of
persecution from which the Church had so recently emerged, the

variety of differing texts that were in use in Christian services, and the pressure of the Roman society within which they had to live.

After he legitimized Christianity, Constantine gathered together at Nicaea Christian theologians from around the empire to address a number of competing views of God, and in particular the nature of the Godhead, including that of Jesus and the Holy Spirit. In that council, convened in 325 A.D., a multitude of positions were debated upon amidst heated controversy and eventually declared to be heretical. Rejected formulations of God's nature included Docetism and Arianism. This council established significant elements of Church doctrine that are still adhered to today in many mainstream Churches.

During the fourth-century debates over Christian doctrine, and particularly at the Council of Nicaea in 325 A.D., a number of divergent views were hotly debated upon. By that time, the Gnostic sect, with its strange views that often clashed with the basics of the Christian faith, was declared to be heretical and tossed out along with their belief in a feminine Holy Spirit. Other divergent views, including Arianism, also were debated upon, with the same pronouncement of heresy. The debate over and rejection as heresy of a number of opposing viewpoints of the faith must have been an exhausting experience for the Church leadership, probably akin to the sharp polarization of Republican and Democratic members of congress in America and their ensuing cross-aisle rancor in recent times. It isn't a stretch to theorize that the weary leadership at some point simply called for an abrupt halt to the debate and imposed their own most welcome controversy-ending pronouncements as to what was acceptable doctrine and what was not. In the process, I suspect, the Gnostics' view of a feminine Holy Spirit got tossed out with the rest of their doctrines while a (weakly) masculine view of the Holy Spirit prevailed, particularly as it supported a removal of sexuality from the Godhead. Perhaps this enormously important pronouncement regarding the Holy Spirit's gender was qualified by the participants, who may have promised to themselves a more thorough investigation of the subject later under more peaceful circumstances. Then, as would be expected, the urgency of the follow-on investigation of the matter diminished with the simple passage of time.

Lively discussion over Church doctrine continued into the Fifth Century A.D., with the convening of over a dozen councils. These included the councils of Carthage, Chalcedon, Ephesus, Hippo and Tours.

Eventually all of the original concerns regarding the viability of the topic and the motivations behind the pronouncements were forgotten. The original pronouncements became cast in the concrete of Church tradition, residing beyond question forevermore. The stripping of Her femininity from the Holy Spirit became established Church doctrine. The versions of New Testament canon in which the Holy Spirit was referred to as "He" prevailed despite the confusion and eventual apathy that the switch created.

By the time that the highly-respected scholar Augustine (354-430 A.D.) arrived on the scene, having been converted to Christianity and ready to expound forth on the topic of sexuality in man and God, the issue already been settled for the most part. Augustine's contribution simply supplied additional cement to the established edifice of God's genderlessness. Augustine's position on the matter reflected his repulsion of his own dissolute pre-Christian years in the enjoyment of the depravity of the surrounding society, which continued on after the Roman state's tolerance of Christianity.

Christianity has endured disagreements and splits over doctrine for much of her history, including the Great Schism of 1064 between Western and Eastern Churches. This split was largely due to the Filioque, which was the Western Church's insertion of the phrase "and the Son" to the creedal statement of the procession of the Holy Spirit from the Father. The later Catholic/Protestant split in the sixteenth century was initiated by Martin Luther in response to his observation of the magnitude of corruption within the Catholic leadership. This parting of the ways was followed by a multitude of theological differences within the various Protestant denominations.

Much later than the Western/Eastern split, when virtually all thought within the Church regarding a gendered God had been removed along with an understanding of how that had come to be, Medieval Italian cleric Jerome Zanchius (1516-1590), a near-contemporary of Martin Luther who post-dated Zanchius by thirty-odd years, offered a pretentious tome entitled *The Doctrine of Absolute Predestination*, which attempted to state with scholarly precision the prevailing viewpoint on the nature of God. This book was snatched up and embraced as holy writ by the Reformed Church, a conservative Protestant offshoot of Christianity. Zanchius is still revered within that sect. If other mainline denominations differ with respect to Zanchius' teachings, they fail to speak up about it. The entire issue of gender and anything related to it seems to be rather a taboo subject within the Church in general.

Zanchius became a bellwether of the descent into ignorance of the Church's misunderstanding of God's actual nature. His passionless God possesses a remote grandeur that overshadows what 1 John 4:8 defines as His greatest attribute, love. This remote perfection, in opposition to the general tenor of Scripture, supports a view of God in which intimacy with Him is replaced with alienation and indifference toward Him.

In opposition to Zanchius, Scripture paints a far more beautiful picture of God, depicting His majestic glory as His willingness to give up the majesty of greatness and power in favor of a love of great fullness and depth. The Gospels appear to support this view, depicting Jesus Christ (as God) as a Being full of the attributes of love as we know it, including passion. Examples that come to mind include His weeping over Jerusalem and Lazarus and His ordeal in the garden of Gethsemane. It is difficult to picture the risen Jesus talking to His followers on the road to Emmaus (Luke 24) in the context of Zanchius' notion of God's remote perfection.

Zanchius' definition of God not only suppressed His most important attribute, but continues to inhibit those to whom Scripture was written from loving Him back. This is a serious issue because it runs counter to His Great Commandment to love Him with all our hearts, and our souls and our minds.

Controversies regarding Bible canon continued until recently, with the removal of the Books of Wisdom and Sirach by Martin Luther from canon in his 1534 version of the Bible. He also unsuccessfully attempted to remove the Books of Hebrews, James, Jude and Revelation. The Book of Wisdom is still accepted canon within the Catholic Church.

Many of the contentious issues that have fractured the Church into a multitude of denominations exist within Christianity to this day. Some recent differences have arisen over the degree to which Churches adhere to Scripture in the face of intellectual disputes over the origins of Scripture and social issues like the LGBQT movement. The most troubling issue facing the modern Church is the apathy of its congregants. This sad state should be no surprise to the thoughtful Christian, given the alienation of man from God due to the stripping away of the family nature of the Godhead.

The collateral damage to our understanding of the Godhead, having once occurred, was probably maintained through all these centuries under a different mechanism.

One very hot summer day in southern California, my wife and I found ourselves in the high desert north of Los Angeles. By the time we reached the town of Baker we were on empty, so we pulled into the nearest gas station. Back then, so long ago that I can hardly remember it, most gas stations were full service. This station was no exception. The attendant walked in front of the car and motioned for me to release the hood latch. He lifted it, looked under it for several moments, and emerged with a frown on his face. "Mister," he said with grave concern, "I'm afraid you have a real problem. Your engine is leaking oil and it's real bad."

I'll give him this – he was a good actor. He should have been in Hollywood. What he didn't appreciate was that with the hood raised there was a gap through which I could myself see under the hood. What I saw there was a hand that came into my field of view. The hand was holding an oil can. The thumb was fiddling with the plunger, going up and down while oil jetted out of the can onto my engine, making a real mess.

If I hadn't been so hot I would have reacted quicker and flashed out of the car to slam the hood down on his scrawny red neck. I'm glad I didn't. Starting the car, I just told him to get out of the way while I peeled rubber out of the station.

Had I asked him why he would do such an evil thing, he almost certainly would have replied that he had seven hungry kids and a wife to feed. The issue would have been survival.

That's often why bad things don't get fixed. That's especially the case when bad things are accepted as good and proper, which returns us to the topic of how the misunderstanding of the gendered nature of the Godhead was maintained for so many centuries. Almost two millennia ago, the attribute of gender was excised from God out of a misguided desire to purify the Church. In the centuries since that happened, the supposed genderlessness of God had become an integral element of Church tradition. The back story of that change was completely forgotten.

As time went on the Church declined, its original nobility and fervor of worship having departed. In its place a different kind of Church leader emerged, for whom self-service was the norm. To this type so distant from the nobility pleasing to God, the Church and its followers became useful tools toward the accumulation of wealth. Stories of the malfeasance of Popes and bishops are commonplace; the accounts are readily accessible. Much of John Foxe's *Christian Martyrs of the World* is devoted to presenting examples of true Christians who suffered greatly at the hands of their religious betters for the sake of ego and greed, a motivation that was present during the terrible Inquisition.

Yet there almost certainly were theologians in every generation who put more thought into the nature of the Godhead than the casual churchgoer. Why didn't these people speak up?

Maybe, being respected theologians and in good standing within their communities they had jobs and reputations to protect. They would have been reluctant to face the wrath and accusations of heresy that would spew forth from their superiors. They would have been even more fearful of being ousted from their lucrative positions into the dark world of the unemployed.

If that indeed was their motivation, in their cowardice they violated the very precepts of their profession. Christianity demands selfless nobility. If it is accompanied by pain, that is what Jesus Himself told them that their lot would be. Selfishness and cowardice go hand-in-hand, but have no place in the realm of God.

Some theologians would be insistent that selfishness is acceptable if it is godly. Godly selfishness? That self-contradictory statement makes a perfect example of an oxymoron. I can't find one place in Scripture where selfishness can be associated with the believer's walk with God, but I can find in there a whole lot of places where selflessness is the order of the day.

Greed and selfishness are attributes of the secular mind that Scripture claims is in opposition to faith. A case in point is the way the material world works. Have you ever wondered why, with all of our technical achievements, most of us seem to be living on the edge, barely able to cope financially? With all the wonderful tools for making our lives easier than those of our more primitive forefathers, why is the good life continually distant for most of us?

Look at the airlines, for instance. An airplane as shown in a very old movie may have been technologically backward, but was a wonder of luxury. The accommodations looked like the dining car of a train of that era, with white tablecloths, vases with flowers, and sumptuous, multi-course meals. Overseas seaplanes were furnished with sleeping berths.

On a trip from Seattle to New York to visit one of our daughters a few years back, we booked a flight on a well-known airline. The booking was admittedly on the el-cheapo side, with a stopover in Chicago's Airport B. When we reached that midpoint, we were told to disembark and await the connecting flight to New York. An hour passed, then two. Eventually an airline spokesman approached the milling crowd and explained that the airplane was docked at its terminal, but that the company was attempting to find a crew to man it. The spokesman promised us that we'd be given something to eat if the delay exceeded three hours.

One member of the crowd spoke up, mimicking the voice of the company man: "Attention on deck: Now hear this: You each will be given a handful of peanuts for your dining pleasure."

The quip obviously was a sarcasm relating to how the airline had gone from serving actual meals to handing out peanuts in the interest of "economy" – read "profit."

Four and a half hours later with no crew in sight, the company made good on their promise of a meal. In wheeled a cart with cans of Coke (the 8-oz size) and packages of crackers, two little squares to a package. There were enough packages to furnish each traveler with two.

Somewhere in the middle of the crowd, a voice shouted in lamentation: "THEY LIED ABOUT THE PEANUTS!"

We eventually went on to New York, laughing along the way, but hungry and convinced by this demonstration that the god of this world was money, and its followers were worshipers of its acquisition.

I'd like to think that the Churches are above this kind of self-centeredness, but, looking around at the variety of self-indulgent messages that are spewed out by way too many of today's Churches, I'm not too sure about that. But maybe even those Churches that consider themselves to be conservative should make the effort to re-examine their doctrines and traditions and, if they find some that are at odds with Scripture, bring them back into alignment with the Word of God.

There are numerous negatives in persisting to view the Holy Spirit as genderless or weakly masculine. I can name four just off the top of my head: falsehood, confusion, alienation and sexual misconduct.

To think of the Holy Spirit as genderless is just plain wrong. It doesn't represent truth. In particular, it contradicts Scripture in key areas, creating a void in the heart toward God. Right at the beginning of the Bible, who can fail to notice how the beginning of Creation in Genesis 1:1 and 2 is supported so beautifully by the feminine Voice in Proverbs 8:22-24, 27, 30 and 31:

> The Lord possessed me in the beginning of his way, before his works of old. I was set up from everlasting, from the beginning, or ever the earth was. When there were no depths, I was brought forth – when there were no fountains abounding with water. . . When he prepared the heavens, I was there; when he set a compass upon the face of the depth; . . . Then I was by him, as one brought up with him; and I was daily his delight, rejoicing always before him, rejoicing in the habitable part of his earth; and my delight was with the sons of men.

Who can't understand the self-centered narcissism and duplication of role with its consequent conflict or vagueness of purpose that would inevitably accompany a triune Godhead void of gender or of the same gender? Or who can't understand with joy the implication in Genesis 1:26 and 27 that our attributes of gender reflect the nature of the Godhead Itself?

And God said, Let us make man in our image, after our likeness; and let them have dominion over the fish of the sea, and over the fowl of the air, and over the cattle, and over all the earth, and over every creeping thing that creepeth upon the earth. So God created man in his own image, in the image of God created he him; male and female created he them.

3
Driven by Shame

Somehow the Church thought that she was doing God a favor by cleansing the Church of sexuality. But she took a big step by altering the Word of God to remove an attribute of God and to denigrate an element of God's own design, part of what, in Genesis 1, He pronounced to be good. That step was way out of line, as God never spoke ill of sexuality, but only of its misuse. He wished to limit its use, for our sakes and for the sake of our obedience to the type of God Himself, to a lifelong relationship between one man and one woman. What problem with sex was so deeply-seated that it caused the Church to go to such an extreme of throwing the baby out with the bathwater?

Much of the misinformation that has been handed down to us, as was the case with the Jewish inability to recognize Jesus, can be traced to the self-interest of the religious leadership and the ignorance of the layperson regarding Scripture. But there is one important error in the Bible that deserves a closer look, whose roots can be traced back to Adam and Eve. This misunderstanding has burdened the Church for centuries, causing Christians to remove intimacy from their connection to God, rendering Him a remote, even alien, Being. Further, it was made deliberately by those who thought they were doing God a favor. To understand how this could have happened, one needs to appreciate how severely the fall of Adam and Eve impacted mankind, and how the impact was further exacerbated by the social conditions experienced by the early Christians.

When Eve was introduced to Adam by God, Adam's words indicate that he was aware of gender and its implications. Significantly, they had no shame regarding their sexuality, or, indeed, in sexuality itself.

And Adam said, This is now bone of my bones, and flesh of my flesh; she shall be called Woman, because she was taken out of man. Therefore shall a man leave his father

*and mother, and shall cleave unto his wife; and they shall
be one flesh. And they were both naked, the man and his
wife, and were not ashamed.*

Their innocence before the fall represented their freedom from
shame rather than their inexperience regarding sexual expression.

Then came the fall, as noted in Genesis 3:6 and 7:

*And when the woman saw that the tree was good for
food, and that it was pleasant to the eyes, and a tree to
be desired to make one wise, she took of the fruit thereof,
and did eat, and gave also unto her husband with her;
and he did eat. And the eyes of them both were opened,
and they knew that they were naked; and they sewed fig
leaves together, and made themselves aprons.*

As suggested in the Genesis account of the fall, the shame of
sexuality appears to be more basic than an attitude acquired by
society, and seems to be particularly prevalent among those who
place great value on goodness and purity. Take Ronald, for example.
By the time that we'd reached the eighth grade, virtually all of us
knew all about the birds and the bees, but it was whispered around that
Ronald remained uninformed. A couple of guys approached Ronald
and let the cat out of the bag, whereupon the unfortunate creature
ran out of class, tears streaming down his face and heading toward
a confrontation with his parents. The event created an atmosphere
of hilarity in the class, the girls participating in the raucous laughter.

The next day Ronald returned to class, red-faced and unhappy. It
didn't help that he was met by a multitude of grinning faces. One boy
thrust a present into his hand. It was a pacifier. The epos associated
with poor Ronald remained with him throughout junior high. He
didn't attend the same high school as the rest of us.

From time to time we all wondered what happened to him. Maybe
he became some kind of religious authority.

But that's not fair. Or is it? It's not that sex is completely taboo
for Christians – it's taboo only in their relationship with God. But
that certainly doesn't let men of the cloth off the hook. We all know
about priests and altar boys. And this blight of hidden sex affects far
more Christians than just men of the cloth. A recent poll discovered

that eighty percent of Christian men, the vast majority, regularly indulge in pornography. But the mere thought of sex as being benign to God, let alone be a legitimate attribute of His own nature, strikes horror in the minds of the faithfully pure. One can only presume from this ubiquitous obsession with stray sex that most male Christians experience an ongoing disconnect between God and their lives in this matter that amounts to a genuine alienation from God. The faithfully pure, on the other hand, would profit from a perception of God at the adult level.

I truly wonder whether Ronald, who was so appalled at the thought of his parents having participated in sex, finally found freedom from such nasty thoughts in the genderless Church. Perhaps he's a priest now, attempting to maintain that mythical situation.

From the Pope on down, the Church needs to read and thoroughly digest Hebrews 13:4:

> Marriage is honorable in all, and the bed undefiled, but fornicators and adulterers God will judge.

There's good sex and there's bad sex, but not all sex is bad. Chastity does not confer purity, and vice versa. Beyond that, there is a noble beauty that is unique to motherhood. If, as stated in John that God is the essence of love, why would God forsake within Himself such a beautiful attribute as loving motherhood arising from an intimate union between complementary others?

This attribute is beautifully encapsulated in two Catholic commentaries on Mary, excerpts of which I placed in my novel *Buddy* and my nonfiction book *Marching to a Worthy Drummer*. The first of these is from Dominican Father Gerald Vann in a book entitled *Mary's Answer for our Troubled Times*, in which he addressed the hatred and suffering in the world during the Second World War. Like the title suggests, he wrote about Mary's own suffering while Jesus was on the cross, a theme which the Catholic Church frequently visits. While Father Vann's scenario may not be historically accurate, it certainly captures the essence of Scripture's portrayal of Mary in a magnificent way. It represents a stunning and deeply moving demonstration of nobility on Mary's part, which is entirely consistent with Scripture's portrayal of a major function of femininity, which is to evoke nobility from her masculine complement.

Father Vann talked of Mary's concentration of gaze and rapt, exclusive focus on Jesus as He endured His suffering. He contrasted the mutual sorrow-laden silence between her and Jesus with the noisier, more self-serving lamentations of the other women, developing a picture of Mary of stoic determination. She had a task, Vann claimed. This task involved the double sorrow of the mother as she watched the torments of the Son, and of the girl who flinched at the sight of naked evil and cruelty destroying innocence and beauty and love. She remained silent, because it was not for her to find an emotional outlet for her grief, for she is here because of Him, to fulfill her vocation as mother by helping Him to fulfill His as Savior. "In her," Vann claims, "there are two conflicting agonies: the longing to save Him from His agony and the effort to help Him to finish His work. It is the second that she must do, giving Him to the world on the Cross as she has given Him to the world in the stable."

Another beautifully noble representation of Mary in Catholic lore is a historic incident that took place just outside Mexico City in the year 1531. In that tale, as related by Father John Macquarrie in his book *Mary for all Christians,* an apparition of Mary appeared to a peasant, one Juan Diego. At the time, Juan's uncle was very ill, to the point of near-death. He spent a day trying to relieve his uncle's sufferings and left him only on Tuesday, to get a priest. An apparition of Mary barred his way. She told him,

'My little son, do not be distressed and afraid. Am I not here who am your Mother? Are you not under my shadow and protection? Your uncle will not die at this time. This very moment his health is restored. There is no reason now for the errand you set out on, and you can peacefully attend to mine. Go up to the top of the hill: cut the flowers that are growing there and bring them to me.'

As Juan's uncle was awaiting the priest, his room was filled with light. A luminous figure of a young woman appeared. He was indeed cured, but that's not the essence of this story. The main event occurs with Juan, who obeys the order to go to the flowers on the hill.

Juan Diego didn't expect to see flowers on the hill because it was the middle of winter. But he did indeed find flowers there. They were Castilian roses. He cut them as Mary had instructed and carried them back to her in his crudely-woven cape. She spent some time arranging the flowers, and then tied the corners of the cape behind his neck to prevent the roses from falling out. She told him to let only the bishop see the sign that she had given him.

When he reached the bishop's palace several servants made sport of him, pushing him around and trying to snatch the flowers from his cape. But the flowers dissolved when they reached for them. Amazed, they let him go. As he approached the bishop, Juan Diego untied the corners of the cape. As the ends dropped the flowers fell out in a jumbled heap. The disappointed peasant became confused as to the purpose of his visit. But then he was astonished to see that the bishop had come over to him and was kneeling at his feet. Soon everyone else in the room had come near and they all were kneeling with the bishop.

Juan Diego's cape now hangs over the altar in the basilica of Our Lady of Guadalupe in Mexico City. Over eight million persons were baptized there in the six years that followed this event. Many millions more since that time have knelt before the two-piece cape, coarsely-woven of maguey fibers, for imprinted on it is an intricately detailed, beautiful figure of Mary. In her graceful posture she appears kind and lovable. She is surrounded by golden rays. Fifteen hundred persons a day still visit the shrine. The image is available on the Internet by Googling on "Juan Diego".

This beautiful story suffers from the fact that the honor attributed to Mary belongs instead to the Holy Spirit. This misplaced attribute was necessitated by the Church's unjustified removal of femininity from the Holy Spirit due to fallen mankind's shame of sexuality.

Sexual shame was a direct result of the fall. The fall caused the spiritual death of mankind, some consequences of which we fail to this day to recognize. Partaking of the Tree of the Knowledge of Good and Evil caused the substitution of the spirit of man for the Spirit of God, giving man a mind of a thoroughly secular nature, one that, while acknowledging the existence of God, was unable to commune with Him with the intimacy that both he and God once enjoyed. Sexual shame became a critical barrier between God and man.

The tragic effect of this shame in the minds of the new Christians is evident in the commentaries of the early Christian fathers. On the personal level, more than one Church Father attempted to remove the allure of sex from himself through castration. An example of this mindset may be found in the writing of Justin Martyr in the middle of the second century A.D.:

"About continence [Jesus] said this: 'Whoever looks on a woman to lust after her has already committed adultery in his heart before God.' And: 'If your right eye offends you, cut it out; it is better for you to enter into the kingdom of Heaven with one eye than with two to be sent into eternal fire.' And: 'Whoever marries a woman who has been put away from another man commits adultery.' And: 'There are some who were made eunuchs by men, and some who were born eunuchs, and some who have made themselves eunuchs for the Kingdom of Heaven's sake; only not all [are able to] receive this.

"And so those who make second marriages according to human law are sinners in the sight of our Teacher, and those who look on a woman to lust after her. For he condemns not only the man who commits the act of adultery, but the man who desires to commit adultery, since not only our actions but our thoughts are manifest to God. Many men and women now in their sixties and seventies who have been disciples of Christ from childhood have preserved their purity; and I am proud that I could point to such people in every nation. . . But to begin with, we do not marry except in order to bring up children, or else, renouncing marriage, we live in perfect continence. To show you that promiscuous intercourse is not among our mysteries – just recently one of us submitted a petition to the Prefect Felix in Alexandria, asking that a physician be allowed to make him a eunuch, for the physicians there said they were not allowed to do this without the permission of the Prefect. When Felix would by no means agree to endorse [the petition], the young man remained single, satisfied with [the approval of] his own conscience and that of his fellow believers."

Among the early Christian Fathers, Justin Martyr also spoke of the rampant and often cruel immorality that was involved in the worship of the false pagan gods. His words show how deeply he felt about it:

"Far be it from every sound mind to entertain such a concept of deities as that Zeus, whom they call the ruler and begetter of all, should have been a parricide [killer of a relative] and the son of a parricide, and that moved by desire of evil and shameful pleasures he descended on Ganymede and the many women whom he seduced, and that his sons after him were guilty of similar actions. But, as we said before, it was the wicked demons who did these things. We have been taught that only those who live close to God in holiness and virtue attain to immortality, and we believe that those who live unjustly and do not reform will be punished in eternal fire."

"Secondly, out of every race of men we who once worshiped Dionysus the son of Semele and Apollo the son of Leto, who in their passion for men did things which it is disgraceful even to speak of, or who worshiped Persephone and Aphrodite, who were driven mad by [love of] Adonis and whose mysteries you celebrate, or Asclepius or some other of those who are called gods, now through Jesus Christ despise them, even at the cost of death, and have dedicated ourselves to the unbegotten and impassible God. We do not believe that he ever descended in mad passion on Antiope or others, nor on Ganymede, nor was he, receiving help through Thetis, delivered by that hundred-handed monster, nor was he, because of this anxious that Thetis' son Achilles should destroy so many Greeks for the sake of his concubine Briseis. We pity those who believe [such stories], for which we know that the demons are responsible."

"That we may avoid all injustice and impiety, we have been taught that to expose the newly born is the work of wicked men – first of all because we observe that almost all [foundlings], boys as well as girls, are brought up for prostitution. As the ancients are said to have raised herds of oxen or goats or sheep or horses in their pastures, so now [you raise children] just for shameful purposes, and so in every nation a crowd of females and hermaphrodites and doers of unspeakable deeds are exposed as public prostitutes. You even collect pay and levies and taxes from these, whom you ought to exterminate from your civilized world. And anyone who makes use of them may in addition to [the guilt of] godless, impious, and intemperate intercourse, by chance be consorting with his own child or relative or brother. Some even prostitute their own children or wives, and others are admittedly mutilated for purposes of sodomy, and treat this as part of the mysteries of the mother of the gods – while beside each of those whom think of as gods a serpent is depicted as a great symbol and mystery. You charge against us the actions that you commit openly and treat with honor, as if the divine light were overthrown and withdrawn – which of course does no harm to us, who refuse to do any of these things, but rather injures those who do them and then bring false witness [against us]."

As was noted in the previous chapter, foremost in the minds of many of the early Christians were the lewd and disgusting bacchanalias associated with the devotions to the Greek and Roman gods, who themselves were prone to bouts of lust and sexual perversions. In sharp contrast to the gross depravity of these gods, Jesus stood apart, radiant in shining moral splendor. At a time of rampant sexual excess, Jesus' Words sparkled like swords of righteousness and were taken deeply to heart. Among these were His own pronouncements of the place of sexuality within the Christian economy, which stressed single male/single female lifetime relationships.

Not rejected about the time Constantine legitimized the Church, although it should have been immediately discarded as contradictory to Scripture, was the shift in perception of the Holy Spirit's gender from feminine to weakly masculine. The shift probably came about through the prevailing disgust with the sexuality of secular society along with exasperation over the seemingly endless contention over heretical issues. The clerics must have been quite relieved over putting an end to the controversies through their final declaration of Church doctrine. Looming above these lesser considerations, of course, was the sexual shame associated with the fall.

As doctrine continued to mature in the Western Church, several oddities formed in it through this misconception of the Holy Spirit's gender.

It must be stressed that the idea of God without gender is extra-Biblical. Despite some Scriptural passages that are sometimes quoted in defense of this concept, including Paul's commentary regarding women in 1Timothy 2:11-15, Scripture in a wider sense rather uniformly supports the opposite view. The Scripture in question is quoted below:

> *Let the woman learn in silence with all subjection. But I permit not a woman to teach, nor to usurp authority over the man, but to be in silence. For Adam was first formed, then Eve. And Adam was not deceived, but the woman, being deceived, was in the transgression.*

> *Notwithstanding, she shall be saved in childbearing, if*
> *they continue in faith and love and holiness with sobriety.*

As Gail Wallace noted in a 2014 Internet article, the translation doesn't do justice to what Paul was attempting to get across. A proper translation would have emphasized the belligerent, domineering nature of the woman of which he was speaking. Furthermore, Paul was instructing Timothy regarding the problem of false teaching, which in Ephesus was being spread largely through the womenfolk. Finally, Paul may have been looking back on Eve's failure, by responding to the serpent instead of the Word of God, to represent the Holy Spirit's functional role as executive to the Divine Father. This latter possibility actually supports a gendered God as well as a feminine Holy Spirit.

In the fourth century A.D., Augustine's shame of sexuality mirrored that of the earlier Church Fathers. The strength of his feelings in that regard are demonstrated throughout his book *City of God*, an example of which is given in Chapters 4 and 5 of Book II:

"When I was a young man I used to go to sacrilegious shows and entertainments. I watched the antics of madmen; I listened to singing boys; I thoroughly enjoyed the most degrading spectacles put on in honour of gods and goddesses – in honour of the Heavenly Virgin, of Berecynthia, mother of all. On the yearly festival of Berecynthia's purification the lowest kind of actors sang, in front of her litter, songs unfit for the ears of even the mother of one of those mountebanks, to say nothing of the mother of any decent citizen, or of a senator; while as for the Mother of the Gods - ! For there is something in the natural respect we have towards our parents that the extreme of infamy cannot wholly destroy; and certainly those very mountebanks would be ashamed to give a rehearsal performance in their homes, before their mothers, of those disgusting verbal and acted obscenities. Yet they performed them in the presence of the Mother of the Gods before an immense audience of spectators of both sexes. If those spectators were enticed by curiosity to gather in profusion, they ought at least to have dispersed in confusion at the insults to their modesty.

"If these were sacred rites, what is meant by sacrilege? If this is purification, what is meant by pollution? And the name of the ceremony is 'the *fercula*', which might suggest the giving of a dinner-party where the unclean demons could enjoy a feast to their liking. Who could fail to realize what kind of spirits they are which could enjoy such obscenities? Only a man who refused to recognize even the existence of any unclean spirits who deceive men under the title of gods, or one whose life was such that he hoped for the favour and feared the anger of such gods, rather than that of the true God."

Mankind's shame of sexuality bore bitter fruit in the sixteenth century, with Zanchius' heartless intellectual effort to describe a genderless God. On the surface, it appears that Zanchius' view of God was driven by the prevailing Ptolemaic understanding of the cosmos as being of absolute perfection in the heavenly realm, the embodiment of simplicity, perfection, unchangeability and independence of being. But underneath this motive lies the misunderstanding of gender's role in the nature of God. This misfortune was the inevitable consequence of his theological predecessors' sexual shame. Zanchius' unscriptural views translated into the following examples of his statements regarding God's nature in his Chapter 1, entitled in grandiose manner "Wherein the Terms Commonly Made Use of in Treating of this Subject are Defined and Explained.":

"HAVING considered the attributes of God as laid down in Scripture, and so far cleared our way to the doctrine of predestination, I shall, before I enter further on the subject, explain the principal terms generally made use of when treating of it, and settle their true meaning. In discoursing on the Divine decrees, mention is frequently made of God's love and hatred, of election and reprobation, and of the Divine purpose, foreknowledge and predestination, each of which we shall distinctly and briefly consider.

"I.—When love is predicated of God, we do not mean that He is possessed of it as a passion or affection. In us it is such, but if, considered in that sense, it should be ascribed to the Deity, it would be utterly subversive of the simplicity, perfection and independency of His being. Love, therefore, when attributed to Him, signifies—

"(1) His eternal benevolence, *i.e.,* His everlasting will, purpose and determination to deliver, bless and save His people. Of this, no good works wrought by them are in any sense the cause. Neither are even the merits of Christ Himself to be considered as any way moving or exciting this good will of God to His elect, since the gift of Christ, to be their Mediator and Redeemer, is itself an effect of this free and eternal favour borne to them by God the Father (John 3.16). His love towards them arises merely from "the good pleasure of His own will," without the least regard to anything *ad extra* or out of Himself.

"(2) The term implies complacency, delight and approbation. With this love God cannot love even His elect as considered in themselves, because in that view they are guilty, polluted sinners, but they were, from all eternity, objects of it, as they stood united to Christ and partakers of His righteousness.

"(3) Love implies actual beneficence, which, properly speaking, is nothing else than the effect or accomplishment of the other two: those are the cause of this. This actual beneficence respects all blessings, whether of a temporal, spiritual or eternal nature. Temporal good things are indeed indiscriminately bestowed in a greater or less degree on all, whether elect or reprobate, but they are given in a covenant way and as blessings to the elect only, to whom also the other benefits respecting grace and glory are peculiar. And this love of beneficence, no less than that of benevolence and complacency, is absolutely free, and irrespective of any worthiness in man.

"II.—When hatred is ascribed to God, it implies (1) a negation of benevolence, or a resolution not to have mercy on such and such men, nor to endue them with any of those graces which stand connected with eternal life. So, "Esau have I hated" (Rom. 9.), *i.e.,* "I did, from all eternity, determine within Myself not to have mercy on him." The sole cause of which awful negation is not merely the unworthiness of the persons hated, but the sovereignty and freedom of the Divine will. (2) It denotes displeasure and dislike, for sinners who are not interested in Christ cannot but be infinitely displeasing to and loathsome in the sight of eternal purity. (3) It signifies a positive will to punish and destroy the reprobate for their sins, of which will, the infliction of misery upon them hereafter, is but the necessary effect and actual execution."

The most destructive consequence of Zanchius' view of a God void of passion is its denial of the suffering, emotional as well as physical, that Jesus underwent in Gethsemane, the various chambers in which He was abused, and on the cross. He undertook that for the sake of His passion toward us, His future Bride. The refutation of that passionate love mocks what should be the Christian understanding of God.

Despite the freedom from sin that Jesus' crucifixion and resurrection obtained for mankind, the Church has continues even now to cling to the shame associated with sex.

To this day both Catholic and Protestant Churches have in common a view of the Trinity in which sexuality is at most a superficial feature and in which vital aspects of femininity are denied altogether. This view leads most investigators into the nature of the Trinity into an admission that the topic is very complex, to the extent that in the end they admit further that, like attempting to understand the duality of light or the logic behind quantum mechanics, they can't comprehend it completely. This limitation has and continues to have a profound influence on the entire nature of Christianity. Didn't any of these investigators grasp a hint in the wake of this inability to comprehend such an important topic that perhaps the standard view of the Trinity might need some revision?

For the most part the Protestant Church, in contrast with her Catholic sister, simply accepts the lack of the feminine and ignores the issue altogether, treating it as beyond the pale of appropriate intellectual investigation. The Catholic Church responded quite differently to the removal of gender from the Godhead. Avoiding an acknowledgment of this complete abandonment of femininity in God, Catholics simply supplied the missing element of the Godhead elsewhere by heaping the feminine attributes that belonged to the Holy Spirit onto Mary and in the process elevating her to a position of near-godhood.

One day in San Diego a week before Easter Sunday, a compassionate but misguided group, being aware of the joyful celebration about to take place in the civilian world, knew also of one lonely group for which the occasion would represent a somewhat bleaker situation. They decided to do something about it. The group, presumably a number of Church women who had banded together for the purpose of Doing Good, approached the powers that be at the locally-situated Marine Corps Recruit Depot with the offer of providing jelly beans for the eating pleasure of the recruits there at the breakfast meal. Their intent was to convey to the recruits the notion that someone loved them. They further offered to perform the tedious task of putting the candies into paper cups for ready distribution to each individual.

The officer with whom the women communicated these benevolent offers, having somewhat less of a compassionate nature than that of the women, was about to give them the boot. Why on earth, he must have questioned, would anyone want to give those sorry-assed recruits the idea that they might be loved? But then a thought intruded into his devious mind. Turning his frown into a broad smile, he said "Sure, why not?"

The result was that when the Marines-to-be were marched into the mess hall that Easter Sunday, they found paper cups filled with gaily-colored jelly beans in front of their places at the tables. There was delight in their eyes until the shouted "Attention!" forced them to look to the grim face of their Drill Instructor. "Each of the cups before you contains exactly seven of those odious pellets of candy bunny crap," the angry face before them said. "You will carry the full cups with you after you've eaten your meal. There you will stand at attention on the Grinder while your cups are inspected for the proper number of pellets. I don't think that you will want to find a count less than seven in your cup. In fact, I'm sure of it. At ease and sit."

The officer with whom the women had communicated the offers made sure that he was in attendance on the Grinder when the first platoon of recruits had exited the mess hall. He couldn't refrain from grinning as the troops lined up in formation, cups in hand. A cursory check of the cups was performed to the accompaniment of epithets of "candy-ass Marines" and "pogey baiters" hurled at them, followed by a command to double-time in place. Very much later another command was issued, this one on top of the previous one. While continuing to jog in place the exhausted recruits were commanded to empty the cups into their mouths.

I know all about it – I was there, attempting to swallow half-chewed jelly beans without choking and entertaining some rather mean thoughts about the persons who had perpetrated the offense of providing jelly beans. None of us had serious problems, and we ended up laughing about it. But we really didn't enjoy those jelly beans a whole lot. It was a case of too much of a good thing.

Purity often is a good thing, particularly in the domain of sexuality. But like many other "good" things, too much of it is not. The attempt to purify God by removing all things sexual associated with Him was unnecessary. It wasn't even Scriptural. Assumptions were made about the Godhead and Mary that elevated purity to the primary reason for Jesus' birth by a virginal Mary, and for Mary's supposed persistent and continuous virginity after Jesus' birth. This move was misguided: the only reason for the virgin birth of Jesus is functional: He had to be both Man and God, born of man and born of God as well.

As for the false notion of Mary's perpetual virginity upon which the Catholic Church is most insistent as driven by the equally false misunderstanding that purity is equivalent to chastity, Matthew 13:55 and 56 say otherwise:

> *Is not this the carpenter's son? Is not his mother called Mary? And his brethren, James, and Joseph, and Simon, and Judas? And his sisters, are they not all with us? From where, then, hath this man all these things?*

The Catholic Church attempts to get around this with the claim that it was common in those times to call cousins brothers and sisters. But Matthew 1:24 and 25 puts the kibosh on that idea with the word "until", which makes Mary's virginity a temporary condition.

> *Then Joseph, being raised from sleep, did as the angel of the Lord had bidden him, and took unto him his wife, and knew her not till she had brought forth her first-born son; and he called his name Jesus.*

Another claim of the Church is that Jesus never married because of His perfection of purity. I think not; people who embrace this notion need to go back and read Ephesians 5. Jesus didn't marry during His first advent because He was already betrothed to the Church. His marriage will take place during His second advent, as foretold in Revelation 19:7:

> *Let us be glad and rejoice, and give honor to him; for the marriage of the Lamb is come, and his wife hath made herself ready.*

It appears that gender, far from being nonexistent within the Godhead, is of great importance. If Jesus thought so little of His own sexuality while in our material world that He remained celibate for the sake of His future marriage in the spiritual domain, doesn't that speak volumes about how superior is the spiritual world to our more limited domain? Why haven't our theologians understood that simple fact?

Instead, the Church continues to defy Scripture in viewing sexuality as something contrary to God. This is particularly evident in Catholic doctrine as displayed in some excerpts presented below as taken from *Mary in the Church Today,* compiled by Father Bill McCarthy. These vignettes are all excerpted either from *Redemtoris Mater* or Pope John Paul II's series of catecheses on the Blessed Virgin:

"Through her mediation, subordinate to that of the Redeemer, Mary contributes in a special way to the union of the pilgrim Church on earth with the eschatological and heavenly reality of the Communion of Saints, since she has already been 'assumed into heaven'. The truth of the assumption defined by Pius XII, is reaffirmed by the Second Vatican Council, which thus expresses the Church's faith: 'Preserved free from all guilt of original sin, the Immaculate Virgin was taken up body and soul into heavenly glory upon the completion of her earthly sojourn. She was exalted by the Lord as Queen of the Universe, in order that she might be the more thoroughly conformed to her Son, the Lord of lords (cf. Rv 19:16) and the conqueror of sin and death.' In this teaching Pius XII was in continuity with Tradition, which has found many different expressions in the history of the Church, both in the East and in the West."

"Mother of the Son, Mary is the 'beloved daughter of the Father' in a unique way. She has been granted an utterly special likeness between her motherhood and the divine fatherhood. And again, every Christian is a 'temple of the Holy Spirit', according to the Apostle Paul's expression (1 Cor 6:19). But this assertion takes on an extraordinary meaning in Mary: in her the relationship with the Holy Spirit is enriched in a spousal dimension, I recalled this in the Encyclical *Redemptoris Mater*: 'The Holy Spirit had already come down upon her, and she became his faithful spouse at the Annunciation, welcoming the Word of the true God. . .' (n. 26)."

"The freedom 'from every stain of original sin' entails as a positive consequence the total freedom from all sin as well as the proclamation of Mary's perfect holiness, a doctrine to which the dogmatic definition makes a fundamental contribution. In fact, the negative formulation of the Marian privilege, which resulted from the earlier controversies about original sin that arose in the West, must always be complemented by the positive expression of Mary's holiness more explicitly stressed in the Eastern tradition.

"Pius XII's definition refers only to the freedom from original sin and does not explicitly include the freedom from original concupiscence [generally, the desires of the flesh in the Catholic vernacular]. Nevertheless, Mary's complete preservation from every stain of sin also has as a consequence her freedom from concupiscence, a disordered tendency which, according to the Council of Trent, comes from sin and inclines to sin (DS 1515)."

"The intention to remain a virgin, apparent in Mary's words at the moment of the Annunciation, has traditionally been considered the beginning and the inspiration of Christian virginity for the Church.

"St. Augustine does not see in this resolution the fulfillment of a divine precept, but a vow freely taken. In this way it was possible to present Mary as an example to 'holy virgins' throughout the Church's history. Mary 'dedicated her virginity to God when she did not yet know whom she would conceive, so that the imitation of heavenly life in the earthly, mortal body would come about through a vow, not a precept, through a choice of love and not through the need to serve; (De Sancta Virg. IV. PL 40 398).

"The angel does not ask Mary to remain a virgin, it is Mary who freely reveals her intention of virginity. The choice of love that leads her to consecrate herself totally to the Lord by a life of virginity is found in this commitment.

"In stressing the spontaneity of Mary's decision, we must not forget that God's initiative is at the root of every vocation. By choosing the life of virginity, the young girl of Nazareth was responding to an interior call, that is, to an inspiration of the Holy Spirit that enlightened her about the meaning and value of the virginal gift of [sic, substitute 'chastity'] heresy. No one can accept this gift without feeling called or without receiving from the Holy Spirit the necessary light and strength."

"It may be presumed that at the time of their betrothal there was an understanding between Joseph and Mary about the plan to live as a virgin. Moreover, the Holy Spirit, who had inspired Mary to choose virginity in view of the mystery of the Incarnation and who wanted the latter to come about in a family setting suited to the Child's growth, was quite able to instill in Joseph the ideal of virginity as well."

These views of Mary's exemption from sexual expression, as described by the highest Catholic authority and seconded by the entire Church, presents Mary with the warmth of humanity. But she, like the Godhead Itself, has been stripped clean of all sexual experience throughout her life except for the pain of childbirth. In thinking about that rampant sexual housecleaning, it seems strange indeed that Peter, the iconic and revered founder of the Catholic Church, was himself married, according to Matthew 8:14 and 15, while his successors and the entire body of clergy were and continue to be prohibited from doing so:

> And when Jesus was come into Peter's house, he saw that his wife's mother laid, and sick of a fever. And he touched her hand, and the fever left her; and she arose, and ministered unto them.

We all know how that worked out in practice: instead of taking wives and thereby participating in a relationship established and condoned by God, the clergy instead took the wives of other men, prostitutes and, ultimately, altar boys.

Perhaps the Church, over the many years since she cast her doctrine in concrete, never has understood that she got it wrong. After all, her initial motivation in defining the Godhead as she did was out of the Church Fathers' purity of intent. Perhaps they never have recognized how important in attempting to right wrongs is the all-too-human failing of reactionary overkill.

Most of us have the desire, when we see something bad having taken place, to correct the problem. Some of us even go so far as to attempt to make certain that this negative situation never arises again.

But there are some Dudley-Do-Rights (DDRs) among us who wish to so thoroughly stamp out whatever evil that has occurred that they indulge in reactionary overkill, otherwise known as throwing the baby out with the bathwater. A distressingly large percentage of situations involving one or more DDRs involves collateral damage so extensive as to create situations that are worse than the ones they attempted to fix,

In their self-satisfied moral superiority, DDRs rarely think beyond the immediate problem, having no clue as to the possibility of unintended consequences.

Here's an actual example proposed by one of my family members, who witnessed an accident caused by a car that had moved into an intersection after stopping at a sign, getting T-boned by a car coming at right angles to him, there being no stop sign in his direction. After fuming a bit over the lack of a stop sign in that other direction, this DDR wrote a long letter about this absence to the city council. But he didn't stop there. He insisted that every intersection in the city be graced with a stop sign, and followed that up by starting a movement to ensure that this happened.

Fortunately, the movement was a one-man show, everyone else understanding that with a stop sign on every block, drivers eventually would get so irritated that they'd make California Stops, greatly increasing the chances for more accidents.

Sometime later the same individual, having read in the paper that a tree had fallen onto a car and injuring the driver, attempted to start another movement to effect the removal of every tree within fifty feet of a street. He wasn't much for aesthetics, so this proposal got axed as well, to the relief of the city's inhabitants (all but one).

As was noted earlier, in the Fourth Century A.D. the Church was faced with having to deal with a negative gender issue on two fronts. On one front the secular population surrounding the Christian community in Rome, the *de facto* seat of Christianity, was given to participating in lewd and depraved celebrations of its pagan gods and goddesses. The associated bacchanalias contrasted sharply with the more noble worship of our Christian God. On another front the Gnostic sect of Christianity, while worshiping a mixed-gender Godhead as did all the early Christians, had adopted some rather bizarre and complicated misunderstandings of God and His origins. The Church Fathers of that time, weary of these potential threats to their faith and all the associated arguments and debates over them, embarked on an effort to maintain the noble purity of their faith through narrowly-defined doctrinal statements and Bible translations that supported those statements.

The result, as I see it, is that in their passion to purify the Church and separate her from questionable perceptions of God, the entire lot became DDRs. They threw multiple babies out with the bathwater, including a gender switch of the Holy Spirit from feminine to weakly masculine and stripping God from all implications of exercised gender.

The denial of the Holy Spirit's femininity, driven fundamentally by the shame of sexuality, has led to speculations that have led to yet further damage to our understanding of Scripture. In the chapter entitled "God and the Feminine" in his book *Mary for all Christians*, Catholic scholar Father John MacQuarrie acknowledges the incompleteness of male alone or female alone without their complements. Thinking more deeply than most of his peers, he goes so far as to touch on the all-important notion of complementary otherness. But then he moves on to other topics rather than pursuing the implications and consequences associated with that essential attribute of gender. In doing so, he overlooks the implication of God's noble selflessness, presented as of key significance throughout Scripture, which is of such paramount importance toward a mature understanding of the nature of God.

Instead, Fr. MacQuarrie proposes his own take on how the Divine Feminine might be incorporated within the Godhead. His idea represents pretty much the precise opposite of complementary otherness. He sets the preliminary groundrule, established before by a host of theologians in open defiance of Scripture, that God transcends sex. Within the walls of that artificial box that he constructed, he goes on to apply the notion that God resides above gender to his perception that a single-gendered Godhead is incomplete by borrowing from psychiatrist C. J. Jung's concept of shared gender within the individual. The result is MacQuarrie's assertion that all the Members of the Trinity share both masculine and feminine attributes. Indeed, Fr. MacQuarrie isn't entirely wrong about this – there must be some overlap of attributes within the two genders, at least to the extent that they can understand each other.

But what MacQuarrie appears to have had in mind was such a high degree of overlap that neither the masculine or feminine attributes dominated over the other within each Member of the Godhead. Such an excess of attribute sharing would weaken the genders to the point of degrading both and creating internal conflicts. This is alien to the human experience and is not what Scripture suggests about the nature of gender in man or God. Nevertheless, many Catholic theologians have gone along with this notion, following this blind guide into a theological ditch.

This attribute, if true, would support standard Church doctrine, which follows the extra-Scriptural Athanasian Creed in viewing each Member of the Godhead as independent and identical to the others with respect to powers and abilities.

Such an attribute, again if true, also would facilitate the slide into homosexuality. In the first place, the concept is logically untenable, as it weakens the male element of both the Father and Jesus Christ, violating the proscription, as noted in Chapter 3 herein, against male sexual neutrality in Deuteronomy 23:1 and against male femininity in 1 Corinthians 6:9 and 10:

> He who is wounded in the stones, or hath his privy member cut off, shall not enter into the congregation of the Lord.

> Know ye not that the unrighteous shall not inherit the kingdom of God? Be not deceived: neither fornicators, nor idolators, nor adulterers, nor effeminate, nor abusers of themselves with mankind, nor thieves, nor covetous, nor drunkards, nor revilers, nor extortioners, shall inherit the kingdom of God.

These Scriptural statements effectively take the dual-gender idea off the table. Both Jesus and the divine Father must be strongly and exclusively masculine. If there is to be any femininity within the Trinitarian Godhead, it would have to apply to the Holy Spirit. Deuteronomy 23:1, in fact, also suggests that Jesus is entire, to use an expression regarding horses, meaning that He is sexually capable.

Moreover, as if the direct problems associated with the gender-neutral or all-male viewpoints of the Godhead aren't bad enough of themselves, they sometimes create collateral difficulties, particularly of sexual sins. It's easy to imagine how a supposedly celibate priest, faced with normal sexual urges, could condone his lust for one altar boy or another on the basis that his "feminine side" is attracted to the male object of his desire. The same danger would apply to other sexual sins as well. Again, it's only in the context of a strongly-gendered Godhead that sexual sins are even relevant to His own nature.

But overriding even that danger, such an attribute would promote an unhealthy misunderstanding of God every bit as wrong as that for which pagan religions have been deserving of denunciation, in which each Member of the Godhead is so self-sufficient that, beyond contradicting the necessity of a Trinitarian Godhead, it supports the evil notion of divine narcissism. Such self-love is so opposed to the general tenor of Scripture that it represents nothing less than blasphemy.

Only a person burdened with the shame of gender can torture Scripture by lopping off the phrase "male and female created he them" from its natural connection to the manner in which our Godhead in the plurality made man in His image according to Genesis 1:26 and 27:

> And God said, Let us make man in our image, after our likeness; and let them have dominion over the fish of the sea, and over the fowl of the air, and over the cattle, and over all the earth, and over every creeping thing that creepeth upon the earth. So God created man in his own image, in the image of God created he him; male and female created he them.

Or who can miss the intimate correspondence between Genesis 2:18 and 22, and Proverbs 8:30:

> And the Lord God said, It is not good that the man should be alone; I will make him an help fit for him. . . And the rib, which the Lord God had taken from man, made he a woman, and brought her unto the man.
>
> Then I was by him, as one brought up with him; and I was daily his delight, rejoicing always before him.

It would be difficult not to see in Adam's pronouncement over his new and beautiful wife in Genesis 2:23 and 24 the fulfillment within the Godhead Itself of Jesus' words in Matthew 22: 37 and 38 (echoing Deuteronomy 6:5), and in Matthew 19:4-6:

> *And Adam said, This is now bone of my bones, and flesh of my flesh; she shall be called Woman, because she was taken out of Man. Therefore shall a man leave his father and his mother, and shall cleave unto his wife; and they shall be one flesh.*

> *Jesus said unto him, Thou shalt love the Lord, thy God, with all thy heart, and with all thy soul, and with all thy mind. This is the first and great commandment.*

> *And [Jesus] answered and said unto them, Have ye not read that he who made them at the beginning, made them male and female; and said For this cause shall a man leave his father and his mother, and shall cleave to his wife, and they two shall be one flesh? Wherefore, they are no more two, but one flesh. What, therefore, God hath joined together, let not man put asunder.*

To top that off, Paul in Ephesians 5:31 and 32 quoted that same statement of Adam's regarding leaving father and mother and cleaving to his wife and the two being one flesh, applying it to the union of Christ with His Church.

Finally, among the negatives of failing to understand God as gendered, with the participation of both male and female, is the seriousness of sexual sin. Given that sexual malfeasance is plainly proscribed in the Bible, including passages in Leviticus 18 and Romans 1, such indiscretions, while acknowledged as disobedient to God, are commonly categorized as misdemeanors. The prevailing thought that a person might engage in, faced with sexual temptation, might be that if God Himself is genderless, why would He care how we humans indulge our desires?

If, however, the understanding of the Godhead includes femininity, sexual sins would represent a violation of type, which would elevate the misdeeds from misdemeanors to felonies.

The gross sexual misconduct of the Church membership now and into the distant past may be laid right at the doorstep of Church leadership of all denominations and sects, who maintain a stubborn refusal to analyze why God might be so against sexual sins, and thereby begin to straighten up their understanding of the gendered nature of the Godhead. Most of us are aware of the predilection of Catholic priests for taking altar boys as sexual partners, a crime that had been covered up possibly for centuries. Lately, a scandal has erupted in the Vatican regarding a number of priests there who have shamelessly engaged in homosexual orgies. They didn't even have the decency to repent of their acts. But this problem is not confined to the Catholic Church leadership. Lest a Protestant layperson shoot out the lip in condemnation, he needs to know that the problem is in his own backyard as well. A recent study by Pew Research has established the astonishing fact that of the eighty percent of Christian men who regularly indulge in the watching of pornography, a full half are addicted to it.

4

God, Scripture and Gender

God's relationship with mankind as detailed in Scripture gives us a natural focus for assessing Scripture's presentation of gender within the Godhead.

The anti-gender presuppositions to which the readers of Scripture are chained force them to interpret these passages in an awkward manner that misdirects them to overlook what the passages may actually say.

In the example presented earlier involving Genesis 1:26 and 27, God creates mankind in two models, male and female, in the same breath by which the plural Godhead claims that mankind is made in God's image.

> *And God said, Let us make man in our image, after our likeness; and let them have dominion over the fish of the sea, and over the fowl of the air, and over the cattle, and over all the earth, and over every creeping thing that creepeth upon the earth. So God created man in his own image, in the image of God created he him; male and female created he them.*

As noted before, any attempt to separate the gender reference from the rest of the passage tortures Scripture, but theological "experts" do it all the time. In my Scofield KJV Bible, the editorial commentary on this passage begins as follows:

"Man was made in the 'image and likeness' of God. This image is found chiefly in the fact that man is a personal, rational, and moral being."

The commentary continues to describe in more detail these three elements, completely ignoring the emphasis that Scripture itself places on gender. The editors simply continue in unquestioning thoughtless adherence to the ancient doctrinal formula of a genderless God despite the clear indication of Scripture to the contrary.

This pattern is ubiquitous. The NKJV Reformation Study Bible also comments on this passage in much the same manner, completely avoiding the strong implication in it that God also is gendered. This unity in the matter in the presence of the diverse divisions within Christianity is to be expected, as the doctrine of religious "purity" was established long before the splits occurred; almost no mainstream Church group thereafter, with the exception of the Moravian Church and a very few others, bothered to even question that doctrine in the face of the departure of its intent from that of Scripture.

Genesis 2:18-22 represents another Scriptural passage suggesting the gendered nature of God that is commonly interpreted in a manner that is vastly different than a natural reading of it would suggest.

> *And the Lord God said, It is not good that the man should be alone; I will make him an help fit for him. And out of the ground the Lord God formed every beast of the field, and every fowl of the air; and brought them unto Adam to see what he would call them: and whatsoever Adam called every living creature, that was the name thereof. And Adam gave names to all cattle, and to the fowl of the air, and to every beast of the field; but for Adam there was not found an help fit for him. And the Lord God caused a deep sleep to fall upon Adam, and he slept: and he took one of his ribs, and closed up the flesh instead thereof; and he rib, which the Lord God had taken from man, made he a woman, and brought her unto the man.*

This passage exalts the complementary otherhood of gender differentiation, the completion of man and the unity intrinsic to his dual-gendered nature. This unity is emphasized in the very next two verses, Genesis 2:23 and 24:

> *And Adam said, This is now bone of my bones, and flesh of my flesh; she shall be called Woman, because she was taken out of man. Therefore shall a man leave his father*

*and his mother, and shall cleave unto his wife; and they
shall be one flesh.*

The account of Eve's creation is usually interpreted as an
afterthought. Since it follows the creation of man and woman
described in Genesis 1, it is sometimes thought to suggest that Eve
was created well after Adam. The more likely interpretation is that
it has nothing to do with the sequence of creation; instead, it was
placed where it was for the purpose of emphasizing gender. Two
statements within the passage point directly to the larger application
of gender to God Himself. The first is God's pronouncement that
it was "not good" for Adam to be without a complementary other,
after He had declared in Genesis 1:31 that His creation was "very
good". It is difficult to imagine why God would frown upon the
lack of an attribute that He Himself also lacked. The second is
Adam's declaration of a man leaving his father and mother to join
his wife to become "one flesh". This declaration of Adam was
repeated by Jesus in Matthew 19:3-6 and by Paul in Ephesians 5:31
and 32, elevating its importance in God's economy and directly
linking gender with Jesus Himself, who, of course, is a Member of
the Godhead.

The referenced passage in Matthew 19 implicates God's deep
involvement in the marital union. If God was "above that kind
of thing" as is usually thought to be the case, particularly among
members of the Reformed Church, it's hard to understand His
commitment to it.

> *The Pharisees also came unto him, testing him, and
> saying unto him, Is it lawful for a man to put away his
> wife for every cause? And he answered and said unto
> them, Have ye not read that he who made them at the
> beginning made them male and female; and said, For
> this cause shall a man leave father and mother, and
> shall cleave to his wife, and they two shall be one flesh?
> Wherefore, they are no more two, but one flesh. What,
> therefore, God hath joined together, let not man put
> asunder.*

That this "joining" involves gender in the form of sexual
communication Paul makes crystal clear in 1 Corinthians 6:15-18:

Know ye not that your bodies are the members of Christ?
Shall I, then, take the members of Christ, and make them
the members of an harlot? God forbid. What? Know ye
not that he who is joined to an harlot is one body? For
two, saith he, shall be one flesh. But he that is joined unto
the Lord is one spirit. Flee fornication. Every sin that a
man doeth is outside the body; but he that committeth
fornication sinneth against his own body.

In Proverbs 8, Wisdom is described in terms of complementary otherness to the Father Himself, a feature that puts the lie to the notion that Wisdom is an attribute of God rather than a Person. The identification of Wisdom as a separate Entity from the Father is supported elsewhere in Scripture, particularly by Jesus in Matthew 12:31 and 32, in which Jesus appears protective toward Her name in His pronouncement of the unforgivable sin:

Wherefore, I say unto you, All manner of sin and
blasphemy shall be forgiven men; but the blasphemy
against the Holy Spirit shall not be forgiven men. And
whosoever speaketh a word against the Son of man, it
shall be forgiven him; but whosoever speaketh against
the Holy Spirit, it shall not be forgiven him, neither in
this age, neither in the age to come.

That Jesus here was speaking of Wisdom is manifestly clear by the associated passage in Proverbs 8:36:

But he that sinneth against me wrongeth his own soul;
all they that hate me love death.

In 1 Timothy 2, Paul engages in what appears to be a rant against womanhood, leading some (a good many, in fact) pastors and their male constituents to consider femininity to be but a dim reflection of masculinity, encouraging a discounting of the value of gender. I've addressed that issue in my book *Marching to a Worthy Drummer*, pointing out that Paul here may be implying something entirely different than the usual interpretation and actually may well be supportive of a gendered Godhead. In this alternate interpretation, Paul may have pointed to Eve as failing to mimic the feminine Holy Spirit as a responder to Her Complementary Other, the Holy Father. The nature of her failure was twofold: in her responding to satan rather than Adam or God she went "off the reservation" by displaying loyalty to the wrong being; also, her disobedient partaking of the forbidden fruit demonstrated her role-reversal in assuming the role of initiator to Adam rather than responder. Adam, by the way, wasn't clean in all of this – where was he when he was supposed to protect Eve from danger? And, more importantly, he also reversed the way that God made him in His image by playing the role of the responder rather than that of the initiator.

A close look at the examples noted above reveals the inconsistency of the perception of the Holy Spirit as genderless.

Moreover, the Book of Proverbs consistently personifies a feminine Entity. How then can Church 'authorities' claim that Jesus is the Person represented by Proverbs, particularly in light of what Paul wrote in 1 Corinthians 6:9?

> *Know ye not that the unrighteous shall not inherit the kingdom of God? Be not deceived: neither fornicators, nor idolaters, nor adulterers, nor effeminate, nor abusers of themselves with mankind, . .*

Again, regarding the specific reference to gender in Genesis 1:27, Why do the same Church 'authorities' insist that this reference has nothing to do with the way God created man in His image?

Yet again, regarding Genesis 2:18, why would God declare that it was not good for Adam to be without a feminine companion if it would be 'good' for God to lack it?

Furthermore, why, if, as Paul wrote in Ephesians 5:31 and 32, would Jesus, as a Member of the Godhead, marry a feminine companion when the other Members would not partake of the same gendered relationship?

Inconsistency leads directly to confusion. That these examples of inconsistency produce confusion is eloquently demonstrated by the admission of multiple 'authorities' (of which two have confessed the same to me) of their confusion regarding the nature of the Godhead and of the Holy Spirit.

Even worse than the inconsistency it produces is the alienation from God that results from a rejection of a feminine Holy Spirit. I fail to see how God can be loved with the fervor commanded by Jesus in Matthew 22:37 and 38 (see above) without an intimate understanding of Him. He certainly cannot be understood sufficiently under the prevailing view of a genderless Godhead to permit obedience to that commandment. If one thinks that he can love God simply through an exercise of his will, he's fooling himself. The fervor that Jesus commands is akin to that which ideally exists between a man and his wife. That kind of love is possessive, best described by the Greek word *eros*. An exercise of the will is wholly insufficient to achieve a love of that intensity. Can anyone disagree with my assertion that there has been a persistent and widespread alienation from God as a result, even among those who claim to be committed Christians? Medieval cleric Jerome Zanchius, noted elsewhere herein, certainly must have considered himself to be a good Christian. However, his descriptions of God remove all possibility of the intimate connection with God that He, according to Scripture, desires. What remains is a worship based on majesty and power. Where is the love in that?

The inconsistency with Scripture of the denial of the femininity of the Holy Spirit can easily lead to misinterpretations of Scripture that are no less than profound. Scripture's silence with regard to Jesus' relationship with women have led to popular speculation of an affair with Mary Magdalene or, worse, His gender neutrality, which would violate Scripture, particularly Ephesians 5. It was asserted in the previous chapter that Scripture strongly suggests that Jesus is both strongly masculine and sexually capable. If Jesus is strongly masculine and sexually capable, why then did He stay celibate during His time on Earth? The answer to that question is quite simple and Scripturally appropriate: as noted earlier, Paul explained in Ephesians 5:31 and 32 that Jesus was already betrothed to his Church. In maintaining the marital model involving the lifetime one man/one woman pairing, Jesus avoided violating God's intent for marriage as prefigured in the creation of Adam and Eve.

> *For this cause shall a man leave his father and mother, and shall be joined unto his wife, and they two shall be one flesh. This is a great mystery, but I speak concerning Christ and the Church.*

Many authorities on Scripture, including pastors, would make light of this "marriage", suggesting that the marriage is only symbolic. It is highly doubtful, considering the emphasis that Scripture placed on the marriage in Cana, that Jesus sees it that way.

In the marriage in Cana as recorded in John 2, Jesus performs His first miracle in celebration of marriage, joyfully changing water to wine. In that passage He obviously is looking forward to His own marriage to His Church. I've commented in other books on the strangeness of the notion that if Jesus marries, being a Member of the Godhead, the other Members would have nothing to do with the exercise of gender. That the notion represents a profound stagger into faulty logic must be self-evident to all but the most rigidly reactionary brain.

One of the most direct pointers to the femininity of the Holy Spirit is in Her role as the Glory of God, or the Shekinah Glory, a connection which spans both Testaments of Scripture.

The Wikipedia entry for "Shekinah" begins as follows:

"Hebrew [Shekinah] is the English spelling of a grammatically feminine Hebrew ancient blessing. The original word means the *dwelling* or *settling,* and denotes the dwelling or settling of the divine presence of God, especially in the temple in Jerusalem."

An accompanying figure shows the Shekinah, or the Glory of God, indwelling the temple as described in 1 Kings 8.

Exodus 40 and 1 Kings 8 provide prominent examples of the *Shekinah* as a precursor to the indwelling Holy Spirit of the New Testament. Exodus 40:33-38 describes the indwelling of the Tabernacle in the wilderness:

> *And [Moses] reared up the court round about the tabernacle and the altar, and set up the hanging of the court gate. So Moses finished the work.*
>
> *Then a cloud covered the tent of the congregation, and the glory of the Lord filled the tabernacle. And when the cloud was taken up from over the tabernacle, the children of Israel went onward in all their journeys; but if the cloud were not taken up, then they journeyed not till the day that it was taken up. For the cloud of the Lord was upon the tabernacle by day, and fire was on it by night, in the sight of all the house of Israel, throughout all their journeys.*

The description "cloud of the Lord", "fire by night" and "taken up" leaves no doubt that this "cloud" is equivalent to the *Shekinah* of the Red Sea adventure and of Isaiah 4:5. The corresponding incident with respect to Solomon's Temple, taken from 1 Kings 8:6-13, is given below:

> *And the priests brought in the ark of the covenant of the Lord unto its place, into the inner sanctuary of the house, into the most holy place, even under the wings of the cherubim. For the cherubim spread forth their two wings of the place of the ark, and the cherubim covered the ark and its staves above. And they drew out the staves, that the ends of the staves were seen out in the holy place before the inner sanctuary, but they were not seen outside; and there they are unto this day. There was nothing in the ark except the two tables of stone, which Moses put there at Horeb, when the lord made a covenant with the children of Israel, when they came out of the land of Egypt. And it came to pass, when the priests were come out of the holy place, that the cloud filled the house of the lord, so that the priests could not stand to minister because of the cloud; for the glory of the Lord had filled the house of the Lord. Then spoke Solomon, The Lord said he would dwell in the thick darkness. I have surely built thee an house to dwell in, a settled place for thee to abide in forever.*

In this passage the meaning of "cloud" is closely linked with "dwelling place" and "glory of the Lord", which again point to the phrase *Shekinah Glory.*

The connection between these precursor events and the Holy Spirit who indwells Christian believers is given in 1 Corinthians 3:16 and Ephesians 2:19-22, wherein Paul asserts that the Church herself, through her constituents, is a temple indwelt by the Holy Spirit:

> *Know ye not that ye are the temple of God, and that the Spirit of God dwelleth in you?*

> *Now, therefore, ye are no more strangers and sojourners, but fellow citizens with the saints, and of the household of God; and are built upon the foundation of the apostles*

and prophets, Jesus Christ himself being the chief corner
stone, in whom all the building fitly framed together
groweth unto an holy temple in the Lord; in whom ye
also are built together for an habitation of God through
the Spirit.

The facts embedded in these passages are no surprise to Christians, who generally accept without question that believers are indwelt by the Holy Spirit and comprise, as the Church, a holy temple. The Holy Spirit is not only our spiritual Mother-in-Law, but She also is our Companion as well in the material world in which we now inhabit. In Her role as the Shekinah Glory, just as she indwelt the Wilderness Tabernacle (Exodus 40) and Solomon's Temple (1 Kings 8), She indwells Christian believers to comfort them in their inevitable distresses, and to help them grow in character as members of Christ's body, the Church.

Noting the female gender of this indwelling Shekinah, we find here by comparing the indwelling presence of the Glory in Solomon's temple with the description in Ephesians 2 of the Holy Spirit indwelling the human temple that Scripture itself, by furnishing this direct comparison, supports an interpretation of the Holy Spirit as a female Entity in the face of conventional Christian thought, as driven by the use in Scripture of the male pronoun in reference to the Holy Spirit.

This feminine gender attribute in Exodus 40 and 1 Kings 8 may have been simply lost in the translation from Aramaic to English, which could have been a result of the lack of gender precision in the English language. (Actually, the first transference from feminine to masculine occurred in the Latin, for which the Holy Spirit was definitely presented as male. Spirit, in Latin, is of the masculine gender.) But there is an associated gender misrepresentation in Isaiah 51:9, 10 that appears to be more deliberate, as both feminine and neuter versions of this verse exist. What the translators did in that passage, which is obvious in the comparison of both versions, was to substitute the grammatically incorrect 'it' for the gender-correct 'she' in reference to Shekinah. In their desire to maintain a fully masculine Godhead, they neutered the feminine.

The value of the Holy Spirit's femininity is appreciated rather indirectly by the Catholic Church, which, unlike her Protestant sister, recognized how necessary a feminine element is to the worship of God. Stubbornly maintaining the false tradition of a masculine Holy Spirit, the Catholic Church compensated for this lack of the feminine by elevating Mary to a position of near-Godhood, placing upon her many attributes that rightfully belong to the Holy Spirit. This compromise position, while basically wrong, is better by far than living with the lack of the feminine as most Protestant Churches do. At least becoming close to Mary as a stand-in for the Holy Spirit acknowledges intimacy with the feminine side of God.

Perhaps the most touching element of the Holy Spirit's intimacy with mankind is in Her role as the Shekinah Glory, in which She indwells Christian believers as Paul was careful to note.

A feminine Holy Spirit renders the Godhead intuitively understandable. The consequence is immediate: confusion flees from the mind at the speed of Light. But this femininity brings even more than clarification to the mind of the Christian believer. The heart also is affected, for God becomes closer to us by nature. The family comes into view as a basic element of God, indeed as the binding force for unity within the Trinity. Romance enters the picture as well, and its product in birth, the Son and our own spouse, Jesus Christ, with His attribute of all of Creation.

All these now-familiar elements of the Godhead draw us closer to Him. He's no longer an alien Being, but through his declaration that we are made in His image He is close to us far above the limited sense forced upon us by the Church's insistence on a genderless God.

This closeness, in turn permits us to love Him without reservation. I will not go so far as to claim that God could not be loved without the understanding of the Holy Spirit's femininity. But I will claim that our love now can be of greater fervor, and with the possessiveness of romance, just as Israel was commanded in Deuteronomy 6:4 and 5, and Jesus commanded His followers in Matthew 22:37 and 38:

> *Hear, O Israel: The Lord our God is one Lord; and thou shalt love the Lord thy God with all thine heart, and with all thy soul, and with all thy might.*
>
> *Jesus said unto him, Thou shalt love the Lord, thy God, with all thy heart, and with all thy soul, and with all thy mind. This is the first and great commandment.*

In addition to the femininity of the *Shekinah Glory*, other sources have pointed to a most interesting situation where the gender-neutral word *God* was substituted in numerous references in the Hebrew Scriptures for a specifically feminine Member of the Godhead denoted by the feminine word *Eloah*. *Eloah* was frequently used to depict the Judeo-Christian God in the original Hebrew Scripture, particularly in the Book of Job. In one count, it was claimed that this word for God was used 57 times in the original Scripture. In addition to that, the grammatically feminine Hebrew words *Ruach ha Kodesh* (*Ruah* in Aramaic) translate to Holy Spirit. *Ruah* and *Eloah* are considered by many to refer to that same Person in the Godhead, the Holy Spirit.

In their attempt to rebut the notion of a feminine Holy Spirit, some authorities would claim that Scripture itself suggests a genderless God. The most prominent passage dealing with the apparent lack of gender in the spiritual realm is Galatians 3:28. Instead of supporting this presupposition, it merely demonstrates the shallowness of the confronter, and of his inability to think outside the box. A similar passage may be found in Matthew 22:30. They read as follows, starting with Galatians 3:28:

> *There is neither Jew nor Greek, there is neither bond nor free, there is neither male nor female; for ye are all one in Jesus.*

> *For in the resurrection they neither marry, nor are given in marriage, but are like the angels of God in heaven.*

On the surface (the very thin top layer), these passages seem to indicate that when we get to heaven we won't be gendered. In a trivial way, that's true. And then in Matthew 22:30, Jesus Himself points out that we won't be married. End of story?

Of course not! Hello – did anyone bother to read Matthew 22:29, the verse immediately preceding Jesus' commentary on marriage in the spiritual realm?

> *Jesus answered and said unto them, Ye do err, not knowing the scriptures, nor the power of God.*

Does anybody think that the phrase "power of God" suggests the removal in the spiritual realm of one of our most important attributes? Doesn't it suggest instead that something bigger is in the offing? That fundamental passage, Ephesians 5:31 and 32, suggests exactly the opposite of how Paul's passage in Galatians 3:28 is usually interpreted:

But there's more to it than that: in John 5:19, Jesus makes a remarkable statement regarding His role during His first advent as the image of the Father:

> *Then answered Jesus, and said unto them, Verily, verily, I say unto you, The Son can do nothing of himself, but what he seeth the Father do; for whatever things he doeth, these also doeth the Son in the same manner.*

Applying this statement of Jesus to the big picture of His objective on earth, Scripture in general identifies it as Jesus' effort to save the souls of the human components of His future Bride through His work on the cross on their behalf. This He did, to the end that He might marry His beloved Church. If that objective is connected to the fact that Jesus did only that which He saw His Divine Father do, then we must conclude that the Father Himself is married. Of course, the only Member of the Godhead available for this union is a feminine Holy Spirit, as a gay relationship there most certainly is off the table.

To recap, in Ephesians 5:31 and 32, Paul speaks of the Church in terms of marriage to Christ. As Paul here echoes Adam's words regarding his wife Eve in Genesis 2:24, this marriage must involve gender. This implication of gender is given additional weight in Matthew 19:4-6. That this marriage bears fruit is asserted in another passage of Paul's, Romans 7:4:

> *Wherefore, my brethren, ye also are become dead to the law by the body of Christ, that ye should be married to another, even to him who is raised from the dead, that we should bring forth fruit unto God.*

How can the lack of gender spelled out in Galatians 3 and Matthew 22 be reconciled with the presence of gender in Matthew 19, Romans 7 and Ephesians 5? Simple! It's so basic that you'd have to be either blind or committed to a preconceived view to miss it.

While in a trivial way, as noted above, it's true that we won't possess gender in the spiritual realm, in a more significant way it's not true at all. The lack of gender in the spiritual realm refers to individuals. The presence of gender in that realm refers to an aggregate of individuals. The Church, as an entity beyond the individual, comprises that collection, and is indeed gendered. It's as simple as that – and profound beyond measure.

The situation is very much like that within our own bodies. Out of all the trillion cells and the numerous components of which we consist, we are gendered only in the complete assembly. Our gender involves many more than one single component, but includes our brains, our hearts (in the Biblical sense), our sight, our limbs, our faces, and last and possibly the least, our genitals. Paul made much about the distinction between the individual component and the entire assembly in the spiritual realm in several passages, including that found in 1 Corinthians 12:4-20.

Now there are diversities of gifts, but the same Spirit. And there are differences of administrations, but the same Lord. And there are diversities in operations, but it is the same God who worketh all in all. But the manifestation of the Spirit is given to every man to profit. For to one is given, by the Spirit, the word of wisdom; to another, the word of knowledge by the same Spirit; to another, faith by the same Spirit; to another, the gifts of healing by the same Spirit; to another the working of miracles; to another, prophecy; to another, discerning of spirits; to another, various kinds of tongues; to another, the interpretation of tongues. But in all these worketh that one and the very same Spirit, dividing to every man severally as he will.

For as the body is one, and hath many members, and all the members of that one body, being many, are one body, so also is Christ. For by one Spirit were we all baptized into one body, whether we be Jews or Greeks, whether we be bond or free; and have been all made to drink into one Spirit. For the body is not one member, but many.

If the foot shall say, Because I am not the hand, I am not of the body is it, therefore, not of the body? And if the ear shall say, Because I am not the eye, I am not of the body; is it, therefore, not of the body? If the whole body were an eye, where were the hearing? If the whole

were hearing, where were the smelling? But now hath
God set the members, every one of them, in the body, as
it hath pleased him. And if they were all one member,
where were the body? But now are they many members,
yet but one body.

Paul continues in that vein, but I think by now you get the point.
Gender applies to the Church, not the individual Christians who
comprise it.

Another passage that those in favor of a genderless God like to
trot out is found in Matthew 19:4-12, where Jesus responds to the
Pharisees' questions regarding divorce while claiming that it is God
who joins man and woman together in marriage:

And he answered and said unto them, Have ye not read
that he who made them at the beginning, made them male
and female; and said, For this cause shall a man leave
father and mother, and shall cleave to his wife, and they
two shall be one flesh? Wherefore, they are no more two,
but one flesh. What, therefore, God hath joined together,
let not man put asunder.

They say unto [Jesus]. Why did Moses then command to
give a writing of divorcement, and to put her away? He
saith unto them, Moses, because of the hardness of your
hearts, permitted you to put away your wives, but from the
beginning it was not so. And I say unto you, Whosoever
shall put away his wife, except it be for fornication, and
shall marry another, committeth adultery, and whosoever
marrieth her who is put away doth commit adultery.

His disciples say unto him, If the case of the man be so
with his wife, it is not good to marry. But he said unto
them, All men cannot receive this saying, except they to
whom it is given. For there are some eunuchs, who were
so born from their mothers womb; and there are some
eunuchs, who were made eunuchs by men; and there
are eunuchs, who have made themselves eunuchs for the
kingdom of heaven's sake. He that is able to receive it,
let him receive it.

The latter part of this statement of Jesus is less direct than that of
Matthew 22 and Galatians 3, but is frequently used as justification
for the assertion that God lacks gender. The gist of the standard

interpretation of it is, as Paul appears to echo in 1 Corinthians 7, that exercised gender in humans, while not exactly frowned upon by God, is a hindrance to a whole-hearted devotion to God. But here again Jesus is talking about individuals, and not every God-loving one at that – Jesus seems to acknowledge here that eunuchs comprise the exception rather than the rule. What the passage implies to me is that while gender is of God and basically good, in us it is but a weak representation of marriage in the spiritual realm, which is far grander. Indeed, in that passage quoted above from Matthew 19, Jesus appears to be talking of Himself, giving His listeners His reason for foregoing marriage in the material realm. Specifically, He was already betrothed to His Church. He must have been looking forward with great anticipation to that future marriage in the spiritual realm.

And then there's that thing about God Himself joining men and women together in marriage.

5
In the Beginning

Whether or not one may adhere to the Athanasian Creed, eternity as presented in it is commonly understood by Christians in the way it is expressed there, and the eternal coexistence of Father, Son and Holy Spirit also is commonly understood in that same way – foreverness – by the universal community of Christians.

But that misunderstanding not only is not taken directly from Scripture, it actually violates it. There was a point in existence when Jesus was entirely within the Father, as an integral part of Him. That's the most we can say of Jesus' existence, that there was this point where Jesus was not an individual personality external to the Father. That was a point where time itself, as we know it, didn't exist. Jesus Himself acknowledged this fact in Colossians 1:15 and Revelation 3:14, where He described Himself as the Beginning of the Creation of God.

The Holy Spirit and Jesus always were part of the Father, but at the very beginning there was no separation. They existed together as One, and that One was the Father, the Divine Will. Being alone and in full command of Himself, He had the choice to remain in that state and retain within Himself absolute power and authority over everything that He would subsequently create.

The theologian Arius picked up on that obvious point, declaring that there was a time that Jesus was not, at least not as an independent Being. As this point is Scriptural according to Revelation 3:14 and Colossians 1:15, Arius had a large sympathetic following, which gave other Church Fathers massive headaches. They ended up declaring him to be a heretic. But what really made Arius a heretic was his take-away from the limitation in time of Jesus' existence. From it, Arius developed the notion that Jesus was less than the Father, and therefore not truly God. That follow-on notion is not a necessary conclusion from Jesus' beginning in time. Arius simply didn't possess the common sense to see that.

Before time began, as I understand it from the early chapters of Genesis and from Jesus' noble act on the cross, the Father decided to act upon love as the greatest of His attributes. I believe that He did so through an irrevocable expression of His will. The decision cost Him dearly, reducing His exalted status from stand-alone Master of the cosmos to one element of a dual partnership. No longer would He be the All-in-All, but would henceforth share all that He was and had with Another. His motivation, to our everlasting gratitude, was the intrinsic quality of His character: His selfless nobility. His desire to have a Partner upon whom He could confer love transcended the benefit of unique greatness.

I see the process by which He accomplished this transformation as lovingly presented to us in Scripture. Do you remember, in Genesis 2 as we mentioned earlier, how God rent Adam's side, from which he extracted the rib from which He formed Eve?

Perhaps this account is not all about Eve. It may well be a reenactment, for those with eyes to see, of something even more profound that took place before time began – the bringing forth of a greater Eve from the Father's own rent side, of His essence still, a part of Him but a different Person.

Yet this beautiful former part of Him, the Holy Spirit, did not remain apart. What he lost, he regained in love, according to Adam's words in Genesis 2 as he gazed upon his new Wife:

> *And Adam said, This is now bone of my bones, and flesh of my flesh; she shall be called Woman, because she was taken out of Man. Therefore shall a man leave his father and his mother, and shall cleave unto his wife; and they shall be one flesh.*

Precisely as He created Eve to be Adam's complementary other, the Holy Spirit, the Father's feminine element, would faithfully reside by His side in the majestic harmony of creative union. To that end, He would maintain His primary role of Divine Will, while She would respond in selfless nobility to implement this Will into the reality of Creation. The story of that epic is found in Proverbs 8:22-31:

> *The Lord possessed me in the beginning of his way, before his works of old. I was set up from everlasting,*

from the beginning, or ever the earth was. When there were no depths, I was brought forth – when there were no fountains abounding with water. Before the mountains were settled, before the hills, was I brought forth; while as yet he had not made the earth, nor the fields, nor the highest part of the dust of the world. When he prepared the heavens, I was there; when he set a compass upon the face of the depth; when he established the clouds above; when he strengthened the fountains of the deep; when he gave to the sea its decree, that the waters should not pass his commandment; when he appointed the foundations of the earth, then I was by him, as one brought up with him; and I was daily his delight, rejoicing always before him, rejoicing in the habitable part of his earth; and my delight was with the sons of men.

Weightier minds than mine have made this connection between the Holy Spirit and the feminine Wisdom of Proverbs. In an article published in 2016 entitled "The Holy Spirit as Feminine: Early Christian testimonies and their interpretations", theologian Johannes van Oort said the following under the heading "The Pseudo-Clementines" in connection first with *Clementines, Homilies, 16, 12, 1* and next with *Wisdom of Solomon* 9:17:

"The text identifies *Wisdom* with the Holy Spirit. . . Wisdom is equated with the Holy Spirit and both are considered to be feminine."

One thing the Catholic Church did for the feminine which the Protestant Church did not was to include the Book of Wisdom within the body of canonical, and therefore considered to be inspired, Old Testament books. This beautifully-written book furnishes several interesting passages suggestive of the identity of Wisdom as the feminine Holy Spirit. Selected passages are presented below from Wisdom 9:2,4,9-11 and 17:

And in your wisdom have established humankind . . . Give me Wisdom, the consort at your throne . . . Now with you is Wisdom, who knows your works and was present when you made the world; Who understands what is pleasing in your eyes and what is conformable with your commands. Send her forth from your holy heavens and from your glorious throne dispatch her that she may be with me

and work with me, that I may know what is pleasing to
you. For she knows and understands all things, and will
guide me prudently in my affairs and safeguard me to
her glory . . . Or who can know your counsel, unless you
give Wisdom and send your holy spirit from on high?

When I first understood the connection between Wisdom and
the Holy Spirit, I found the possible details to be so moving that I
included it in my novel *Buddy*, as I pictured Wisdom relating Her
origin to Earl Cook:

"But then," She said, regaining control over Her emotions, "the
Father did something that was the essence of selflessness. It was of
an order of nobility that transcends everything that came after."

"Even Jesus on the cross?" he asked in wonder. "That was pretty
painful. And humbling."

"Yes. Even that. The Father was first to humble Himself. He set the
standard. And yes, it was painful too. Remember that He possessed
everything that was and ever will be. He chose to give that up."

"What did He do?"

"He chose to create an Other out of Himself, giving up part of
Himself in the process and restricting His portion in everything that
is or ever will be to that of one Member of a Partnership. He decided
to share His exalted position with that Other. But here's the great
beauty of what he did: in relinquishing His singleness He added love
into the mix. And through this love He again became One with His
Other."

In God's economy, the Holy Spirit acts in complementary fashion,
responding to the Father's will by furnishing the means to transform
His desire into reality. Although we have no idea what femininity
looks like in the spiritual realm, we do know that in the most general
sense, femininity is the perfect complement to masculinity. In that
sense, the Holy Spirit is feminine. As the perfect complement to the
Father, the Holy Spirit creates a harmonious coupling of Will and
Means through Her responsive execution of His wishes.

The executive nature of the Holy Spirit, wherein She is responsive
to the will of the Father, fits well with Jesus' words in Matthew 12:50:

*For whosoever shall do the will of my Father, who is in
heaven, the same is my brother, and sister, and mother.*

Hold on. Why should the Holy Spirit be considered to be
feminine when the Bible refers to this Diety in masculine terms?
Isn't Scripture supposed to be inerrant? Besides, for almost two
millennia this masculinity has been traditional in both the Catholic
and Protestant Churches. What gives here?

We might recall here that Scripture is indeed inerrant, but that
inerrancy applies only to the original. Mistakes in the various
translations are frequent and well-known. Most of them are
inconsequential. This one isn't. As for references to a feminine Holy
Spirit in the New Testament, a number of Bible scholars, including
Johannes van Oort, as noted earlier, have discovered that the earliest
Christians worshiped a feminine Holy Spirit.

But wouldn't that be contradicting Jesus' own words, particularly
in the Gospel of John? No, it wouldn't. It would be contradicting
what some arrogant, self-righteous "authority" did in tampering
with Scripture in the name of a false purity. Of particular interest
in this matter is the Sinaitic Palimpsest, discovered by Agnes
Lewis in 1892. (A palimpsest is a text where the original written
information was written over and subsequently retrieved.) Included
in this recovered text is John 14:26, where Jesus refers to the Holy
Spirit as feminine. This issue of deliberate tampering was discussed
in Chapter 2 as well as herein, and will be briefly revisited again in
Chapter 7.

In the original Hebrew Old Testament, the Holy Spirit was of
the feminine gender as well. Thanks to the research of theologians
possessing expertise in ancient Hebrew, Aramaic and Syriac
languages, we have retrieved the understanding that the original
Old and New Testaments both depict the Holy Spirit as feminine.
As noted previously, Dr. van Oort had found that the early Jewish
Christian and Syriac Churches understood the Holy Spirit to be
feminine as well. As acknowledged by a multitude of scholars
who have addressed the topic, the femininity is deeper than a mere
grammatical issue.

Among these modern scholars, Semitic language expert R. P.
Nettelhorst of the Quartz Hill School of Theology was surprised to

discover that in the Old Testament in the original Hebrew the Holy Spirit was unequivocally characterized as feminine. Passages of this nature, including Genesis 1:2, Judges 6:34 and, in fact eighty four such passages in the Old Testament alone, forced him to change his mind and take a tack in opposition to the prevailing understanding of the Holy Spirit's gender.

Although I've said it before, I wish to emphasize that the problem is not with the original Scripture. It always has resided above falsehood. The problem is in the multitude of translations of Scripture, some of which were made with an agenda in mind, that of assuring the purity of the Church in the face of the lewdness of the surrounding society.

In his book *Destined for the* Throne, Paul E. Billheimer noted that the Church had come from Jesus' side riven by the centurion's spear, drawing a parallel with the creation of Eve out of Adam's side. As was noted earlier, this remarkable similarity begs a question: could the divine Father Himself have brought forth the Holy Spirit out of His own parted side, establishing the first precedent for that beautiful act, such that He created His own complementary Other? If so, should Genesis 1:26 and 27 be interpreted in an entirely different way than it typically has been, such that the passage involves God as well as man? The Bible speaks often about gender, particularly with regard to mankind. But there also are passages that could well be interpreted as associating gender with God Himself. The creation of Eve out of Adam's side could well be one of these. I comment on this possibility in my book *Marching to a Worthy Drummer:*

"Moreover, I view the Holy Trinity as having existed throughout and beyond eternity either within or outside the Personage of the Divine Will. Eternity in this context began with time at the beginning of Creation. At some point beyond time as we know it, the human race being dimensionally limited, the Divine Father chose in love to separate Himself into two Beings, Father and Holy Spirit, thereby voluntarily in love choosing to reduce his status as All-in-All to one Member of a Partnership. That which the Father lost was reclaimed in love according to the words given to Adam by the Holy Spirit in Genesis 2:23 and 24, and applied to the union between the Divine Will and the Holy Spirit:

And Adam said, This is now bone of my bones, and flesh of my flesh; she shall be called Woman, because she was taken out of man. Therefore shall a man leave his father and mother, and shall cleave unto his wife; and they shall be one flesh.

Understanding the Holy Spirit in feminine, motherly terms, we can now appreciate in Genesis 1:1 and 2 how the Holy Spirit moved in response to God's will in bringing creation to reality.

In the beginning God created the heaven and the earth. And the earth was without form and void; and darkness was upon the face of the deep. And the Spirit of God moved upon the face of the waters.

According to Genesis 1:3-5, the Holy Spirit gave birth to Jesus in the process.

And God said, Let there be light; and there was light. And God saw the light, that it was good; and God divided the light from the darkness. And God called the light Day, and the darkness He called Night. And the evening and the morning were the first day.

(Recall that the sun and the moon were established on the fourth day.)

Jesus is the glory of implemented Creation, the Reality that arose from the union of the Holy Father and His lovely Partner, as expressed in John 1:1-7:

In the beginning was the Word, and the Word was with God, and the Word was God. The same was in the beginning with God. All things were made by him; and without him was not anything made that was made. In him was life; and the life was the light of men. And the light shineth in darkness; and the darkness comprehended it not.

There was a man sent from God, whose name was John. The same came for a witness, to bear witness of the Light, that all men through him might believe.

The beginning to which Moses and John referred was the birth of Jesus Christ, as acknowledged by Jesus Himself in Revelation 3:14. It was also the beginning of time as we know it, which began with Creation.

> And unto the angel of the church of the Laodiceans write: These things saith the Amen, the faithful and true witness, the beginning of the creation of God.

This origin of Jesus in which Jesus Himself apparently concurred with in the passage quoted above (Colossians 1:15 is similar), is considered by many to be a heresy. Nevertheless, a recent study showed that eighty percent of the American Christian population holds to that same "heresy", which an article wrongly identified as the old and famous "Arian Heresy".

This position is not the Arian Heresy, nor is it a heresy. A heresy is a belief that contradicts Scripture. The belief in the creation of Jesus does not contradict Scripture. What it does contradict is the various Church creeds, particularly the Athanasian Creed, which in essence stated that Jesus and the Holy Spirit coexisted eternally with the Father, and that none of these Members of the Trinity was created.

But the Athanasian Creed is extra-Scriptural, formulated at a time when the Church Fathers, fed up to their eyeballs with all the endless debate going on over Arius' position that Jesus was inferior to the Father and not truly God, clamped down on the discussion with the blanket statement that Jesus was indeed God and, furthermore, wasn't created. The Church Fathers indulged in overkill in taking this position. It's the creeds that are faulty in their claim that Jesus wasn't created, not Scripture. The heresy actually rests with Church tradition.

Arius, however, also deserves to be thought of as a heretic, not from his understanding that Jesus was created, but from what he concluded from that thought, namely that if Jesus was created by the Father, then he was inferior to the Father. Since when does being a son make one inferior to his father? Or, in Jesus' case, less than God?

One of Jesus' identifying names was Son of David. In Matthew 22:41-45, Jesus refers to David's Psalm 110:1, in which David refers to Jesus as his Lord, the implication being that this descendent (Son) of David would be greater than him. The passage in Matthew is given below:

While the Pharisees were gathered together, Jesus asked them, Saying, What think ye of Christ? Whose son is he? They say unto him, The Son of David. He saith unto them, How, then, doth David, in the Spirit, call him Lord, saying, The Lord said unto my Lord, Sit thou on my right hand, till I make thine enemies thy footstool? If David, then, call him Lord, how is he his son?

It appears that Arius failed to have read that passage, or perhaps failed to have recalled it.

The Jews certainly understood Jesus to have claimed that He was indeed God. That's why they tried to kill him, and eventually succeeded, but all according to God's will to our great benefit.

One clear example of Jesus' claim to be God is found in John 8:53-59:

Art thou greater than our father, Abraham, who is dead? And the prophets are dead. Whom makest thou thyself? Jesus answered, If I honor myself, my honor is nothing; it is my Father that honoreth me, of whom ye say, that he is your God. Yet ye have not known him; but I know him. And if I should say, I know him not, I shall be a liar like unto you; but I know him, and keep his saying. Your father, Abraham, rejoiced to see my day; and he saw it, and was glad.

Then said the Jews unto him, Thou art not yet fifty years old, and hast thou seen Abraham? Jesus said unto them, Verily, verily, I say unto you, Before Abraham was, I am.

Then took they up stones to cast at him; but Jesus hid himself, and went out of the temple, going through the midst of them, and so passed by.

We know from this passage that Jesus claimed to be one and the same Great I AM of Exodus 3:14 who spoke to Moses out of the burning bush, and whom the Israelites worshiped as their God. We also know, from the threat of His being stoned, that the Jews interpreted His words that way. But how certain can we be that Jesus really was that same God?

We can be very sure about that from an event that went beyond Jesus' words to action in John 18:3-6:

> *Judas, then, having received a band of men and officers from the chief priests and Pharisees, cometh there with lanterns and torches and weapons. Jesus, therefore, knowing all things that should come upon him, went forth, and said unto them, Whom seek ye?*
>
> *They answered him, Jesus, of Nazareth. Jesus saith unto them, I am. And Judas also, who betrayed him, stood with them. As soon, then, as he had said unto them, I am, they went backward, and fell to the ground.*

According to the early Jewish Christians who referenced the Gospel of the Hebrews, which is no longer in existence, Jesus also acknowledged His birth by the Holy Spirit prior to His incarnation through Mary.

"Just now, my Mother, the Holy Spirit, took me up. . ."

The early Christians welcomed the Holy Spirit into their hearts as their own spiritual Mother as well, a form of worship that was taken up much later by the Moravian Church in the mid-seventeen hundreds in America under the guidance of Count Nikolaus Ludwig Graf von Zinzendorf. The Moravian Church was exceptionally successful while they practiced that devotion.

These Churches had good cause to do so. Their justification may be taken directly from Scripture in John 3:5 and 6:

> *Jesus answered, Verily, verily, I say unto thee, Except a man be born of water and of the Spirit, he cannot enter into the kingdom of God. That which is born of the flesh is flesh; and that which is born of the Spirit is spirit.*

The pattern that God established for the bringing forth of His complementary Other he repeated for the creation of Eve out of Adam, and, later for the creation of the Church out of Jesus' side, rent by the Roman spear.

This understanding of Jesus as the beginning of creation and time differs somewhat from the Christian creeds that have Jesus co-existing with the Father throughout eternity. Which version is correct? I'll place my bet on Scripture, which has Jesus Himself stating that He is the beginning of the creation of God. In my opinion, those who formulated the various creeds attempted to understand time in the sense that is not understandable to the limited human mind.

Here's something a little extra to think about: does the multi-member composition of the Church point to a similar arrangement within the Holy Spirit? I think it does, and I'll tell you why. Back when I was writing my first Christian book *Family of God*, I had not yet learned of the large amount of evidence that points to multiple versions and translations of Scripture having been tampered with to the extent that the Holy Spirit was changed from feminine to masculine (the "He" issue). Yet, I had already become convinced of the Holy Spirit's functional femininity. Accepting that notion while maintaining an aversion to any thought of Scripture being less than inerrant, I had come to the conclusion that the Holy Spirit consisted of an aggregate of elements, such that the individual members, like in the same situation with respect to the Church, could rightly be considered male, being of the substance of the Father, while the combination could be functionally feminine, also just like with the Church. That still could be the case, but there now is so much evidence that suggests a switch in Scripture from feminine to masculine that my original supposition doesn't matter.

Again, it's not that I entertain any thought that the original Scripture could have been corrupted. The change occurred in the revisions and translations.

But the possibility of the Holy Spirit having an aggregate composition may be an important factor in understanding where angels belong in God's economy. If - like the individual persons comprising the functionally feminine Church, which as a collection are thought of as masculine (mankind is collectively designated as masculine) – the functionally feminine Holy Spirit also may well be a collective of individuals, wherein these individuals may be angels. There is a hint to that effect in Matthew 22:28-30:

> *Therefore, in the resurrection whose wife shall she be of the seven? For they all had her. Jesus answered and said unto them, Ye do err, not knowing the scriptures, nor the power of God. For in the resurrection they neither*

> *marry, nor are given in marriage, but are like the angels*
> *of God in heaven.*

Obviously, like the individuals within the Church, angels are intended to be neither male nor female, the fallen angels of Genesis 6 representing a violation of that intent. This raises the possibility that it is in the collective in the case of both the Church and the Holy Spirit that gender is functionally exercised. And, like the Church, that gender is functionally feminine. It is difficult to conceive of gender being absent in the collective, given Jesus' reference to the power of God, which suggests that something even greater is in play in the spiritual realm.

6
Agape is Not Enough

When as teens my brother and I went on vacation with our parents to the Sunshine Coast of British Columbia, our interest was keenly focused on the girls in the area. We'd have big bonfires on the beach, which would warm us as we lay on blankets with our arms around female representatives of the local population. A few years before that our interest lay in fishing. An in-between year was taken up in a fascination with snakes. We'd have contests as to who could catch the most in an hour. The record, as I recall, was forty seven.

Many years later, Carolyn and I took to the road in our recreational vehicle. A favorite spot was an RV campground next to a tiny little town in a high-desert valley close to Cochise Stronghold south of Willcox, Arizona and north of Bisbee and Sierra Vista. The owner of the park was into the Old West, and he arranged his campground to suit, parking the RVs in a circle around a central campfire, reminiscent of wagons circling at night. Benches were placed in a circle between the fire and the RVs. He'd light the fire at night, and expected a good turnout of campers to occupy the benches. The turnout was indeed good, as he was given to telling tales of the Old West with the drama of a natural storyteller. The black cowboy hat he wore added authenticity to his tales.

One night he entered the circle darkly, the spurs on his boots jingling, and sat down very close to the fire. Looking down at the coals with a black sky above, he told us of a gold mine he owned up in the Dragoon Mountains to the west that overshadowed the park. He wanted to open the mine to his campground buddies, he said with piercing stares at the rest of us, as the light from the fire highlighted his cheeks and forehead, making black holes of his eye sockets and rendering his face a skull. Our eyes were riveted on him as he explained the problem with the mine. The mine was a pit, he said, the first level being a hole about twenty feet in diameter and about ten feet deep. At the bottom of this first pit was a shelf that occupied half the area. The other half was another hole that went down vertically another hundred feet or so. At the bottom of that abyss was a tunnel that led to the vein, now worked out.

He wanted to give visitors access to the top hole, the shelf of which he'd eventually board up to close off the deeper hole. But he couldn't do that right then, because it was too dangerous. The mine already was occupied, he said with a frown. Just then, his right eye glinted with a reflection of a snapping ember. A boot jingled as he stamped on the ground. Something was underfoot, maybe a scorpion. The occupants of the pit, he said, were snakes. Big, mean rattlers, who inhabited dens in the pit. Maybe they were Mohave Greens, the most deadly of the species. He wanted to do this thing himself, he said, but his bad back prevented him from climbing down the ladder into the pit.

He scanned the crowd, electrifying his audience with two short, terrifying words: "Any takers?" The womenfolk got up to leave, offended with his boldness. They glared at their husbands as if to say they'd better not entertain any ideas of volunteering. A few men left with their wives, but the owner had cast a spell over us. The Old West had returned with a new sheriff in town, and we were the hand-picked posse. Several of us agreed to go take a look in the morning. Carolyn was angry with me for a bit, but calmed down fairly quickly, as she's an adventurous sort herself.

A few of us loaded our guns with snake shot that night, and fashioned snake-catchers out of PVC tubing, into which we inserted doubled-up electrical wires to grab them behind their venom-filled triangular heads.

In the morning we headed out to the mine in the back of the owner's truck. I don't know how it happened, I really didn't expect to be the one who'd enter the pit. But when we got there and we all peered down into that hole, one guy volunteered to take pictures of the event with a video camera that he'd brought along. Another rather quickly offered to hold the ladder at the top where the end rose a foot above the ground. Eventually they all found themselves important tasks to perform on top, which left me, the dummy, to go below.

Resigned to my fate, I descended the ladder with my PVC snake-catcher, beneath the light from a flashlight held above by one of the courageous volunteers. When I got to the bottom, I saw big holes in the face of the wall of the pit. It was very dim down there, so I asked for a flashlight that I could shine into the holes. Another noble soul extended his arm down as far as he could reach, allowing me to climb but a few short steps of the ladder to grasp the light. When I shone the light into the holes, a multitude of beady eyes glared back at me.

To be honest, the snakes were somewhat lethargic, being in hibernation and all. But still I was apprehensive, the more so as the evil-looking creatures had a green cast to them. One by one, I removed the snakes from their resting places and climbed the ladder partway with the snake held by the catcher, one hand maintaining pressure on the wires as I handed the assembly back up to the top. After each such trip I'd hear a gunshot as the snake was relieved of its head.

I became careless with the last snake, the biggest of the lot. I tripped on one of the ladder legs and twirled around, losing my balance. I couldn't grab anything for support, as both hands were occupied with the snake and the catcher. For an instant my back was turned to the ladder, the snake whirling above my head, and I looked down to face the deep shaft that I was perilously close to falling into. But my twisting took me back around and, with great relief, I found myself leaning against the ladder. Very carefully I proceeded to hand up the snake to the brave crowd above, then returned to retrieve the flashlight. When I climbed out, I thanked God for preserving my life.

When we returned back to the park I had every intention of passing off the event to Carolyn as a routine affair. The guy with the camera put the ax to that as he regaled the crowd with the evidence. Carolyn was incensed with me. She needn't have worried. If something like that ever was to happen again, I'd be the one to find a brave and important task above ground.

In our society one person's possessiveness toward another is not thought of as either good or healthy. It is often seen as evidence of mental instability, or at least as an unhealthy selfishness. The independence of the individual is a treasured asset.

Why, then, did Carolyn feel that she had the right to be angry with me over my little adventure? And why did I feel that she had that right as well?

Independence is not a universal need. There is an important exception to its appeal. In marriage and the family it produces, at least up to the childrens' teenage years, it is rare to find family members wishing for independence. In those cases where the need for it is present, the family is seriously dysfunctional.

The tie between man and wife is uniquely close. Carolyn was angry with me because I came close to stealing from her a prized possession – me. I belong to her and she belongs to me. We own each other in a bond that God Himself ordained.

Perhaps possessiveness is a bad feature in most human associations, but that's not the way God intended it to be viewed for marriage. In the marital union, possessiveness is the glue that holds the partners together, differentiating the nature of their relationship toward each other from the benign friendship of an *agape* association to the more intense *eros*-driven romance between lovers. Gender and possession go hand-in hand. Without mutual possession, there would be no long-term commitment to each other as God intended for marriage.

Is God "above" a possessive nature of that sort? Exodus 20:2-5 and Hosea 1:2 say otherwise:

> *I am the Lord thy God, who have brought thee out of the land of Egypt, out of the house of bondage. Thou shalt have no other gods before me. Thou shalt not make unto thee any carved image, or any likeness of anything that is in heaven above, or that is in the water under the earth; thou shalt not bow down thyself to them, nor serve them; for I, the Lord thy God, am a jealous God, visiting the iniquity of the fathers upon the children unto the third and fourth generation of them that hate me;*
>
> *The beginning of the word of the Lord by Hosea. And the Lord said to Hosea, Go, take unto thee a wife of harlotry and children of harlotry; for the land hath committed great harlotry, departing from the Lord.*

In the context of a gendered God, possession is as natural within the Godhead as it is for married humans, as the above passages suggest. For a genderless God, however, passages like Jeremiah 10:12 convincingly point to wisdom as an attribute of the Father Himself, as the Church usually interprets it.

> *He hath made the earth by his power; he hath established the world by his wisdom, and hath stretched out the heavens by his understanding.*

Even so, there are problems with the interpretation that God lacks gender. If wisdom is an attribute of the Father, then it does not represent a separate sentient Being. If that is the case, the function and role of the Holy Spirit becomes vague and confusing. Why is the Holy Spirit even necessary under that understanding?

Indeed, the necessity for the Holy Spirit as a Person within the Godhead has been debated by Christian theologians. Some sects even make that all-too-inevitable denial. Other theologians openly admit to confusion regarding the necessity for and role of the Holy Spirit.

In the gendered context the problems and associated confusion go away. If the Godhead enjoys more than an *agape* love among its Members, if their bonding love is the more intense, romantic and family-oriented love associated with *eros*, which is the type of love that bonds human families together, the Members of the Godhead own each other. *Eros* is joyfully possessive. One Member is the willing possession of another, exactly like a husband is a possession of his wife and children, a wife is the possession of her husband and children, and the children are possessions of both husband and wife. Society alludes to the possessive nature of *eros* by naming the wife after her husband. Adam alluded to it in Genesis 2:24 by claiming unity between man and wife, as did Jesus and Paul. Moses alluded to it in Genesis 5:2 by naming the wife after the man and in Exodus 20:14 by declaring adultery off-limits. In Ephesians 5, Paul also alluded to it by speaking of marriage (both between man and wife, and between Christ and His Church) in terms of mutual submission.

In the context of the possessive nature of love in the *eros* form, passages such as Jeremiah 10:12 may quite naturally be interpreted as God establishing the world through His beloved Holy Spirit, the feminine embodiment of wisdom.

This vast difference in interpretation points to the importance of presuppositional thinking in the interpretation of Scripture. Both interpretations are consistent with their respective understandings of the nature of the bond among the Members of the Trinity. But only one represents the truth.

If you've ever read The Song of Solomon, you know that it's pretty racy, but in a beautiful manner. While avoiding tawdriness, it elevates through romance the gendered relationship. If, however, gender isn't an element of the nature of God, what is this book doing in the canon of Scripture? That it doesn't apply merely to man is manifest in the very nature of the writing. Besides, if God resides above gender, the book simply wouldn't belong in the Bible, regardless of whether it applied only to man or had a larger purpose.

The application of this book to God was recognized by the editors of the KJV Schofield Bible, who included in a commentary of it that one of its purposes was an allegory of "Christ's love for His heavenly bride, the Church". Paul assures us in Romans 7:4 that this marriage is not sterile; it is more than a mere figure of speech, as theologians are given to understand.

> *Wherefore, my brethren, ye also are become dead to the law by the body of Christ, that ye should be married to another, even to him who is raised from the dead, that we should bring forth fruit unto God.*

In the context of gender in the spiritual realm as well as of the material world in which we find ourselves at the present time, we marvel at the prospect that God has laid before us in Revelation 19:7-9:

> *Let us be glad and rejoice, and give honor to him; for the marriage of the Lamb is come, and his wife hath made herself ready. And to her was granted that she should be arrayed in fine linen, clean and white; for the fine linen is the righteousness of saints. And he saith unto me, Write, Blessed are they who are called unto the marriage supper of the Lamb. And he saith unto me, These are the true sayings of God.*

The presence in Scripture of the Song of Solomon, John 2, and Ephesians 5 puts the issue of romance at rest. The romantic nature of the Song is possessive as well. *Eros* is in play here with God. As for the issue of a possessive nature, Exodus 20:5 and 34:14, and Deuteronomy 4:24, 5:9, and 6:15 inform us that God is jealous toward us. If jealousy doesn't imply a possessive attitude, nothing does.

More directly, as was noted earlier, Proverbs 8:22 describes the Father romantically possessing Wisdom, which we equate to the feminine Holy Spirit:

The Lord possessed me in the beginning of his way, before his works of old.

Agape love, as far as I know, does not connote the kind of ownership that Scripture describes God as possessing, either within or without the divine Godhead. Romance and possession go hand-in-hand; one becomes trivial, actually meaningless, without the other. *Agape* love just doesn't do the job.

Recall that Paul Billheimer captured the essence of the relationship between Jesus and His Church in his book *Destined for the Throne*. Billheimer claimed that the single purpose of Creation was the production and preparation of an eternal Companion for Jesus, called the Bride, the Lamb's Wife. He deduced from that purpose that romance is key to all existence. Noting that in Genesis 2 God had declared that it was not good for His Son to be alone, Billheimer asserted that God's purpose from the very beginning was that Jesus Christ should have an "Eternal Companion to sit by His side upon the throne of the universe as a bona fide partner, a judicial equal, to share with Him His sovereign power and authority over His eternal kingdom."

Billheimer sees in 1 Corinthians 6:2-3 a confirmation of his assertions regarding the sharing of Jesus' heavenly throne:

Do ye not know that the saints shall judge the world? . . .Know ye not that we shall judge angels?

Billheimer stopped short of asserting that the Church, in her spiritual form, may be integrated into the Godhead, nor did he directly imply that a feminine element exists within the Trinity. For example in his Chapter 2, page 37, he commented: "As sons of God [speaking of the individuals within the Church], begotten by Him, incorporating into their fundamental being and nature the very 'genes' of God, they rank above all other created beings and are elevated to the most sublime height possible short of becoming members of the Trinity itself."

But Billheimer came very close to those two intimately related associations. Two pages earlier, on page 35, he stated "Thus, through the new birth – and I speak reverently – we become 'next of kin' to the Trinity, a kind of 'extension' of the Godhead." Even more telling, in a footnote at the end of that chapter, he claimed "There is a clear and convincing implication in Genesis 1:27 that sex, in its spiritual dimension, constitutes an element of the image of God."

Paul Billheimer forcefully presented a relationship between Jesus and His Church that transcended *agape* love, describing a Jesus with whom we can relate with joyful anticipation.

7

The Stubborn, Intractable Church

Have you ever felt as helpless to control your destiny as a dumpster-rooting dog, looking up through rheumy eyes at a universe that doesn't seem to regard your existence as essential? Years ago after I retired from my engineering job, Carolyn and I would travel part of the year in one kind of RV or another. At various times we've had two tow-behind trailers, a motor home, and a fifth-wheel trailer. At one time during this routine, Carolyn and I would travel from the Seattle area to San Antonio, Texas, to operate a Christmas tree lot. We'd plan on arriving there just before Thanksgiving in order to be set up and selling trees immediately afterward as intended by the owner of the large multiple-lot operation. On one trip we made it to Kerrville just up the road from San Antonio by Thanksgiving Day, where Carolyn had planned to provide for us a splendid turkey dinner. We spent much time at the local grocery store picking out the perfect turkey. The RV had a microwave convection oven, into which we placed the beautiful bird. The cooking time was five hours, during which the mouth-watering scent grew ever stronger and my hunger increased to match. There was a window in the microwave into which I could peer as the turkey turned into dinner.

While the turkey roasted Carolyn had the trimmings cooking on the stove. Meanwhile, I was attempting to put the increasingly luscious smells out of my mind with a novel. The effort was largely unsuccessful. I must have consulted my watch a thousand times.

At last the time came to remove the turkey from the microwave. With great anticipation I pressed the button to open the door.

But the door wouldn't open. The plastic components of the latch mechanism had melted from the extended duration of the cooking process. The turkey was trapped inside the oven.

I, on the other hand, was trapped outside the oven.

Like a dog whose owner had cruelly pulled back the Beggin' Strips, I just stood there, staring helplessly at the evil microwave oven that refused to release its treasure. I didn't whine, pant or lick my chops, but I was very close to doing just that. I did break out into a sweat.

What reduced the accessibility even more, the microwave was embedded into cabinetry. My frustration overrode the complexity of the arrangement and after two hours I had pieces of cabinetry and a disassembled microwave on the dining table, out of which I finally plucked the turkey.

It was dark while we ate, but the meal turned out to be quite delicious. After dinner was over and the messes cleaned up, we both laughed.

I have the same dog-like feeling of helplessness in the face of the Church's refusal to address the issue of the femininity of the Holy Spirit. It's one thing for Church authorities to err with respect to it, and for the seminaries that they attended to teach such a massively harmful falsehood. It's quite another thing for these religious authorities to pass on this misinformation to the multitude of their congregants. But it's even worse than that – the authorities, seminaries and pastors both, are perfectly comfortable in their lack of any initiative to pursue the truth.

There are lots of reasons why a genderless God isn't such a hot idea. If this untruth represented a minor, inconsequential misunderstanding, it wouldn't be so important. But that's not the case. The consequence is painfully obvious in the indifference of the public toward what remains of the Church.

For one thing, it makes God different than us. Given the extent to which our sexuality impacts our humanity, that difference is a very big deal. At the very least, the vast difference leads to alienation.

Moreover, such a big difference is confusing. Many, if not all, explanations justify it on the notion that God is above sexuality.

But why, then, would God have endowed mankind with sexuality (Genesis 1:26 and 27) in the same breath that He claimed that we were made in His image, and afterward called His creation very good (Genesis 1:31) when such an attribute was beneath Him? In the same vein, why would God declare it "not good" for Adam to be without a female companion (Genesis 2:18) if He corrected that deficiency with gender if He was the least bit contemptuous of the inevitable result? By viewing God as having made us with an attribute that He considers unworthy of Him, we make a mockery of God's talent for design as well as fostering a rather bleak picture of the spiritual realm as static and uncreative.

Beyond the confusion in this matter regarding the heavenly role of mankind, there is even more confusion with respect to God Himself. In endowing mankind with an attribute for which He is above, this difference represents a very large hole in God's set of attributes. Being a deficiency, this lack contradicts our basic notion of God's completeness. Horse breeders understand this fact intuitively, calling an animal that has not been neutered "entire". This is not a trivial issue; it involves more than the mere inability to copulate, impinging on God's ability to love with the possessive nature of *eros*, constraining Him to the *agape* version of love, which, while being benign, lacks passion.

As was noted earlier, medieval cleric Jerome Zanchius saw this difference clearly. Unfortunately, he applauded it and attempted to formally codify it in his pretentious tome *Absolute Predestination.* In his definitions there of some of God's more important attributes, including love, passion and hatred, he saw God as quite different than man with respect to those qualities, God coming out as lacking the basic ability of conjuring up fervor in anything. The resulting representation of God has Him being benign in a rather hazy way, but an indifferent Sort. The Reformed Church enthusiastically bought into this garbage, which deviates demonstrably from what Scripture has to say about God's ability to emote. Other Churches followed suit, not realizing how far they were straying from the representation of God in the Bible. Scriptural examples of a God who differs radically from Zanchius' concept of Him include Genesis 1:27, Genesis 2, Deuteronomy 32:16, Psalm 79.5, Song of Solomon, John 2 (Cana), Ephesians 5, Deuteronomy 6:4 and 5, Matthew 19:6-8 and Matthew 22:37. These examples provide a mere taste of Zanchius' remoteness from Scripture. There are many more indeed.

Another confusing aspect of a genderless God is attempting with that view to understand God as both one and three. How, in the face of God's lack of gender, can one get perfect unity out of committee of three as set forth in Deuteronomy 6:4 and 5? It's hard to picture that kind of oneness with a binding force of common interest and *agape* love with no hint of family. Such an arrangement of one in three is more than confusing: it's logically inconsistent. Given the essential nature of this issue, why has the Church been so indifferent to this confusion?

Gender renders its possessor capable of romance. A God who can't experience romance? Give me a break. If that's the case, the Song of Solomon doesn't belong in the Bible. Nor does Jesus' first miracle at Cana, nor Paul's numerous depictions of Jesus' romance with His Church, particularly that in Romans 7:4 and Ephesians 5. I expect that someone will come along pointing out that Jesus didn't exercise His gender during His first advent, "proving" that gender doesn't belong to God. Of course Jesus didn't exercise His gender! As noted before, He was already betrothed to His Church, waiting for a future consummation. Zanchius and his followers make a mockery of this upcoming marriage, denying that it will be anything more than a shadow of the real thing. This denial distorts beyond recognition God's intent for gender to foster intimacy among the complementary others in the marital union. And that says nothing about procreation, a highly significant element of the function of gender.

A genderless God doesn't procreate. Some Christian creeds have cast this "fact" in concrete by declaring that all three Members of the Triune Godhead have coexisted throughout eternity, being uncreated Beings. Really? Actually, that notion doesn't square with Scripture either, contradicting Colossians 1:15, in which Jesus is described as the first-born of all creation, and Revelation 3:14, in which Jesus describes Himself as the beginning of the creation of God. In my estimation, the depiction of Jesus as uncreated was an over-the-top response to what has come to be called the Arian Heresy, wherein in the fourth century A.D. the Libyan priest Arius, in declaring that there was a time when Jesus was not, followed that up with the notion that therefore Jesus was beneath the Father, not worthy of Godhood. But it's simply common sense to understand that if Jesus was created, it doesn't necessarily follow that He cannot be God. The early Church Fathers, weary of all the heretical notions that kept cropping up during that period, failed to come to that obvious conclusion. Instead, they threw the baby out with the bathwater, embarking on a path that took them ever farther away from a Scriptural understanding of God.

In today's anything-goes society, sexual deviation generally has been placed rather forcibly by a loudly contentious minority into the realm of normal behavior. Yet, despite the trend of mainstream Churches to go with the flow on this, there are many Christians who vehemently oppose it, considering it to be an example of society's degeneration. What I can't understand is why, if these same Christians consider God to be genderless, as many of them do, they're so upset about it. After all, why should a genderless God, particularly if He doesn't engage in procreation Himself, concern himself with the manner in which humans engage in their sexuality? To be sure, in Leviticus 18 and Romans 1, God does admonish us not to participate in homosexual behavior. But these proscriptions can be explained away rather easily as simply being God's intent for us to multiply by referring to the passage in Genesis 1:28 where God calls us to procreate and fill the earth with ourselves.

But it just may be from the passage in Genesis 1:27 where God links His creation of man in His image to our gendered natures that God actually meant what He said here from a far deeper motivation: that mankind's gendered nature is a representation of God's own gendered nature. In fact, it amazes me how this passage is typically parsed such that our gendered nature has nothing to do with God's having created us in His image. If this verse is read as others are, sexual deviation of any kind, including adultery, would represent a violation of type, which is a far more serious matter than such deviation would be to a genderless God. Again, with our present misunderstanding of the nature of God, why the fuss?

In viewing God as lacking gender, we lessen the hope of being obedient to God's greatest commandment (Matthew 22:37 and 38), that we love God fervently. As I've noted before, attempting to love through the intellect just doesn't cut it.

Just as there are lots of reasons to consider a genderless God to be a bad idea, there are many reasons why a gendered God is a good one.

Among the most important of these reasons is Scriptural accuracy. Scripture interpreted naturally and understood in its entirety points directly without ambiguity toward a God who in unity represents the essence of Family. Such is evidently why Paul, in Ephesians 3:14-19, made that identical association, while at the same time mentioning all three Members of the Godhead:

> *For this cause I bow my knees unto the Father of our Lord Jesus Christ, of whom the whole family in heaven and earth is named, that he would grant you, according to the riches of his glory, to be strengthened with might by his Spirit in the inner man; that Christ may dwell in your hearts by faith; that ye, being rooted and grounded in love, may be able to comprehend, with all saints, what is the breadth, and length, and depth, and height, and to know the love of Christ, which passeth knowledge, that ye might be filled with all the fullness of God.*

Second is the ability, with this understanding, to intuitively grasp the nature of the Godhead without the slightest element of uncertainty or confusion. As noted before, even a child can comprehend such an arrangement. God has intentionally structured our lives around the core configuration of family, with its masculine father, feminine mother, and its fruit consisting of children, in order that we might naturally see in this structure a pattern of Him.

Third is our consequent ability, in perceiving the unity of family with its diversity of members, to love God as we love our own nuclear family, just as He commands us to do in Deuteronomy 6:4 and 5, and Matthew 22:37-40. Love of this kind and magnitude doesn't take effort – we don't have to go off on our own to contemplate this as an exercise in deep thinking, although at times we may wish to spend time alone in God-thought for the sheer joy of it. We can simply live our lives naturally, secure in our image of God in the same way we might at times reflect on the joys within our own core families (provided, of course, that the core family experience has been a good one). If the thought of a joyful family is iffy for you, be assured that the Family of God in heaven is more perfectly loving than the ones here on Earth.

We can even, in the context of the Family of God, appreciate negative life experiences as paths to growth toward the end of developing in us the selfless nobility that Jesus seeks in us as His spouse. Having an intimate relationship with our future Mother-in-Law, the Holy Spirit, in the face of life's downers, we can accept the compassionate comfort of Her indwelling feminine presence to help us through the experiences that act to strip us of our selfishness and thus render us capable of the love necessary to enjoy full communication and companionship with God.

Moreover, gender has a purpose. Actually, it has a multiplicity of useful, even essential, features, most of which go completely over the heads of our Church authorities.

It is quite possible that you could spend a lifetime as a churchgoing Christian without obtaining the slightest comprehension of the nature of God, other than superlatives of attributes like omnipotence, omniscience, omnipresence, and a host of other "omnis" that denote perfection with respect to capabilities. To most Christians including pastors with whom I have been acquainted, God is a superman with a crown, lacking only tights and a cape. Some see Him as a glorified Santa as well. But very few Christians, as far as I'm aware, venture beyond ultra-shallow assessments of that nature that might bring Him closer to our hearts.

On the day that Ronald was clued in to the role of gender with respect to procreation, he was forced to discover some of its essential meaning. Gender definitely furnishes other benefits besides reproduction, as the manufacturers and users of contraceptives are well-aware, but the most prominent function requires both male and female partners. It's obvious that birth - the continuation of life from one generation to the next - demands both masculine and feminine participants, or, in essence, complementary otherness. But complementary otherness is useful beyond procreation. There are certain activities supportive of life for which males are best suited, and the same can be said of females. The pairing of male and female supports their respective strengths such that in the whole – the family unit – their respective weaknesses vanish.

One wonders, though, whether Ronald ever realized the truly beautiful aspects of the blessings that sexuality, properly exercised within the boundaries that God Himself placed on the experience, confers on us humans. Above all, it fosters intimacy between the pair who have made lifelong vows toward each other. That, in turn, takes the focus off self and places it directly upon the other. The otherness between male and female discourages narcissism in the relationship. The differences between partners of a heterosexual union preclude notions of self-sufficiency and promote selflessness in their mutual love, encouraging nobility within the relationship. Nobility of spirit, I would think, is the ultimate benefit of sexuality, as it leads directly to a loving relationship with God.

Reproduction itself is a generator of beauty in love. Within the loving family, the child evokes a sense of responsibility within the parents, extending their nobility yet further. The child, in turn, receives the comfort of caring and stability – all in the context of loving intimacy.

Greatest of all, given the insight that the human family is representative of the Godhead, is that the family intimacy reaches outward toward a loving intimacy with God Himself, comfortable in the knowledge that despite the vast differences between God and ourselves, there is a familiar family tie that links us closely with Him. He is fully knowable in that very important sense which removes the element of alien from our relationship with Him.

So why, if gender is such a wonderful thing on so many levels, do Church authorities consider it to be so bad, particularly when applied to God?

Our uncle and aunt ran a ranch that was large enough to have its own machinery graveyard. Our fascination with engines began there at the age of twelve when we first visited that final resting place of nonrepairable mechanisms. The heady smell of gasoline and sagebrush permeated the air as we peered and poked at the rusted pieces, trying to decode the means by which the intricate assemblies had once performed their tasks. The engines captured the bulk of our interest. Through the cracked block of one we could catch glimpses of pistons and connecting rods, and from another we could see where the other ends of the connecting rods attached to the crankshaft to convert reciprocating into rotary motion.

My love of engines remained with me partway into high school, all the way up to the time when the back seats of my cars eclipsed the engine compartments as the focus of my interest. But even then I harbored no ill-will toward them. They were still quite useful in conveying me and my companion to places where the back seat could come into play.

My resentment toward engines began later, after I'd started a family and bought a house. The property included a yard with grass. The grass, in turn, required a lawn mower. My first foray into domestic maintenance began with a lawn mower that I had cleverly purchased in a garage sale.

Had I been more clever yet, the fact that behind the items for sale stood a brand-new lawn mower would have registered in my brain. The old lawn mower was for sale. The new one was not. There was a reason for that, as I found out when the time came to start the engine and begin cutting the nearby grass. That was most strange, as I had started the mower before I had bought it. I have since come to suspect that the previous owner had sprayed a liberal quantity of starting fluid (ether) into the carburetor to bag a sucker like me. By the time I finally got the engine to start I was exhausted. My mind also was heading toward a dark place, one where the engine was capable of understanding the pain I wished to inflict upon it. Eventually I rid myself of it, and in a more noble manner than the other owner: I took it to the junkyard, where it never again could shatter the family harmony of another poor sap.

Engines aren't the only balky things. People can be balky too. They can be so hide-bound that they refuse to entertain any thought that resides outside the confines of their mental boxes, regardless of whether or not a particular thought might be more truthful than the blatant falsehood that rests so comfortably within the person's box.

There was plenty of motivation within the early Church for her to embrace the falsehood that God lacks gender. After shame, among the most pressing of these drivers was the sexual misconduct associated with the pagan rituals and the Church's corresponding desire to distance herself from that kind of behavior; a similar driving issue was the Gnostic sect of the young Christian community, which, while perceiving God as gendered with the Holy Spirit as feminine like the earliest Church did, also held to some pretty bizarre misunderstandings of God. Their odd theology led the more mainstream Church to throw the baby out with the bathwater, ridding God of gender altogether.

More than a millennium has passed since these issues were factors in how the Church came to define herself. They are no longer relevant. Nor is the Church's attitude toward gender in the Godhead. Yet they reside in the box of mainstream Church thought and hidebound "authorities" refuse to contemplate their removal. Perhaps the laypersons of the Church need to stand up and explain to their theological betters why gender is a useful attribute of the Godhead Itself.

Not that there haven't been heroic attempts to explain away the confusion, the only problem being that those highly-qualified theologians such as Benjamin Warfield and Alister McGrath who have engaged in this work have stubbornly refused to either address or take seriously the real issue, the proper gender of the Holy Spirit.

Earlier on, I had described a situation in which I felt like a helpless dog. Here as well I have the same frustrating feeling, which puts me in mind of an event that took place as we returned home from selling Christmas trees in San Antonio. Our favorite route northwest from San Antonio to the Seattle area took us close to the Texas/Mexico border, where we'd stop for a night at Marathon, sitting outside in the quiet evening looking southward at the vast desert in front of us, seemingly untouched by human hands until a freight train would interrupt us with its own kind of entertainment. The next day would continue to take us westward, where we'd end up at the pretty and very interesting town of Alpine, Texas. Besides its college, Alpine also boasted a relatively high elevation for a Texas town. Indeed, within an hour's drive up the nearby Mount Locke at an elevation of around 7800 feet is the McDonald Astronomical Observatory run by the University of Texas – Austin. Closer to the town is Fort Davis, a National Historic Site showing remnants of the era of Indian wars.

There is so much of interest to the traveler in the Alpine area that we stayed there a week in a nice, secluded RV park run by an attractive young woman. Our first night there she volunteered a must-see attraction, the Marfa Lights. Marfa is located fifteen miles to the west of Alpine. The next evening after dark Carolyn and I went there and found a parking area specifically designated for viewing the "Lights". We pulled into the last empty space and turned off the engine. After straining our eyes to no avail, we then became distracted by the goings-on around us. Some cars were playing music; all consisted of couples engaged in heavy petting. At intervals they would break off their embraces to lift bottles to their lips, after which they'd carry on as before. What the heck, we decided. When in Rome. . . We didn't have anything to drink, but we did enjoy each others' company, glancing out the windshield on occasion to attempt a sighting of the "Lights".

The next morning the operator was out and about, and as I approached she asked me how the "sighting" went. I grinned a little and said, "it was okay, but we didn't see any lights."

She grinned back and scratched her head. "I don't know," she responded. "Did you bring along a six-pack?" When I told Carolyn about our short conversation, we both cracked up.

The next day things turned serious. A couple of years back, I had developed a heart condition that called for the insertion of a stent. I understood the symptoms of the condition and now I felt a recurrence. I also knew that it was mild, so I wasn't in any real danger. Nevertheless, we went to the nearby clinic for an evaluation. I was examined by a young nurse, who checked my vitals. After the brief examination, she very calmly asked me to return to the waiting room. With a smile, she closed the door. When I was out of sight, she immediately called the heart doctor at the nearby hospital, picked up my folder and, hair flying in the wind, ran headlong out to her car, threw it into gear and screeched out of the parking lot speeding toward the hospital.

In the meantime, I was sitting down in the waiting room watching the entire drama play out through the large picture window facing the parking lot. I knew that I wasn't having a heart attack, so I could only laugh at the surreal scene and the nurse's attempt to keep me in the dark about what she thought was a life-endangering situation. I was still laughing when she returned and called me back in. She admitted that maybe she overreacted. I told her that it was good entertainment but that I kind of felt like a helpless dog. I made sure afterward that she knew I was grateful for her concern on my behalf.

As I said before, my "helpless dog" feelings come back whenever I think of the blind adherence to unscriptural dogma that besets our theological authorities. They simply fail to think things through, preferring to confine themselves to very small intellectual boxes.

Despite the general official refusal of the Protestant Churches to address the void caused by the removal of functional gender from God, a number of earnest theologians, well informed regarding most theological issues but smugly self-satisfied while dismally lacking with regard to this one, have attempted to explain the nature of the Holy Spirit in a way that, while conforming to Church doctrine, presents the Holy Spirit in a logical and, as they struggle to achieve, a warm manner.

Both the Father as the divine Will and the Son as Jesus Christ, the divine Word, are well-defined in Scripture as to their general natures and their functional roles. Of the three Members of the Trinity, the Holy Spirit is by far the most enigmatic. It is the lack of understanding, or perhaps simply the misunderstanding, of the nature of this divine Member from which the confusion and apparent complexity of the Trinity has arisen. A substantial part of this confusion is the obviously apparent but discomforting feature of the Holy Spirit's character as embracing specifically feminine elements in contradiction to the general view of the Trinity as being either gender-neutral or masculine.

Many expositors of the Holy Spirit see in Genesis 1 the active participation of the Holy Spirit in the act of creation. This is the position taken by respected scholar of Scripture Benjamin B. Warfield, who describes this functional attribute of the Holy Spirit in Chapter Seventeen of his book *The Holy Spirit*:

"His offices in Nature – The 'Spirit' or personal 'Breath' is the Executive of the Godhead, as the 'Son' or 'Word' is the Revealer. The Spirit of God moved upon the face of chaos and developed cosmos (Gen. 1:2). Henceforth he is always represented as the author of order and beauty in the natural as of holiness in the moral world. He garnished the astronomical heavens (Job 26:13). He is the organizer and source of life to all provinces of vegetable and animal nature (Job 33:4; Ps. 104:29, 30; Isa. 32:14, 15), and of enlightenment to human intelligence in all arts and sciences (Job 32:8; 35:11; Ex 31:2-4)."

Dr. H. A. Ironside, in a little tome first printed in 1941 entitled *The Holy Trinity,* also interprets Genesis 1:2 as asserting that the Holy Spirit, in concert with the Father, was actively involved in creation. Interestingly, in referencing Isaiah 66 as an Old Testament reference to the Trinity he quotes from verse 13:

As one whom his mother comforteth so will I comfort you.

Although Ironside invariably interprets the Holy Spirit in terms of the masculine pronoun 'he', he also confesses a lack of full understanding of the nature of the Trinity. Yet the passage quoted above, by associating the word 'mother' with 'comfort', furnishes a key argument for the feminine function of the Holy Spirit. For Jesus, in John 14:16 and 17, directly links the Holy Spirit with the name (implying role) Comforter:

And I will pray the Father, and he shall give you another Comforter, that he may abide with you for ever; Even the Spirit of truth; whom the world cannot receive, because it seeth him not, neither knoweth him: but ye know him; for he dwelleth with you, and shall be in you.

Could it be that the masculine pronouns in this passage, as well as elsewhere in Scripture, refer to the substance of the Holy Spirit rather than functional nature? Or is it even more likely that the original "she" was deliberately changed to "he" in opposition to the maintenance of Scriptural integrity, as indicated by John 14:26 in the original Sinaitic Palimpsest, which refers to the Comforter as "She". This issue was touched on in Chapters 2 and 5, and will be revisited in Chapter 9.

Dedicated theologian Dr. Bruce A. Ware makes similar statements as Warfield regarding the executive (implementation of will) role of the Holy Spirit in his work *Father, Son, & Holy Spirit*. In fact, this executive role of the Holy Spirit is a general theme among theologians. In his own work, Ware encapsulates the roles of Father, Son and Holy Spirit as follows: Father – Grand Architect; Son – Submission to the Father in doing (displaying) His Will; Holy Spirit – Carrying out the work of the Father.

Alister McGrath, who wrote the work *Understanding the Trinity*, provides a representative viewpoint of this genre, yet also furnishes some remarkably fresh insights. He stands on what I humbly perceive as firm soil in his eloquent and moving descriptions of God and the incarnate Jesus in chapters 1 through 6. In reading it for a second time quite recently, I realized afresh how his treatment of the Trinity had influenced my own work *Family of God* (original edition). It was Dr. McGrath, in fact, whom I mentioned on pages 24 through 26:

"Some theologians, having briefly noted the one intuitively satisfactory functional description of the Trinity, reject this particular answer quite abruptly, justifying their rejection on the basis of insufficient logic. They proceed from there to hammer out tortuously-derived and ultimately insufficient, emotionally empty alternatives. One such expositor, who otherwise paints with highly readable and insightful words a delightful description of God, mentions the Trinity with profound understanding and then quickly discards it as a misapplication of a familiar model in an attempt to apply too much of what is, after all, just a simplistic and imperfect model to the reality of God Himself. In his haste to reject that application, however, he violates the same logical guidelines which he carefully presented in the immediately preceding pages of his discussion.

"This same theologian, in viewing the Trinity in the uncontroversial terms of man's encounters with God, explains it as different facets of His nature through which God has chosen to reveal Himself to man. God, he asserts, is altogether too vast for man, with his limitations in time and space, to acquire a complete picture of His entire nature. We can sample portions of this Divine Entity, however, and by thinking through the implications of the composite picture that He has given us through Scripture, we perceive His Trinitarian nature and the necessity for it. This experiential description is, I think, a valid one and has the advantage of being safely neutral with respect to gender. It is certainly the most intuitively satisfying characterization of the Trinity that I have seen to date. Yet such an exclusively man-centered description yields a disappointing poverty of information about God Himself, leaving the reader to ask why, if God does indeed have a Trinitarian nature, He is so reluctant to share a picture of that characteristic with us in terms of His intrinsic functional attributes. It would seem, after all, that a God-centered intuitive understanding would naturally lead to a greater appreciation of Him, and consequently a greater love toward Him on the part of His subjects. One might easily suspect, as a matter of fact, that those individuals in the past who were named in the Book of Hebrews, did indeed have personal insights into the nature of God beyond those which the usual churchgoer might have access to via his pastor or his reading of Scripture."

The description of the Trinity that Dr. McGrath presented with profound understanding and subsequently discarded in haste begins on page 57 of *Understanding the Trinity*. An important continuation is presented twelve pages later, where the author appears to wish to tone down his rejection of the earlier model by presenting some qualifying remarks which suggest that perhaps he himself had some persistently lingering thoughts about the nature of the Holy Spirit that he didn't wish to assert directly:

"It was therefore assumed that light also needed to travel through something [as was the case for sound, upon which light was modeled], and the word 'aether' was coined to describe the medium through which light waves traveled. If you read old radio magazines, or listen to old radio programmes, you'll sometimes find people referring to 'waves traveling through the aether'. But by the end of the century it had become clear that light did not seem to need any medium to travel through. What had happened was simply that the logical necessity of one aspect of the model (sound) had initially been assumed to apply to what was being modeled (light), and this assumption was gradually recognized to be incorrect as the experimental evidence built up.

"And so it is with models of God. For example, we often use 'father' as a very helpful model of God, emphasizing the way in which we are dependent upon God for our existence. But for every human child there is a human mother as well as a human father. This would seem to imply that there is a heavenly mother in addition to a heavenly father. But this assumption rests upon the improper transfer of the logical necessity of an aspect of the model (father) to what is being modeled (God), in just the same way as the necessity of one aspect (the need for a medium of propagation) of the model (sound) was transferred to what was being modeled (light). . ."

Whew! Cutting to the essence of that, he's saying that parallels aren't always exact.

". . . Although the strongly patriarchal structure of society of the time inevitably meant that emphasis was placed upon God as father (e.g., Jeremiah 3:19; Matthew 6:9), there are several passages which encourage us to think of God as our mother (e.g., Deuteronomy 32:18). We shall be considering these two images together, and ask what they tell us about God.

"The first, and most obvious, point is that God is understood as the one who called us into being, who created us. Just as our human parents brought us into being, so God must be recognized as the author and source of our existence. Thus at one point in her history, Israel is chided because she 'forgot the God who gave [her] birth' (Deuteronomy 32:18; cf. Isaiah 44:2, 24; 49:15).

"The second point which the model of God as parent makes is the natural love of God for his people. God doesn't love us because of our achievements, but simply because we are his children. 'The Lord did not set his affection on you and choose you because you were more numerous than other peoples, for you were the fewest of all peoples. But it was because the Lord loved you' (Deuteronomy 7:7-8). Just as a mother can never forget or turn against her child, so God will not forget or turn against his people (Isaiah 49:15). There is a natural bond of affection and sympathy between God and his children, simply because he has brought them into being. Thus God loved us long before we loved him (1 John 4:10, 19). Psalm 51:1 refers to God's 'great compassion, and it is interesting to note that the Hebrew word for 'compassion' (*rachmin*) is derived from the word for 'womb' (*rechmen*). God's compassion towards his people is that of a mother towards her child (cf. Isaiah 66:12-13). Compassion stems from the womb."

A delightful feature of Dr. McGrath's discourses, remarkable for its rarity, is a description of God's loving relationship to mankind in romantic terms, a facet of God with which I wholeheartedly agree. Another feature of his presentation which I admire is his lengthy discussion of the necessities of Jesus' essence as both man and God, and of His resurrection. Yet another interesting item that he presents in his chapter entitled *A Personal God* is his strong intimation of free will with respect to salvation in the face of his self-proclaimed deep interest in Martin Luther. Here he makes statements such as "In no way does God force us to respond positively to him." He goes on to liken the notion of God's exclusive influence over our salvation as akin to rape rather than love. This item is worthy of further exploration.

Unfortunately, Dr. McGrath appears to be on less stable ground in his discussion of the Trinity. In his presentation of this dogma he avoids delving too deeply into God's intrinsic nature or attributes by substituting in its place a lengthy experientially-based account of Him in terms of His interaction with mankind. He is careful near the outset of his discourse, however, to distance himself from any notion that the Trinity includes a female Persona. He does so in his chapter entitled *Thinking About God* by noting that intellectual models are subject to misapplication through the improper assumption that every attribute of a model must apply to its counterpart in reality. As already noted, he cites as an example the wave characteristic of sound as a model for light, as was quoted directly from his work above.

But is the assumption of a Divine Mother in the economy of God necessarily a misapplication of the human parent model? It could be, but that's a long way from must be. Nowhere does Dr. McGrath justify the necessity that he associates with that application. Instead, he elevates a mere illustrative example to the status of a law, which easily could be construed as either less than honest or less than brilliant. (Actually, I recognize my lack of qualification to cast such judgment on a man who possesses doctorates in both theology and science; indeed, I suspect quite strongly that he is neither dishonest or less than brilliant. Rather, I think that his presentation here is an overzealous attempt to distance himself from an extremely controversial topic.)

Moreover, and again as we have already noted, a short twelve pages further along, Dr. McGrath equivocates a bit regarding the possibility of motherhood in God's economy, citing a number of Scriptural passages that describe God in a role more appropriate to motherhood than to fatherhood.

Almost at the end of his book it can be seen how Dr. McGrath rescues himself from this apparent inconsistency: as discussed in more detail below, he does not posit a distinct member of the Godhead who possesses the attributes of femininity; instead, he attributes this characteristic to the same Person as the Father. But rather than solving the problem of the feminine side of God, he comes dangerously close both to ultra-monotheism and modalism. Beyond that, he defines a God with gender characteristics indeed, but in the same Person. According to 1 Corinthians 6:9, 10, this suggests a model for a human malady known as hermaphroditism, which is contrary to Scripture, even to the extent of being labeled as unrighteous:

> *Know ye not that the unrighteous shall not inherit the*
> *kingdom of God? Be not deceived: neither fornicators,*
> *nor idolaters, nor adulterers, nor effeminate, nor*
> *abusers of themselves with mankind, nor thieves, nor*
> *covetous, nor drunkards, nor revilers, nor extortioners,*
> *shall inherit the kingdom of God.*

I find it hard to believe, given its treatment in Scripture, that in His own organization God would wish even to hint at sexual perversion, or even sexual difficulty.

The essence of McGrath's description of Jesus may be encapsulated in this passage, found in his chapter entitled *God as Three and God as One*: "The difficulties really begin with the recognition of the fundamental Christian insight that Jesus is God incarnate: that in the face of Jesus Christ we see none other than the living God himself. Although the New Testament is not really anything like a textbook of systematic theology, there is nothing stated in the great creeds of the church which is not already explicitly or implicitly stated within its pages. Jesus is understood to act *as God and for God:* whoever sees him, sees God; when he speaks, he speaks with the authority of God; when he makes promises, he makes them on behalf of God; when he judges us, he judges as God; when we worship, we worship the risen Christ as God; and so forth."

Dr. McGrath goes on to characterize Jesus in his incarnate form as not actually comprising the fullness of God, but merely as a representative sample of God suitable for furnishing humanity with some comprehension, consistent with their limitations, of the far more complete spiritual God who resides in heaven. He claims in a similar vein that the Holy Spirit, like Jesus, is another manifestation of God, in this case one that indwells the believer, that furnishes another way by which redeemed mankind can encounter, or experience, God.

A comment regarding Dr. McGrath's comparison above of Scripture with "the great creeds of the Church": I contend that in at least the areas of the eternal coexistence of the Members of the Godhead, and of their interrelationship, the creeds are at variance with Scripture. That I'm far from alone in this contention is demonstrated by the "Great Schism" between the Western and Eastern branches of the Church over the issue of the Filioque.

Dr. McGrath ends with this commentary:

"We can now see why Christians talk about God being a 'three-in-one'. One difficulty remains, however, which must be considered. How can God be three persons and one person at the same time? This brings us to an important point which is often not fully understood. The following is a simplified account of the idea of 'person' which may be helpful, although the reader must appreciate that simplifications are potentially dangerous. The word 'person' has changed its meaning since the third century when it began to be used in connection with the 'threefoldness of God'. When we talk about God as a person, we naturally think of God as being *one* person. But theologians such as Tertullian, writing in the third century, used the word 'person' with a different meaning. The word 'person' originally derives from the Latin word *persona*, meaning an actor's face-mask – and, by extension, the role which he takes in a play.

"By stating that there were three persons but only one God, Tertullian was asserting that all three major roles in the great drama of human redemption are played by the one and the same God. The three great roles in this drama are all played by the same actor: God. Each of these roles may reveal God in a somewhat different way, but it is the same God in every case. So when we talk about God as one person, we mean one person *in the modern sense of the word*, and when we talk about God as three persons, we mean three persons *in the ancient sense of the word.* It is God, and God alone, who masterminded and executes the great plan of salvation, culminating in Jesus Christ. It is he who is present and active at every stage of its long history. Confusing these two senses of the word 'person' inevitably leads to the idea the God is actually a committee, which, as we saw earlier, is a thoroughly unhelpful and confusing way of thinking about God."

One certainly could not accuse Dr. McGrath of being a tritheist. On the other hand, despite his denial on the back cover of the book that he entertains the heretical notion of modalism, he's on shaky ground there, being right on the edge or over it according to his own words.

Dr. Mcgrath is somewhat unique among other well-established theologians in that his scientific training has furnished him with an ability to be objective in his presentation and make use of useful intellectual tools such as models to make his points. Further, he at least addresses some notions that others avoid like the plague, as if they themselves might be infected by ideas they may have been taught were close to blasphemous. He has in common with the others, however, several notions regarding the Holy Spirit that are generally accepted within faithful Christendom: while all Members of the Trinity possess the same substance and are fully and equally God, they differ with respect to functional role; the role for the Holy Spirit conforms most closely to that associated with executive companion and motherhood; the Holy Spirit is a background Entity, more self-effacing than Father and Son; the Trinity (as confessed by the Church) is a mystery beyond man's comprehension. The 'others' who share these particular view with Drs. McGrath and Ware include Dr. Peter Masters (*The Faith*) and James R. White (*The Forgotten Trinity*).

I agree quite thoroughly with all of these points except the last, regarding the mystery which appears to be beyond comprehension, with which I disagree quite thoroughly. To me, the incomprehensibility in understanding the Trinity is another typical case of man's brain outsmarting his heart. What should be an extremely simple and intuitive understanding, man has turned into a riddle, in the process wrapping himself tightly around the intellectual axle.

A case could be made that in the many attempts made by scholars of Scripture to describe the Holy Spirit, they end up implying an association of the Holy Spirit with Wisdom. Wisdom, of course, is given a lengthy treatment in Proverbs, with a female gender association.

As I have noted, I appreciated Dr. McGrath's extensive use of models. I believe that they are so effective, as a matter of fact, that I'd like to offer one of my own: that of a war ship. In this model the commanding officer, or CO, would be the functional counterpart of the Father. Under rigid shipboard discipline there is only one leader of the entire vessel, and that is the CO. He must make the tough decisions and live with the consequences; correspondingly, it is his will, and his alone, that must be instantly obeyed by the rest of the crew. The counterpart of Jesus in this model is the action that results from the CO's orders. The next in the chain of command is the executive officer, or XO. The XO has the responsibility of executing, or carrying out, the CO's commands; like the XO's counterpart the

Holy Spirit, it is the XO who makes the will of the CO actually happen. While the XO is subordinate to the CO, he is in an understudy mode, being in constant readiness to assume command should some misfortune befall the CO. Therefore, the XO is capable of being CO, but willingly assumes a subordinate position for the sake of the ship's welfare. One can readily perceive that the CO and XO are an interdependent pair, each having different but complementary functions. It is in these complementary functions that the CO serves in a male role and the XO in a female role. One might well argue that on a warship, both CO and XO are eminently masculine. Both, to be sure, are cut from the same masculine cloth, just as (I perceive) the Holy Spirit is male with respect to substance, proceeding from the Father. On the functional side of things, however, one must be careful to note that the XO doesn't initiate the basic commands, but rather responds to them in a subordinate manner by carrying them out in fulfillment of the CO's will. This responsive characteristic, I would assert, is eminently feminine. Note in this context the synergy in the complementary interaction, which indeed is suggestive of a male-female relationship. The only thing that could bring it closer and more effective would be the level of communication and mutual empathy intrinsic to a love-based relationship, i.e. the marital union, which for that reason, in my mind, remains a more representative model of the relationship between Father and Holy Spirit than the shipboard chain of command.

8

A Church that Got it Right (Temporarily)

Recently as I was browsing the Internet I came across a fascinating article written by Dr. Craig D. Atwood entitled *Motherhood of Holy Spirit in 18th Century*.

According to Dr. Atwood's biography, his current title is the rather lengthy "Charles D. Couch Associate professor of Moravian Theology and Ministry Director of the Center for Moravian Studies". He is a faculty member of the Moravian College and Theological Seminary located in Bethlehem, Pennsylvania, where he teaches Moravian theology and history, Christian history, religion in America, and history of Christian thought.

His present interests include a desire to help the Christian community in general to "rediscover the riches of the Moravian theological heritage". There is a hint in this aspiration, supported in the article noted above, that he sees that something quite valuable was lost in the transition of the Moravian Church away from its unique early dogma toward a more mainstream perception of our Trinitarian Godhead.

The perception that was abandoned by the Moravian Church is identified in the title of the article: The Femininity of the Holy Spirit.

The article itself, which was delivered in a presentation to the faculty of the Moravian College in 2011, traces the history of the Moravian Church in America during its most controversial (and possibly its most fruitful) period, the two decades of the 1740s through the 1750s. From the establishment of the Moravian community of Bethlehem in 1741 on a 500-acre plot purchased from the estate of George Whitefield, the Church initially adhered to the theology of Moravian (now Czechoslovakia) Count Nicholas Ludwig von Zinzendorf.

Zinzendorf's theology is rooted in the Czech reform movement of the fourteenth century, in which John Hus' protests against the Catholic Church a full sixty years before Luther landed him astride a stake, where he was burned as a heretic in 1415. Followers of Hus organized the Moravian Church in 1457 in the village of Kunvald, about a hundred miles east of Prague. The Church spread into Poland through heavy persecution in the sixteenth century. Continuing persecution in the seventeenth century contributed to a relative stasis in the Church. It enjoyed a revival in the eighteenth century as the Church planted roots in Bethlehem, Pennsylvania under the leadership of Count Zinzendorf.

According to Dr. Atwood, Bethlehem, which lies on the outskirts of Allentown in southeastern Pennsylvania, just north of Philadelphia and west of the New Jersey border, enjoyed particular favor from God, as the community was one of the most successful in pre-revolution America. Atwood implies that this favor resulted from the unique theology of the Moravian Church, in which the Holy Spirit was considered the Spouse of the Holy Father and Mother of Jesus and His Church.

This perception of the Holy Trinity continued at least for the twenty years following the establishment of Bethlehem, but following the death of Count Zinzendorf and his wife and son, the far-weaker post-Zinzendorf Church leadership fell away into a desire to conform more closely to the more popular "mainstream" dogmas of the Protestant Churches in the surrounding communities. They completed their abandonment of dogma by burning Zinzendorf's writings.

Dr. Atwood appears to lament this transition toward "normalcy", implying that Bethlehem and the Moravian Church did not continue in the favor of God thereafter. He expresses disappointment in the manner in which this transition was handled during the time he was a student of the Moravian seminary, claiming that in continuing embarrassment Church historians label the two initial decades of the Moravian presence in America as "a time of sifting', wherein the theological "experimentation" of the time eventually led to the more "stable" dogma of mainstream Christianity. In opposition to this false and rude dismissal, Dr. Atwood claims that a substantial segment of the Moravian Church continues in the initial dogma even to this day.

Dr. Atwood himself seems to be seeking a re-establishment of that early doctrine of the Holy Spirit, not only for its intrinsic truth but for the good of the Church and perhaps even America. As he commented regarding Zinzendorf's view of the Godhead as a divine family in another article entitled *Holy Spirit as Mother*, "This is a language that even a child can comprehend. It is the best language to communicate spiritual reality for all people because it does not depend on abstract reasoning or speculation on unfathomable realities."

One can be so devoted to his intellect that he completely misses the simplicity of God's presentation of Himself to us through Scripture. The situation calls to mind what Jesus said to His disciples in Mark 10:15:

> *Verily I say unto you, Whosoever shall not receive the kingdom of God as a little child, he shall not enter into it.*

Here's my take on this account of accommodation to popular thought: as the reader of my blog postings is well-aware, I consider the perception of the femininity of the Holy Spirit not only to represent truth, but to be the only viable way to worship our Judeo-Christian God with the love that He demands of us. Beyond that, the transition of the Moravian Church to "normal" is just another sad tale in a very long litany of similar ungodly, cowardly acts of appeasement to majority thought, begun in the New Testament by Peter's threefold denial of Jesus and continuing on to this very day, where we see, among other examples of falling-away, large elements of the mainstream Church's attempt to accommodate herself to the secular and thoroughly false notion of evolution.

In a previous chapter I identified selfishness as a cause for clinging to beliefs that don't square with Scripture. That certainly applies here as well, linking selfishness with ego. I'm willing to bet there are some ego issues involved in the alignment of the Moravian Church with the surrounding religious society, as well as the accommodation of a good many Christians to secular values and beliefs. It's natural for people to want to be liked and respected. You can see it quite often just by driving from home to the store catching the glare of the sun off spotless new sports cars, bikes, Caddies, you name it, or if you observe bumper stickers like I do, just count the number of stickers that brag about their other cars, which usually are airplanes or boats, or their childrens' honors, like soccer, baseball, softball, football, or, if they're older, where they're going to college or the armed forces.

Christians are supposed to get over their ego thing, but there are a lot of Christians I know who haven't. I'd be a hypocrite if I didn't admit to some of that myself. I do ask God to forgive me for that. And I do appreciate a different kind of bumper sticker when it comes along. One such was stuck to the rusty bumper of a trashed-out pickup truck that was spewing blue smoke out of its exhaust. As I approached the truck from behind (it was maxed out at forty-five on the freeway) I read: "My Other Car is a Piece of Crap Too". I gave the guy a thumbs-up as I whizzed by. About the childrens' achievements, a sticker on the topic caught my eye and made my day: "My Son Was Voted Inmate of the Month at Walla Walla".

About the beautiful person inside the vehicle, there's "I Have PMS and I Own a Gun", or for the loving couple who look like they're sharing the same seat, there's "We're Staying Together for the Sake of the Cats". One that I didn't understand, as it was begging for hurt, was a big sign on the trunk of a hot rod that read: "Pay Cuts for Cops". More and more bumper stickers can be seen shamelessly proclaiming one odd sexual orientation or another. Somebody came up with a spoof on that which reads: "Help! I'm a Transfinancial, A Rich Person Born in a Poor Person's Body".

Bumper stickers also can be pithy sources of profound wisdom, like "Be the Person Your Dog Thinks You Are". Even more profound are the Christian logos that can be seen on a few good cars.

9
A Person Who Got it Right

A ctually, a number of Christian scholars have gotten it right, and the number is growing. But I single out R. P. Nettelhorst as the most prominent recent advocate of the Holy Spirit's femininity, because he possesses the right scholastic background to effectively rebut those who would insist that he is wrong. While an important attribute of a theologian is his or her mastery of Scripture, it is as important for a particular element of the controversy regarding the Holy Spirit's femininity to be an expert in the Hebrew language. The particular element that I address here is the suspicion that the original Hebrew of the Old Testament was tampered with as to the gender of the Holy Spirit, and that the tampering has been allowed to continue unopposed right up to the present time. What is particularly annoying about this issue is that often, when one wants to go back to the original language to verify the accuracy of its translation into English, and that person's knowledge of the original language is lacking and he or she must rely on available translations, he or she encounters versions that don't accurately correspond to the original writing.

Case in point: responding to assertions on the Internet that in the original Hebrew the Holy Spirit was addressed as "She" rather than "He", I attempted to verify through interlinear Hebrew/English translations of Scripture, also available on the Internet, this original use of the feminine gender in referencing the Holy Spirit. Most of these translations referred to the Holy Spirit as masculine. The same dead-end happened when I attempted, through the available interlinear Aramaic/English translation corresponding to verse John 14:26 in the Sinaitic Palimpsest (a palimpsest is a document in which the original text has been written over by later text).

Enter R. P. Nettelhorst, Academic Vice-President of Quartz Hill School of Theology, who placed on the Internet a few years back a remarkable document in which he claimed, through his understanding of Hebrew and Syriac, that quite often in the original text of Scripture the Holy Spirit was depicted as feminine.

Nettelhorst stated in that document, which was entitled *More Than Just a Controversy: All About the Holy Spirit*, that he first encountered this femininity while working on a doctoral dissertation in reading the apocryphal Acts of Thomas. In that text the Holy Spirit was described in terms of motherhood.

Attempting to adhere to the prevailing understanding of the Holy Spirit, Nettelhorst simply assumed that the Syriac Orthodox Christianity, from which this text was extracted, was somewhat heretical. Later, he encountered, this time in the Hebrew language, the same association of femininity with the Holy Spirit in Judges 3:10. This time he pursued the subject in more detail, finding to his great surprise that a significant number of original Scriptural passages, including Genesis 1:2 and multiple instances in Judges, refer to the Holy Spirit (Spirit of God, Spirit of Yahweh, etc.) as feminine. He also found, contrary to opposing claims that the grammatical association is trivial, that the original wording unequivocally attaches the feminine gender to the Holy Spirit. The association is anything but arguable.

Following this revelation, Nettelhorst accepted this femininity, perceiving that for a very long time the standard Christian concept of the Godhead was in error. Pursuing the topic in yet greater depth, he also discovered that the association with femininity led to a very natural, consistent understanding of God, which he included in his Internet commentary.

In support of Nettelhorst's revelation, scholar Steve Santini, among others, wrote of the Sinaitic Palimpsest, discovered by Agnes Lewis as noted earlier, in which the earlier writing was found to include John 14:26, where in the original Aramaic Jesus Christ also referred to the Holy Spirit in feminine terms.

Close on the heels of Dr. Nettlehorst in presenting strong theological evidence for a feminine Holy Spirit is Dr. Johannes Van Oort, who undertook a review of significant early Christian Jewish documents, coming to the conclusion that the earliest Christians understood the Holy Spirit to be feminine and worshiped Her as such. An article of his entitled *The Holy Spirit as Feminine: Early Christian testimonies and their interpretation* is also available on the Internet under the search phrase "feminine Holy Spirit".

In his book *The Spirit of Life,* respected theologian Jurgen Moltmann also claimed that the Holy Spirit should be "termed a 'feminine' Spirit". He linked that understanding with the nature of the Godhead, asserting that "In Trinitarian theology, the image of the divine family raises the Spirit to the same rank as the Father, and puts the Spirit before the Son."

In a commentary under the heading "How the Treasure Got Lost" in an article posted on the Internet entitled *Desperately Seeking Sophia*, author Joyce Rupp points to several reasons why the Constantine-era Christians switched the gender of the Holy Spirit from feminine to masculine. The motivations she presented make a lot of sense and served to support my own conclusions. First, she identified the continuing popularity of the goddess cults at the time. These pagan cults, while supporting lewd sexual behavior, also attached the attribute of wisdom onto their objects of worship. The similarity of this attribute with a feminine Holy Spirit was a major source of discomfort. Second, a popular offshoot of Christianity at the time was the Gnostic sect, which also worshiped a feminine Holy Spirit. Gnosticism was declared a heresy for other reasons' which added to the discomfort with the femininity of the Holy Spirit. The mainstream Church didn't want to be associated in any way with Gnosticism, of which the divine feminine was an integral component. Rupp also mentioned a confusing association of Sophia with the Logos by which Jesus Christ is often identified, which also contributed to Church doctrine distancing itself from a feminine Holy Spirit. Perhaps, as she noted, the prevailing patriarchy also had something to do with losing the feminine in the Holy Spirit.

I like what Joyce Rupp said later: "We need Sophia now more than ever. We need her compassionate presence and ability to help us see clearly in the midst of a world that cries out for wisdom and love."

10
Glimpses of the Spiritual Realm

Even after Adam's fall from grace, in which he took some of the world down with him, much of God's Creation remains magnificent. Carolyn and I live in a rural area, and we wouldn't have it any other way. Here we often are blessed with the sight of deer on our road and in our yard, and of elk in the nearby woods. We also have the good fortune to catch sight of bald eagles, huge and magnificent in flight. Such noble creatures!

Well, maybe noble. Lately, they've been hanging out at a nearby landfill. Driving down the highway, we can see them perched on trees like vultures, waiting for an easy meal. I counted seven of them the last time we drove by.

A few years back, before we became aware of the landfill-eagle connection, we had two people bid on a project to enclose our patio, replacing the plastic roof with glass. It didn't happen – we still have the open patio, and during the rare times when it gets hot, we're glad that we do. But while they were there estimating the cost, an enormous eagle flew over, dropping a large, live trout on our lawn. While it flopped around, one of the workers said "Gee, I've never seen that before."

I guess not. When I told a neighbor about that, he shot back, "Did you tell him that it was just Fred, bringing your morning breakfast? Did you tell him that Fred was late today?" I wish that I'd had the presence of mind to tell the estimator that, but I still enjoyed the image as we laughed over it.

Magnificent as this material world is, there's a better one waiting for us where landfills don't exist.

For several years after becoming a Christian, I didn't think often of the spiritual realm. When I did, it wasn't with much enthusiasm, because to me the spiritual realm was a misty, insubstantial place where nothing much happened. Stasis was the apparent order, making me wonder whether eternity was all that desirable. How could the residents of heaven handle an eternally boring existence?

The Church didn't help with that view, as nothing that came from the pulpit opposed that view. I began to wonder if something was wrong with me – shouldn't I be content to be sitting on a cloud singing praises to Jesus on a continual basis?

When I really read John 20:19-31 for the first time, everything changed for me:

> *Then the same day at evening, being the first day of the week, when the doors were shut where the disciples were assembled for fear of the Jews, came Jesus and stood in the midst, and saith unto them, Peace be unto you. And when he had so said, he showed unto them his hands and his side. Then were the disciples glad, when they saw the Lord. Then said Jesus to them again, Peace be unto you; as my Father hath sent me, even so send I you. And when he had said this, he breathed on them, and saith unto them, Receive ye the Holy Spirit. Whosoever's sins ye remit, they are remitted unto them; and whosoever's sins ye retain, they are retained.*

> *But Thomas, one of the twelve, called Didymus, was not with them when Jesus came. The other disciples, therefore, said unto him, We have seen the Lord. But he said unto them, Except I shall see in his hands the print of the nails, and put my finger into the print of the nails, and thrust my hand into his side, I will not believe. And, after eight days, again his disciples were inside, and Thomas with them; then came Jesus, the doors being shut, and stood in the midst, and said, Peace be unto you.*

> *Then saith he to Thomas, Reach here thy finger, and behold my hands; and reach here thy hand, and thrust it into my side; and be not faithless, but believing. And Thomas answered and said unto him, My Lord and my God. Jesus saith unto him, Thomas, because thou hast*

seen me, thou hast believed; blessed are they that have not seen, and yet have believed.

And many other signs truly did Jesus in the presence of his disciples, which are not written in this book; but these are written, that ye might believe that Jesus is the Christ, the Son of God; and that believing ye might have life through his name.

After His resurrection, Jesus returned to the spiritual realm. But He was able to return to the material world. Moreover, He had the ability to pass through walls while still appearing as solid to His observers. He was able to be felt as one who possessed flesh and bones. The same can be seen as Jesus talked to two men on the road to Emmaus, Luke 24. There He also possessed the appearance of solidity. He had the ability to eat as well.

Jesus, while belonging to the spiritual realm, obviously didn't behave after His resurrection as a static Entity. Perhaps, then, neither would we when we, too, attained to the heavenly domain. In Matthew 22:30, Jesus spoke of us as being like the angels in the spiritual realm. We know from Genesis 6 that although they did so in disobedience to God, the fallen angels were capable of behaving like humans, even to the extent of taking human wives. Their natures were anything but ephemeral.

The passages referred to in Luke and John also suggest something else: the spiritual domain possesses at least another dimension beyond that of the material realm that we now inhabit. Otherwise, Jesus in that passage of John may have been required to open the door and enter the usual way into the room where His disciples were. Other passages where the prophets speak of the future with such astonishing accuracy also suggest at least another dimension where time extends beyond our perception of it in the material domain. Examples are numerous: Isaiah naming Cyrus (Isaiah 44:28); Daniel foretelling Jesus' entrance into Jerusalem to the very day; and Ezekiel, in Chapter 4 supported by Leviticus 26:18, foretelling Israel's return to nationhood in 1948.

The spiritual domain, then, is grander than ours. Moreover, there is no reason to perceive that it is a place where stasis reigns. We can expect, in opposition to prevailing opinion, that it is both colorful and lively.

Our limited understanding of time, if we pursue it, is seen to impact our perception of time without end, which is how we usually interpret eternity. Eternity means to us time without boundary, both past and future. We incorporate that notion into our various creeds. The Athanasian Creed, according to the Christian Reformed Church's statement of it, for example, contains as part the following declaration of faith:

"That we worship one God in Trinity and the Trinity in unity, neither blending their persons nor dividing their essence. For the person of the Father is a distinct person, the person of the Son is another, and that of the Holy Spirit still another. But the divinity of the Father, Son and Holy Spirit is one, their glory equal, their majesty coeternal.

"What quality the Father has, the son has, and the Holy Spirit has. The Father is uncreated, the Son is uncreated, the Holy Spirit is uncreated. The Father is immeasurable, the Son is immeasurable, the Holy Spirit is immeasurable. The Father is eternal, the Son is eternal, the Holy Spirit is eternal."

Beyond the notion of eternity, can anyone intuitively wrap arms around the meaning of "person" and "essence" in this creed? I can't, and I've done a lot of thinking about it. Not that my mind is superior in any way to that of another, but I suspect, from listening to others, that nobody else, given the prevailing understanding of the Godhead, can either. I've had two intelligent and well-read theologians confess to me that they don't understand the Godhead, nor do they understand the essence of "essence". A commentary in my Schofield Bible declares as well that the Trinity is a concept that can't truly be understood completely. In fact, there is nobody of whom I'm aware, except those who share my views, that with confidence has been or can be able to shed light on the nature of the Godhead.

This nature can indeed be understood, and understood intuitively. That's the good news. The bad news is that for the Trinity to be understood, Christians must first shed some of the traditional understandings that the Church has presented to her members.

In no way does this imply that Scripture itself is in error. It isn't, at least not in the original.

The Athanasian Creed, like the Nicene and Apostles' Creed, are extrabiblical; they don't necessarily adhere to Scripture. They are wonderful distillations of biblical truth in most respects, but they don't represent biblical truth in other important respects. A case in point is the concept of eternity. To virtually all Christians, eternity means forever, or time without end. But time as we know it began with the Creation Epic of Genesis 1. Before the Creation, time as we understand it simply didn't exist.

In actuality, we know nothing about 'time' before creation. We know nothing about the meaning of existence before that event, nor about sequence in general. We'll never know while we're in the material world, because we're a dimension or two short of the ability to comprehend it. Here's a brief mental exercise to demonstrate that limitation: think about the edge of the universe. The universe must have an edge; it must be bounded, as our minds can't accept anything else. But then if it does have an edge, what's on the other side of it? How is that otherness bounded? The mind simply can't grasp this conundrum.

But some of us have thought that we can. Their arrogance in this regard reminds me of Augustine of Hippo (354-430 A.D.). Augustine had a brilliant mind but, like many modern clerics and scientists, he didn't recognize its limitations. Nor did he understand the limitations of the age in which he lived. He was well versed in Scripture for the most part, but there is one passage that he failed to embrace: Daniel 12:4-13:

> *But thou, O Daniel, shut up the words, and seal the book, even to the time of the end; many shall run to and fro, and knowledge shall be increased.*
>
> *Then I, Daniel, looked and, behold, there stood two others, the one on this side of the bank of the river, and the other on that side of the bank of the river. And one said to the man clothed in linen, who was above the waters of the river, How long shall it be to the end of these wonders? And I heard the man clothed in linen, who was above the waters of the river, when he held up his right hand and his left hand unto heaven, and swore by him who liveth forever, that it shall be for a time, times, and an half; and when he shall have accomplished the breaking up of the power of the holy people, all these things shall be finished.*

And I heard, but I understood not. Then said I, O my Lord, what shall be the end of these things? And he said, Go thy way, Daniel; for the words are closed up and sealed till the time of the end. Many shall be purified, and made white, and tested, but the wicked shall do wickedly; and none of the wicked shall understand, but the wise shall understand. And from the time that the daily sacrifice shall be taken away, and the abomination that maketh desolate set up, there shall be a thousand two hundred and ninety days. Blessed is he that waiteth, and cometh to the thousand three hundred and five and thirty days. But go thy way till the end be; for thou shalt rest, and stand in thy lot at the end of the days.

In other words, Daniel wasn't given to understand the prophetic words of the Lord. It wasn't his time. It wasn't the time, in fact, for anyone to understand these words until knowledge drastically increased and with it the great shift in the means of transportation.

Augustine lived in an era well before that late date in which the books of Daniel 12 would be open,. Yet he attempted to reason out the Book of Revelation, with its obvious references to a world where technology was very far advanced from his time. Failing to understand the text with a natural interpretation, as only those of the late twentieth and the twenty-first century who are well-versed in modern technology can, Augustine arrogantly and without justification decided that this book was to be understood allegorically as pointing to deeper truths. In that context, he viewed the text as representing something other than actuality.

Having placed Augustine in her unreserved favor, the Church followed suit. Catholic seminaries from that time on have adhered to this interpretation and continue to do so to this day. Consequently many among, the Catholic clergy adhere without justification to that view, when the Book of Revelation has obviously been open to all for several years inviting a far more natural interpretation. The clergy's stubborn refusal to understand this falsehood has, over the years, borne bitter fruit, particularly with respect to the anti-Semitic stance of Replacement Theology.

I think that the Church's position with regard to the eternal co-existence of Father, Holy Spirit and Son also was generated by minds that failed to understand their limitations. This view, I believe, is equally false and with very damaging implications.

According to the quantity of books published that have addressed the large and increasing number of near-death accounts, the reality of the spiritual realm appears to be well-established. Furthermore, most of those who have died, entered that realm and subsequently returned to tell about it promote it as a happy place. A loving Jesus is often encountered, and the one undergoing this experience senses a strong bond with Him. It is heaven, they say, and it is an altogether happy, delightful place.

Scripture suggests the same. In 1 Corinthians 15:12-19, Paul lays out the hope that Christians possess regarding the next world:

> *Now if Christ be preached that he rose from the dead, how say some among you that there is no resurrection of the dead? But if there be no resurrection of the dead, then is Christ not risen; and if Christ be not risen, then is our preaching vain, and your faith is also vain. Yea, and we are found false witnesses of God, because we have testified of God, that he raised up Christ, whom he raised not up, if so be that the dead rise not. For if the dead rise not, then is not Christ raised; and if Christ be not raised, your faith is vain, ye are yet in your sins. Then they also who are fallen asleep in Christ are perished. If in this life only we have hope in Christ, we are of all men most miserable.*

The bottom line is that there really does seem to be a better world up there than the material world we now find ourselves in. Otherwise, Paul wouldn't have suggested that heaven is well-worth what struggles Christians may undergo in our material realm. This is a recurrent theme for Paul; one can find it in many places throughout his letters. Paul should know, because when Jesus laid hold of him on the road to Damascus (Acts 9), He not only took him to the woodshed and gave him what-for, but in order to strengthen him for the work that lay ahead, He showed Paul some of the riches of the heavenly realm. Many Christians, including me, believe that Paul himself was the person of whom he wrote in 2 Corinthians 12:1-4:

> *It is not expedient for me, doubtless, to glory. I will come to visions and revelations of the Lord. I knew a man in Christ above fourteen years ago (whether in the body, or out of the body, I cannot tell: God knoweth) – how*

he was caught up into paradise, and heard unspeakable
words, which it is not lawful for a man to utter.

Paul got the message five-by-five: there's a big world out there
beyond the material one, and it's incomparably better as well. It's
indescribably great, in fact, as he wrote in 1 Corinthians 2:7-9:

> *But we speak the wisdom of God in a mystery, even*
> *the hidden wisdom, which God ordained before the*
> *world unto our glory; which none of the princes of this*
> *world knew; for had they known it, they would not have*
> *crucified the Lord of glory. But as it is written, Eye hath*
> *not seen, nor ear heard, neither have entered into the*
> *heart of man, the things which God hath prepared for*
> *them that love him.*

Not that heaven comes without cost. There's a big reason for that
cost: we know that Jesus has a selfless, noble nature. He wishes to
adore that same quality of character in His wife, as Paul explains in
Ephesians 5:24-28:

> *Therefore, as the church is subject unto Christ, so let the*
> *wives be to their own husbands in everything. Husbands,*
> *love your wives, even as Christ also loved the church,*
> *and gave himself for it, that he might sanctify and cleanse*
> *it with the washing of water by the word; that he might*
> *present it to himself a glorious church, not having spot,*
> *or wrinkle, or any such thing; but that it should be holy*
> *and without blemish.*

Paul knew about that cost, and accepted it willingly, as he notes
in 2 Corinthians 12:5-10:

> *Of such an one will I glory; yet of myself I will not glory,*
> *but in mine infirmities. For though I would desire to*
> *glory, I shall not be a fool; for I will say the truth. But*
> *now I forbear, lest any man should think of me above*
> *that which he seeth me to be, or that he heareth of me.*
> *And lest I should be exalted above measure through the*
> *abundance of the revelations, there was given to me a*
> *thorn in the flesh, the messenger of Satan to buffet me,*
> *lest I should be exalted above measure. For this thing I*

*besought the Lord thrice, that it might depart from me.
And he said unto me, My grace is sufficient for thee; for
my strength is made perfect through weakness. Most
gladly, therefore, will I rather glory in my infirmities,
that the power of Christ may rest upon me. Therefore, I
take pleasure in infirmities, in reproaches, in necessities,
in persecutions, in distresses for Christ's sake; for when
I am weak, then am I strong.*

The Gospels hint at much the same thing – both the desirability
and the cost of heaven - as does the Book of Hebrews: this world
of ours and the trials we undergo here are insignificant next to the
beauty of heaven, the spiritual world that is open to the faithful in
Christ. A taste of this is found in Matthew 5:10-13 in the beatitude
regarding persecution:

*Blessed are they who are persecuted for righteousness,
sake; for theirs is the kingdom of heaven. Blessed are
ye, when men shall revile you, and persecute you, and
shall say all manner of evil against you falsely, for my
sake. Rejoice, and be exceedingly glad; for great is your
reward in heaven; for so persecuted they the prophets
who were before you.*

In this message Jesus is specific as to where the bummers are –
here on earth – and where the blessings are – in heaven. In effect,
Earth is not worthy of comparison with heaven.

In Matthew 6:19 and 20, Jesus elaborates on this theme:

*Lay not up for yourselves treasures upon earth, where
moth and rust doth corrupt, and where thieves break
through and steal, but lay up for yourselves treasures in
heaven, where neither moth nor rust doth corrupt, and
where thieves do not break through nor steal;*

As Revelation 21:9-11 promises, we, through the Church, will
participate in marriage in the Spiritual domain. Our Husband will be
Jesus, the Lamb of God:

*And there came unto me one of the seven angels who had
the seven bowls full of the seven last plagues, and talked
with me, saying, Come here, I will show thee the bride,*

the Lamb's wife. And he carried me away in the Spirit to a
great and high mountain, and showed me that great city,
the holy Jerusalem, descending out of heaven by God,
having the glory of God; and her light was like a stone
most precious, even like a jasper stone, clear as crystal;

I have personally known a person who claims to have had a near-death experience. From my talks with her, enlarged upon by my own reading of Scripture, I think that I have caught the tiniest glimpse of what heaven may look like. In that picture is an almost overwhelmingly beautiful scene, in which Jesus is about to take the Church to wife. As He gazes into her eyes, he sees the beauty for which He has waited so long and patiently. His eyes travel over her face, to the bruises and scars that speak of the afflictions that have rendered her so nobly selfless, and He is near tears. He sees in them an even greater beauty, one that has whitened her garments to pristine condition, and His heart beats in love for the character so worthy to receive a Medal of Honor for her valor in resisting the whiles of satan. He is overwhelmed by a great tenderness, and a desire to forever share His life with her.

In the wisdom he was granted in such abundance, Solomon understood that in the spiritual domain, gender didn't reside in the individual but in the aggregate. He also may have anticipated Jesus, and of His future marriage to another aggregate, the Church. Looking forward to the marriage of Jesus with that aggregate, Solomon may have attempted to represent Jesus with his seven hundred wives and three hundred concubines. God may have applauded that attempt. Or perhaps instead God saw it a mistake, wherein Solomon failed to realize that this gender arrangement applied only to the spiritual domain.

Whether Solomon's actions in taking so many wives was acceptable to God or not, Solomon intimately understood the romance involved in God's interrelationship and its image in the Church's relationship with Jesus. Verses 12 through 16 of Song Chapter 1 are typical:

While the king sitteth at his table, my spikenard sendeth
forth the fragrance therof. A bundle of myrrh is my
well-beloved unto me; he shall lie all night between my
breasts. My beloved is unto me as a cluster of camphire
in the vineyards of Engedi.

*Behold, thou art fair, my beloved, yea, pleasant; also our
bed is green.*

Even the same Bible commentators who have shied away
from openly declaring the role of gender in the economy of God
understood the implications regarding the Song of Solomon. The
introductory commentary to the Song in my Schofield Bible reads
as follows:

"Nowhere in Scripture does the unspiritual mind tread upon
ground so mysterious and incomprehensible as in this book, whereas
saintly men and women throughout the ages have found it a source of
pure and exquisite delight. That the love of the divine Bridegroom,
symbolized here by Solomon's love for the Shulamite maiden,
should follow the analogy of the marriage relationship seems evil
only to minds that are so ascetic that marital desire itself appears to
them to be unholy.

"The book is an expression of pure marital love as ordained by
God in creation, and the vindication of that love as against both
asceticism and lust – the two profanations of the holiness of marriage.
Its interpretation is threefold: (1) as a vivid unfolding of Solomon's
love for a Shulamite girl; (2) as figurative revelation of God's love
for His covenant people, Israel, the wife of the Lord (Isa. 54:5-6;
Jer. 2:2; Ezek 16:8-14, 20-21,32,38; Hos. 2:16,18-20); and (3) as an
allegory of Christ's love for His heavenly bride, the Church (2Cor.
11:1-2, refs., Eph. 5:25-32).

While I would suggest that item (2) above would more
appropriately describe the intra-Godhead relationship, I think you
get the point of where this commentary has been heading: that God
is both gendered and romantic.

The discussion of asceticism put Ronald back to mind, and our
theologians as well.

Appendix 1-1
Copious Scriptural Affirmation

In the interest of brevity, I summarize below the ten reasons that I consider to be the most important Scriptural implications of a feminine Holy Spirit. These items are consistent with a view of the Bible as inspired and inerrant in the original.

ONE: The original Old Testament Scripture in the Hebrew language described the Holy Spirit in feminine terms. Evidence of this has been furnished by several language-expert Bible scholars, among whom is R. P. Nettelhorst of the Quartz Hill School of Theology. Dr. Nettelhorst's specific examples include Genesis 1:2 that pointed to the role of the Holy Spirit in Creation and Judges 3:10, which represented a turning point in his understanding of God. He claims that there are 75 instances of either a feminine or indeterminable reference to the Holy Spirit, and no instances, other than descriptors of the Father, where in the original Hebrew the word "Spirit" is described in masculine terms. Other investigators have listed a multitude of specific Old Testament Bible passages that describe the Holy Spirit in feminine terms. Other passages, including Isaiah 51:9 and 10, furnish evidence of a deliberate switch of the Holy Spirit (Arm of the Lord) from feminine to neuter, as both feminine and neuter translations still exist, the feminine version being the earliest.

TWO: The original New Testament Scripture in the Greek/Aramaic language described the Holy Spirit in feminine terms, exposing a deliberate switch in descriptors from feminine to masculine. Evidence of this has been furnished by several Bible scholars, among whom is Johannes van Oort of Radboud University, Nijmegen, the Netherlands, and the University of Pretoria, South Africa. Dr. van Oort, another language expert, claims that the

primitive Christian Church, until at least through the second century
A.D., and in some places through the fourth century A.D. spoke
of the Holy Spirit as feminine. His sources include the Gospel of
the Hebrews, which, while now lost, was quoted widely by early
Christians, who noted that the Holy Spirit in that Gospel was
described as feminine. He observed from the extensive quotations
from that Gospel that it apparently was quite popular among the
early Christians. Dr. van Oort notes that more modern Christian
leaders, including John Wesley and Count von Zinzendorf of the
Moravian Church, were influenced by quotes from that Gospel.
Other investigators, including S. Santini and R. Nettelhorst, point
to the Sinaitic Palimpsest, the earliest currently known of Gospel
passages still extant, as quoting Jesus in John 14:26 as referencing
the Holy Spirit in feminine terms. It is the originals that are to be
respected for inspiration and accuracy, not the various translations.
Next in line for respect, the earliest available versions are generally
considered to be the most faithful to the original. Other passages,
including Romans 9:25, retain an understanding of the Holy Spirit
as feminine. It is important to note also that some of the interlinear
translations of the Bible in Hebrew, Greek and Aramaic have also
adjusted the language to conform to the Church tradition of replacing
the feminine with the masculine or neuter.

   THREE: **The first Chapter of Genesis in commonly
available translations and versions (including the King James)
unequivocally depicts the Holy Spirit as feminine, regardless
of the attempts to suppress that aspect of the Holy Spirit's
nature.** The passage most strongly indicative of a feminine Holy
Spirit is Genesis 1:26 and 27, which identifies the gendered nature
of mankind as conforming to God's own nature. While modern
commentators on this passage refuse to address this gender issue,
they have no basis to do so other than participating in a slavish
conformance to Church tradition, and are dishonest in their attempts
to remove this characteristic from the image of God. Direct support
of the depiction in Genesis 1 of the Holy Spirit's feminine nature
is found in Psalm 94:9, wherein God describes attributes of man,
specifically ears and eyes, asking why man can't understand that
God possesses the same attributes. In that context, it would be
appropriate for God to ask why, if man was made a gendered being,
why God Himself wouldn't possess as well that same profoundly
important attribute.

FOUR: The account of the creation of Eve in Genesis 2 is a statement of the importance to God of gender. In opposition to the generally-accepted notion that the account of God's creation of Eve in Genesis 2 took place well after the creation of Adam as an incidental afterthought, the Genesis 2 account is so central to the intention of God that it is more detailed than the original description and is presented again for the purpose of emphasis. Back in Genesis 1:26-31, God already had created both Adam and Eve as gendered and capable of reproduction. Furthermore, it is in Genesis 1:31 that God describes His creation, including gendered humanity, as very good. In Genesis 2:18, God describes Adam without Eve as being not good, which would be a contradiction to the earlier account in Genesis 1 if Genesis 2 represented anything other than an emphatic revisit of Eve's creation. Yet more, in Matthew 19:4 and Mark 10:6-8, Jesus strongly defended the gendered nature of mankind as being the express intent of God from the beginning of Creation, pointing to its importance within the Godhead itself. This emphasis suggests the importance of Eve's creation from Adam to the extent that it says something about the gendered nature of the Godhead, which could easily be interpreted as a continuation of the information presented in Genesis 1:27 that the creation of Eve amounts to a reprise in mankind of God's own family nature.

FIVE: Only a union of a romantic, possessive nature between a male and a female is capable of fulfilling the passion intrinsic to God. Despite Church tradition that, influenced by the odd, cold theology of Zanchius and others of his cloth, the attributes of God include passion, and that passion includes romance. Scripture often attributes passion to Jesus and the other Members of the Godhead, most notably so in the Song of Solomon. The Song of Solomon is an overt description of gender-driven passion. Many respected Bible commentators see in this book a connection between Jesus and His Church in the spiritual domain, which places the attribute of gender firmly within the Godhead. Given the romantic, passionate nature of that Book, if romantic, possessive passion was not an attribute of God, the Song wouldn't belong in the canon of Scripture. Moreover, according to Jesus' greatest commandment to us in Matthew 22 (echoing Deuteronomy 6) God demands that same passion of us with respect to our relationship with Him. If God was incapable of experiencing that same passion, the commandment would be meaningless.

SIX: **The selfless nobility intrinsic to God suggests a union within the Godhead of a harmony built upon complementary otherhood, which can only be fulfilled through gender differentiation.** The Bible in its entirety, most emphatically presented in the work of Jesus on the cross, depicts God as selflessly noble. The alternatives to gender differentiation of an all-male or genderless Godhead would encourage narcissistic selfishness. The demand to love God with fervor requires us to view God in a family context as well. Any alternative to that view leaves us with confusion and a profound inability to obey the commandment of love that Jesus expressed in Matthew 22. The confusion is quite real: the confusion and lack of understanding has been confessed to me multiple times by theologians who possess impressive credentials, but who remain committed to a genderless or all-male Godhead. It is difficult to understand how a person who is confused about such an intimate detail regarding the nature of God would be able to worship Him with fervor.

SEVEN: **In Ephesians 5, Paul claims that Jesus and His Church will be married, attributing functional gender to attributes within the Godhead.** In Genesis 2, Adam states that Eve is bone of his bones and flesh of his flesh, and that therefore shall a man leave his father and his mother, and shall cleave unto his wife, and they shall be one flesh. The latter phrase represents the very words that Jesus repeated in Matthew 19:5 and 6, and in Mark 10:7 and 8. The importance of this phrase is confirmed in Ephesians 5:31 and 32, where Paul repeats it yet again, and then goes on to claim that it applies to the union of Jesus and His Church. Here, the Bible explicitly states that Jesus and the Church are fully gendered and will, in the spiritual domain, unite in marriage. That this union will be productive is asserted in Romans 7:4. The fact that Jesus is a Member of the Godhead and is slated to be married plainly suggests that the other two members of the Godhead are also gendered, and, in fact, are united with each other.

EIGHT: **The Old Testament Shekinah Glory, generally acknowledged to be feminine, is revealed in the New Testament as the Holy Spirit.** Paul goes to great lengths to describe the Church as a spiritual composite of individual Christians, in which the individuals are contributing elements of a whole, each individual being somewhat akin to the various organs that comprise a human body. In that context, gender is not important with regard to the individual (how would a gendered heart work?), but is a vital necessity, as in the complete human body, to the complete Church. An important aspect of the integrated spiritual Church is the indwelling Holy Spirit. As Paul declares in 1 Corinthians 3:16 and Ephesians 2:19-22, we Christians comprise a temple of God, wherein the Holy Spirit dwells. This temple described by Paul is a fulfillment of the type described in the Old Testament, where the Shekinah Glory indwelt the Tabernacle of the Wilderness and Solomon's Temple at their dedications (Exodus 40 and 1 Kings 8). The Shekinah Glory is generally acknowledged to be feminine in nature; the indwelling fulfillment in Christians identifies the Shekinah as the Holy Spirit.

NINE: The Book of Proverbs describes as feminine the Holy Spirit in Her role as complementary other to the Father. Proverbs 8:22-36, in particular, describes the Holy Spirit working alongside the Father in the Creation. That the feminine *Persona* of the Holy Spirit in Proverbs is far more than simply a figure of speech, is confirmed by Jesus Christ, who in Luke 7:35 described the Holy Spirit in terms of a sentient Mother. The connection between Wisdom and the Holy Spirit is also made in the Book of Wisdom, which, while having been removed from the canon of Protestant Scripture during the Reformation, remains canonical in the Catholic Church. In that book, Wisdom as a feminine Being is directly linked to the Holy Spirit.

TEN: In multiple passages, Jesus describes the Holy Spirit in feminine terms. In the Gospel of John, Jesus frequently links the Holy Spirit with feminine descriptors, such as "Comforter" and "Helper". This association is most direct in John 3, where Jesus connects the Holy Spirit with spiritual birth. Birth, of course, is an eminently feminine function. Moreover, many theologians see in Scripture the role of the Holy Spirit as an executive one. An executive function is feminine in nature, representing the essence of complementary otherhood in the carrying out of the will of the Father. More generally, even in translations that corrupt the original description of the Holy Spirit in feminine terms, the Holy Spirit in Genesis 1:2 is described as creatively responsive to the Father's will. A responsive role is a feminine one.

COMMENTARY

Having demonstrated that Scripture itself points to the Holy Spirit's femininity, perhaps it should be stressed how important this gender issue truly is. The usual response to my multi-year heartfelt presentations of the Holy Spirit's femininity is glassy eyes and a shrug of the shoulders. *So what?* The body language says with eloquence. *Why should I care? Whoever or whatever God is or isn't, I'm a believer, so my faith is the only thing that really matters.*

But is it all that matters? More to the point, is faith without love really faith? In Matthew 22:37, Jesus echoes Moses' words in Deuteronomy 6:5 by claiming that the greatest commandment of God is that *Thou shalt love the Lord, thy God, with all thy heart, and with all thy soul, and with all thy mind.* Jesus stated that not as a suggestion, but as a commandment. Jesus also said in John 14:15 *If ye love me, keep my commandments.* These two passages can be paraphrased to say that your love must be fervent to truly be love.

Our faith itself must involve fervent love; otherwise, it isn't really faith at all, just some meaningless mind-exercise performed for the sake of acquiring peace of mind over the issue of where one goes after the game's up here on earth. But the faith of most of us is exactly that – fire insurance. Our worship of God seems to be based on a self-centered desire not to be left out of the joys of heaven (if heaven actually does exist, as we wonder within ourselves, and if it actually is joyful).

Fervent love toward God is far more than an exercise of the mind, because fervor doesn't come from the mind. It is an imprinting upon the soul akin to the passionate, possessive love between a man and a woman. It must be of such a magnitude that the thought of its removal invokes the same sense of desperate grief as the loss of a lifelong mate. It is the way that God made us to love Him. Anything less is not love, nor is it faith. Less than fervent love has the potential of crumbling at the first threat to well-being. We see it happening now in the mass exodus from Church following the recent marginalization of Christians.

Here is where the issue of loving faith collides with our understanding of the nature of God. How can we possibly love that which we so imperfectly know? The Church for centuries has treated the Trinitarian Godhead as either void of gender or somewhat masculine, all three Members having essentially the same nature. The problem with that misrepresentation is that the Godhead and the functional roles within it are both alien and confusing. Some theologians, in recognizing that problem, have put forth the idea that each Member of the Godhead is endowed with traits belonging to both genders. But such theologians failed to use their heads: on a moral basis alone God's nobility resides far beyond such a narcissism-promoting arrangement as that would encourage. Beyond that issue, gender duality within each Member leaves unsolved the confusion of roles. Yet further, the gender ambiguity would attribute to God Himself gender traits which Scripture discourages in us. Because of the multiplicity of issues associated with it, most Churches recognize the problems inherent in that assignment, leaving us with the basic genderless or all-male model of the Godhead, returning us to confusion and alienation regarding the matter, which has led most Churches to ignore the issue completely.

But the issue is so important that it demands to be heard, for it involves faith. How can we worship God with the fervor He demands of us without even a basic understanding of who He is, and what little that we do know of Him is alien to us? That is exactly why the majority of self-styled Christians, lacking the love that God asks of us, are in blatant disobedience to God, holding to nothing more than a shallow semblance of faith. Most of us think more highly of ourselves than that, visualizing how we will hold fast to our faith in the face of persecution. But that kind of self-aggrandizing attitude is nothing but self-centered chest-pounding that will vaporize under any real threat.

The importance that I attach to this issue of the Holy Spirit's gender raises another issue of grave importance to all the millions of Christians who have lived and died over the many centuries that the Church has mischaracterized the Holy Spirit: has their failure to obey their God with the ardent love that He commanded denied them the eternal fellowship with God that He promised to His believers? Personally, I don't think that to be the case, particularly since the misleading came from the Church, not them. My belief that God is far more compassionate and merciful than that is reinforced by the numerous descriptions in Scripture of godly people who, at one time or another, failed to the extent of disobeying God's commandments.

I certainly hope that He is that merciful, because I, for one, have been disobedient to God with distressing frequency.

Yet, if disobedience in loving God the way we should doesn't forever prohibit us from attaining favor with God, the issue of the Holy Spirit's feminine gender remains important to us regarding the depth of our commitment to God and to the advantages that are conferred upon us in the here and now for that understanding. For it is a great blessing to fellowship with God, and the closer we come to Him, the nearer that He comes and displays His love toward us. Then, of course, there is the matter of a shallow faith being subject to abandonment in the face of trouble, which is an issue that is not a threat to those closer to God.

In an enormous contrast to the prevailing state of affairs with the Church's misconception of God, an appreciation of a feminine Holy Spirit introduces the archetype of family into an understanding of the Godhead, instantly clarifying the respective roles of the individual Members and immediately removing all sense of confusion regarding the nature of God.

Most importantly, God is no longer alien to us, but One with whom we can identify through the personal experience of life itself. We can know this God intimately, and this intimacy grants us access to the kind of love that produces real faith in obedience to Jesus' command, a faith that is capable of withstanding all the negatives that life as Christians can bring us.

Principally because of the issue of holding fast to our faith under the pressure of worldly pleasures and the threat of persecution, the understanding of the Holy Spirit as of the feminine gender does indeed matter – under certain situations, it can be as important as the destination of our eternal souls.

There's still another reason for appreciating the Holy Spirit's feminine gender. Equipped with that understanding, a reading of Genesis 1 and 2 becomes a breathtakingly beautiful endeavor. For in the reading the prospect becomes convincing that these passages speak not only of the creation of mankind, but of the arrangement and roles within the Godhead itself of the Members comprising it. Is it not possible, then, that the Holy Spirit Herself was formed out of the Father's side in His effort to place Love above all other attributes of God, irretrievably far beyond self?

Appendix 1-2
Implications of a Genderless God

What is the meaning of a genderless God? Such is a God wherein the Trinitarian Godhead is an assembly of Members void of gender but possessing both masculine and feminine secondary characteristics. According to Church tradition, in which all Members of the Godhead are addressed in the male gender, and references to the Holy Spirit in Bible versions available to the Christian community also are male, masculine characteristics apparently prevail over the feminine ones. Character traits associated with masculine ideals are emphasized: will, courage, strength of purpose, and omniness are idealized in this association.

There are certain implications associated with this view of God. Some have to do with our relationship to Him, and others with our relationships among ourselves. This appendix is devoted to the exploration of these implications and the prevailing indifference to them.

How do we worship a genderless God? We do so intellectually, as a God without gender is different than us in a manner that makes Him alien to our hearts. He doesn't possess the same passions that so influentially drive us and form such a major part of our lives. He stands above us, and when we look up to him, we must empty ourselves of our lesser feelings to appreciate the radiant glow of His benign superiority. We must demand of our minds that our love toward Him be fervent, as that is His greatest command to us, and our obedience to this requirement must be fearfully executed, even if it is forced. We then congratulate ourselves for our obedience to Him. We refrain from contrasting this intellectualized love with the natural manner in which we imprint our spouses to our hearts in unfeigned fervor.

How do we understand and carry out our sexuality, those of us who see God as genderless? Our sexual impulses, residing so far beneath God's purity, are removed from God entirely. In matters of sex, we indulge in any number of lurid fantasies and permutations of couplings within and without the bounds set by God, being assured within our minds that in our sexual behavior God has nothing to do with us or that kind of thing. The extreme separation between God and us in this matter permits us to enjoy our desires wherever they may take us, as God is not involved in any way beyond our understanding of his desire for us to be obedient to His Word. But this understanding is secondary at best, because the expression of our sexual desires is of itself often so shameful as to represent disobedience to Him or at the very least the removal of ourselves from His presence. This, in truth, equates to our removal of Him from our own presence, shutting him into a closet of nonexistence during the time it takes to fulfill our sexual needs. Consequently, it matters little whether we fulfill our baser needs in the manner prescribed by God or whether we prefer to look upon those of our own gender with lustful thoughts, or whether we wish to behave as those of the other gender and physically and emotionally remake ourselves in conformance to that wish. The majority of us place God in a position of almost unapproachable purity, putting ourselves so far beneath that ideal that we ignore it altogether. There are exceptions: a few of us – a very few – attempt to achieve on their own something close to that perceived purity, remaking themselves in the name of chastity into something different and lesser than God created them.

How, as a result of perceiving God as genderless, do we look upon the notion of purity, an essential feature of a God who stands so radiantly above our baser desires? We begin with lumping chastity in with the qualities associated with purity, although the two are innately very different concepts. The more godly among us, treasuring the notion of chastity, contemplate becoming eunuchs for the sake of becoming closer to God as did Church Father Origen. It has been common practice among the Church faithful to point to Jesus' own avoidance of marriage as evidence of purity while failing to understand that Jesus never married because He was already betrothed to the Church, His future wife, and wished to remain faithful to her. Those godly people who equate purity with chastity but who shy away from such a drastic step as changing the way that God made them, must learn to suppress their baser desires, doing so with some pain but quite successfully, albeit often conflicted. Unless, of course, a particularly attractive wife of a congregant makes inappropriate overtures, or an altar boy catches the eye.

How do we treat Paul's revelation in Ephesians 5:31 and 32 that the Church will be the wife of Christ? Given the mainstream insistence upon the absence of gender in heaven, this marriage must be in name only. The only problem with that is that we're conditioned by the very way we're made to think that such an arrangement represents a severe loss, and not only of the sexual part, but the intimacy and belonging that goes along with it. Such an arrangement doesn't square with Jesus' words in Matthew 22 that the heavenly arrangement displays the power of God. Nor does it harmonize with the notion in Genesis 1:26 and 27 of man, and here gender is emphasized, being created in the image of God:

> And God said, Let us make man in our image, after our likeness; and let them have dominion over the fish of the sea, and over the fowl of the air, and over the cattle, and over all the earth, and over every creeping thing that creepeth upon the earth. So God created man in his own image, in the image of God created he him, male and female created he them.

In fact, how do we properly handle Genesis 1:26 and 27, where God in the plural describes man's creation in His image as male and female? Mainstream commentators parse out this attribute of God with absolutely no justification, and in open defiance of logic. The mainstream Church simply goes along with it without questioning this distortion of truth that so blatantly suppresses the Word of God.

Nor does a genderless God match the implication of Psalm 94:9, that He possesses the features, including gender of what He created in man:

> He who planted the ear, shall he not hear? He who formed the eye, shall he not see?

A genderless marriage, though, well-represents the mainstream view of the arrangement within the Godhead, evoking thoughts of an all-masculine Trinity actually participating in a marriage of sorts, elevating *agape* love almost (but not quite) to the level of romance and giving us pause to think, perhaps, that gay marriages shouldn't be looked down upon by Christians as much as they are.

How do we perceive the emotional nature of a genderless God? He must also be above passion as well, passion being so earthy. Medieval cleric Jerome Zanchius expounded on that very topic in his tome *Absolute Predestination*, presenting to the Christian community a God so far above passion that He is limited to benign approbations and sorrowful cluck-clucks, these in direct contradiction to the presentations made of God's personality in His Word. Interestingly, many of those who treasure Scripture and should know better don't seem to get that, as a large proportion of them approve of or fail to denounce Zanchius' arrogant, godless pomposity without thinking through the implications. Speaking of Church Greats, those within the Reformed community who think so highly of Martin Luther fail to acknowledge or appreciate that apparently he was quite comfortable with the notion of a feminine Holy Spirit. (Note: the attribution of this remains to be verified.)

What on earth do we do with Solomon's Song of Songs? There it blatantly sits nested in Scripture, belonging in the canon approved by the mainstream Church and glaring out at the Church's disapproval of gender in God as it extols the virtues of erotic love. Mainstream commentaries point to its relevance to Jesus' future marriage to the Church in disregard of the mainstream notion that this marriage will be in name only.

Why do Church "authorities" think that when God declares us as individuals to be genderless in the spiritual domain (Galatians 3:28 and Matthew 22:30) they stop there with the notion that heaven itself is genderless, failing to pursue the issue at any depth to the point where they understand that it is the spiritual collective that is gendered? In failing to understand that, the Church reads Paul's numerous references to the spiritual collective (e.g. 1 Corinthians 12) in dumb lack of comprehension of what Paul was really trying to say regarding the distinction between attributes of the individual Christian and of the Church in the aggregate. Perhaps, like the prepubescent child who reacts in shock and anguish to the revelation that his parents created him through sexual union, Church leaders refuse to believe that God could do such things. They need to grow up and look at God through adult eyes, forsaking the milk and begin partaking of the meat of the Word as described in Hebrews 5:11-14.

Why is it unthinkable to an adult Christian leader to consider that when God refers to characteristics, as in Jeremiah 10:12, they may refer not to His own attributes, but of those belonging to His possession in love, His complementary Other? In a genderless Godhead, perhaps the notion of one Member possessing another in love is off the table. The "committee" within the genderless Godhead simply cannot be tied that close together. The situation is very different for a gendered Godhead; in that arrangement, romance and its attendant possession are very much in play.

Many mainstream Churches have come to appreciate that the Person speaking in Proverbs is a sentient Being rather than a figure of speech. Given that understanding, the feminine Persona of Proverbs is troubling and contradictory to the notion of a genderless God, which deprives the reader of Proverbs of its intrinsic vitality.

Why do those attached to the idea of a genderless God find the nature and role of the Holy Spirit so confusing, as they all appear to do? While they await their entrance into heaven to answer their questions regarding the Holy Spirit, those who see God as gendered already have satisfactory answers.

Why do mainstream Protestants look down upon the Catholic elevation of Mary to near-Godhood, probably in the Catholic response to an awareness of a void of femininity in the Godhead, when they themselves refuse even to think about that lack of femininity and its implications? In denying women any representation in God, mainstream Protestants are closer in that particular respect to the Muslim faith than to the essence of Christianity.

The denial of gender in God corresponds to a companion denial of family as the core integrating factor within the Godhead. With that denial, family is not an essential feature of God. The downgrading of family in that manner opens the door to a plethora of social ills, as can readily be seen in today's misguided world. The denial of gender in God opens the door as well to confusion regarding subordination and its application within the Godhead. While to a gendered God family would represent the highest level to which all three Members of the Trinity would voluntarily subordinate themselves, no such meta-level higher than the individual Members is apparent in the view of a genderless God, leading either to questions regarding their relationship to each other or a blind, intuition-void insistence on their co-equality.

The mainstream Church suffers from an utter lack of intuitive understanding of how Jesus became the Son of God. The Athanasian Creed does have an explanation, pointing to the eternal co-existence of Father, Son and Holy Spirit, but this extra-scriptural creed violates the Word in Revelation 3:14. Beyond that, eternity has no meaning before Creation, the point at which time began.

How can the Holy Spirit's function of giving spiritual birth, as described by Jesus in John 3, be reconciled with the notion that God is genderless? The birth function obviously is a major part of femininity, and attempting to associate it with a lack of gender is a self-contradictory pursuit.

Some theologians have proposed that the three Members of the Trinity share secondary characteristics of both sexes. That proposition is influential among Catholics, including Fr. John MacQuarrie, who presented it in his usually insightful book *Mary for all Christians;* the same is also heard from local theological authorities. Has anybody made the effort to assess the collateral damage to Christianity that such a view can produce? In the first place, having both genders in one individual diminishes both the masculine and the feminine in that being, leaving a gender weakness to suffer with. The malady is called hermaphroditism, and it is not viewed with approbation, either by society or by the Bible. Perhaps that's exactly how the Members of the Godhead are supposed to be, according to the genderless view. However, I for one insist upon a robust masculinity for my Jesus. More importantly, God Himself frowns upon a watered-down masculinity. He makes that quite plain in His Word in Deuteronomy 23:1 and 1 Corinthians 6:9 and 10, as quoted earlier.

Having described a number of reasons, particularly those associated with a plain reading of Scripture, as to why the attempt to render God genderless is fraught with absurd consequences, it becomes apparent that the effort to do so begs a question: why do some Christians, especially those possessing theological credentials, insist upon claiming that God lacks gender in the face of such massive Scriptural evidence to the contrary and of such enormous negative consequence?

The most reasonable answer to that question harks back to the Garden, and the fall of mankind through the malfeasance of Adam and Eve. A key pointer to the damage caused by the fall was a statement made in Genesis 2:25 before that happened: *"And they were both naked, the man and his wife, and were not ashamed."* A major result of that fall was evidenced by the prime couple, who attempted to hide their private parts with leaves. They did so in response to the sexual shame that they experienced as an immediate consequence of their disobedience to God. From that time on, sexuality was treated as a base instinct, its fulfillment dark and even disgusting. That disassociation of sex with goodness, even in the face of its design by God Himself, persists to this day, remaining a heavy influence on how many perceive their God. To them, it must be unthinkable that God might participate in some form of gender.

Another possible reason for the reluctance to view God as gendered might be the "slippery slope" issue. An important part of Christian belief is the understanding that Scripture is inspired and infallible in the original. Most Christians, knowing that errors crept into the various translations, pass them off as inconsequential. The difference between gender and no gender in God is far from trivial, however, raising the issue that if a change in Scripture is made at this very late date, it might well open the door to a wholesale skepticism regarding the truth of Scripture. But here is a basic difference in viewpoint regarding this issue: it all depends on holding fast to the notion that "I'm right and you're wrong." The defender of a genderless God thinks that he's right, that Scripture wasn't tampered with at any time, and therefore has every reason to consider a change to that view as a "slippery slope" toward the full-scale rejection of all Scripture. The believer in a feminine Holy Spirit, on the other hand, thinking that he's right and the other side of the argument is wrong, sees the "slippery slope" as having been entered a very long time ago, perhaps as early as the fourth or fifth century A.D. The damage already has been done, he thinks, so it's too late now to worry about the implications of change. To him, the issue has become irrelevant. The believer in a gendered God has another argument he can make: at some point near the time of the Reformation, over a millennium since the canonization of Scripture, the Protestant community removed some books from the canon. Among these was the book of Wisdom, which remains in the Catholic canon of Scripture. This interesting little book overtly associates the Wisdom of Proverbs with the Holy Spirit, and directly associates femininity with the Holy Spirit as well. It is revealing that those who had embraced a genderless God had themselves indulged in "slippery slope" activity, making their objection on that basis to the gendered-God viewpoint rather hypocritical.

A further possibility is that some of those who view God as genderless have a vested interest in resisting change, from the standpoint of ego, faithfulness to what respected theologians had taught them, and the practical element of maintaining their credibility within their Church group. This would apply primarily to pastors and Church leaders, who wish to remain loyal to the seminaries from which they emerged and to the God whom the seminaries attempted to present to them. They should realize that the seminaries themselves, as well as the standard regimen of instruction conducted by pastors, already has suffered from such bad, Scripturally-indifferent theology that even laypersons are beginning to recognize that as a serious problem.

There's yet another possibility, one that probably furnishes the most likely scenario for the resistance to change. This is the almost preposterous nature of a claim fraught with the potential for such a vast theological reorientation that it suffers a lack of credibility and defeats a motivation for change at the very outset. Moreover, the claim stands in stark opposition to the nearly universal belief held by credentialed Christian theologians over a very lengthy stretch of time that God stands above gender. How could so many doctrinal authorities say differently for so many centuries? And it's not just an issue of so many – it's more about their virtually complete unanimity. But that's the very point in favor of its actual plausibility – it would take a substantial amount of courage to oppose such a large and influential body of theological experts with such a miniscule chance of changing minds. One can see how so many potential supporters of change wouldn't consider it to be worth the effort. One can picture the years sliding by as generation after generation of Church authorities rethought the gender issue, paused to count the cost, and rationalized the issue away. The situation with respect to that issue is much like the one with a number of secular intrusions into Scripture, the theory of evolution being the most obvious. Regarding that issue, science itself already has undermined Darwin's theory to the point where any rational, scientifically knowledgeable person can see the cracks in its foundation. Yet mainstream science continues to insist upon its credibility while practitioners in the field of biology support it for the sake of their grants, their jobs, and their relationships with their peers. Given the persistence of that falsehood, it's really not too hard to accept that the same thing has happened with respect to the issue of gender in the Christian Godhead, even over a duration of centuries. It also is easy to understand how this reluctance to admit of error in the perception of God has led the Catholic Church to elevate Mary to her position of near-godhood as those in the Church who were motivated to set the gender issue straight without suffering the consequences started heaping feminine attributes belonging to the Holy Spirit onto Mary. My own pastor is brave. Fortunately, he has approached the issue with sufficient courage to address it in depth. I'm proud of him for that, as he has much at stake in maintaining his current understanding of God as genderless. Perhaps in his thorough investigation of this controversial topic he'll come to see the Holy Spirit as gendered and feminine. If so, it would be a happy occasion for me. If not, he will at least have been sufficiently exposed to the relevant information as to appreciate the mindset of those who firmly and passionately believe in a feminine Holy Spirit.

APPENDIX 1-3
CONFRONTING
1 PETER 3

There are some passages in the Bible that are almost untouchable, especially those that seem to place women in a subordinate position to men. One glaring instance is 1 Timothy 2:9-15, in which Paul relegates women to silence in the Church, also telling them not to teach or place themselves in authority over men. Most pastors refuse to go near that passage, being tempted to write off Paul as a misogynist. Braver ones do address it, but their exposition of it is as harsh as the passage itself.

Was Paul a misogynist, as those who have difficulty in accepting that passage believe? An affirmation of that judgment is difficult. For one thing, this passage has been included in the canon of Scripture, something that can't be taken lightly given the expectation of Christians that Scripture is inspired by the Holy Spirit and inerrant (in the original). Almost as important, Scripture elsewhere, and particularly in Ephesians 5, presents Paul as respectful of women. Most contradictory to this position is the fact that Paul isn't the only one who wrote in Scripture who took this same position regarding the subordination of women to men. Peter also did in 1 Peter 3:1-6:

> *In the same manner, ye wives, be in subjection to your own husbands that, if any obey not the word, they also may without the word be won by the behavior of the wives, while they behold your chaste conduct coupled with fear; whose adorning, let it not be that outward adorning of braiding the hair, and of wearing of gold, or of putting on of apparel, but let it be the hidden man of the heart in that which is not corruptible, even the ornament of a meek and quiet spirit, which is in the sight of God of great price. For after this manner in the old*

time the holy women also, who trusted in God, adorned themselves, being in subjection to their own husbands. Even as Sarah obeyed Abraham, calling him lord; whose daughters ye are, as long as ye do well, and are not afraid with any terror.

Subordination to men is not usually considered by women to be a pleasant prospect, particularly having been commanded by God and therefore irrefutable. It appears to be a punishment, a confirmation of which many find in Genesis 3:1-6, and 16:

Now the serpent was more subtle than any beast of the field which the Lord God had made. And he said unto the woman, Yea, hath God said, Ye shall not eat of every tree of the garden? And the woman said unto the serpent, We may eat of the fruit of the trees of the garden; but of the fruit of the tree which is in the midst of the garden, God hath said, Ye shall not eat of it, neither shall ye touch it, lest ye die. And the serpent said unto the woman, Ye shall not surely die; for God doth know that in the day ye eat thereof, then your eyes shall be opened, and ye shall be as God, knowing good and evil. And when the woman saw that the tree was good for food, and that it was pleasant to the eyes, and a tree to be desired to make one wise, she took the fruit thereof, and did eat, and gave also unto her husband with her; and he did eat. . . Unto the woman he said, I will greatly multiply thy sorrow and thy conception; in sorrow thou shalt bring forth children; and thy desire shall be to thy husband, and he shall rule over thee.

For most people that's the end of the story. Because of Eve's misdeed in the garden, women are to constrained to be subordinate to men.

But this answer, unsatisfactory as it is, compels one who is troubled by it to probe a little deeper into the interpretation of these passages. A better answer is indeed available, one that, while it supports rather than contradicts these troubling passages, softens the message considerably.

This happier interpretation requires one to appreciate the entire meaning of another passage, Genesis 1:26 and 27:

And God said, Let us make man in our image, after our likeness; and let them have dominion over the fish of the sea, and over the fowl of the air, and over the cattle, and over all the earth, and over every creeping thing that creepeth upon the earth. So God created man in his own image, in the image of God created he him; male and female created he them.

Here God in the plural, implying that the Father emphasized the inclusion of His Holy Spirit in this pronouncement, created mankind in His plural image, specifically male and female. The result is that the Godhead, in which the Father is eminently masculine, includes femininity, which can only be fulfilled with an eminently feminine Holy Spirit. That this interpretation is Scripturally correct has been thoroughly explored, being the subject of numerous writings. The Godhead is comprised of complementary Others, Father and Spirit, in a harmonious relationship in which the Father exercises the Will and the Spirit responds by creatively transforming the Will into Reality in the Person of Jesus Christ.

In summary, the Father is the initiator and the Spirit the responder. This complementary initiative and responsive relationship may be seen in the manner in which human men and women differ as a reflection of how they were created in the image of God: it is in the nature of men to initiate, and in the nature of women to respond.

Both Adam and Eve were indeed punished for their transgression, but the punishment differs from the popular interpretation. Eve's punishment was not her subordination to Adam. Originally, she was to be quite happy in the fulfillment of her responsive role; it was the way she was made. But after the transgression, Eve's nature was subtly changed, in that she was no longer fully content in this role, but longed to participate in Adam's role as well.

The regenerated Christian woman who understands the full meaning of Genesis 1:26 and 27 may well be content in her responsive role, happy that it is not only compatible with her own nature, but reflects the nature of God the Holy Spirit. God intended to for them to understand this through the exhortations, not at all harsh, of Moses, Paul and Peter.

PART TWO

The Curse and the Promise

Contents for Part Two

Preface to Part Two

There are at least two basic reasons why some individuals view Jesus as less than God or irrelevant to our modern world. The reasons are related. The first is simple ignorance of Scripture, at least in the depth in which it was intended to be accepted into the heart. Much of the blame for this lack of understanding can be laid directly at the foot of the Church, the shallowness of its message and its faulty interpretation of Scripture. Part One set out to address the issue of wrong interpretation and the correction of some potential blank spots in our vision of God.

Primarily, however, ignorance of Scripture usually comes from an indifference toward it, an attitude that leads inexorably toward a misunderstanding of its message. That relates to the second reason for perceiving Jesus to be no more than human, and the one that is addressed in Part Two herein: some people simply don't want to see God. If people with this attitude read Scripture at all, they are motivated by a desire to support their *a priori* conviction that it is not inspired by God.

Secular education plays to this attitude. Those who integrate into their own minds the several myths that they've been taught in school and society in general can say *'I thought so all along'*, remaining comfortable with the pursuit of their own self-serving objectives in life. The motive of the unbeliever is most probably a desire to continue in a lifestyle that is less than noble. His justification, however, is usually presented in terms that reflect a disappointment in God's own apparent lack of nobility. We shall review one very common objection tossed out by the non-Christian to explain away his unbelief, exposing its basic emptiness.

Much of the material in this essay follows from the development of Part One. As with that essay, it is timely because of its relevance to the family. It also offers a new and exciting picture of the Christian's future with his God.

1
The Utility of Evil

I have had interesting theological discussions with many people. In the process I've watched some faces turn surly. Perhaps it's because I didn't observe the cardinal rule of what our society has defined as decent behavior: don't talk about politics or religion with family, neighbors, or often even friends. It also could be my oafish manner, for some of these people were angry enough not to change the subject when the chance came up. Instead, they trotted out the argument that has served for centuries as the means to reduce the offending party to uncomfortable silence. "Why," they say, "if this God of yours really exists and is so good as you're trying to peddle, does He permit all this suffering to go on in the world?"

It is common for the unsaved individual to justify his rejection of God on the basis of the obvious evil in the world. The notion of a God, especially a supposedly benevolent and loving one, appears to him as contradictory to the pain and injustice that fill our planet. Virtually every person on earth, through the media or personal experience, has seen an evil person receive an unwarranted reward for his ill treatment of others. In his rejection of God, the unsaved person attempts to rub God's nose into this moral excrement. As he casually reflects on the existence of these negatives he likens God to a wizened old incompetent, or one that stumbles on crutches or rides in a wheelchair. Or one that is dead or simply never existed.

I've often noted that these same people who speak so loudly about the pain in the world aren't suffering themselves. Most of them are living comfortably. The only pain they see is what they read and watch on the news as they sit quite passively on the sidelines. Nevertheless, at first the remark would shut me up, much to the satisfaction of my temporary adversary. But it got me to thinking of all the terrors and suffering and violence which form such a substantial part of Scripture. Despite that, and perhaps even in a way connected with it, I had formed my impression of God as the embodiment of love of the most pure kind. In reviewing the grand sweep of Scripture and discussing the issue with those who impressed me as having an understanding of theology, I was happy to affirm that the reasons for this impression were good ones.

After man chose to disobey his Maker, the entrance of evil was necessary, just as each victory over evil turns it on its head from a negative to a positive. Jesus suggested that necessity when He accompanied His pronunciation of woe upon His betrayer Judas Iscariot with the comment that His betrayal was nevertheless required. It certainly was, for without the betrayal of Judas Jesus could not have performed His substitutionary death for our sins as forecast throughout the Old Testament.

Through its demonstration of selfless love, the act of Jesus on the Cross subjected evil to the Will of the Father by turning it around into a means to glorify God. Through the selfless acts of Jesus and His followers, God's love toward mankind is inevitably exercised in the process. While it was our choice to allow evil to enter into the world, God will, in the fullness of time, turn it into good. That is a specific promise, as Paul said in Chapter 8 of his letter to the Romans:

> *And we know that all things work together for good to*
> *them that love God, to them who are the called according*
> *to his purpose.*

The community of believers has an answer to the existence of evil, but it comes across to the unbeliever as rather glib. With some correctness they say that evil came into the world through the fall of Adam. Having said that, they say no more, allowing the unbeliever to perceive the intrinsic unfairness of having to put up with imperfect natures in an imperfect world all because of Adam's little problem. A person may be satisfied with that reasoning for a while, descending into mean little contemplations of Adam. But eventually even believers come to the point of scratching their chins and asking why God made an Adam that was even capable of succumbing to the devil, or why the devil was even allowed to exist in the first place.

A more satisfactory answer to these questions, as hinted above, may lay in a mature understanding of the meaning of our existence in the context of the loving nature of God. As God has plainly stated, we do not live for ourselves. Each of the billions of us that has ever lived, or lives now, or ever will live on earth has a purpose, and that purpose is to glorify God. The glorification of God does not imply a pettiness or selfishness on His part. To the contrary, in accordance with the nature of the Godhead its glorification is the exaltation of Love in its purest form and its ultimate selflessness in the context of Family. God has conveyed in Scripture the fact that man was created in this kind of love with the expectation of its return. As promised in Ephesians 5:31 and 32, Jesus will marry His Church. Our time on earth, if we spend it wisely, will permit us to acquire the nobility to love Him with the fervor appropriate to our part in that great event to come.

If God is the embodiment of such perfect, selfless love, the demonstration of that love to mankind demands the existence of evil. How, except under duress, can true selflessness be evoked? Only in the context of God's own sacrifice can man understand and appreciate the depth of His love toward us. Only by returning the same to God under our own duress in absolute trust and obedience are we capable of that unity with God which He intended from the beginning of Creation.

Of necessity man was endowed with at least the appearance of free will in order that he might return the love of God out of choice. Having sufficient free will to possess the ability to choose between good and evil, the first couple eventually (how long was that time?) chose to partake of the Tree of Knowledge against the instruction of God. The first evil enacted by man was his loss of absolute trust in the love and benevolence of God. The second evil, as was demonstrated in Part One, was the violation of gender type as enacted first by Eve in initiating the transgression, and then by Adam in responding to Eve. The evil of sexual shame followed immediately thereafter. But God in all probability foreknew this turn of events from the outset of Creation. Its enactment must have been an integral part of His grand design from the very beginning.

Not only does the Glory of God shine through the overcoming of evil, but our own fallen natures are compatible with the existence of its curse, provided that we look to God for our fulfillment. Life must have been idyllic for Adam and Eve before they partook of the forbidden fruit. It must have been perfect. But it may also have been without struggle and its attendant drama, as it was after Adam's fall that God pronounced the curse upon the ground, forcing Adam to sweat for its produce. Despite our failure to appreciate it, however, the drama of the struggle is the very thing that we require, in our fallen state, to add color and richness to our lives. We must have been quite different before the fall, necessarily so, since the perfection that existed may not have been tolerable to our present natures. Not only may we have lacked knowledge, but our mental and emotional composition must have been in perfect harmony with that lack of knowledge. Perhaps, then, the Tree of Knowledge supplied not only knowledge but also the ability to receive it.

God apparently doesn't treat us all the same. Even Christians seem to experience vastly different lives, one from the other. Some, and even perhaps most, churchgoing families get to live out their lives in relative peace and contentment. But there are others, maybe not more than a few dozen out of every thousand families, that get caught in the worst of life's meatgrinders. With these people, abuse gets heaped upon offense, seemingly without respite. Their lives reflect that of the Apostle Paul. Like with Paul and Daniel and Esther and all the great ones in the Bible, God with loving approval formed these people with their potential for valor under duress, their inherent nobility. Despite the pain, suffering and injury they had to endure to reach their final state, they are to be envied.

As a Marine in World War II, Russell Davis fought the Japanese on the little Pacific island of Peleliu. In his memoir of the battle, *Marine at War*, Davis describes the rifleman on the front lines as the reason for all the ships and aircraft and the huge logistics organization that had massed for the assault. According to him, those lonely, tough, and courageous men were important quite beyond their rank and numbers: the outcome of the battle, and of the war itself, would rest on their deeds:

> From the base of the hill, we could pick out each man and follow him until he got hit, went to ground, or climbed to the top. Not many made the top. As they toiled, caves and gullies and holes opened up and Japanese dashed out to roll grenades down on them, and sometimes to lock, body to body, in desperate wrestling matches. Knives and bayonets flashed on the hillside. I saw one man bend, straighten, and club and kick at something that attacked his legs like a mad dog. He reached and heaved, and a Japanese soldier came

end-over-end down the hill. The machine-gunners yelled encouragement.

As the riflemen climbed higher they grew fewer, until only a handful of men still climbed in the lead squads. These were the pick of the bunch – the few men who would go forward, no matter what was ahead. There were only a few. Of the thousands who land with a division and the hundreds who go up with a company of the line, there are only a few who manage to live and have enough courage to go through anything. They are the bone structure of a fighting outfit. All the rest is so much weight and sometimes merely flab. There aren't more than a few dozen in every thousand men, even the Marines. They clawed and clubbed and stabbed their way up. The rest of us watched.

These men who overcome their fear to fight for their love of country and fellow soldiers may receive recognition for valor in combat, but their true rewards are the attainment of selflessness. For some the battles may live on in their hearts for the rest of their lives, not so much for the negatives of death and destruction but more for the knowledge that they experienced a time of horror and came through on the other side having maintained the courage they had desperately wished for at the time.

When we ponder the meaning of our miserable little lives, questioning the wisdom or the capability of a God who permits a world to exist that is so thoroughly inhabited by the negatives of fear, and sorrow, and suffering, we should consider the alternative. Could our present fallen natures handle the absence of the curse of evil without going insane from sheer boredom? Perhaps the tapestry of life, if it is woven of entirely white threads, might well be intolerable for us in our fallen state. It is with the inclusion of the darker threads that a pattern becomes possible, an image forms. Not in the threads themselves, of course, but in the larger picture created by both dark and light together.

We all become so immersed in the process of attempting to live in harmony with our own perceived needs that we often fail to comprehend the poverty of a life without trial. But in reflection can we not see in unrelieved gratification a complete shallowness of existence and an utter lack of nobility? How quickly we all lose sight of God and strive for the quick reward and the easy life! How often we remain utterly oblivious to how our search for pleasure might impact the lives of our neighbors, even those whom we profess to love!

Given that they emerge intact, who has not gone through a trial of passage, one that involves pain or sorrow, or one that demands the discomfort of personal courage, and passed through to the other side without being grateful for the opportunity? Even those who have come through ordeals with permanent disabilities might take comfort in the strength of character acquired through these situations. Such experiences give us the understanding that, with the help of our Lord, the intrinsic negative can yield to a more profound positive, even to the opportunity to glorify God in our own lives. A person may be tempted to avoid doing something that intrigues him, or from which he perceives that he might gain by performing it, simply because he is fearful of injury or failure. Each of these events, regardless of the outcome, gives the individual the opportunity to enrich his life. When he emerges on the other side of whatever events demand discomfort or courage, his experiences are usually so compatible with God's own nature and His design of mankind as to be cherished for the remainder of his life.

Our present compatibility with the existence of evil encourages our love and obedience to God. In opposition to this, those who have been born into and raised in comfort live in win-directed societies in which God is largely perceived as irrelevant to their daily lives. They learn from their schools and our media to handle difficult times and evil people with a martial spirit. They put away their gentle and kind facades, adopting the role of warriors to overcome and conquer. They topple and trample, and if they can't do it without help they turn ourselves into generals and hire lawyers, the mercenary soldiers of modern society, to do it for them.

That is why some of us have such a difficult time understanding Jesus. On the surface, Jesus didn't win big on the Cross. To the reckoning of those who would pose as rugged individualists, who fail to perceive the real issue for which He fought, Jesus lost big. With this mindset, many of us have no desire whatsoever to emulate that behavior, choosing instead to distance ourselves from that loser mentality with a vacant attitude of pious worship. We either do that or we reject Him completely.

But upon reflecting on this, we see that it takes a great deal more courage to maintain a constant character than to change faces according to circumstance. It takes guts to remain kind and thoughtful of others in the face of mistreatment or misfortune than to promote self by striking out in rage. The real hero and the person of great faith is the individual who can subordinate self in times of stress. God didn't promise anyone an absence of stress. The Christian above all people should understand this quite well, for, as Jesus said in His Beatitudes (Matthew Chapter 5),

> *Blessed are they which are persecuted for righteousness' sake: for theirs is the kingdom of heaven. Blessed are ye, when men shall revile you, and persecute you, and shall say all manner of evil against you falsely, for my sake. Rejoice, and be exceeding glad: for great is your reward in heaven: for so persecuted they the prophets which were before you.*

In the context of our relationship with God, that statement of Jesus pretty much takes the win orientation of our secular society off the table. The simple truth is that we as individuals are defined less by our triumphs and joys than by our adversities. Our characters are both formed and exposed by the trials that come our way and the manner in which we handle them. It is easy, for example, to show ourselves as nice and caring people when everything is going our way. Most of us do that as an incidental matter, and then pat ourselves on our backs for being so friendly and pleasant. But to show that same face in times of trouble - that is what real heroes are made of, the kind that are rare and precious. It is only through adversity that this kind of spiritual beauty can shine forth.

We have already noted that Judas Iscariot, in fingering Jesus to the Pharisees, allowed Him to fulfill His mission on the cross. God also applies the presence of evil to the fulfillment of prophecy regarding mankind, and particularly the Jews.

Those who lived under the Nazi regime undoubtedly remembered with sorrow how Germany ruled Europe and used that raw power to embark upon a quest of genocide, creating factories that produced death. But hopefully they also remembered that the ultimate victory in that battle, as always, was God's, for He used that brief time after the end of the Second World War when the world felt sufficient compassion for Jewry to end the Diaspora in fulfillment of the thirtieth chapter of the book of Deuteronomy and in remarkable alignment with Ezekiel's prophecies. Not only did the Holy Spirit through Ezekiel foretell in Chapters 36 and 37 the rebirth of Israel as a single nation but, as the late Bible scholar Grant Jeffrey discovered, in his Chapter 4, Ezekiel foretold its occurrence to the very day in 1948. This astonishing prediction has gone so unrecognized that it deserves to be retold herein. The topic is covered in Appendix 2-1.

The well-documented excesses of the world against Jewry are nothing short of astonishing, appearing to fulfill in every detail the prophecy of Moses in Deuteronomy chapter twenty-eight. It is an awful truth that a good portion of this abuse has been heaped upon them by their misguided Christian brothers in the name of Replacement Theology and its false claim that the Church has replaced Israel with the respect to God's covenants. Someday, however, the sons of Jacob will be a blessing to the entire earth as God demonstrates the steadfastness of His Word, for He will never forsake Israel. As Joseph served as a model for Jesus (see Appendix 2-2), so also will he serve as a precursor for the Jewish believers to come. They may yet bring more people to a saving knowledge of Jesus than all the evangelists who ever lived. Is there not a beauty in the demonstration of this kind of love, despite the terrible injustice in which it grew and developed?

How, in the absence of our own hurt and anguish, could we begin to see the magnitude of God's love toward us in Jesus' agony on the cross? How could Abraham see the depth of the Father's lament toward Jesus if he hadn't come to within a hair of carrying out his sacrifice of Isaac? How could a person possibly show compassion toward the sick, or the handicapped, or the elderly, or the abused, if he was born into perfection and comfort and avoided pain throughout his entire life?

How could David have known the beauty of exercised faith had he not had the courage in the face of overwhelming odds against him to confront Goliath with nothing but a sling, or the ineffable mercy of his Descendent Jesus to come had he not experienced the sorrow of his own terrible sin against Uriah?

Understanding the love enacted by Jesus on the cross, the committed Christian should see adversity in quite a different light than the win-oriented, gratification-seeking world at large. The understanding Christian, upon reflecting on the notion of faith, is irresistibly drawn to the Book of Hebrews, where in the eleventh chapter he encounters the people before him whose God, through their faith, had fashioned lives of heroic stature. These men and women defined the meaning of real faith, the kind with substance behind it that gave them character and grit.

After he recounts the faith of individuals from Adam to Moses and what that faith had wrought, the writer of Hebrews makes a summation of the subject:

> *And what more shall I say? I do not have time to tell about Gideon, Barak, Samson, Jephthah, David, Samuel and the prophets, who through faith conquered kingdoms, administered justice, and gained what was promised; who shut the mouths of lions, quenched the fury of the flames, and escaped the edge of the sword; whose weakness was turned into strength; and who became powerful in battle and routed foreign armies. Women received back their dead, raised to life again. Others were tortured and refused to be released, so that they might gain a better resurrection. Some faced jeers and flogging, while still others were chained and put into prison. They were stoned; they were sawed in two; they were put to death by the sword. They went about in sheepskins and goatskins, destitute, persecuted and mistreated - the world was not worthy of them. They wandered in deserts and mountains, and in caves and holes in the ground.*
>
> *These were all commended for their faith, yet none of them received what had been promised. God had planned something better for us so that only together with us would they be made perfect.*

Faith, to the Christian, is the wellspring of courage. Faith provides the wherewithal to stand fast in the many battles that the man of character must face, whether they are the repression of lust, confrontation involving the danger of bodily harm, or the maintenance of intellectual objectivity in the face of strong, often hatred-laden, opposition. Paul, in recounting his own trials in 2 Corinthians 6:5, provides an excellent example of faith under fire:

Are they ministers of Christ? (I speak as a fool,) I am more; in labors more abundant, in stripes above measure, in prisons more frequent, in deaths oft. Of the Jews five times received I forty stripes save one. Thrice was I beaten with rods, once was I stoned, thrice I suffered shipwreck, a night and a day I have been in the deep; In journeyings often, in perils of waters, in perils of robbers, in perils by mine own countrymen, in perils by the heathen, in perils in the city, in perils in the wilderness, in perils in the sea, in perils among false brethren; In weariness and painfulness, in watchings often, in hunger and thirst, in fastings often, in cold and nakedness. Besides those things that are without, that which cometh upon me daily, the care of all the churches. Who is weak, and I am not weak? Who is offended, and I burn not? If I must needs glory, I will glory of the things which concern mine infirmities.

The God and Father of our Lord Jesus Christ, which is blessed for evermore, knoweth that I lie not.

Sometimes we dwell overly much on perceived hurts and the unfairnesses that come our way without allowing God, in His infinitely superior wisdom and omniscient perspective, to set things right again in His own way. How devastatingly sad to think of all the souls who lack the faith to overcome that attitude, for they are doomed to continually revisit their hurts. Hurts for which they will have no harmonious resolution in either this life or the next!

When we question God's Will in allowing the presence of pain in our lives, we also must appreciate that in the context of our immortal souls, the time of pain is indeed slight. And there is no pain that we have experienced that our Lord didn't have the greater portion. The cross was indeed terrible. And we can only guess at Jesus' horror as His Father in Heaven forsook Him to His descent into hell covered with the filth of sin.

The gift that God has given us in allowing us to participate in His great prophetic drama surely far outweighs the pain that we all experience from time to time, some more than others. The only question regarding this participation is how much of it God uses and retains. Nobody has the answer to that one, but it seems fairly clear from His Word that He might have a pretty selective focus on love, the kind of love that is other-directed.

The initial presence of evil, subsequently vanquished by the greater power of God, is a familiar pattern in the development of Scripture as well as in human affairs in general. Evil itself furnishes a contrasting backdrop by which the glory of God shines most brightly. Maybe we ourselves, at the times that we rise above our negative circumstances to demonstrate real love toward Him or others, are capable only then of the kind of behavior of lasting value to God. Perhaps those small snapshots of us at our finest will be the only portions of us that God will retain throughout eternity. If that is the case, it would go a long way toward explaining the injustices with which we are constantly surrounded. Of drug lords who acquire wealth and comfort on the misery and tears of the people that they enslave into addiction. Of robbers and rapists that escape a dysfunctional civil justice system to commit their crimes again and again. Of power-thirsty control freaks who are rewarded with governments of their own, dirty little adult playgrounds within which they commit without restraint insane acts of cruelty and lust. Of parents that abandon their children, or sell them into abuse, or commit the abuse themselves.

Each of these abominable acts provides a human being the opportunity to touch another with help, or comfort, or compassion. When the game is over, the robbers and the rapists and the cruel dictators will be gone and forgotten. But the love and the sharing and the courage that shine through the adversities will remain forever in the heart of our Lord.

And that is the positive side of evil – its utility: while pain has an end, it provides an opportunity for love, which is eternal. As David said in the thirty-fourth Psalm,

> *The eyes of the Lord are upon the righteous, and his ears are open unto their cry. The face of the Lord is against them that do evil, to cut off the remembrance of them from the earth. The righteous cry, and the Lord heareth, and delivereth them out of all their troubles. The Lord is nigh unto them that are of a broken heart; and saveth such as be of a contrite spirit. Many are the afflictions of the righteous: but the Lord delivereth him out of*

*them all. He keepeth all his bones: not one of them is
broken. Evil shall slay the wicked: and they that hate the
righteous shall be desolate. The Lord redeemeth the soul
of his servants: and none of them that trust in him shall
be desolate.*

It is only from a self-serving point of view that the evil of this
world appears to contradict the notion of a kind and just God. But
from a God-centered point of view, this earthly life and the evil
therein is but a tiny part of His immense plan for us, for out of this
life Jesus is fashioning for Himself a wife, one that He will cherish
and adore.

If we lived for ourselves only, it would be entirely appropriate to
question the existence of evil in our lives, or even the awareness of
evil in the world. But we do not live for ourselves. We never did.
We live for our maker and our lover, Jesus Christ, who is fashioning
out of our trials a noble bride. As Paul wrote in Romans Chapters
14 and 18,

*For none of us liveth to himself, and no man dieth to
himself. For whether we live, we live unto the Lord;
and whether we die, we die unto the Lord: whether we
live therefore, or die, we are the Lord's. . .For I reckon
that the sufferings of this present time are not worthy to
be compared with the glory which shall be revealed in
us. . .For I am persuaded, that neither death, nor life,
nor angels, nor principalities, nor powers, nor things
present, nor things to come, Nor height, nor depth, nor
any other creature, shall be able to separate us from the
love of God, which is in Christ Jesus our Lord.*

When a friend expressed his difficulty reconciling God's goodness
with the evil in the world, I asked him to read what I had written
above, much of which was in the original version of my book *Family
of God.*

"I think I understand what you wrote about bad things happening
to people," he began with a shake of his head, "because most people
deserve it. But what about when bad things happen to *good* people?"

He still didn't get it. Hebrews 12:6-8 says it well:

> *For whom the Lord loveth he chasteneth, and scourgeth*
> *every son whom he receiveth. If ye endure chastening,*
> *God dealeth with you as with sons; for what son is he*
> *whom the father chasteneth not? But if ye be without*
> *chastisement, of which all are partakers, then are ye*
> *bastards, and not sons.*   .

But even if he'd understood that God takes corrective measures (bad things) particularly with whom He loves, and with the loving motive of developing character within us, he didn't get it either that there aren't any good people among us, as Isaiah noted in Is 64:6. Paul reminded us of that often, Romans 3:9 and 10 being a representative example:

> *What then? Are we better than they? No, in no way; for*
> *we before proved both Jews and Gentiles, that they are*
> *all under sin; as it is written, There is none righteous,*
> *no, not one.*

I think that the biggest problem here is that the doubter limits his focus to self, contradicting the purpose of our lives. Having been created by a loving God for His Glory, He wishes to develop us from the self-centered persons we are into the nobility fitting for our future relationship with Jesus as His Bride. That means that our present physical existence is simply a kind of training for our future spiritual existence. This spirituality is the real kicker: those who complain about bad things that happen to people are mentally and emotionally stuck in the mire of our limited three-dimensional physical universe, having no concept that the larger spiritual world inhabited by God is much grander than what we are presently able to experience.

Compared to God's selfless nobility, we're all mired in the slime of self-interest, which is exactly why we can't storm the gates of heaven on our own merit. For our reconciliation with a holy God, we desperately need God's substitutionary atonement on the cross for our evil natures, as enacted by Jesus Christ: it is to the cross that we must look for that, not to ourselves.

This is the core problem with countless unfortunate, lost, people: not troubling themselves to read the Bible, they have bought into the devil's own lie about the meaning of Christianity. Considering themselves to be basically 'good', they claim to be Christian. It is hard to picture any attitude that can be more fundamentally in opposition to Christianity. In the first place, with that attitude they don't need Jesus at all. Completely disregarding Jesus' own words that nobody comes to the Father except through Him, they arrogantly think that they just need their own good works, making a mockery of the cross. In the second place, they are so comfortable with the prevailing attitude toward self and self-gratification that they fail to appreciate just how bad off we all are. None of us is good. Persons having the mindset that they are 'good' think that they can even perform 'good' acts with nothing but 'good' consequences, when history is full of the collateral damage caused by 'good' acts that have met with unintended but disastrous consequences.

In sharp contrast, the real Christian is humble enough to admit to his own shortcomings, thereby enabling him to gladly accept Jesus' very difficult work on his behalf on the cross.

Throughout his letters canonized in Scripture, Paul noted often that his fellow Christians shouldn't expect their faith to result in the lavishing of physical blessings upon them. It is in the spiritual world instead upon which they should set their sights and to which they should look with hope. Nowhere does he present this focus on another world more clearly than in 1 Corinthians 15:12-19:

> Now if Christ be preached that he rose from the dead, how say some among you that there is no resurrection of the dead? But if there be no resurrection of the dead, then is Christ not risen; And if Christ be not risen, then is our preaching vain, and your faith is also vain. Yea, and we are found false witnesses of God, because we have testified of God that he raised up Christ, whom he raised not up, if so be that the dead rise not. For if the dead rise not, then is not Christ raised; And if Christ be not raised, your faith is vain, ye are yet in your sins. Then they also who are fallen asleep in Christ are perished. If in this life only we have hope in Christ, we are of all men most miserable.

Jesus and His apostles explained numerous times just what Christians should expect during their time here on earth. Among these comments is Paul's summary given in Philippians 1:29:

For unto you it is given in the behalf of Christ, not only to believe on him but also to suffer for his sake, having the same conflict which ye saw in me, and now hear to be in me.

Golly, that doesn't sound like fun. Oddly, though, there is actual joy in living the Christian life despite the apparent negatives. First is the Christian's peace with God and the certain knowledge of His love. An intimate part of this peace is the great advantage possessed by the Christian in having the indwelling of the Holy Spirit, something that is completely unexplainable to the unbeliever, who has little idea of what he is missing. Then, too, there is the peace and satisfaction of selfless living. Mature Christians understand the difference between this life and the next quite well, having perceived the necessity of life's trials in producing men and women of selfless nobility who are fit to inhabit the spiritual kingdom of God. Here's where the nature of the Holy Spirit comes into play, by indwelling the believer to comfort him as would a mother to reconcile the loving nature of God with the suffering that the believer must face to strip him of his selfishness and thus render him capable of the love necessary for him to enjoy full communication and companionship with God.

2

The Promise of God for the Life to Come

Under the extraordinary circumstance of disaster or war, a man might bond with his companions through the sharing of hardship and fear. In some cases, this bond may become so close that he will lay down his life for them. But the individual character and the conditions that might bring this about are so unique that medals are granted for altruism of this order. More typically, man is, at best, indifferent to the welfare of his neighbors and acquaintances. At his worst, he regularly places those with whom he is in contact at a disadvantage for his own profit, caring little about his victims' consequent loss and discomfort. He lies, cheats, covets, and steals, doing these things with impunity under a pragmatic and often twisted legal system. He may do them with little sense of wrongdoing. Hidden behind the mask of a false face or the tinted glass of his automobile, he often indulges in nasty, mean-spirited thoughts: he hates; he is quick to take offense and visualize a bad end for the offender. In this manner he might, in his mind, break most of God's commandments without hesitation during a simple drive from home to work.

But there is a unique relationship in which that same individual will often behave in an altogether more altruistic manner. That relationship is his family, his spouse and children. Historically, most people on earth have willingly belonged to this unit, exercising their responsibilities to it and taking pleasure and comfort from it. The individual intuitively understands and accepts the principle that while every member of the family unit deeply and permanently belongs to him, he also belongs to them in that same way. He accepts as natural the principle of sharing: of shared responsibilities, shared activities and recreation, shared possessions and, most importantly, shared intimacy. Within the impositions and limitations of the larger society to which he belongs, the individual will also usually accept as natural and beneficial that particular division of function and labor which will result in the most secure and orderly maintenance of the family unit. Beyond that, he will often behave as nobly as the heroic soldier in the protection of his family members from harm.

In behaving as he does with respect to his family, man elevates the unit to position greater than himself. He does so naturally and without reservation, sensing no conflict in this behavior with the essential components of his individual identity. There is no conflict because the integrating factor is love in a variety of different manifestations. Love produces harmony in place of friction, and results in unity rather than separation.

Given the imperfect and often base nature of fallen man, his historic nobility in the family setting is quite different than his behavior with respect to the rest of mankind. It is, in fact, so different that it is unique. That man must function so well in the context of family merely to survive is incidental. He was designed to operate that way. As we have seen, God created man in His own image, one that included the Godhead as an integral feature. As my brother Jon once noted, there's also a hint of gender and role differentiation within the divine Family in that upper-level relationship in the closing sentence of the Lord's prayer (Matthew 6:13), the essence of which Jesus captured from David's prayer in 1 Chronicles 29:11. As Jesus instructed us to pray, He included this line:

For thine is the kingdom, the power and the glory, forever.

These words are a gift to the beloved of God, implying as they do the three distinct roles of the Members of the Trinitarian Godhead. As the treatment of gender in Part One described, this gift would indeed be an amazing one. Just as Jesus is the Son of the Divine Will, He may well assume that future function of Will in the context of Family. And, using His Church as the Means of implementing that new Will, He may bear the universe a new Child in its Implementation. That Child also would belong to us, the Church, as the Wife of Jesus, as hinted at in Romans 7:4 and declared in Revelation 21 and 22.

As God designed it, the family operates as a wonderfully effective means to bring individuals into a unity larger than themselves. A man and a woman share a romantic love. Through that love they form an intimate union of body and soul. That union, in turn, creates a new life that is also shared between them, and expands their shared love into a new form. Through the nurturing of that larger love the life they created develops and grows. Along the way, the couple may have struggled to develop a farm or a business, so that as the child matures, it can first participate to the benefit of the existing family unit, and eventually acquire it for the benefit of his own new family. During this entire process the constituents of the family function not as individuals but as components of the unit.

The family provides the only natural context in which man will willingly give up his individuality. There are other human institutions in which individuals contribute to a greater whole, but they are artificial and contrived. Within these other institutions are inevitably found strife, backbiting, self-service, forced participation, and a host of other evils. Because of its unique bond of love involving the creation and nurturing of life, the family stands alone as a cohesive unit in which its members can claim: we are one.

If imperfect man represents the family as well as he does, the Godhead in its greater perfection exhibits all the elements of love in such a perfectly harmonious interaction that its result is a transcendent Unity. This Unity is of an order of perfection that permits God to speak of Himself as One. As we have already noted, its perfection is not only functional; it is romantic:

> *Thou hast ravished my heart, my sister, my spouse; thou hast ravished my heart with one of thine eyes, with one chain of thy neck. How fair is thy love, my sister, my spouse! how much better is thy love than wine! and the smell of thine ointments than all spices!*
>
> *Thy lips, O my spouse, drop as the honeycomb: honey and milk are under thy tongue; and the smell of thy garments is like the fragrance of Lebanon. A garden enclosed is my sister, my spouse; a spring shut up, a fountain sealed. Thy plants are an orchard of pomegranates, with pleasant fruits; camphire, with spikenard*

The Song of Solomon, from which verses 4:9-13 above typify, illustrates this romance. But it has a further significance. Although it applies first to the Godhead, it also describes a future relationship between Jesus and humanity as the Church for which our family institution is simply the prelude. On what basis is this extravagant claim made? Turning first to Genesis 1:21-24, we find a depiction of the beginning, essence and basic significance of family:

> *And the Lord God caused a deep sleep to fall upon Adam, and he slept: and he took one of his ribs, and closed up the flesh instead thereof; And the rib, which the Lord God had taken from man, made he a woman, and brought her unto the man.*

> *And Adam said, This is now bone of my bones, and flesh of my flesh: she shall be called Woman, because she was taken out of Man. Therefore shall a man leave his father and his mother, and shall cleave unto his wife: and they shall be one flesh.*

In the context of this description, note the incredible statement that Paul makes in Ephesians 5 starting with verse 17:

> *Wherefore, be ye not unwise, but understanding what the will of the Lord is. And be not drunk with wine, wherein is excess; but be filled with the Spirit; Speaking to yourselves in psalms and hymns and spiritual songs, singing and making melody in your heart to the Lord; Giving thanks always for all things unto God and the Father in the name of our Lord Jesus Christ; Submitting yourselves one to another in the fear of God.*

> *Wives, submit yourselves unto your own husbands, as unto the Lord. For the husband is the head of the wife, even as Christ is the head of the church: and he is the saviour of the body. Therefore as the church is subject unto Christ, so let the wives be to their own husbands in every thing. Husbands, love your wives, even as Christ also loved the church, and gave himself for it; That he might sanctify and cleanse it with the washing of water by the word, that he might present it to himself a glorious church, not having spot, or wrinkle, or any such thing; but that it should be holy and without blemish. So ought men to love their wives as their own bodies. He that loveth his wife loveth himself. For no man ever yet hated his own flesh; but nourisheth and cherisheth it, even as*

> *the Lord the church. For we are members of his body, of his flesh, and of his bones.*
>
> *For this cause shall a man leave his father and mother, and shall be joined unto his wife, and they two shall be one flesh. This is a great mystery: but I speak concerning Christ and the church.*
>
> *Nevertheless let every one of you in particular so love his wife even as himself: and the wife see that she reverence her husband.*

Herein Scripture plainly shows that when Jesus shall perform His new functional role as Divine Will on earth, He shall do so with redeemed mankind at His side. Mankind, too, shall have a new functional role in this long-awaited heavenly order, that of Jesus' wife. Just as a child, as it approaches maturity, is given to understand the significance of male and female and begins to anticipate a future as a spouse, our eyes will eventually open to what Scripture has already told us. Jesus awaits our coming of age. This was the beautiful mystery of which Paul wrote to the Ephesians.

There has been some speculation over the centuries as to whether Jesus may have had a hidden romance. He has often been linked in this regard with Mary of Magdalene. After all, it is rather difficult to think of an all-powerful God taking the time and effort to come to earth as a man and then leaving without once having tasted of the greatest delight obtainable on the planet. His supposed celibacy somehow makes Him incomplete in many minds.

But His celibacy did make Him incomplete! As the Son of God He was already betrothed to His church. That is the mystery of which Paul spoke and His great promise of future joy to those who love Him, that without His church He is indeed incomplete. That is the wedding for which He is yet waiting, and which He joyfully anticipated at the ceremony in Cana. Just as He permitted the prophets to define Him before he came to earth, he permits his Church to complete His function as a man. In the fullness of God's time, mankind will yet serve again in the function of implementation, this time alongside the risen Jesus as His partner in marriage.

The grand design of God that included man as an eventual member of the Heavenly Family was foreshadowed in Genesis 24 and the romantic book of Ruth. From the very beginning of man in Adam, God has jealously guarded the bloodline of the Jesus to come. This was well understood by the rulers of this world, from Pharaoh to Herod. At times that were interpreted as Messianic, these rulers were given to killing off the male forebears of Mary. They instinctively knew that the bloodline was intended to remain within the Semites, passing down through the Hebrews to the Israelites under Abraham. It was to rest on the specific tribe of Judah, through whom came King David, his son Solomon, and, finally, both Mary and her husband Joseph.

But an exception was granted, one of a very few in number. There was a gentile woman named Ruth who, after the untimely death of her first husband, demonstrated a godly loyalty to her Israelite mother-in-law Naomi:

> *And Naomi said, Turn again, my daughters: why will ye go with me? are there yet any more sons in my womb, that they may be your husbands? Turn again, my daughters, go your way: for I am too old to have an husband. If I should say, I have hope, if I should have an husband also to night, and should also bear sons; Would ye tarry for them till they were grown? would ye stay for them from having husbands? nay, my daughters; for it grieveth me much for your sakes that the hand of the Lord is gone out against me. And they lifted up their voice, and wept again: and Orpah kissed her mother in law; but Ruth clave unto her.*

> *And she said, Behold, thy sister in law is gone back unto her people, and unto her gods: return thou after thy sister in law.*

> *And Ruth said, Intreat me not to leave thee, or to return from following after thee: for whither thou goest, I will go; and where thou lodgest, I will lodge: thy people shall be my people, and thy God my God: Where thou diest, will I die, and there will I be buried: the Lord do so to me, and more also, if ought but death part thee and me.*

So Ruth followed Naomi back to her people, and in poverty gleaned corn in the field of Boaz. As kinsman to Naomi, Boaz also took her as wife to redeem the name of Naomi's family. Ruth conceived a child through this man. His name was Obed:

And Naomi took the child, and laid it in her bosom, and became nurse unto it. And the women her neighbours gave it a name, saying, There is a son born to Naomi; and they called his name Obed: he is the father of Jesse, the father of David.

Now these are the generations of Pharez: Pharez begat Hezron, And Hezron begat Ram, and Ram begat Amminadab, And Amminadab begat Nahshon, and Nahshon begat Salmon, and Salmon begat Boaz, and Boaz begat Obed, and Obed begat Jesse, and Jesse begat David.

This genealogical record is repeated in the Gospels of Matthew and Luke. As noted in Matthew:

. . .And Salmon begat Booz of Rachab; and Booz begat Obed of Ruth; and Obed begat Jesse; And Jesse begat David the king; and David the king begat Solomon of her that had been the wife of Urias;. . .And Jacob begat Joseph the husband of Mary, of whom was born Jesus, who is called Christ.

It is striking how the Bible can so dramatically convey passion by means of a simple genealogical list. By the grace of this exception that is immortalized in the begats like a medal of honor, the gentiles were permitted to participate in the creation of the physical Jesus. This gentile participation in the bringing forth of the Jewish Messiah is a type of the participation of man in the Godhead. Like her descendant Mary, Ruth is indeed blessed among women.

Regarding our own union with Jesus, the book of Revelation clearly states that His church will be raised up on the seventh day, to reign with Jesus for a thousand years on earth. Our reign with Jesus will represent that of our Divine Mother the Holy Spirit as we furnish the means that, in union with the Will of our Lord Jesus, gives birth to a new Creation. It will be a marriage of great joy, as specifically confirmed by our Lord in the second chapter of John. As John recounts, Jesus reserved the first miracle that He performed on earth to demonstrate this to us by turning water into wine at the wedding ceremony in Cana.

The implications of this possibility are large. It confirms the nature of the Holy Spirit as diffuse, consisting of many components, possibly angelic, and explains why our God may have deliberately discouraged us from falling into the worship of a female deity. For to worship this entity would be dangerously close to worship of self, or at least to self as it might exist in the future next to Jesus, our Lord and our husband. Even now a false, arrogant, and self-serving form of this hope is manifest in the New Age belief that we ourselves are gods.

In the context of Jesus as the Husband of His church, an interesting topic for further speculation is this as the Jewish procedure for divorce is recalled: In thrice denouncing the Pharisees, did Jesus annul his relationship with the religious leaders? And in his threefold request of Peter to feed His sheep, was He in effect betrothing Himself to His church? We do know this: when Jesus in John 14 gave us the promise of a place in heaven, he was speaking according to the custom, current at that time in that society, of the preparations that the bridegroom makes for his wife:

> *Let not your heart be troubled: ye believe in God, believe also in me. In my Father's house are many mansions: if it were not so, I would have told you. I go to prepare a place for you. And if I go and prepare a place for you, I will come again, and receive you unto myself; that where I am, there ye may be also.*

We also see in viewing Jesus as Husband the potential for a union that bears fruit. In Part One we arrived at the fascinating notion of the Godhead as a dynamically continuous Family process, a recursive drama in which the human pattern of one generation receiving the scepter of activity from its predecessor and passing it on to its descendents is truly an image of its Godly counterpart. There may be large differences, of course. The original God must still be active in an open and expanding universe rather than lying dead in some heavenly grave. But the essential functional passing of the torch, at least with respect to earth, yet may be a reality.

One very happy corollary to this view of our eventual relationship with Jesus is a picture of heaven that is more substantial and infinitely more interesting than the usual ephemereal place of clouds, harps, and a rather boring stasis. To the contrary, our future time with Jesus appears to be a busy one, full of creative effort, quite possibly rich with adventure, and certainly with love.

In whatever direction our new roles shall lead us, the next time that we shall see Jesus, we shall truly see Him as our God. And when we do, we shall be alongside Him as His intimate companion. A glimpse of that sight is given in the Book of Revelation:

> *And he shewed me a pure river of water of life, clear as crystal, proceeding out of the throne of God and of the Lamb. In the midst of the street of it, and on either side of the river, was there the tree of life, which bare twelve manner of fruits, and yielded her fruit every month: and the leaves of the tree were for the healing of the nations.*
>
> *And there shall be no more curse: but the throne of God and of the Lamb shall be in it; and his servants shall serve him: And they shall see his face; and his name shall be in their foreheads. And there shall be no night there; and they need no candle, neither light of the sun; for the Lord God giveth them light: and they shall reign for ever and ever.*

3
Isaac's Trial and His Later Joy

Two events in the life of Isaac described in Genesis Chapters 22 and 24 provide an interesting overview of the issues covered in the two chapters above regarding the issues of suffering in our lives and the joy that Christians have to look forward to as components of the Church, the future bride of Jesus Christ.

Chapter 22 of Genesis describes one of the greatest tests of faith that God would impose upon Abraham or, for that matter, upon any human. In that chapter, God tells Abraham to sacrifice the son whom he dearly loved.

And it came to pass after these things, that God did tempt Abraham, and said to him Abraham: and he said, Behold, here I am. And he said, Take now your son, your only son Isaac, whom you love, and get you into the land of Moriah; and offer him there for a burnt offering upon one of the mountains which I will tell you of.

And Abraham rose up early in the morning, and saddled his ass, and took two of his young men with him, and Isaac his son, and split the wood for the burnt offering, and rose up, and went to the place of which God had told him. Then on the third day Abraham lifted up his eyes, and saw the place afar off. And Abraham said unto his young men, Stay here with the ass; and I and the lad will go yonder and worship, and come again to you.

And Abraham took the wood of the burnt offering, and laid it upon Isaac his son; and he took the fire in his hand, and a knife; and they went both of them together. And Isaac spoke to Abraham his father, and said, My father: and he said, Here am I, my son. And he said,

197

Behold the fire and the wood: but where is the lamb for a burnt offering? And Abraham said, My son, God will provide himself a lamb for a burnt offering: so they went both of them together. And they came to the place which God had told him of; and Abraham built an altar there, and laid the wood in order, and bound Isaac his son, and laid him on the altar upon the wood. And Abraham stretched forth his hand, and took the knife to kill his son.

And the Angel of the Lord called to him out of heaven, and said, Abraham, Abraham: and he said Here am I. And he said, Lay not your hand upon the lad, neither do any thing to him: for now I know that you fear God, seeing you have not withheld your son, your only son, from me. And Abraham lifted up his eyes, and looked, and behold, behind him a ram caught in a thicket by his horns: and Abraham went and took the ram, and offered him up for a burnt offering in the stead of his son. And Abraham called the name of that place Jehovah-jireh: as it is said to this day, In the mount of the Lord it shall be seen.

Abraham actually had more than one son, but Isaac was the only son who was born of his wife Sarah, and the Bible carefully showed that it was to be through Isaac's bloodline that the promises of God to Abraham eventually would be realized. It was in the sense that Abraham's seed through Isaac would be the one to bear fruit to God in the bloodline to Judah that Isaac was considered to be Abraham's only son.

Unfortunately, many Christians question why God would call for such brutality as to command Abraham to sacrifice his son. They see only God's apparent cruelty in this directive. They don't understand the significance of it in demonstrating the nobility of God's own character, His enormous love toward His Son Jesus and the pain that He would have to endure for our sake in handing Jesus over to the cross for our own salvation. In brief, this episode was a foretelling of God's plan of salvation for mankind in the form of a passion play.

God clearly intended this event in the life of Abraham and Isaac to foretell the sorrow that would be the Holy Father's lot as his only begotten Son Jesus was sacrificed on the cross at Calvary. What God held back from requiring of Abraham, He Himself had to do in this magnificent expression of His sacrificial love toward mankind.

Abraham was blessed for his faith. The importance of it was not just that he was willing to suffer the sorrow of losing his son. The greater part of his faith was that he was willing to represent the drama between the Father and Jesus in the most significant moment in the history of mankind: Jesus' passion on the cross.

Genesis Chapter 24 involves Isaac again, but under considerably happier circumstances. Isaac is now old enough to marry, and his father Abraham is choosy about whom he shall have as a bride. Sarah has died, so the task of selecting the proper wife for Isaac falls on the shoulders of Abraham's trusted servant, who is told to go to the country of Abraham's kinfolk. We pick up the narrative at verse 10:

And the servant took ten camels of the camels of his master, and departed; for all the goods of his master were in his hand: and he arose, and went to Mesopotamia, unto the city of Nahor. And he made his camels to kneel down outside the city by a well of water at the time of the evening, even the time that women go out to draw water. And he said, O Lord God of my master Abraham, I pray you, send me good speed this day, and show kindness to my master Abraham. Behold, I stand here by the well of water; and the daughters of the men of the city come out to draw water: and let it come to pass, that the damsel to whom I shall say, Let down your pitcher, I pray you, that I may drink; and she shall say, Drink, and I will give your camels drink also: let the same be she that you have appointed for your servant Isaac; and thereby shall I know that you have shown kindness to my master.

And it came to pass, before he had done speaking, that, behold, Rebekah came out, who was born to Bethuel, son of Milcah, the wife of Nahor, Abraham's brother, with her pitcher upon her shoulder. And she was very fair to look upon, a virgin, neither had any man known her: and she went down to the well, and filled her pitcher, and came up. And the servant ran to meet her, and said, Let me, I pray you, drink a little water of your pitcher. And she said, Drink, my lord: and she hasted, and let down her pitcher upon her hand, and gave him drink. And when she had done giving him drink, she said, I will draw water for your camels also, until they have done drinking. And she hasted, and emptied her pitcher into the trough, and ran again to the well to draw water, and drew for all his camels. And the man wondering at her held his peace, to wit whether the Lord had made his journey prosperous or not. And it came to pass, as the camels had done drinking, that the man took a golden earring of half a shekel weight, and two bracelets for her hands of ten shekels weight of gold; and said, Whose daughter are you? Tell me, I pray you: is there room in your father's house for us to lodge in? And she said to him, I am the daughter of Bethuel the son of Milcah, which she bare to Nahor. She said moreover to him, We have both straw and provender enough, and room to lodge in. And the man bowed down his head, and worshiped the Lord. And he said, Blessed be the Lord God of my master Abraham, who has not left destitute my master of his mercy and his truth: I being in the way, the Lord led me to the house of my master's brethren. And the damsel ran, and told them of her mother's house these things.

As this account went, Abraham's servant went into the house of Rebekah's brother Laban and told them of his mission to find a wife for Abraham's son Isaac. He related how God had led him directly to Rebekah and had confirmed that she was the one whom he had sought. After this, the servant asked for their consent to take Rebekah back with him and present her to Isaac. Upon receiving their consent, the servant lavished Rebekah and her family with gifts. As he prepared to return home, the family stalled off, asking that Rebekah stay with them for at least ten more days. He, wishing to return immediately, asked them to reconsider the delay, whereupon they called Rebekah into the meeting and asked her for her consent. Having received it from her, the servant then returned home with her and she became Isaac's wife.

At this point, Scripture had already identified Isaac as representing Jesus on the cross. Now, the circumstances of his marriage to Rebekah just as clearly show him as representing Jesus who will wed a very special bride. As the Bible brings out in the New Testament, the bride that Rebekah foretold will be the Church; moreover, Rebekah's own consent was down in the weeds of apparent importance, but it was there, suggesting that while the lion's share of initiative toward our salvation belongs to God, He did leave a tiny portion of it to us.

Appendix 2-1
Ezekiel's Prophesy of Israel's Rebirth in 1948

According to Bible scholar Dr. Grant Jeffrey, God had foretold in Scripture not only the return of Israel as a nation into her land in 1948, but the exact date of that event. Dr. Jeffrey claims that he was given the ability by God to piece together the items of Scripture by which that event was foretold, thus demonstrating two points: first, that Scripture is supernaturally accurate, and second, that God had everything to do with the return of Israel as a modern nation in bold opposition to those who would claim that Israel is no longer the apple of God's eye.

Before addressing the specifics of Jeffrey's research in this area, we note that his conclusions are corroborated elsewhere in Scripture. The Book of Hosea contains prophecies regarding Israel's lengthy dispersion and her subsequent revival as a nation. While not as precise as the prophecies that Dr. Jeffrey investigated, they are quite remarkable in their own right as to the accuracy of the general timing of Israel's revival after two millennia of dispersion. The dispersion itself is addressed in Hosea 4:4 and 5:

> *For the children of Israel shall abide many days without a king, and without a prince, and without a sacrifice, and without an image, and without an ephod, and without teraphim; Afterward shall the children of Israel return, and seek the Lord, their God, and David, their king, and shall fear the Lord and his goodness in the latter days.*

Hosea 6:2 addresses the general time frame of Israel's return, in which a day is interpreted as a thousand years according to Psalm 90 and 2 Peter 3:

After two days will he revive us; in the third day he will
raise us up, and we shall live in his sight.

Returning to Dr. Jeffrey's work regarding Israel's return as a nation, he received his first clue regarding the nature of Israel's return from Ezekiel Chapters 36 and 37, in which the 'dry bones' connect together, are clothed with flesh, and are given life. Many eschatologists view these chapters as applicable to the Jews having been given new life and a return to their homeland after the Holocaust they suffered in Nazi Germany.

As to the timing of their return to their homeland, Dr. Jeffrey received his initial clue regarding that topic from Ezekiel 4:4-6:

Lie also upon your left side, and lay the iniquity of the
house of Israel upon it; according to the number of the
days that you shall lie upon it, you shall bear their iniquity.
For I have laid upon you the years of their iniquity,
according to the number of the days, three hundred and
ninety days; so shall you bear the iniquity of the house of
Israel. And when you have accomplished them, lie again
on your right side, and you shall bear the iniquity of the
house of Judah forty days. I have appointed you each
day for a year.

Here the Word of God specifically laid on Israel a judgment of a year for each day that Ezekiel was commanded to lie on his side. Adding 390 and 40 together, Dr. Jeffrey arrived at a total of 430 years of God's judgment upon Israel. Ezekiel himself was a captive in Babylon, so Dr. Jeffrey assumed that the judgment was to begin at the beginning of Israel's or Judah's captivity. Israel was captured by the Assyrians in the eighth Century B.C., while Judah became captive to Nebudchadnezzar somewhere between 606 and 605 B.C. Dr. Jeffrey attempted to apply the 430 years directly to each of these dates, but came up with no historically meaningful end date.

Pursuing this topic in greater detail, Dr. Jeffrey came to an astonishingly relevant passage in Leviticus 26:17, 18, 27 and 28:

And I will set my face against you, and you shall be slain
before your enemies; they that hate you shall reign over
you, and you shall flee when none pursues you. And if
you will not yet for all this listen to me, then I will punish

you seven times more for your sins. . . And if you will not
for all this listen to me, but walk contrary to me, Then I
will walk contrary to you also in fury; and I, even I, will
chastise you seven times for your sins.

Here is where Dr. Jeffrey demonstrates the power of the Holy Spirit and the depth of his knowledge of Scripture. He realized in connection with this passage that during Ezekiel's time, the northern tribes of Israel had been under continuous captivity while Judah was undergoing a punishment that, according to Jeremiah 25:11, would last for precisely seventy years. Jeffrey also realized that the passage in Leviticus quoted above was conditional upon the Jews failing to turn back to God after an initial punishment. Judah's captivity did indeed end after seventy years, when the Persian King Cyrus, who was called by name by Isaiah over a century before his birth (Isaiah 44:28), decreed at some time between 536 and 535 B.C. that Israelites could return to Jerusalem to rebuild their temple. The fulfillment of that prophetic message is recorded in the Book of Ezra. (This prophetic event is not to be confused with the fulfillment of Daniel's prophecy in Daniel 9 regarding the appearance of Messiah 483 years after the commandment permitting the Jews to rebuild the city of Jerusalem. That prophecy was fulfilled in the beginning event by Artaxerxes Longimanus in 445 B.C. as recorded in the Book of Nehemiah and at the conclusion by Jesus' triumphal entry into Jerusalem in 32 A.D.)

Grant Jeffrey appreciated that the outcome of Leviticus 26 would depend on the behavior of the Jews following the termination of their captivity in Babylon, which meant that the 70-year period of their captivity must be subtracted from the 430-year period of Ezekiel 4 prior to the application of the sevenfold punishment of Leviticus 26. The resulting calculations are:

430 - 70 = 360

360 x 7 = 2520 (prophetic) years x 360 = 907,200 days

Applying a 907,200-day interval to the assumed earlier date of the end of the Babylonian captivity results, according to Jeffrey, in an end date of 1948, the precise year that Israel became a modern nation in fulfillment of Isaiah 66:7 and 8:

> *Before she travailed, she brought forth; before her pain*
> *came, she was delivered of a man-child. Who hath heard*
> *such a thing? Who hath seen such things? Shall the earth*
> *be made to bring forth in one day? Or shall a nation be*
> *born at once? For as soon as Zion travailed, she brought*
> *forth her children.*

This calculation may be roughly confirmed first by assuming that the Babylonian captivity ended sometime between 535 and 536 B.C., the two dates most commonly noted by Biblical historians. Multiplying 536 solar years by the number of days in a solar year of 365.25 results in 195,774 days between the end of the Babylonian captivity and the end of the B.C. era. Subtracting 195,774 from 907.200 results in 711,426 days remaining in the A.D. era to the completion of the prophetic time interval. In converting this to years it is noted that the A.D. era starts at A.D. 1 rather than A.D. 0, requiring the addition of 1 to the conversion:

Years A.D. = 1 + (711426/365.25) = 1 + 1947.7782 = 1948.7782

This roughly-calculated date of 1948+ is extremely close to the actual date of the beginning of the modern nation of Israel of May 15, 1948. differing from it at most by less than a year. Indeed, the difference may be brought to zero by assuming an initial day (Cyrus' proclamation) of only a few days later in the year than the end date of May 15.

Dr. Jeffrey, in fact, makes that very claim, asserting that the precise date of Cyrus' proclamation results in the foundation of the nation of Israel May 14, 1948, the exact day when she became a modern nation. Until I have been able to verify that claim, I will refrain from making the same assertion. Nevertheless, having a prediction actually come to pass within a year over 25 centuries after it was made is entirely sufficient to demonstrate beyond all doubt the supernatural origin of the prophecy.

Nevertheless, the rough verification made above, viewed in the context of the remarkable prophecy of Hosea 6:2 noted earlier and the equally remarkable prophecy of Israel's return as a nation made in Ezekiel Chapters 36 and 37, is more than sufficient to demonstrate both the supernatural source of Scripture and God's continuing love of Israel. That it represents absolute truth follows from the richness of the details involved in the prediction, the very long time between its prediction and fulfillment, and the fact that the entire world saw its fulfillment in 1948.

Appendix 2-2
The Story of Joseph

The story of Joseph in the Old Testament is long. It begins in Chapter 37 of the Book of Genesis, and goes through Chapter 45. The Bible gives it so much attention because it beautifully shows a very important feature of the Jesus who we'll come to know more fully in the New Testament. There are many such stories in the Old Testament like that, that point directly to Jesus. These tales actually define the Jesus who will later come in the flesh. God's like that. He didn't need to do it that way, but he involved mankind in showing itself just how Jesus would appear when He came down to earth to live among us.

Of the twelve sons of Jacob, whom God renamed Israel, Joseph was the most loved by him. That status of his didn't particularly sit well with the others, and his own actions only made things worse. He was given to telling his father of his brothers' evil deeds, and then when he told them of his dreams in which he was their leader, even over his own father and mother, they'd had it up to their eyeballs with him. They were in a remote field when he came upon them again to check up on them, and, unable to take his attitude any more, they rid themselves of him by selling him to a band of Ishmaelites who were traveling with goods into Egypt. By doing so, they handed him a sentence of lifelong slavery. They covered his coat with the blood of a goat and told their father Jacob that Joseph had been killed by a beast.

This was the beginning of a remarkable adventure of Joseph, one that spanned years of slavery and jail, times of distress in which there was no possibility of freedom except for a miracle from God. But that is just what happened. As God raised up the prophet Daniel many centuries later through the circumstance of dreams, He did the same with Joseph by giving the king of Egypt, who is called Pharaoh, a dream of seven fat and seven emaciated animals. The dream troubled this king greatly, but when he commanded his advisors to explain what it meant, they were unable to do so. But Joseph, still in jail, had already interpreted the dream of a fellow prisoner, Pharaoh's butler, who had been released and restored to his former position as Joseph had predicted would happen. When Pharaoh, the lord of Egypt, had heard of this ability of Joseph, he was released from jail to appear before him and interpret the ruler's own dream. Joseph responded by explaining that the dream foretold of seven future years of plentiful harvest, to be followed by another seven years of drought and famine. He went on to recommend to Pharaoh that he appoint an overseer to supervise the storage of surplus food during the good years to offset starvation during the lean years to follow. Pharaoh, recognizing the hand of God in Joseph's talent, not only released him from jail, but appointed him to be that very supervisor. This commission came in Joseph's thirtieth year, as it was for Jesus when He was baptized for His mission. In a grand demonstration of God's power to raise up the humble, Joseph carried out his assigned duty, in the process becoming a mighty ruler, second in command to Pharaoh over all of Egypt.

As years of plenty passed and were replaced by years of drought, the stores of grain laid up by Joseph began to be used. Now the supervision of Joseph turned to the distribution of food to the needy. Meanwhile, the widespread famine extended outside the borders of Egypt. Other people were beginning to starve, and among these were Joseph's Israelite brothers. Their father Jacob, seeing the plight of his people and the relative ease with which the Egyptians were weathering the drought, sent ten of his sons to Pharaoh to plead for food. Of all his sons, only the youngest, Benjamin, remained behind.

In one of life's great ironies, the Israelites were granted an audience with the Egyptian potentate in charge of distribution, who, of course, was their brother whom they had abused so many long, eventful years ago. Because so much time had passed during which they thought he was dead, they failed to recognize him. As for Joseph, he knew immediately, but declined at that time to make the connection known.

At this point Joseph must have struggled pretty hard with feelings of hurt and anger. He was obviously in control over their very lives. Now Joseph was in the perfect payback position and he knew it. He had the ideal chance to even the score and he began to cash in on the opportunity with harsh words and harsher terms. He did give them some food, but kept Simeon behind as a hostage, refusing to release him unless they brought Benjamin to him as surety that they were not spies. Eventually they were forced by the continuing famine to return for more food, bringing Benjamin with them to the terrible distress of their father Jacob. Joseph played a bit with their fear, framing Benjamin for theft and insisting that he stay behind as his slave. Faced with calamity, they spoke among themselves with shame and guilt of God's retribution for the evil manner in they had treated their brother so long ago. Finally, still not recognizing that it was his brother he was standing before, Judah repented of his evil deeds before Joseph, offering his substitutionary enslavement for the freedom of Benjamin.

Throughout this drama Joseph was beset with mixed feelings of hatred and love. Now, in the wake of Judah's repentance the situation changed dramatically. In one of history's great defining moments, Wisdom was imparted to Joseph such that he understood the events shaping his life in the context of the magnificent loving hand of God. Casting away the temptation to indulge in his petty retribution, he decided to obey his God. I particularly like what Joseph said to his brothers in Genesis Chapter 45:

> *Then Joseph could not refrain himself before all them that stood by him; and he cried, Cause every man to go out from me. And there stood no man with him, while Joseph made himself known to his brothers.*

> *And he wept aloud: and the Egyptians and the house of Pharaoh heard. And Joseph said to his brothers, I am Joseph; does my father yet live? And his brothers could not answer him; for they were troubled at his presence.*

> *And Joseph said to his brothers, Come near to me, I pray you. And they came near. And he said, I am Joseph your brother, whom ye sold into Egypt. Now therefore be not grieved, nor angry with yourselves, that you sold me here: for God did send me before you to preserve life. For these two years has the famine been in the land: and yet there are five years, in which there shall neither be plowing nor harvesting.*

> *And God sent me before you to preserve you a posterity in the earth, and to save your lives by a great deliverance.*

So now it was not you who sent me here, but God: and he has made me a father to Pharaoh, and lord of all his house, and a ruler throughout all the land of Egypt. Haste you, and go up to my father, and say to him, Thus says your son Joseph, God has made me lord of all Egypt: come down to me without delay. And you shall dwell in the land of Goshen, and you shall be near unto me, you, and your children, and your children's children, and your flocks, and your herds, and all that you have: and there will I nourish you; for yet there are five years of famine; lest you, and your household, and all that you have, come to poverty.

The importance of Joseph's life, and this story of it, is that Joseph was given the privilege of presenting a very important part of Jesus' selfless character to the world at large. What Joseph did was to suffer on behalf of those who caused his suffering, who hated him. At the end he did it willingly, to save them from starvation and death. Jesus did that very thing – He suffered on behalf of those – us - who, still being in our sins, hated and rejected Him. He did it voluntarily, out of love, for our salvation.

PART THREE

What is Truth?

Contents to Part Three

Preface to Part Three

Having attempted in the previous essays to counter the view of Jesus presented in most of our Churches with a God more worthy of our worship by reason of His intrinsic nature and more believable by reason of His Old Testament credentials, I wish to address general aspects of the modern mindset and the misunderstandings associated with it that inhibit our ability not only to see our God in all His glory, but also to understand some causes of the numerous problems our society faces. The cumulative lack of understanding is so profound that diverse intimately connected topics are commonly perceived to be unrelated to each other. These unseen connections, if properly known, could well have an important potential impact on our individual and collective welfare.

A number of misconceptions in our society have their origins in deliberately propagated falsehoods, the most fundamental being the presumptive denial of the actuality of the Judeo-Christian God. The maintenance of these falsehoods in the presence of their own internal contradictions and the most powerful arguments to the contrary is carried out with a fervor of religious proportions, leading one to suspect that this is the time of which Paul spoke in 2 Timothy 4:3, and 4:

> *For the time will come when they will not endure sound doctrine; but after their own lusts shall they heap to themselves teachers, having itching ears; And they shall turn away their ears from the truth, and shall be turned unto fables.*

1

The Perversion
of Truth

To Pontius Pilate, faced with the distasteful task of condemning an innocent man to an unpleasant death, truth boiled down to situational ethics. He mouthed his famous line "What is truth?" as he attempted to distance himself, both physically and emotionally, from the political necessity of performing an act that violated his own conscience.

The man who stood before Pilate claimed to be the very embodiment of truth. In the context of this personification, there is nothing to question about truth. It is absolute and it is a controlling factor in our lives. Paradoxically, the control has a positive quality: it has the power to set men free to live in harmony with our nature.

Truth perverted has the power to enslave us. In the two thousand years since the death of the innocent man who was thrust before Pilate, battles have been fought and countless people have suffered in the struggle to define truth for gain. No one knew this with more clarity than Niccolo Machiavelli, the fifteenth century Florentine who set out in *The Prince* to describe the means by which an ambitious man might acquire and maintain power over others. It has been recognized for centuries as a handbook on deception and betrayal in which the manipulation of truth is wielded with the objective of obtaining unfair advantage over innocent people. This kind of self-service is the very antithesis of the Judeo-Christian God; it represents a horrifying death of the soul. Below, in his own words (translated by N. H. Thomson), Machiavelli relates a classic instance of the application of duplicity:

"In our own times, during the papacy of Alexander VI, Oliverotto of Fermo, who some years before had been left an orphan, and had been brought up by his maternal uncle Giovanni Fogliani, was sent while still a lad to serve under Paolo Vitelli, in the expectation that a thorough training under that commander might qualify him for high rank as a soldier. After the death of Paolo, he served under his brother Vitellozzo, and in a very short time, being of a quick wit, hardy and resolute, he became one of the first soldiers of his company. But thinking it beneath him to serve under others, with the countenance of the Vitelleschi and the connivance of certain citizens of Fermo who preferred the slavery to the freedom of their country, he formed the design to seize on that town.

"He accordingly wrote to Giovanni Fogliani that after many years of absence from home, he desired to see him and his native city once more, and to look a little into the condition of his patrimony; and as his one endeavor had been to make himself a name, in order that his fellow-citizens might see that his time had not been misspent, he proposed to return honourably attended by a hundred horsemen from among his own friends and followers; and he begged Giovanni graciously to arrange for his reception by the citizens of Fermo with corresponding marks of distinction, as this would be creditable not only to himself, but also to the uncle who had brought him up.

"Giovanni accordingly, did not fail in any proper attention to his nephew, but caused him to be splendidly received by his fellow-citizens, and lodged him in his house; where Oliverotto having passed some days, and made the necessary arrangements for carrying out his wickedness, gave a formal banquet, to which he invited his uncle and all the first men of Fermo. When the repast and the other entertainments proper to such an occasion had come to an end, Oliverotto artfully turned the conversation to matters of grave interest, by speaking of the greatness of Pope Alexander and Cesare his son, and of their enterprises; and when Giovanni and the others were replying to what he said, he suddenly rose up, observing that these were matters to be discussed in a more private place, and so withdrew to another chamber; whither his uncle and all the other citizens followed him, and where they had no sooner seated themselves, than soldiers rushing out from places of concealment put Giovanni and all the rest to death.

"After this butchery, Oliverotto mounted his horse, rode through the streets, and besieged the chief magistrate in the palace, so that all were constrained by fear to yield obedience and accept a government of which he made himself the head."

One does not need to look closely to see applications today of the methods of deception set forth by Machiavelli and his disciples. Problems are created by governments for which the only solution is more state control. Information is hidden and compartmentalized in the name of national security. Groups who oppose state-sponsored agendas are isolated through public marginalization.

A number of political observers have written much about the use of duplicity to further the shallow, selfish, and potentially harmful interests of persons and groups. Several recent best-selling authors have expressed with sharp clarity how truth has been stretched and often distorted by politicians, bureaucrats, and the media in the United States. They demonstrate with detailed understanding how the manipulation of truth has supported a host of self-serving purposes, including the creation of false images and the implementation of personal agendas. Multiple members of Congress, for example, have recently taken positions in direct contradiction to the best interest of our country in order to expand their contstituency and maintain control over the electorate. Perhaps this is a minor example, although it could well end up being of extreme importance; regardless, it occurs with such frequency that it demonstrates how ubiquitous is the exercise of duplicity in American politics. More recently, in his book *The Death of a Nation,* Dinesh D'Souza describes how the American Democratic Party attributes negative characteristics to the Republican Party while they of themselves exercise those very same characteristics. According to him, the real fascists, for example, are groups like *Antifa,* who shout so loudly against Republican "fascism." Other examples are even more serious: the destruction of individuals, the compromise of morality, and the endangerment of national security have all been accomplished with horrifying regularity in the Washington power grab. There is no reason to single out the United States, however. One can find the same self-serving deception rampant in governments around the globe. Members and leaders of the United Nations organization pervert the truth with disgusting regularity to further their personal agendas.

If the manipulation of truth represents power, control over the sources of public information furnish the ability to make that power absolute. Dictatorships exercise overt control over the media for that purpose. Modern democracies are more subtle in their control, ensuring by private means that the agenda of the media coincides with that of the relevant power structure, which ultimately resolves to the acquisition of control. In their subtlety they compound the magnitude of their deception.

We can see the effectiveness of bureaucratic manipulation in the spectacular successes of several recently-pursued social engineering projects. Regardless of whether the results are viewed as positive or negative, they represent the deliberate application of intrusive manipulation upon the public. The public now views cigarette smoking and gun ownership with distaste while accepting as natural what once was considered shocking sexual immorality. Control over the raising of children resides more with the state than with parents. Christians are increasingly viewed with suspicion. To be considered a 'fundamentalist' was once a source of pride. Now it is an epithet, a brand representing a number of false judgments.

But governmental politics is not the only arena in which the manipulation of truth is indulged. Virtually every field of human endeavor which offers some measure of control over the minds or actions of the general public is subject to the infiltration of the bureaucratic mentality which seeks to acquire and preserve power with a shocking lack of care as to whether it does so at the expense of truth. When religion has offered this kind of control, such power was exercised to the complete contradiction and perversion of the principles upon which that religion was based. Examples persist today within both the Catholic and mainline Protestant Churches even in the face of the current decline in religious fervor. One can only say that such behavior does not represent Christianity, indicating that those within Christian institutions who participate in the abuse of power have fallen away from the faith and are driven by other than Godly motives. Jesus alluded to this in choosing Judas Iscariot as one of His twelve disciples.

Christians, at least those who call themselves such, are certainly capable of being taken in by deceptive leaders, and many are. But, contrary to common opinion, they may be less naïve in this regard than the general public. In the first place, given their Scriptural understanding that all unregenerate humans share Adam's fall from grace, Christians do not trust in the basic honesty of mankind. Secondly, those who have taken the time to read Old Testament Scripture understand in the depressing regularity of Israel's backsliding that all human institutions are capable of falling away from their noble beginnings, and rather quickly at that. Third, Christians share the hope of God's future intervention in human affairs. Unbelievers do not have this hope. They can only hope, despite what history so plainly tells them, that man and his governments can achieve justice and equity for all without outside intervention. Having no other hope, unbelievers have no choice but to trust the institutions maintained by their fellow men. That necessity alone makes them dangerously naïve.

Having the necessity to trust in those institutions which have such a large impact on the quality of their lives, unbelievers are capable of being forced further into their unbelief, especially in times of political crisis. The situation can rapidly feed upon itself, impacting their general view of the world about them and especially their regard for Christians.

Christians have no choice: they must not only live among them, but must love them as well.

2

The Secular Marginalization of Christianity

In the domain of science, truth is not the absolute one might expect given its logic-based methodology and the nature of its inquiry. At times it is a relative thing just as it is in the political arena, something wielded for the sake of expedience or to further an agenda. This situation is demonstrated with striking clarity in the ongoing controversy between science and religion. Science presumes to be the sole authority for objective truth, having formalized this claim in the proclamation of the National Academy of Sciences that "religion and science are separate and mutually exclusive realms of human thought whose presentation in the same context leads to misunderstanding of both scientific theory and religious belief."

In this audacious move in the science/religion turf war, science thus seeks with all the duplicity of Machiavelli to divorce truth, in terms of physical reality, from belief, in the form of religious faith. In the process, religion is granted the domain of 'spiritual truths', those moral and basically social concepts which are inherently untestable and about which existing information is apparently both necessary and sufficient. Science arrogates to itself everything else, ultimately including everything to which reason is applied in the acquisition of knowledge.

This usurpation should not be surprising to anyone. With the ascendancy of science as a dominant factor in the affairs of man and its consequent politicization has come the inevitable perversion of truth for the sake of power. The 'hard' sciences, such as mathematics and physics, have been relatively immune to corruption simply because of their precision and consequent testability. The natural sciences, however, are considerably more speculative in nature, so much so that the application of the term 'science' to the associated intellectual endeavors is often of itself less than truthful. It is in this domain that rampant deceptions have taken place to further agendas which have little to do with science itself. Because the deceptions involve the perversion of truth, they inevitably create conflicts with research findings. Such conflict is most evident where valid advances are endowing the historically more speculative sciences with a precision approaching that found in the 'hard' sciences, furnishing research conclusions with a testability not previously available. The results of this new testability, so damaging to the false sciences, are being suppressed by ever more blatantly Machiavellian tactics.

Foremost among the scientific disciplines which have been infected by unproven speculation is the field of biology, where the controlling paradigm remains the theory of evolution. Ironically, the sometimes spectacular recent advances in biology have been made in spite of this most general paradigm and stand in stark conflict with it, causing a divided house. In the field of microbiology, for example, the discoveries of the DNA code and of details of cellular structures, revealing their previously unsuspected system complexities, furnish evidence in direct opposition to the premises upon which the theory of evolution is based. Nevertheless, the most vocal spokespersons for the natural sciences insist upon hiding this fact from the public, attempting instead to create the perception that recent findings are entirely compatible with the collapsing edifice of evolutionary theory and the gradualism upon which it is based. Recognizing the problem among themselves but hardly daring to publicize their concerns, they consciously suppress the alternative paradigm more compatible by far with their discoveries, that of the existence of a Creator.

There are infrequent leaks. When they occur, they are like a refreshing breeze which cleans out the stink in the air. Once in a while, a researcher noted for his scientific expertise in his field will come out with an honest statement regarding the truth of the matter. The late Dr. Grant Jeffrey, for example, in his book *Creation,* attributes the following quotation to embryologist Soren Lovtrup:

> I believe that one day the Darwinian myth will be ranked
> the greatest deceit in the history of science.

The motive behind this deception is clear. As both Grant Jeffrey and Philip Johnson have clearly demonstrated from secular sources, there is a fear within the secular scientific community that the simple truth would allow God to get His foot in the door of science.

The theory of evolution, currently taught as basic fact in public schools, is an inherently atheistic presumption. If it represented truth in the same manner as a physical law, this would not necessarily be the case: there is a modicum of truth in the theory, but only for the most tiny of changes. Anything approaching a change in a creature's form, and especially the development of life from non-life, is as far from its capability as a club is from a 747 airplane. An overview of the intellectual fallacies associated with the theory of evolution is presented in Appendix 3-2: A Commentary on the Incompatibility of Macroevolution with Both Judeo-Christian Scripture and Physical Reality.

It is quite appropriate for religion to accommodate useful knowledge without considering it to be a threat to the omnipotence of God. Instead, such information should be regarded as illumination of a specific way that God has chosen to organize and operate His universe. That is certainly the way Sir Isaac Newton saw it as he developed the mathematical branch of calculus and the basic laws of physics, both of which were necessary precursors to our present technological sophistication. Given today's prevailing attitudes on science and religion, it is ironic that a major edifice of our secular science was constructed by a profoundly religious Christian. Oddly, however, support for the prevailing secular theories, as well as for the separation of science and religion, sometimes is granted by misguided Christians.

It is not appropriate to blindly subordinate Christian faith to "science." It is especially foolish to allow self-proclaimed authorities to elevate a theory based on shallow conjecture above the word of God. Christians, even those who are inclined toward a literal interpretation of Scripture, are often tempted to compromise with evolutionary theory. But any attempt to accommodate Christianity with evolution is entirely unnecessary, for the theory of evolution is not even compatible with the sciences that proclaim it to be truth.

What gives the theory of evolution its evil flavor is its bankruptcy – its flaws and the poverty of useful information that can be derived from it. It's simply bad science. The manner in which it has been thrust upon the public in the face of its intellectual uselessness only serves to bring to light the motives of its proponents in attempting to furnish an alternative to divine design.

Many creative proposals have been put forth in which Scripture and evolutionary theory are adjusted such that some measure of compatibility may be obtained. All such efforts represent some form of appeasement which weakens the interpretation of Scripture. No such accommodation is justified. Evolutionary theory is now in a state of disarray as recognized by the experts themselves. The principle is presently in conflict with more fundamental physical laws and profoundly so with the recently-acquired and growing body of knowledge associated with the basics of life. It is embarrassingly unable to account for observations made in the field and the laboratory.

Many authors have noted that at the highest level of theoretical physics, evolution contradicts the Second Law of Thermodynamics. This law states without reservation that natural processes invariably tend toward disorder, the usual secular attempt to distinguish between closed and open systems being nothing more than a false red-herring argument. The disorder associated with a mechanical process can be quantified. The term which expresses this amount is called entropy. In the field of thermodynamics, the evaluation of the entropy of processes has produced valuable and lasting results. By means of this variable, the efficiency of steam and internal combustion engines was greatly improved. The diesel engine was demonstrated to be superior in efficiency to the gasoline engine and the perpetual motion machine was demonstrated to be a practical impossibility. Yet, despite the apparent universal applicability of the law, the world at large embraces the theory of evolution, blithely ignoring the fact that the increase in order involved in the chance occurrence of life would represent the natural equivalent of a perpetual motion machine.

At a more practical level, field observations fail to square with theory. In strata identified as belonging to the Cambrian Period, a great number of fossils are found representing a variety of complex, fully developed creatures for which no trace of predecessors can be found. In the context of evolution, this amounts to the sudden formation of life forms out of either nothing or of much more primitive transitional forms.

Recent investigations into genetics, the mechanics of cells, and other microbiological processes have introduced the notion of 'irreducible complexity', a term coined by Dr. Michael Behe in his book *Darwin's Black Box* to describe a system requiring multiple components operating in concert to perform a meaningful function. The ability to create irreducibly complex systems is beyond the creative capacity of non-intelligent creative sources, such as the random processes common to evolutionary theories. Being unable to anticipate, they are left out in the cold regarding the development of the very numerous irreducibly complex systems found associated with and necessary to life. Certain systems associated with living creatures, such as the immune system, are of such startling complexity that they have been likened to the workings of a laptop computer. Moreover, all components of these systems must be present and operating for the system to be functional at all. This kind of necessary complexity is also found in the structure of cells, which are virtual factories. To the investigator, their sophistication has the flavor of space-age technology. Such sophistication was not anticipated by the early naturalists who proposed and defended the theory of evolution and its associated mechanics. The implication of the mere existence of these amazing but necessary components of life is that they must have arrived fully developed. Otherwise, the evolutionary process, which is perceived as working incrementally, would operate in successive stages to improve that which is nonfunctional to begin with, contradicting the premise of natural selection. But a sudden emergence of a structure of that complexity also runs counter to the incrementalism intrinsic to the suppositions behind the evolutionary process. This paradox is a strong indicator that the most basic suppositions of evolution are in serious error.

There are other problems with the evolutionary notion. The large majority of possible mutations are known to be harmful, reducing the ability of a life form to survive. Others are merely neutral, leaving a tiny minority, perhaps a nonexistent remnant, possessing beneficial features. In attempting to reconstruct specific sequences of mutations associated with the characteristics of a particular creature, investigators find the apparent involvement of mutations having a neutral impact. But natural selection does not apply to such processes. Even in cases where natural selection would apply, such as in the development of wings, it is difficult to perceive a transitional form which would not have a more difficult time surviving than its simpler predecessor that did not have to carry around the useless baggage of some future capability.

It is one thing to refuse to accept fact. It is quite another to openly lie about it. The conflict within the natural sciences has not been disseminated to the public at large, and the internal confusion has not given rise to the appropriate response in either the scientific or religious community. Many evolutionists thoroughly understand the inability of evolutionary mechanics to account for observations and current knowledge in specific areas. Yet many 'experts' cling to these outmoded concepts of gradualism and evolution as representing the 'best available fit', knowing full well that they are defending indefensible notions, often for the sake of their academic positions.

The entire structure of 'evolutionary knowledge' is based on the unproven, even undemonstrated, axiom that life formed without the aid of design. By common agreement within the secular community, design is not a permissible option. If such were introduced as a possibility, God would necessarily be involved in creation at some level, whether on earth or some distant planet. But, also by the common secular definition, as we have noted, God and science are mutually exclusive: the involvement of God would preclude any attempt to intellectually or scientifically arrive at an understanding of the creation of life. It is in that context that evolution remains the 'best available fit' despite its many problems and contradictions.

Ironically, it may be in the acknowledgment of design that the concept of evolution may prove to have the greatest utility. As noted by more than one Biblical scholar, the notions of creation and evolution are perfectly compatible if design, rather than chance, is the driving factor. All that is required is that the Grand Designer go the extra mile to put a mechanism in place that would allow creatures to adapt in limited ways to various foreseen environmental circumstances. The possible mechanism might involve the ability of living creatures to employ certain normally superfluous and unused DNA sequences under the appropriate trigger conditions, substituting them for ones in previous use. The actual deployment might be thought of as similar to that of the air bags mounted in modern vehicles, which are normally well-hidden and of no apparent use under normal operating conditions. But they exist, if unseen, and deploy in the event of an accident, replacing the function of the steering wheel. As a matter of fact, our very complex immune systems serve that same kind of emergency function. Given the amazing complexity of existing life systems, the kind of design that permits adaptation to emerging situations would require a miniscule effort compared to, say, the human brain. If this is indeed the case, as might be suggested by the latitude-associated skin pigmentation of humans, or the great variety of some animal species, it would have certainly made Noah's task a great deal easier, permitting him to place on board his ark merely the prototypes of animal species, which would then have diversified under local conditions as they expanded to fill the earth following the flood.

Given the prevailing control over the educational process by politicized science, the public has, over several generations, been indoctrinated quite thoroughly in the false notion that God is secondary to science. Whereas this process has been executed more overtly in communist regimes in the past, it has been carried out with no less vigor in the western democracies and is now becoming quite overt. Consequently, in America as well as Russia the majority of the public suffers under the misconception that the theory of evolution enjoys considerably more success than is justified by detailed research. More generally, the public commonly views religion and science as being at odds with each other, with religion occupying the dunce position at the corner of the classroom.

It is inevitable, given the unjustified perception that science represents reality whereas religion does not, that those who remain faithful to their religious beliefs will be viewed as being bound by some deficiency. For if God is confined to the moral boundaries defined by science, He can be neither omniscient nor omnipotent; He is nothing but an inner need, generated by some human lack or weakness.

Whether the majority of religious individuals really understand this point, it is precisely where they are placed by society at large. They have been marginalized. History bears out that those who are marginalized will eventually be abused.

The attack on Christianity by politicized science represents but one of at least three fronts in the secular war against the Judeo-Christian God. On another front in the United States, the judiciary branch of government, urged along by powerful secularist groups like the American Civil Liberties Union, is waging a one-sided battle against Christians with the rallying cry of 'separation of church and state'. On yet a third front, American schoolchildren are being indoctrinated in secular values on a massive scale in what amounts to a full-blown brainwashing campaign.

The doctrine of the separation of church and state as viewed within the liberal community is an outright lie. The doctrine as it stands now supposedly represents the intent of the original founders of the United States Constitution. It does not, as anyone familiar with the background writings of the framers will say without equivocation. To the contrary, our wiser forefathers knew full well that religion, and particularly the Judeo-Christian system of values and morals, were absolutely necessary to the successful operation of a democratic form of government. The real intent of the doctrine was to ensure that, insofar as governmental interaction with religion was concerned, no single religion or sect would be favored above others, thus guaranteeing the right of every individual to practice his faith according to his own conscience. When one considers that secularism is itself a matter of pure faith, the current perversion of the separation doctrine by the courts has granted this particular belief system a dominant status in exact opposition to the original objective. In the name of religious tolerance, any public expression of Christian faith is simply not tolerated. Can anyone recognize in this the 'newspeak' that so terrified Winston in George Orwell's *1984*?

The campaign on this particular front has been hugely successful. Any public display of a Christian motif is now frowned upon by society at large. It is considered offensive. Thirty years ago this prevailing attitude would have created public outrage. Thirty years is a very short time for such a complete turnabout of the public mind. It smacks of social engineering.

We complain in America about the relocation of jobs to Asia, India and other overseas areas while our children are being indoctrinated in comforting mental imagery, social docility and the exploration of their sexuality. Will this equip them for the high-tech jobs of the future? Even if it did, would they have the necessary mental discipline to pursue careers in such fields? It doesn't take much common sense to see that our children are not even being prepared to participate in a democracy. They shall reap the fruit of the weeds we are sowing in their paths: emptiness; poverty of mind and soul; an increasingly dictatorial form of government, and drug-induced docility. Their forced exposure to the false concept of evolution is but one facet of their worthless education. The exclusion of any balance in the form of the Creation alternative is virtually total. Whenever an attempt is made, however cautious, to furnish any Creation-based information in the public schools, it is squashed with a cry of outrage. Such attacks are quick, vicious, and usually final in their outcome. They are purely emotional in form, representing the secular faith and a complete absence of logic. The outcries express a mindless hatred belying the tolerance their perpetrators pretend to espouse. They, too, represent a perversion of truth.

This three-front war against the Judeo-Christian God has already marginalized the Christian faithful. If it continues unopposed, the marginalization will turn ugly for everybody as society degenerates into a state where democracy is unsupportable.

3

The "Christian" Marginalization of Christianity

The timidity with which religious spokespersons have reacted to the outrageously unilateral maneuvers of secularists is an amazing spectacle. Their silence regarding the secular definition of what knowledge is appropriate to the domain of religion has amounted to a tacit acceptance of this most unnatural and logically untenable restriction. Moreover, some religious spokespersons overtly agree with the most intrusive penetration of science into religion, the naturalistic claim of evolution as the principle governing the origin of life. As we have noted, this acceptance has no justification whatsoever, even in terms of the knowledge which science claims as its exclusive domain.

Unfortunately, the shortcomings of this theory have been overlooked by many Christian spokespersons in their haste to accommodate their beliefs to the popular paradigm imposed by secularists. These weak Christians have simply assumed without question that the secularists knew what they were talking about.

Such double-minded Christians have actually bought into the false assumption that the workings of God are unknowable in secular terms. The atheist or agnostic might be excused for having this mindset. It is much more difficult to understand the prevalence of this attitude among Christians. One can see examples of it throughout the Christian community. Pastors and theologians accept the evolutionary concept and attempt to work around it. Most of them avoid it entirely. Other subjects considered to be secular matters are also avoided as if they don't belong in God's domain. If Scripture is simply taken at face value, by contrast, one should come instead to a quick appreciation that God Himself desires man to understand both Him and His Creation in as great detail as possible.

Why have so many Christian 'authorities' knuckled under so readily? Why did they not hold fast to their faith? Perhaps they had little faith to begin with. For many, what faith they might have had may have been destroyed in those seminaries that were infected by the teachings of Higher Criticism. Among other things, these teachings claimed, on the basis of literary flavor alone, that several prophetic passages of Scripture, such as the Books of Isaiah and Daniel, were written not by a single author but by several. Furthermore, they claimed, these books were written over a lengthy time period, including the New Testament era. The result, of course, is the claim that key prophesies were written after the fact, not before, and were therefore not supernaturally inspired. By the time this dubious reasoning was proven untrue by, among other things, the discovery of the complete text of Isaiah in the Dead Sea Scrolls, the damage had been done: generations of pastors laden with untruth went out among the people to spread their false teachings.

This hints at the reason why Church leaders have allowed false secular teaching to subordinate and undermine the teaching of Scripture: these leaders may not be Christian at all.

In reading the Gospels, one comes to the conclusion that Jesus reserved His anger neither for Jew nor the Gentile. He had little to do with the Roman secular authorities. His anger, when it occurred, was directed toward those who used the name of God for their own purposes: the Pharisees and the temple peddlers; the religious leadership.

In Chapter 7 of Matthew's Gospel, Jesus is recorded as saying that not everyone who claims a relationship with Him is of Him:

> *Not every one that saith unto me, Lord, Lord, shall enter into the kingdom of heaven; but he that doeth the will of my Father which is in heaven. Many will say to me in that day, Lord, Lord, have we not prophesied in thy name? and in thy name have cast out devils? and in thy name done many wonderful works?*
>
> *And then will I profess unto them, I never knew you: depart from me, ye that work iniquity.*

The Pharisees were the religious authorities. They claimed to be spokesmen for God. It was they who rejected Jesus to preserve their elevated status among the people. It matters very little whether they were Jews or Gentiles. Historically right down to the present, precisely the same attitude of portions of its leadership has occurred within the Christian community as well. As soon as Christianity assumed a measure of status and power among men, the corruption began. To be sure, one cannot claim that the corruption is universal among Christian leaders. But its extent, if it were known, would probably be surprising and disheartening. That is why Scripture makes it clear that the Church does not reside in a collection of grand cathedrals, nor in a particular sect. Nor are spokepersons for the Church or any other individuals who claim authority over Church matters necessarily associated with the God of Scripture. The Church is simply the body of believers, wherever they may be scattered or to whatever group, small or large, with which they choose to associate. Only God truly knows who comprises His Church, but He gives us a yardstick by which we can evaluate those who claim to speak in His name: by their fruits you shall know them.

One does not have to look far to see the excesses of Church leadership throughout its history. Centuries ago the Catholic Church imposed the Inquisition upon its subjects. Today the corruption runs to pomp, alcoholism and pedophilia, each of which is so completely in opposition to Scriptural teaching that one can be quite sure that such leaders are followers of Satan instead of Jesus. There is no reason whatsoever to single out the Catholic Church as an example of corruption. The same dismal falling away has occurred within the Protestant churches. Their greatest failing is the perversion of truth to those they presume to instruct.

After a minor run-in with the law as a teenager, I was directed by my atheistic parents to attend a church for moral instruction. After hearing half a dozen mediocre sermons at this Methodist Church, I listened with a keen disappointment as the pastor concluded his talk with the observation that 'no one now expects Jesus to actually come in the flesh a second time'. Returning home after the service, I confronted my parents, telling them that if religion was nothing but a fairy tale, there was nothing of moral value that I could obtain from church. They reluctantly agreed, and for the next two decades I never set foot inside a church.

Years later, I became a Christian not through a church but through an adult appreciation of the immense beauty and self-consistency of Scripture itself. The reading of Scripture was an overwhelming experience; eventually I found myself attending an Episcopal Church noted for the fervor of its charismatic worship service. One day the priest told his flock not to bother with reading Scripture, saying "After all, the Bible is just a book" but to listen to the 'spirit' instead. At that point I stood up abruptly and walked out the door. I never returned to that church. Everyone there should have done the same thing. Scripture, provided it is in the original manuscript displaying the influence upon the writer of the Holy Spirit, is both inspired and inerrant, as professed by both Paul and Peter. I discuss this inerrancy and its impact on the reader at length in Appendix 3-1, *The Inerrancy of Scripture*.

I have heard some (but by no means all) televangelists perverting the Word of God in terrible ways. I have watched the spectacle of money-worship in the house of God conducted with such blatant abandonment of common decency as to have symbolically made the ancient temple money-changers wince in shame. I have witnessed wolves in sheeps' clothing glibly leading their flocks down the path to perdition, peddling a religion that can appeal only to selfish and crass moral dwarfs.

I had an associate at work who was a follower of Ramtha, the New Age icon who supposedly subordinated the soul of J. Z. Knight. He was a Presbyterian until his pastor convinced the congregation to follow him *en masse* over to Ramtha.

I eventually became a Baptist. I still am, but I don't go to the same church. That church is now defunct, having been desecrated by the Baptist central authorities in the name of money. I adhere to some, but not all, tenets of the Baptist faith, or those of other "mainstream" Protestant Churches, possessing a strong conviction that the Church erred in her understanding of God in some highly-significant areas, and is too wrapped-up in false pride and shallowness of thought to appreciate it.

When my brother came to the Lord, he took his wife, son, and daughter to the nearest Episcopal Church. In his open lack of guile, he joined committees and developed a friendship with the priest, only to have his trust betrayed by the priest's lust after his son. And we all know of priests in other churches who have had an unusual interest in little boys and girls. Jesus had a special word for such monsters:

But whoso shall offend one of these little ones which believe in me, it were better for him that a millstone were hanged about his neck, and that he were drowned in the depth of the sea.

Woe unto the world because of offenses! For it must needs be that offenses come; but woe to that man by whom the offense cometh!

The World Council of Churches claims to be the ultimate authority for the mainstream Protestant Churches. Given their record of attitudes and projects, I have little doubt that Jesus would disagree with their self-assessment.

One can only arrive at the conclusion that many clerics assume a career in theology for personal reasons that have nothing to do with God. Some may do so as a means to control people; others may seek comfort, wealth, or status. Whatever the errant reason, Scripture has forewarned us of this trend. Foremost of the trend is the gravitation of persons of poor morals and motives to the highest positions of authority. It may have started with the Pharisees, but it certainly continues to this day. In retrospect, it should not be surprising at all that such have succumbed to the false teachings of the secularists. After all, many of them, too, are secularists at heart.

Nevertheless, there are good Churches out there, and my wife and I do go to one of them. At least it's the best we can find within a reasonable distance from our home. Still, we disagree on some articles of doctrine and would wish our pastor to be less dogmatic regarding notions to which the Church adheres but are not Scripturally-justified.

We have seen how our tacit acceptance of false knowledge mislabeled as truth has led to the marginalization of Christians. Unfortunately, at some level their marginalization by society at large also colors the way a great many Christians view themselves and their churchgoing peers. Society has forced them to attempt to accommodate their religion to a dominant pseudoscience, not realizing that God must either be everything or nothing. Given the definition of God in Judeo-Christian Scripture, there is simply no possible middle ground.

As long as the mythical conflict between science and religion is permitted to persist in its gross untruth, the marginalization of the Christian as clinging to something beneath reality will become more overt with time. The threat is that in its ignorance of the truth, mainstream Christianity will become demoralized and gravitate to a casual, basically empty form of faith and worship. Underestimating the tremendous power of Scripture, nominal Christians will fail to read and comprehend it, further eroding their faith and leaving them susceptible to secularist propaganda. The problems the Catholic Church presently faces are indicative of this trend. Indifference will be rampant, leading to the most egregious abuses. Those who continue to hold fast to a strong faith worthy of their religion will face increasing antagonism, not only from the public at large, but from a mainstream Christianity that has fallen from its original faith. But then Jesus has forewarned us:

> *And unto the angel of the church of the Laodiceans write; These things saith the Amen, the faithful and true witness, the beginning of the creation of God; I know thy works, that thou art neither cold nor hot: I would thou wert cold or hot. So then because thou art lukewarm, and neither cold nor hot, I will spew thee out of my mouth. Because thou sayest, I am rich, and increased with goods, and have need of nothing; and knowest not that thou art wretched, and miserable, and poor, and blind, and naked: I counsel thee to buy of me gold tried in the fire, that thou mayest be rich; and white raiment, that thou mayest be clothed, and the shame of thy nakedness do not appear; and anoint thine eyes with eyesalve, that thou mayest see. As many as I love, I rebuke and chasten: be zealous therefore, and repent. Behold, I stand at the door, and knock: if any man hear my voice, and open the door, I will come in to him, and will sup with him, and he with me. To him that overcometh will I grant to sit with me in my throne, even as I also overcame, and am set down with my father in his throne. He that hath an ear, let him hear what the Spirit saith unto the churches.*

4
Truth and Knowledge Richness

Although much has been said about the morality of truth and how one might distinguish it from falsehood, there is one aspect about it that might be given more attention than has been given it in the past. It would seem reasonable to expect that truth would intrinsically provide more richness of information regarding a topic than any corresponding misrepresentation.

Given the prevailing secular reluctance to confer an absolute meaning on truth, one might confront the information-seeking secularist on his own terms. It would be difficult for anyone to deny that information-richness would be a useful yardstick for evaluating the truth of an intellectual proposition, if only as a working guideline.

The correctness of this supposition is borne out by experience. The laws of physics, for example, are considered to be truths insofar as they can be operated on mathematically to furnish detailed and accurate predictions of behavior. The more such manipulations such truths allow, the more fundamental they are considered to be. Information richness also demands a strong thread of internal consistency, for the extraction of information associated with a subject tends to bog down at junctures of conflict. It is universally recognized by intellectually mature persons that consistency and truth are closely related.

In a Christian context, information-richness can be applied to a variety of topics to provide a useful criterion for separating truth from fiction.

Scripture, for example, has been interpreted in a number of radically different ways, depending on such diverse factors as the perceptions of whether God actually exists, miracles actually occur, and who was the ultimate author of Scripture. Because of the subject matter, emotional preconceptions often color the attempt to understand the text, adding to the disparity of differing approaches. Nevertheless, where differing interpretations give rise to conflicts, only one approach can be correct. It would be reasonable to expect that the correct approach would furnish the most information.

Those who adhere to the Historical Jesus approach characteristically consider Jesus to have been fully human. There is a general denial of the miraculous. Scripture is perceived as having been written by men without the aid of God. Consequently, the approach to interpreting Scriptural text is essentially similar to a book review: apparent inconsistencies are readily resolved in terms of author error; prophetic passages are discounted, often leading to the establishment of unconventional dates to place them after the occurrence of the foretold events. Given this casual interpretation of Biblical text, it is natural to attribute the tales of grand, sweeping events, of which Noah's Flood is a typical example, to myth and allegory, denying the possibility that these events may have been so massive as to have been planetary in scale. This temptation to downplay the enormity of Biblical events becomes virtually irresistible to those who continue to subscribe to the gradualist philosophy associated with Darwinism.

With an allegorical emphasis in the interpretation of Scripture, there is little in the Creation account of Genesis that makes much sense. Moreover, whatever it might say about the world is of little consequence anyway, as whatever content is of importance is perceived as exclusively moral in nature. The rest is merely mythical background, described by people of considerably less sophistication than the members of our own more advanced civilization. While wisdom may be attributed to the text, it is seen as dealing with man alone and not the larger world about him. To this mindset, it says nothing about nature or the workings of the physical universe. In this light, it is easy to see how secular science might think that its subject matter has no relationship with religious matters.

Under that mindset little value is placed on those portions of Scripture dealing with natural topics, and an *a priori* attitude is brought to bear in the interpretation of them. The poverty of information associated with this attitude is extreme: no information is produced at all. At the very least, the approach is suspect simply for its virtually absolute lack of information.

Ultra-conservative interpreters reside at the other end of the spectrum and lack balance in their thinking as well. They are so concerned with defending the faith that offense is taken at any speculative adventure. Such straying from the path of rigid, traditional interpretation is viewed with suspicion as a moral threat, a frivolous exercise applied to a serious topic. To this mind, the knowledge sufficient for their forebears is sufficient for any true believer. Unfortunately, this attitude involves precisely the same kind of *a priori* thought processes as the other extreme. This kind of irrational defense of the faith itself demonstrates a lack of faith. If its ultimate author is indeed God, Scripture does not require that kind of defense. Nor does a literal interpretation require the resolution of apparent inconsistencies in terms of error, or the ascription of allegory to topics relating to the natural world. For these reasons, a common-sense, literal interpretation of Scripture is capable of furnishing a great cornucopia of information in the domain claimed by science. Nevertheless, a rigid, *a priori* interpretive attitude freezes such information, stagnating it to its state of development as it rested in the distant past. This violates the whole character of Scripture itself, in which God makes it abundantly clear that the Revelation of His nature and that of His Creation is progressive.

It is in the middle ground, where a literal interpretation of Scripture is perceived as representing truth, but where our understanding of it is acknowledged as still incomplete, that the most rich reward of information can be obtained from it. Not only is this the most scientific approach but it represents the most faith, for it addresses the subject of God without fear of what it may uncover. On the other hand, even for the investigator who may question the ultimate truth of Scripture regarding its exposition of the natural world, it is the most reasonable entry position to take, for it seeks testable concepts.

Appendix 3-1
The Inerrancy of
Scripture

Given the singularly important function of Scripture to provide man with a glimpse into the nature and character of God, it must necessarily be inerrant, for to deny this attribute is equivalent to stating that God does not possess the ability to make Himself known in sufficient depth to the centerpiece of His creation to permit His subjects to carry out His commandments to them. The outcome of this, of course, is to define a God who contradicts the attributes usually associated with Godhood, and who therefore is altogether unworthy of the love that He requests of us.

The only way that the skeptic of Scriptural inerrancy can avoid confronting this dilemma is to attribute the source of Scripture to man rather than God. It is amazing how many so-called 'authorities' do just that. But if a contradictory God is unworthy of our love, so is a God who is so small and powerless as to leave something as important as the presentation of Himself to mankind up to the inconsistencies, biases, self-interest and faults of unsupervised man. Another major problem with making this claim is that Scripture itself claims as its ultimate Author God Himself in the Person of the Holy Spirit. The prophets quite regularly spoke of God as the source of their information; much of what they wrote was written as a direct commandment from God to do so. It is common knowledge that just as directly, both Peter (2 Peter 1:20) and Paul (2 Timothy 3:16) clearly declared Scripture to have been written as men were led by the Holy Spirit.

As we shall demonstrate later, there are many other logically powerful reasons for attributing the source of Scripture to God rather than man. For now, as we explore the effect on the skeptic of assuming that Scripture contains errors, the issue of whether

Scripture came from man or God is not even relevant. Either way, the result of denying its inerrancy will be the same.

More simply stated, regardless of whether Scripture came from God or from man alone, either it is inerrant or it is as worthless as the pseudo-God that it purports to represent.

Lest the equation of Scriptural error to its utter lack of value be too large of a leap to digest all at once, we shall break up the logical process that led to it into more manageable chunks by examining sequentially the consequence of attributing error to Scripture.

Suppose, for example, that in reading Scripture an individual (call him Jack) comes across an item A in one passage that doesn't seem to square with an item B in another. Because both item A and item B appear to be peripheral issues at best, Jack discounts the importance of their accuracy and applies the most logical way to handle it (given that he already knows more than Scripture can tell him, a really safe assumption in today's world), which also happens to be the simplest: he accepts the implied error and moves on. But the next day Bill points out to him a larger error in Scripture, one that does have some importance to Jack's understanding of God. Jack might struggle with this for a while, but because he has already accepted the possibility of error in Scripture, he gives up the effort a little more prematurely than he should, coming to the conclusion that Bill's opinion of the nature of God is better than his was. A few days later he comes across another difficult passage in Scripture, which he automatically reconciles as another error. This time he changes his opinion of God again, to something different than that which either he or Bill had previously held.

Forget the fact that this readjustment of opinion is probably ever downward, constantly diminishing the attributes by which he measures his God. The key issue here is that Jack's understanding of God is becoming as dependent on man's opinion as it is on Scripture. But how can man, with his lack of omniscience, differentiate those portions which are true from those which may represent myth or embellishment, or simply contain mistakes? Now Jack, in his inability to see this obvious consequence of accepting error, is open to any number of charlatans, prosperity-claiming megachurch leaders, and other scurrilous individuals who also come calling with their own patently false sets of opinions regarding the nature of God.

Most unfortunately, Jack is now also open to the opinions of man regarding conflicts between items A in Scripture and items B outside of Scripture. He places as much or more reliance on the attitude of the secular world than Scripture regarding the nature of God and of His place in society. If the Academy of Science tells him (as it does) that God's domain is purely moral and that the physical world is the exclusive domain of science, well, then it must be so. His esteem of Scripture, of course, goes down several notches with that, because any contradiction between mainstream science and Scriptural accounts of the physical world must then be resolved in favor of science. There are, of course, a whole lot of contradictions between Scripture and mainstream science, the most glaring at the present time being uniformitarianism, with its notion of vast time spans, and the theory of evolution, with its insistence that life did not require God to get started.

Well then, if God's Word cuts corners on time, and if God isn't that necessary for life, maybe God is not relevant to our own lives. Multitudes of people have already formed that opinion, and with the Bible having been put in its place as far as he is concerned, why shouldn't he listen to them? Jack gets the picture loud and clear from all the major sources of information. He can't even go to a state or national park or just about any public place at all without getting a dose of these opinions that masquerade as science. By this time, poor Jack just can't get into the reading of Scripture at all. He certainly doesn't know enough about God to love Him. If he goes to church at all, it's only to collect a few tips on how to succeed. But since the rest of the country is working on different rules than he's getting at church, it's only a matter of time before he drops out.

What, now, if Jack and his ilk become the majority? For starters, having learned not to consider God as relevant to their lives, they speed up the process of removing Him from the public square. They do so with anger, thinking meanly of all the restrictions that have been placed on their lives by a God who probably doesn't exist to begin with. Having done that, they place their faith in a truly bad demagogue, who they willingly place over them as their leader, a lord worthy of their submission to him. Eventually realizing their great error in doing so, they listen to sincere political commentators like Glenn Beck, hoping to find some way to recover their country and their sanity. But they can't do that, because God has finally abandoned them to their own self-centered desires and in attempting to find purely political solutions to their problems, they will be unable to find God.

Is this the inevitable outcome of just a miniscule little supposition of Scriptural error? Yes, pretty much – it's a sharp slope toward perdition, and Satan has greased it well by pandering to our own self-absorption, which is really the root cause of our growing disbelief. The supposition of Scriptural error, no matter how apparently insignificant, requires the skeptic to assume at the very outset a judgmental role on a level dangerously close to that of God Himself. Despite the humility he might feign, only the self-centered individual has the wherewithal to do that. Just look around you, at the people you know, at your government, at your own lifestyle. When you ponder this mess, don't say 'How did this happen?', because deep down you know exactly how it did.

Let's now consider another individual, Charles, who happens to come across the same passage in Scripture that got Jack moving in his downward spiral. Like Jack, he struggles with it. But, already possessing some degree of passion (and respect) for God and His Holy Word, he struggles harder. Eventually he comes to a point of reconciliation between items A and B and, in the process of doing so he discovers item C, a concept that not only permits the reconciliation but leads him toward a significantly deeper understanding of God than he had before the exercise. Out of this effort, Charles, most happily, has increased his understanding of God, his love of God, and his faith in the Word of God. When Bill comes along with his more serious discrepancy, Charles applies the same exercise to it as he did with his more trivial issue, this time coming up with concept D, which represents an enormous breakthrough in his understanding of God. Having mined Scripture for the richness of information which he believed it contained, he was rewarded for his effort.

When the charlatans show up in his life, which they inevitably must, Charles, armed with concept D (and E, and so on, as he becomes ever more enamored with God through Scripture), is equipped to see these snakes for what they are. If they lead his church, he finds a better one, or so illuminates that place with the knowledge of Christ that the congregation itself finds better leaders.

Charles, having refused to be subdued by the false opinions of his supposed brothers and sisters in Christ, also stands firm against the equally false opinions of the secular world, regardless of how exalted they may be in the public mind. Having steadfastly opposed the theory of evolution, for example, he is now finding, to his further happiness, that he is in increasingly eminent company, for to his surprise he has come to the realization that a growing number of microbiologists and other heavy thinkers are offering substantial arguments, on the secularists' own terms, in support of the intellectual bankruptcy of the theory.

Charles, however, shares his world with Jack the doubter. Inhabiting the same country that had rid itself of God, they both suffer under the same governmental usurpation of their basic rights. One might consider this to be an unhappy situation for Charles, uncalled for and totally unjust because of his lack of involvement in bringing about that mess. It is not. It is neither unjust nor unhappy, because Charles is busy bringing the light of Christ to a lost world. If he must suffer in the process, he is joyful at it, because he is living not for himself but for his Lord, whom he loves with all his heart. As the world descends into darkness, his light shines ever brighter.

Now that we've contrasted Jack's unhappy state with Charles' happier one, it's time to present their differences in greater detail. First, there is no perceived error in Scripture that is not trivial. The issue reaches beyond the effect on the doubter to touch the character of God Himself, for as one manifestation of the Word of God it is intimately linked to the embodiment of the Word, Jesus Christ. Jesus was careful to note the necessity of His fulfillment of Scripture, intimately associating Himself, as God, with it. In explaining how He fulfilled Scripture to His companions on the road to Emmaus (Luke 24), Jesus expected them not only to comprehend this intimacy, but to treat Scripture as sacred truth. The Bible scholar cannot appreciate this closeness while also asserting either that fallen mankind is the creator of Scripture, or that Scripture is errant. One has only to review the prologue (Chapter 1, verses 1-18) to John's Gospel to grasp this fact.

In his Gospel, John presented Jesus as a direct representation of God to man, that through his understanding of Jesus in the flesh, man might come to have an intimate knowledge of his God. But John went further than that. At the very outset of his Gospel, he claimed that by the power of God the representation was the physical embodiment of the Word of God. As the Living Word, the representation Itself was God. As John wrote,

> *In the beginning was the Word, and the Word was with God, and the Word was God. . . And the Word was made flesh, and dwelt among us, (and we beheld his glory, the glory as of the only begotten of the Father,) full of grace and truth. . .For the law was given by Moses, but grace and truth came by Jesus Christ.*

John's Gospel describes the Word as the substance of Creation Itself, for he wrote with boldness and without equivocation,

> *The same was in the beginning with God. All things were made by him; and without him was not any thing made that was made.*

With that single statement, John places Jesus as preceding His birth in the flesh through Mary, existing as God with the Father at the beginning of the Creation. In fact, in the first verses of the first chapter of his Gospel, John has already firmly established Jesus as the embodiment of the Word, as truth, as life, as light, as God, and as the pre-existing Creator. If Jesus is a representation of God, Scripture itself is a direct representation of Jesus, and if Jesus is both the Word and truth, the Word as Scripture must be truth. If the embodiment of the Word is also the Creator, then the truth of the Word must extend to all of creation as well as Scripture, including the world that is perceived as 'real'. It must be absolute.

The entire Bible with its two testaments is one self-consistent representation of the Word of God. As the New Testament fulfills the Old, so does the Old flesh out the New. It is absolutely necessary, to fully understand either of the testaments, to understand both and how they complement each other to form the single Word. This Word is to be honored and treasured above all, for as a representation of Jesus it is a representation of God. And it is yet more than that: as a part of the Creative Act in which God moved upon generations of mankind in a cosmic drama to develop it, Scripture is an integral part of the Divine Word.

It is of enormous significance that just as John identified Jesus with Creation, Jesus so thoroughly identified Himself with Scripture. In the Gospel of Matthew, Jesus is quite explicit regarding His relationship with Scripture. In Matthew 5, for example, He equates His ministry with its fulfillment:

> *Think not that I am come to destroy the law, or the prophets: I am come not to destroy, but to fulfill. For verily I say unto you, Till heaven and earth pass, one jot or one tittle shall in no wise pass from the law, until all be fulfilled.*

Here Jesus, the Word of God, asserts without reservation that He Who represents Creation Itself is bound, even defined, by the Word of Scripture. Through Him, Scripture is an integral part of the Creative Word. It is alive. Like Jesus, it is a representation of God.

In the eighth chapter of John, Jesus links His nature as the Living Word of God with the Word that was given to mankind in Scripture:

> *I am the living bread which came down from heaven: if any man eat of this bread, he shall live for ever: and the bread that I will give is my flesh, which I will give for the life of the world. The Jews therefore strove among themselves, saying How can this man give us his flesh to eat? Then Jesus said unto them, Verily, verily, I say unto you, Except ye eat the flesh of the Son of man, and drink his blood, ye have no life in you. Whoso eateth my flesh, and drinketh my blood, hath eternal life; and I will raise him up at the last day. For my flesh is meat indeed, and my blood is drink indeed. He that eateth my flesh, and drinketh my blood, dwelleth in me, and I in him.*

As John wrote, ". . . and the word became flesh. . .". How else can one partake of Jesus' flesh but by digesting Scripture, the profound manifestation of the Word of God that defines Jesus to mankind? How else could one perceive Him to the point of loving Him, not just for the sake of loving, but for the sake of those attributes of His that are worthy of our love? If we have no absolute gauge of the reliability of Scripture how can we be certain that those attributes actually exist?

Since this same Gospel (as well as Scripture in general) equates Jesus with the truth and with Creation itself, it is quite difficult to comprehend a Scripture with the inability to get the facts of creation together without error. One might just as well call Jesus a liar, for if Jesus is the embodiment of the Word, and if the truth of the Word is less than absolute such that it is not actually literal in a natural sense, we enter a world of confusing contradiction. For then we are left with a Jesus for which the religious truth that He represents may be higher, but yet different than the truth of the creation that He is also supposed to represent, making Jesus as the Living Word not who He said He is. In particular, He is not God in the flesh, and the entire structure of the Christian faith is but a house built of straw. One must conclude from this that faith itself demands a corollary insistence upon the inerrancy of the Bible with respect to its presentation to man of the nature of God, which necessarily includes the nature of His creation. This requirement applies not to Jesus alone, but to every Member of the Godhead. There is no room for compromise with this fact. Anything less than absolute truth must inevitably lead to the conclusion that the Biblical God of both the Old and the New Testaments does not exist. For if God is to be worthy of our worship as God, then He must possess those attributes which are appropriate to Godhood: omniscience, omnipotence, omnipresence, and, most importantly, given the greatest of His commandments to us, love in perfection.

If His Word is inaccurate in any way, not only is He a liar, but He would possess gaps in His abilities that mock the very attributes that make Him God.

He would also mock His own commandment to us to love Him, for one cannot love without intimacy, and one cannot be intimate with God without knowledge of Scripture.

There are other reasons why it is not possible for a devout Christian to look upon Scripture with reservations as to its accuracy or internal consistency. Some of these reasons are personal. As we have noted, the individual who like Jack has doubts will suffer from such an intellectual disadvantage that he will miss much of the profound beauty and richness of Scripture that only Charles can see as he struggles to reconcile item A with item B. It is unlikely that Jack will have the slightest inclination to study Scripture unless he does so with the motive of reinforcing his doubts. Suppose, however, that this improbable event does occur. Upon arriving at a point therein where he encounters a perceived conflict, he will immediately say 'aha!' and claim error. In that state, he will remain at precisely the intellectual level where the conflict is most apparent, never permitting his understanding to rise to the higher level that furnishes the context in which the conflict is resolved. Such individuals will fail to notice the prophetic link to Jesus in the Levitical rituals, the writings of the prophets and the very lives of Biblical heroes. They will remain blind to the fact that on the cross Jesus kept the Mosaic feasts and especially the Passover in both pattern and timing. The torment of Abraham at the sacrifice of Isaac will have no meaning to them. Joseph will have suffered at his brothers' hands for no real purpose. Daniel and Isaiah will become lesser prophets. David and his psalms will not have been inspired. Jonah will have allowed himself to be cast into the sea for nothing of lasting importance. Doubters like Jack will have completely missed the many incidents in the Old Testament that pointed to Jesus as the Yahweh of Israel, destined for the cross before the beginning of Creation. To them, He would be just a man burdened with significant emotional problems and we would remain burdened with our sins. As he turns to the New Testament his position of doubt only hardens. Comparing Gospel with Gospel, he notes with despair (or is it satisfaction?) that item A in Luke is completely missing in John, or that Item A in Mark differs somewhat from item A in Matthew. He expects the Gospels to be identical in every respect, missing the point that such a state of affairs would represent a redundancy so profound as to constitute a wholesale lack of information, and that the Gospels differ from writer to writer as the Holy Spirit chose to emphasize some facet of Jesus in one Gospel and a different facet in another.

Missing the point of whatever portion of Scripture which he deems to be beneath his consideration, the doubter of inspiration cannot perceive the God of love who is so dear to the heart of the believer. Failing to see Jesus in the sacrificial traditions of the Israelites, the doubter sees a monster instead who feasts on the blood and gore of uncountable thousands of sacrificial animals. Moreover, in failing to satisfactorily resolve apparent conflicts, the doubter never reaches that point where he can grasp the fact that rather than containing errors, Scripture is remarkably free of them, being spectacularly consistent to the smallest details through the thousands of years and the multitude of writers that contributed to its content. Unable to recognize pearls of knowledge containing enormous significance in the minutiae of Scripture, the doubter allows such facts as the equivalence of Abel's lifetime with that of Jesus, or the age at which Joseph began serving Pharaoh being the same as the age at which Jesus began His public ministry, or the prophetic nature of Isaac's marriage to Rebekah, or the exponential nature of the decline of lifetimes following the Great Flood, or a host of similar relationships, to pass over his head completely unnoticed.

It happens that there is a name for the capability of the Bible to harmonize minute details from Scriptural accounts that are widely separated in time and conditions, and that this capability has long been considered as evidence for the divine inspiration of the Bible. In the chapter entitled 'The Phenomenon of "Undesigned Coincidences" of his book *The Signature of God*, Grant Jeffrey describes a number of issues that would be interpreted most readily by the casual reader of Scripture as puzzling inconsistencies (of the kind between item A in Scripture and item B in Scripture) or irrelevancies which might best be allocated to the error file, but which, on careful comparison with obscure passages that might be thought of as bearing no relation to the problem areas, astonishing answers are found that give the reader a sense of awe as to the truth of the Bible. Indeed, these Eureka! moments are encountered by virtually all serious students of Scripture and are treasured as rewards for diligent pursuit of the truth.

Noting that the first overt description of the phenomenon of "Undesigned Coincidences" was made in 1738 by Dr. Philip Doddridge in a commentary on Paul's letters, Dr. Jeffrey goes on to cite several examples, including the mysteries of why David's loyal counselor Ahithophel turned so strongly against him during Absalom's rebellion (Ahithophel was Bathsheba's grandfather, who took umbrage at the way David acquired Bathsheba by putting Uriah to death); why David picked up five stones when coming against Goliath (Goliath had four brothers); and why, when all the neighboring kingdoms used horses in battle, Israel did not (Israel was commanded by Moses in Deuteronomy 17 not to multiply horses to themselves). These answers are thrilling in that in their seeming insignificance they speak so powerfully against Scriptural error.

Most importantly, the doubter will inevitably become an unbeliever because he cannot recognize throughout Scripture the absolute love and lordship of Jesus Christ. He must fail in this endeavor because he lacks the wisdom to do so. Scripture is clear that the beginning of wisdom is the fear of the Lord. The doubter, in rejecting truth as much as the full-blown unbeliever but lacking even the courage to acknowledge his rejection, lacks the Holy Spirit, the embodiment of wisdom and knowledge, and is lost in his blindness of sight and deafness of hearing. He is destined himself eventually to fully accept his unbelief. Not trusting in the faithfulness of Scripture to represent the full truth, it is virtually certain that he will eventually succumb to popular secular teachings regarding the world about him.

Contrast again the unhappy state of the doubter to the blessed condition of the man of faith. The doubter, unwilling to remove himself from the world, knows full well how the Christian individual is perceived by the world at large. Faith, to the secular individual, is blind. As the man of the world openly claims in his many commentaries on the practice of reason, faith is intolerable, being antithetical to the openness of mind required for the dispassionate evaluation of the world about us. The scholar of religious orientation, to the secular world, is limited by his faith to the most trivial sort of mundane and unrealistic perception of reality. Worse, the doubter fully understands that to the secular scholar the notion of religious faith carries with it the stigma of cowardice, a lack of intellectual courage. It represents a self-imposed stifling of the imagination borne out of a weakness of the mind, a need for a crutch, an inability to face the world as it really exists with all its imperfections, pains and magnificent challenges. The closet doubter who maintains a false claim of faith is the unhappiest of all, as he perceives full well his position as the object of ridicule as a foxhole digger, a creature content to hide behind the protective blanket of a nonexistent God, never willing to venture out into the real world. The doubter will bow to the pressure of this attitude sooner than later, because he has insufficient reason or capability to withstand it.

The believing Christian, of course, sees faith in quite a different light. The fully committed believer in Scripture enjoys the benefit of having already exercised his faith through his thorough digestion of God's Word and stands equipped for the larger trials to come. Upon reflecting on the notion of faith, he is irresistibly drawn to the

Book of Hebrews, where in the eleventh chapter he encounters the people before him whose God, through their faith, had fashioned lives of heroic stature. These men and women defined the meaning of real faith, the selfless kind with substance behind it that gave them character, grit, and, above all, nobility.

After he recounts the faith of individuals from Adam to Moses and what that faith had wrought, the writer of Hebrews makes a magnificent summation of the subject:

> *And what more shall I say? I do not have time to tell about Gideon, Barak, Samson, Jephthah, David, Samuel and the prophets, who through faith conquered kingdoms, administered justice, and gained what was promised; who shut the mouths of lions, quenched the fury of the flames, and escaped the edged of the sword; whose weakness was turned into strength; and who became powerful in battle and routed foreign armies. Women received back their dead, raised to life again. Others were tortured and refused to be released, so that they might gain a better resurrection. Some faced jeers and flogging, while still others were chained and put into prison. They were stoned; they were sawed in two; they were put to death by the sword. They went about in sheepskins and goatskins, destitute, persecuted and mistreated – the world was not worthy of them. They wandered in deserts and mountains, and in caves and holes in the ground. These were all commended for their faith, yet none of them received what had been promised. God had planned something better for us so that only together with us would they be made perfect.*

Faith, to the Christian, is the beginning of courage, the wherewithal to stand fast in the battles that God inevitably brings his way. Some of these battles might be against the Christian's own lustful nature; others may be physical, where the Christian is placed into harm's way. Or they may be of an intellectual nature. In this arena, however, faith is more than a prerequisite to courage. It is also a necessary prerequisite to a logical investigation of God. To perceive God in anything more than the most mundane, trivial way our gift of reason must be tempered with the wisdom to understand that we must do so on His terms. And His terms begin with faith, the kind of faith that demands that we accept the Word of God as inerrant and accessible to our hearts and minds.

Indeed, with today's explosively expanding technology, the intellectual battle may be the most significant of all. Here, in the midst of the many intellectual cults engaged in the worship of their computers and cell phones, the Christian of faith is being called upon to exercise that faith, to demonstrate the logical viability of his God as at once more grand by far and the ultimate ruler of the secular god of scientific achievement. It rests upon persons of faith to present to the modern world the magnificent face of a God who, though ancient as time itself, yet is the ultimate Creator of the science and technology that His scoffers so lovingly embrace.

All of these pursuits, for the man of God who actually possesses selfless courage, are capable of representing the most incredibly exciting, wonderful adventures. But to the person who is drawn to the intellectual arena, the most awesome challenge awaits, and with it the most wonderful rewards. For it is here that so many citadels of science falsely so called stand on the brink of collapse. The geological sciences, having been recently embarrassed by the matter of the ubiquitous tell-tale layer of iridium ash at the sites of dinosaur bones, were forced into retreat over the unwelcome implication of that association as pointing to an extraterrestrial source of violence. They eventually acknowledged with great reluctance the encroachment of catastrophism into the domain formerly occupied exclusively by uniformity. Now geology awaits a bold Christian researcher who can re-open the breach initiated by Dr. Velikovsky over six decades ago and so profoundly expose the catastrophic events accompanying the Exodus that the breach will remain open, never to be shut again by narrow-minded and godless politicians who masquerade as scientists. The same doorway beckons the Christian biological scientist, for whom, despite the frantic proclamations of foolish liberals to the contrary, the collapse of macroevolutionary theory is already underway. Thanks to the brilliant efforts of a growing number of pioneering researchers to peer into the incredibly complex and sophisticated world of molecular biology and to write honestly about what they see, as well as the many dedicated Christians who have taken it upon themselves to disseminate these findings to the Christian Community, evolution is being brought down to its rightful place in God's amazing economy of life.

But of all the intellectual pursuits that await the Christian explorer, the theological one beckons the most warmly. We seem indeed to be at the time of the end spoken of in Daniel 12, where the book that has been sealed for so long finally is being opened. Scientific knowledge is now increasing at an exponential rate, providing Christian researchers with the tools and information to look anew at Scripture, probing deeper into favorite topics and investigating hitherto untapped areas: Bible codes, mathematical relationships, the startling relevance of Mosaic law to the life and earthly mission of Jesus Christ, archaeological confirmation of Bible stories, the fulfillment and prospects for further fulfillment of prophetic statements and, more generally, the reconciliation to a higher level of understanding those Scriptural topics that appear to the shallow observer to conflict with each other.

How ironic it is that just as these exciting opportunities for Christian research and thought have become available, so many so-called Christians have given up, having surrendered in abject cowardice to an enemy who is weaker by far than the mighty God whom we Christians claim as our own.

We shall now leave the personal aspect of our inquiry behind and move on to demonstrate that Scripture is indeed worthy of being trusted in its entirety as representing absolute truth, not requiring the device of allegory for its interpretation. In other words, rather than continue in terms of the benefit to us of faith in inerrancy and the consequence to us of a lack of such faith, we shall focus on the attributes of Scripture that speak of inerrancy.

In addition to the support which we have noted above in the 'phenomenon of Undesigned Coincidences' for the notion that for the items A and B in Scripture that we might come across there do exist reconciliatory concepts C and D, we shall demonstrate that the Holy Spirit has furnished the believer with numerous proofs of both the inspiration and the accuracy of Scripture, removing all doubt as to its divine origin.

Foremost among these proofs is the proven accuracy of the Biblical prophets. In Isaiah 53, for example, the very purpose of Jesus' mission on earth as a man is detailed in startling accuracy. But long before Isaiah, the Law in its rituals and observances not only foretold that same mission, but pointed to the day in which its fulfillment would be completed; beyond that, these feasts pointed to the formation of the Church following Jesus' resurrection. Yet even before the Law, the very clothing of Adam and Eve pointed to the cross, as did the animosity between their sons Abel and Cain over their gifts to God. The first book of the Bible, Genesis, contains so much information about Jesus, in fact, that it is often named among the Gospels. Included in this information are moving accounts of Abraham, Isaac and Joseph in which facets of their lives preenacted Jesus' sacrificial love with startling precision. This theme is also presented elsewhere in the Old Testament, as in the story of Jonah, in such depth that it is remarkable that Jesus was not immediately recognized for His Old Testament credentials by everyone who came into contact with Him either by His physical presence or by reading of Him in New Testament Scripture.

There is a good reason why believers insist on the supernatural endowment of prophets such as Isaiah with truth in the face of scholarship that suggested (prior to the discovery of the Dead Sea Scrolls) that their books were written after Jesus came to earth and therefore did not embody elements of the supernatural. Above all, they do so because they possess faith, without which it is impossible to please God. But their faith has also been rewarded with plenty of corroboration in the exposure of the doubters' suggestions as fraudulent. Among the Dead Sea Scrolls, for example, which have been dated by modern methods as preceding the life of Jesus, is the complete text of Isaiah, including that all-important Messianic Chapter 53. The same can be said of Daniel's prophecy which foretold to the day Jesus' entry into Jerusalem precisely 483 years (69 weeks) from an event that was over a century in the future to Daniel. In Chapters 44 and 45, the prophet Isaiah called Cyrus of Persia by name even farther into the future. Before Isaiah and Daniel, David accurately described Jesus' suffering on the cross in Psalm 22 a thousand years before the great event. Micah foretold the place of Jesus' birth. A host of other prophecies describe many other details of Jesus' life and mission. In Chapter 28 of Deuteronomy, Moses foretold the Diaspora of the Jews and gave the reason for it. Both Moses, in Chapter 30 of Deuteronomy, and Ezekiel, in Chapters 36 and 37, foretold in great detail the return of Israel to their land. In the Book of Revelation, the apostle John foretold a currency system that is impossible to implement without modern electronics and computer science. In addition to the overt words of the prophets,

Scripture has defined with astonishing accuracy the purpose of God in its record of the lives of Biblical characters.

Then too, Scripture involves a precision of time of which most Christians are largely ignorant today, but which occupied great minds in the nineteenth and early twentieth centuries. Men such as Sir Edward Denny and Henry Gratton Guinness, having uncovered some of these time patterns, could only describe the precision of prophetic fulfillment as supernatural. Denny, having verified that Daniel's prophecy of 69 weeks from Artaxerxes' command to Nehemiah to rebuild Jerusalem to the coming of Messiah was fulfilled to the very day, then went on to identify the ubiquity of 70-week (490 year) intervals throughout the Scriptural history of man, of which a total of twelve spanned a 5880-year time from Adam to what he expected would be the thousand-year reign of Christ. He noted in particular that if the times during which Israel had strayed from representing God's plan of redemption (e.g. the time from the birth of Ishmael to the birth of Isaac) were not counted, the time of Israel spanned the middle four 70-week intervals as follows, with each interval being marked by profound events in the history of Israel and mankind: the birth of Abram to the Exodus, 490 years; the Exodus to the dedication of Solomon's temple, 490 years; the dedication of Solomon's temple to Nehemiah's commission from Artaxerxes to rebuild Jerusalem, 490 years; and from Nehemiah's commission to Messiah's crucifixion, 490 years. He then noted that since the Jubilee years were observed in parallel with the 49th year of one Jubilee interval and the first year of the next rather than being inserted between them, these special years dedicated to God would, if they were added to each 49-year interval to make 50 years, result in transforming the 5880-year span of man's history to six thousand years. Furthermore, the placement of the Jubilee year between the 49th year of one cycle and the first year of the next in overlapping fashion leads to the surprising understanding that Jesus, in His crucifixion during the Passover of the Jubilee year, fulfilled the Levitical feasts of both the first month of that year and the seventh month of the first year of the next Jubilee cycle. That understanding is but one item among the multiplicity of rewards that God offers those who seek His wisdom.

Guinness approached this precision of time issue from an entirely different tack than Denny. He arrived at the conclusion, both from

Scripture and astronomical data, that God has ordered time in sevens. From Scripture, for example, he observed that the creation week contained seven days as does the sabbath week, that a week of years is a sabbath year, that a week of weeks of years is a Jubilee year, that Abraham's lifetime of 175 years spanned seven 25-year time periods of which the end of each marked a major event in his life, that Daniel's prophecy of weeks contained a multiplicity of sevens, and that Jesus Himself made remarks involving sevens. Noting next that the duration of Jesus' time on earth was 33.6 years, and assuming that Abraham's lifetime was a cameo of mankind's history on earth, he substituted one 33.6-year lifetime of Jesus for each year of Abraham's 175-year life, arriving at seven periods of 840 years each. The amazing thing about it is that the total duration of 5880 years exactly matches Denny's duration for mankind. This duration can also be factored into 49 intervals of 120 years apiece. If a 50th Grand Jubilee of 120 years is added to this sum, it yields a period of six thousand years. Guinness also apprehended grand cycles of 2520 years, each of which contains three intervals of 840 years. Three such 2520-year cycles fit easily into his seven periods of 840 years by overlapping one 840-year interval of one cycle with the next, such that the middle cycle has two overlapping 840-year intervals and one non-overlapping 840-year interval. The astonishing thing about these various cycles is their harmonious relationship among each other as well as their intimate relationship with Jesus Christ.

Moreover, Michael Drosnin in writing of Bible Codes, notes that at the dawn of the modern age Sir Isaac Newton, one of the greatest mathematicians the world has produced, suspected the existence of hidden information embedded in the text of the Hebrew Scriptures. As noted by Bible Scholar Grant Jeffrey, in Proverbs 25:2, Scripture itself furnishes a tantalizing hint of that possibility:

> It is the glory of God to conceal a matter, but the glory of kings is to search out a matter.

Perhaps having been spurred on by this passage, Newton, who was an avid scholar of Scripture when not engaged in inventing the calculus or developing the basics of physics, devoted many hours in a search for a code embedded in the Bible. (As a side point, his calculus, while usually considered to be a purely secular mathematical tool, displays such intrinsic beauty, majestic elegance and universal utility that one can easily attribute its invention to divine inspiration.

Newton himself certainly did.) He also may have known of the work of rabbi Rabbeynu Bachayah in the fourteenth century, who discovered an encoding pattern in the Torah (our Pentateuch), as noted by Bible Scholar Grant Jeffrey in his *The Signature of God*. However, the first real progress in uncovering the code was initiated by rabbi Dov Weissmandl in the early years of the twentieth century, who discovered that he could form meaningful words by assembling sequences of characters separated by fixed intervals of skipped characters. Describing this process as the creation of 'equidistant letter sequences' (ELS), Weissmandl was forced by the lack of technology in his day to perform the work meticulously by hand. Given the difficulty of the task, he was unable to say with certainty that his results were more than coincidental. That issue was resolved nearly a half century later by Israeli mathematician Eliyahu Rips, who, along with Doron Witztum and Yoav Rosenberg, applied the emerging computer technology to the process. The results were so spectacular as to convince the researchers that they had come face-to-face with the supernatural. As the price of computers dropped while they increased in speed and capability, a host of interested parties joined the ELS search. Among the claims made for the results are those published in *Bible Code I and Bible Code II* by Michael Drosnin, which indicate that the encoded data includes a number of fulfilled prophecies, many of which relate to our own time.

One of the earlier results may well be the most spectacular. As noted by scholars Grant Jeffrey and Chuck Missler, an examination of the Torah revealed that a 50-character ELS interval yielded the word 'Torah' in the books of Genesis, Exodus, and Numbers, and that a 49-character interval yielded the same word in Deuteronomy. In Leviticus, the only book of the Torah that failed to produce that word, an 8-character sequence formed the word 'God'. Curiously, while in the books of Genesis and Exodus the word 'Torah' is spelled in the forward direction, it is spelled backwards in Numbers and Deuteronomy. Upon their noting the sequence of these five books with Leviticus in the center, they were surprised to observe that 'Torah' in each book pointed toward 'God'.

Chuck Missler notes another authentication code in the Bible that is completely separate from the ELS code. This time it is found in the New Testament Greek. This code has to do with the pattern of the text, which evokes the number seven in so many various ways that the improbability (impossibility, actually) of its being generated by the hand of a human immediately places it among the supernatural manifestations of God. The first instance of it occurs at the very beginning of the New Testament, in the geneology of Jesus Christ as presented in the Greek version of Matthew 1, verses 1 through 11. In this passage, there are a number of various text elements precisely divisible by seven: words; letters; vowels; consonants; words beginning with a vowel; words beginning with a consonant; words occurring more than once in the passage; words that occur in more than one form; words that occur in only one form; nouns; non-nouns (only 7); names; male names; and generations.

Missler attributes this discovery to Dr. Ivan Panin, who was born in Russia December 12, 1855, and emigrated first to Germany and then to the United States, where he graduated in Harvard in 1882 with a PhD. in mathematics. He discovered this structure of sevens in 1890, after which he devoted the remainder of his life to a study of the Bible. According to Missler, Panin generated 43,000 pages of discoveries before his death in October of 1942. Oddly, the disputed final twelve verses of Mark (Mark 16:9-20) are among the other texts where the number seven was found to be prominent. Most translations of the Bible carry a footnote to these verses to the effect that they were missing from important Scriptural sources, such as the Alexandria codex. However, Missler emphasizes that Irenaeus quoted from them around 150 A.D., as did Hypolatus in the second century, whereas the Alexandria codex came several hundred years later. Missler notes that this virtually proves that the verses were part of the original Gospel of Mark and later expurgated, rather than having been added later as claimed by some modern scholars. He also notes that Chapter 16 of Mark's Gospel requires these final verses to tie up what otherwise would be loose ends.

Again, in verses 9-20 of Mark 16 the following text elements are precisely divisible by seven: words; vocabulary; letters; vowels; consonants; words found elsewhere in the Gospel of Mark; words only found in these verses; and the words found in the Lord's address (verses 15-18).

As noted earlier, Scripture itself claims to have been inspired by God. Paul, in 2 Timothy 3:16 and 17 states with certainty that the text came directly from God:

All Scripture is given by inspiration of God, and is profitable for doctrine, for reproof, for correction, for instruction in righteousness: That the man of God may be perfect, thoroughly furnished unto all good works.

Again, in 2 Peter 1:20 and 21, that apostle affirms Paul's assessment of Scripture:

Knowing this first, that no prophecy of the scripture is of any private interpretation. For the prophecy came not in old time by the will of man: but holy men of God spake as they were moved by the Holy Ghost.

Of course, the ultimate authority on this matter is Jesus Christ. Scripture records numerous instances of His quoting directly from it. Moreover, in Matthew 5:17 and 18, and in John 10: 35 and 36, He claimed that Scripture had the authority of God behind it:

Think not that I am come to destroy the law, or the prophets: I am not come to destroy, but to fulfill. For verily I say unto you, Till heaven and earth pass, one jot or one tittle shall in no wise pass from the law, till all be fulfilled.

If he called them gods, unto whom the word of God came, and the Scripture cannot be broken; Say ye of him, whom the Father hath sanctified, and sent into the world, Thou blasphemest ; because I said, I am the Son of God?

The Greek word *theopneustia,* meaning 'inspiration from God', describes this movement of the Holy Spirit upon the souls and minds of men, directing their thoughts, actions and words. It is key to note that divine inspiration has impacted the lives and actions of the people of God as well as what they wrote in Scripture, for much of its instruction comes from its recalling of historical events and deeds of people other than the writers. Nevertheless, these lives and actions had the ultimate purpose of furnishing the information that went into Scripture. A good part of Joseph's life, when recalled in the Bible, was a defining forecast of Jesus, as were those of many of the characters of the Bible, which obviously include the Patriarchs and the prophets. A casual glance at the Book of Acts is sufficient to perceive the grand movement of the Holy Spirit upon the actions of the Apostles. After Paul's conversion from a vehement Christian-hater to a dedicated

Christian, his very life was directed continuously and fully by the Holy Spirit. The point of this is that if one is inclined to doubt the inspiration of Scripture, he must apply that same reservation to the actions of all the Biblical heroes, including those of Paul and the other Apostles, to the extent of questioning their motivation, ability to heal or perform other inspired works and even their general conduct. At best they would be terribly conflicted in their denial of the indwelling Holy Spirit on persons of faith, for who could deny the inspiration behind the willing, self-sacrificial martyrdom of Christians throughout history and the radically changed lives of dedicated Christians to this very day?

Why then, if so many proofs exist of Scripture's inerrancy, are there so many doubters? One would think that in the interest of eternal self-preservation these people would be inclined to give God the benefit of the doubt. Why isn't that the case?

In our world of technological sophistication and moral degeneration, there are two very powerful obstacles to the man on the street's acceptance of Scripture as infallible. The first obstacle is a matter of character and has been noted in Scripture as the ultimate reason for the rejection of God: scoffers of God and the Bible do so not on the basis of intellect but for the sole reason of their selfish lusts. They just don't want God telling them what to do (or, more to the point, what not to do). Appreciating subliminally if not overtly that Christianity implies selfless nobility, they want none of that. They want instead to maintain the right to put self above others – to get what they claim as their due, regardless of the implications regarding those who also want the same. They wish to continue rooting around in the filth of pornography, or to pursue those sexual deviations which so deliciously capture their imaginations. They want to get high whenever they like. They'd hire lawyers to sue their wealthier family members if they could get away with it. They live in the world of 'To Thine Own Self be True', which amounts to 'Me First'. Understand what Paul in 2 Timothy 3:1-9 and Peter in 2 Peter 3:3-10 have to say about that sort of person:

> *This know also, that in the last days perilous times shall come. For men shall be lovers of their own selves, covetous, boasters, proud, blasphemers, disobedient to parents, unthankful, unholy, without natural affection,*

truce-breakers, false accusers, incontinent, fierce, despisers of those that are good, traitors, heady, high-minded, lovers of pleasures more than lovers of God; having a form of godliness, but denying the power thereof: from such turn away. For of this sort are they which creep into houses, and lead captive silly women laden with sins, led away with diverse lusts, ever learning, and never able to come to the knowledge of the truth. Now as Jannes and Jambres withstood Moses, so do these also resist the truth: men of corrupt minds, reprobate concerning the faith. But they shall proceed no further: for their folly shall be manifest unto all men, as theirs also was.

Knowing this first, that there shall come in the last days scoffers, walking after their own lusts, and saying, Where is the promise of his coming? For since the fathers fell asleep, all things continue as they were from the beginning of the creation. For this they willingly are ignorant of, that by the word of God the heavens were of old, and the earth standing out of the water and in the water: whereby the world that then was, being overflowed with water, perished. But the heavens and the earth, which are now, by the same word are kept in store, reserved unto fire against the day of judgment and perdition of ungodly men. But, beloved, be not ignorant of this one thing, that one day is with the Lord as a thousand years, and a thousand years as one day. The Lord is not slack concerning his promise, as some men count slackness; but is long-suffering to us-ward, not willing that any should perish, but that all should come to repentance. But the day of the Lord will come as a thief in the night; in the which the heavens shall pass away with a great noise, and the elements shall melt with fervent heat, the earth also and the works that are therein shall be burned up.

The other obstacle to the acceptance of Scripture as inerrant appears to be an intellectual one, but it is not – it is rooted in materialism and the placement of the world and its things and delights over God, thereby putting it into the same category as the first obstacle. This obstacle is the belief, as most of us have been taught in school, that modern science clashes with Scripture with Scripture as the loser. It is not. Informed Christians, if not the public at large, are well aware of the many frauds that have been perpetrated in the name of science, particularly over the past century or so. Examples include the numerous fossil 'discoveries' of missing links between ape and man that turn out to be fakes (including the highly-touted Lucy), the circular reasoning behind the dating of strata, the glaring lack of a complete geological column, dating hanky-panky (and the constant revisions thereto), the intrusion of catastrophism on uniformitarian turf (an unwelcome turn of events that modern scientists have been forced to accept with great reluctance after realizing, from the ubiquitous presence of iridium ash wherever dinosaur bones were found, iridium being rare on earth but a common component of asteroids, that the dinosaurs died *en masse* and quite violently), the disturbing features of Venus and Mars that corroborate our recently-acquired picture of the dinosaur extinction event, and the development of devastatingly logical scenarios for the world as described by Scripture prior to the Flood, and for the Flood itself (which, as many have demonstrated, had to be universal). The driver behind many of these false beliefs is itself the greatest of the frauds, the theory of evolution. Before specifically addressing that item, it is worth noting that a Biblically-based reconstruction of the Flood naturally accommodates several apparent anomalies that mainstream science has been incapable of explaining and has therefore largely ignored. These include: the findings of mammoths flash-frozen in place, still edible, at least in the early 1900s, having well-preserved buttercups between their teeth, in regions where buttercups cannot grow and where insufficient food is available to maintain a mammoth population; the discovery of coal and oil in polar regions; the discovery of human artifacts embedded in coal; and the finding of fossilized trees in the upright position extending through multiple layers of strata that are supposedly separated in time by millions of years.

Unfortunately, we believe what we want to believe, and we believe who we want to believe. Given a set of false beliefs to begin with, we have an uncanny ability to construct logical proofs of their validity. Here is what Scripture, in 1 Timothy 6:20 and 21, and has to say about the matter:

> *O Timothy, keep that which is committed to thy trust, avoiding profane and vain babblings, and oppositions of science falsely so called: which some professing have erred concerning the faith.*

By what right does the arrogant skeptic think that science, metaphysics, and religion must be mutually exclusive domains? The truly exciting thing about the Word of God is that, if it is indeed given to us by Divine Inspiration by the Lord of creation, it will necessarily contain knowledge and wisdom about that creation. It will teach of things that we usually allocate to science and metaphysics rather than to the presently-assigned domain of the purely theological. We have noted a number of items presented in Scripture that serve not only to demonstrate its divine origin, but to give us understanding of the world about us that we usually attribute to the domain of science. Impressive as these numerous factors are, they represent but a tiny fraction of the information with which God has provided man to substantiate the truth of His Book. Furthermore, the accumulated knowledge of mankind over the millenia since our history began has opened but a tiny foothold in our ability to understand the depth of wisdom and knowledge contained in that Book, for even to our best and most devoted, godliest minds the unsearchable riches of Scripture remain largely untapped. Is it not the ultimate objective of the scientist and the metaphysician to comprehend the universe that God created? Does this universe not include even the mind that was made to comprehend it and its interaction with the world that it sees? And does it not also include the tools, both mathematical and physical, that man develops to facilitate that comprehension?

Yet, as we have said, we believe what we want to believe.

We have attempted in this summary presentation to establish through a diverse assortment of perspectives the inherent truth of Scripture and its corresponding infallibility as to its basic message, the presentation of God to man. These various corroborating factors have included: the teaching of Scripture itself regarding its inspiration and truth; its influence on the lives of those who have believed in its truth and, conversely, the inability of the nonbeliever by his lack of the indwelling Holy Spirit to comprehend it; the gold mine of information embedded in Scriptural minutiae and apparent inconsistencies; the precision and detail with which prophecies have been fulfilled; the precision of timing in the events of Israel and the nations at large throughout history; the Bible Codes; and the recent overthrow of major tenets of science falsely so called which have contradicted Scripture, including uniformitarianism and the theory of evolution with its inability to create life from non-life or any kind of being from a lesser kind.

With so much ahead of us remaining yet to be understood, it is a tragic thought that so many of our best minds might fall short of the attempt to acquire that wisdom, and for no reason except that they willingly believe a lie. Knowing that Scripture represents absolute truth, and knowing further that true believers in Christ must have the ability to understand Scripture sufficiently to love Him and obey His commandments, we find that this same Scripture fully and without equivocation identifies those who are unable to comprehend the truth which it contains.

In John 14:17, for example, Jesus associated the Holy Spirit with truth. In the process of making that association, Jesus also identified those who, in their inability to receive the Spirit, could not comprehend truth. Of the Holy Spirit He said

> . . .whom the world cannot receive, because it seeth him not, neither knoweth him: but ye knoweth him; for he dwelleth with you, and shall be in you.

Here Jesus was speaking to His disciples who, as He noted, were indwelt with the Spirit as believers in Him. The world at large stood in opposition to them as unbelievers who were unable to receive the Holy Spirit.

Scripture often declares understanding to follow belief. Conversely, faithlessness is presented in Scripture as bereft of understanding. To declare, then, that one cannot understand Scripture is fully equivalent to declaring one's unbelief. An inability to understand the Word of God does not proclaim meekness and humility. It is, instead, a declaration of a skepticism so profound as to cause dullness of hearing and sightless eyes. In Chapter 6, verses 9 and 10, Isaiah spoke of this situation:

> *And he said, Go, and tell this people, Hear ye indeed, but understand not; and see ye indeed, but perceive not. Make the heart of this people fat, and make their ears heavy, and shut their eyes; lest they see with their eyes, and hear with their ears, and understand with their heart, and convert, and be healed.*

In Matthew 22, verses 10 through 16, Jesus repeated these words, acknowledging that Isaiah was speaking on His behalf. According to Matthew,

And the disciples came, and said unto him, Why speakest thou unto them in parables? He answered and said unto them, Because it is given unto you to know the mysteries of the kingdom of heaven, but to them it is not given. For whosoever hath, to him shall be given, and he shall have more abundance: but whosoever hath not, from him shall be taken away that which he hath. Therefore speak I to them in parables: because they seeing see not; and hearing they hear not, neither do they understand. And in them is fulfilled the prophecy of Esaias, which saith, By hearing ye shall hear, and shall not understand; and seeing ye shall see, and shall not perceive: For this people's heart is waxed gross, and their ears are dull of hearing, and their eyes have closed; lest at any time they should see with their eyes, and hear with their ears, and should understand with their hearts, and should be converted, and I should heal them.

The apostle John just as boldly associated through this statement of Isaiah a lack of understanding due to a fatal unbelief. Later, Luke attributed that statement to Paul in Acts chapter 28, associating it again with unbelief. In John 12, verses 35 through 41, he records what Jesus had to say on that subject:

Then Jesus said unto them, Yet a little while is the light with you. Walk while ye have the light, lest darkness come upon you: for he that walketh in darkness knoweth not whither he goeth. While ye have light, believe in the light, that ye may be the children of the light. These things spake Jesus, and departed, and did hide himself from them. But though he had done so many miracles before them, yet they believed not on him: That the saying of Esaias the prophet might be fulfilled, which he spake, Lord, who hath believed our report? and to whom hath the arm of the Lord been revealed? Therefore they could not believe, because that Esaias said again, He hath blinded their eyes, and hardened their heart; that they should not see with their eyes, nor understand with their heart, and be converted, and I should heal them. These things said Esaias, when he saw his glory, and spake of him.

This same association between unbelief and an inability to understand Scripture may be found elsewhere and often throughout its pages.

In Psalm 14:1-4, for an example from the Old Testament, David speaks about unbelief and its implications:

The fool hath said in his heart, There is no God. They are corrupt, they have done abominable works, there is none that doeth good. The Lord looked down from heaven upon the children of men, to see if there were any that did understand, and seek God. They are all gone aside, they are all together become filthy: there is none that doeth good, no, not one. Have all the workers of iniquity no knowledge? who eat up my people as they eat bread, and call not upon the Lord.

Proverb 1:1-7, for another example, states the issue in a positive sense, directly equating understanding with wisdom, and wisdom with belief:

The Proverbs of Solomon the son of David, king of Israel; To know wisdom and instruction; to perceive the words of understanding; To receive the instruction of wisdom, justice, and judgment, and equity; To give subtilty to the simple, to the young man knowledge and discretion. A wise man will hear, and will increase learning; and a man of understanding will attain unto wise counsels: To understand a proverb, and the interpretation; the words of the wise, and their dark sayings. The fear of the Lord is the beginning of knowledge: but fools despise wisdom and instruction.

Returning to the New Testament, Paul describes in a particularly damning manner the character of those who persistently fail to apprehend the truth. In 2 Tim 3:1-9, he as this to say about such people:

> *This know also, that in the last days perilous times shall come, For men shall be lovers of their own selves, covetous, boasters, proud, blasphemers, disobedient to parents, unthankful, unholy, Without natural affection, trucebreakers, false accusers, incontinent, fierce, despisers of those that are good, Traitors, heady highminded, lovers of pleasures more than lovers of God; Having a form of godliness, but denying the power thereof: from such turn away. For of this sort are they which creep into houses, and lead captive silly women laden with sins, led away with divers lusts, Ever learning and never able to come to the knowledge of the truth. Now as Jannes and Jambres withstood Moses, so do these also resist the truth: men of corrupt minds, reprobate concerning the faith. But they shall proceed no further: for their folly shall be manifest unto all men, as theirs also was.*

In this same letter, Paul exhorts Timothy to present Scripture to others as understandable to salvation before a time to come when many who will claim to be Christians will be unable to receive the truth. In 2 Tim 3:15-17; 4:1-4, Paul specifically claims that:

> *And that from a child thou hast known the holy Scriptures, which are able to make thee wise unto salvation through faith which is in Christ Jesus. All Scripture is given by inspiration of God, and is profitable for doctrine, for reproof, for correction, for instruction in righteousness: That the man of God may be perfect, thoroughly furnished unto all good works. I charge thee therefore before God, and the Lord Jesus Christ, who shall judge the quick and the dead at his appearing and his kingdom; Preach the word; be instant in season, out of season; reprove, rebuke, exhort with all long-suffering and doctrine. For the time will come when they will not endure sound doctrine; but after their own lusts shall they heap to themselves teachers, having itching ears; And they shall turn away their ears from the truth, and shall be turned unto fables.*

In a nutshell, our incapability of understanding truth equates to an incapability to know God, which itself is equivalent to lacking the Holy Spirit Who indwells believers. Throughout Scripture there is a consistent theme as to why that is, but Paul, in Romans 1 and throughout his letters makes it very clear what causes that lack: it is a moral issue. Intellect has little or nothing to do with the unbeliever's decision to harden his heart, reject Jesus and remain in unbelief. Here again, the truth is presented with such clarity that it is accessible to all but those who may be burdened with the most profound mental disorder.

If you would give Scripture the credit it deserves for representing truth, listen to Paul in this matter:

> *For I am not ashamed of the gospel of Christ: for it is the power of God unto salvation to every one that believeth; to the Jew first, and also to the Greek. For therein is the righteousness of God revealed from faith to faith: as it is written, The just shall live by faith.*

> *For the wrath of God is revealed from heaven against all ungodliness and unrighteousness of men, who hold the truth in unrighteousness; Because that which may be known of God is manifest in them; for God hath showed it unto them. For the invisible things of him from the creation of the world are clearly seen, being understood by the things that are made, even his eternal power and Godhead; so that they are without excuse: Because that, when they knew God, they glorified him not as God, neither were thankful; but became vain in their imaginations, and their foolish heart was darkened.*

> *Professing themselves to be wise, they became fools, And changed the glory of the uncorruptible God into an image made like to corruptible man, and to birds, and to four-footed beasts, and creeping things.*

Appendix 3-2
A Commentary on the Incompatibility of Macroevolution with Both Judeo-Christian Scripture and Physical Reality

Introduction:

We are in a war, and as Christians we are in the front lines. The war is a spiritual one, in which we are fighting for human souls. Our opposition is the humanist camp, which already has achieved a position of dominance over our media, our schools, and our government.

One of the main battles in this warfare is over the general acceptance of evolution as the factual paradigm of the origin of life. In this battle, our opposition has largely succeeded. Despite the claims of some Christians that Christianity and evolution are compatible, they are not. Committed Christianity, as noted by both Peter and Paul, demands the acceptance of Scripture as inerrant as to substance and as divinely inspired. Evolution directly undercuts Scripture and ultimately disposes of the necessity for God.

This appendix addresses the theory and scientific/intellectual shortcomings of naturalistic evolution. In its broadest sense, this theory embraces Darwin's theory of evolution, Neo-Darwinian evolution and in general all theories of the origin of life that propose that life originated without the necessity of a Designer.

Claims for evolution of the magnitude sufficient to create life or even a new kind of creature are generally associated with what is called 'macroevolution', which is distinct from 'microevolution'.

Dr. Michael Behe has demonstrated that microevolution actually works, but only for the tiniest, most insignificant of changes, at the cost of huge amounts of time, and always at the cost of information loss.

The adaptive ability of living creatures, or the very small-scale evolutionary process by which living things undergo superficial changes in response to changes in their environments, is within the ability and scope of microevolution. An example of such changes are the modifications of coloring in some moths as a result of changes in environment, or the mutational changes to viruses and bacteria by which they evade measures taken by the immune systems of animals to ward off diseases. Books dealing with the topic of evolution, particularly those offered to the public and students, often deceptively resort to microevolutionary changes to demonstrate the viability of macroevolution.

It is a fact, as noted above, that evolution as proposed by Charles Darwin in his book *The Origin of the Species,* first published in 1859, does indeed work under some very limiting constraints. It has been demonstrated recently to work at the micro-evolutionary level by Dr. Michael Behe[1], the science professor who wrote the controversial book *The Edge of Evolution*. In that work he also demonstrated, on the basis of a detailed study of the interactive evolution of both malaria and the human body's response to it, that micro-evolutionary changes occur at the cost of information loss. He further demonstrated the complete failure of Darwin's theory and its more modern expressions to account for changes beyond one or at most two tiny steps. As we shall show herein, his demonstration of evolution's failure is intellectually convincing. Indeed, it is more convincing than the so-called 'proofs' cited by evolution's supporters of its supposed basis in fact. Moreover, Dr. Behe's work is not a singular effort, but is supported by the works of a growing number of professionals in the fields of molecular biology, mathematics, and philosophy.

The material in this appendix focuses in general on the non-viability of macroevolution, or the inability of evolution to accomplish functionally beneficial large-scale changes in living beings, and particularly its failure to account for the generation of life from nonliving matter. A side discussion will speak to the demonstrable futility of attempting to reconcile evolution with Christianity. For the sake of brevity in the following work, the term 'evolution' shall be used with the understanding that the term refers to naturalistic macroevolution.

The theory of evolution is precisely what this descriptor suggests: evolution is a theory. It is not a natural law like gravity, but merely a proposition. It is merely a proposition because it is unproven and unverified in accordance with the standard that science itself has erected for differentiating a law from a mere theory[2].

Informational literature in some quasi-official publications, including National Geographic Magazine, school textbooks, governmental placards located in National Parks and other popular tourist attractions, do indeed present evolution as fact. They do so in violation of that scientific standard. Every so-called 'proof' of evolution to date, including the numerous 'missing links', has subsequently been exposed as either an intentional fraud or a misapplication of scientific tools or knowledge[3].

In 2 Thessalonians 2, Paul talks about the mystery of iniquity as the world approaches the end of the Church age. In verses 8 through 12, he describes a grave indifference to the truth represented by the Word of God. Paul then indicates that because of this indifference, God will allow those who are infected with this attitude to be deluded even more:

> *And then shall that wicked one be revealed, whom the Lord shall consume with the spirit of his mouth, and shall destroy with the brightness of his coming. Even him whose coming is after the working of Satan with all power and signs and lying wonders, and with all deceivableness of unrighteousness in them that perish,*

because they received not the love of the truth, that they may be saved. And for this cause God shall send them strong delusion, that they should believe a lie, that they all might be damned who believed not the truth, but had pleasure in unrighteousness.

Evolution is just such a falsehood that is generally accepted as truth in today's sophisticated, technology-embracing world, and it is glaringly overt in nature. God tells us in First Timothy Chapter 6:20 and 21 that such a condition will prevail in the last days. Moreover, the falsehood will be distinctly scientific in character, and it will even be accepted among some ill-informed Christians:

O Timothy, keep that which is committed to thy trust, avoiding profane and vain babblings, and oppositions of science falsely so called. Which some, professing, have erred concerning the faith. Grace be with thee. Amen.

Peter sheds further light on the nature of this falsehood. According to Second Peter 3:3 and 4, the lie will involve a deep sense of the unpunctuated continuity of the earth and life within it, such as is embodied in the principle of uniformity. This principle embraces the notion of the great age of the earth, wherein all geological changes are of extremely modest proportions that produce measurable results only over vast intervals of time:

Knowing this first, that there shall come in the last days scoffers, walking after their own lusts, and saying, Where is the promise of his coming? For since the fathers fell asleep, all things continue as they were from the beginning of the creation.

Interestingly, the principle of uniformity as expressed here by Peter represents such a necessity to the viability of Darwin's theory of evolution that uniformity and evolution may be considered to be two halves of a common philosophy.

The reason why uniformity is so key to the viability of evolution is that evolution is an intrinsically weak process. The theory, in its vehement rejection of design of any sort, demands change unguided by thought, either human or otherwise. It relies on chance as the prime mover: the random process of tiny mutationally-driven changes, collectively summing to large-scale functional variations in living creatures, and even to the production of living creatures from nonliving matter. Given the readily-acknowledged extreme unlikelihood of even one ultimately beneficial mutation, the process demands for viability truly enormous quantities of time. This necessity, in turn, demands a uniformitarian view of the processes that have shaped the world we live in.

The problem with this is that, aside from its support of evolution, there is no logical justification whatever for the claim that uniformitarian processes governed the earth's history. Demanding its validity is equivalent to demanding that the earth be flat, or that something is true merely because we wish it to be so. The 'standard geologic column' as developed out of uniformitarian presuppositions, does in fact exist in its entirety nowhere on earth. The fossil basis for its construction shows circular reasoning, proving nothing.

The theory of uniformity, as a matter of fact, has already been overtaken by the acceptance within the scientific community of facts that contradict it. These facts include the well-known discovery by the Alvarez team of the extinction of the dinosaurs by an asteroid impact event. The theory of uniformity had led the scientific community to categorically deny the possibility of a catastrophic event of that magnitude to have occurred. After being confronted with uncontestable proof that the event did indeed occur and was indeed of enormous proportions, the scientific community quite reluctantly backed off from its rigid stance in opposition to the reality of catastrophism. They made no effort to convey this radical change in position to the schools or to the public at large, nor did they consider or wish to address the implications of this change on evolutionary theory.

The Christian doesn't have to accommodate his understanding of the world to the theory of evolution, because despite the extensive hype about evolution put out by the superficial popular media, an increasing number of experts in the field of microbiology have themselves rejected the theory as an unworkable folly. In other words, to be blunt about it, science itself is backtracking away from the evolutionary notion, leaving the general public holding the bag of science falsely so called.

The intellectual retreat from evolution has been slow and quite reluctant, to be sure. Many scientists who privately reject the theory continue to espouse it publicly for the simple reason that they fear for their careers if they don't go with the flow. Eminent professors, despite the presumed safety net of tenure, have lost their positions by politically being on the wrong side of this issue, as have competent scientists.

But more courageous souls are becoming involved in the issue, and their works quite thoroughly explain why the theory of macroevolution cannot work. Among these works are what are becoming classics in the genre: *Darwin's Black Box* and *The Edge of Evolution* by Michael Behe; *Intelligent Design* by William Dembski; *Reason in the Balance* and *Objections Sustained* by Phillip Johnson; *What Darwin Didn't Know* by Geoffrey Simmons; *Creation* by Grant Jeffrey; *Dismantling Evolution* by Ralph Muncaster; and the seminal work *Signature in the Cell*, by Stephen Meyer.

The discussion to follow briefly examines key demonstrations of the failure of evolutionary theory to perform the functional changes attributed to it by its proponents.

Evolution lacks the ability to anticipate

Naturalistic processes are, by intrinsic definition, non-intelligent[4]. A fundamental feature of non-intelligent processes is that they are unable to anticipate. They can't form *a priori* an objective or goal for a system. If a system function or feature doesn't yet exist, a non-intelligent process cannot envision it, for to do so demands intelligence.

Take the following example, among a very large number in which evolution has claimed the ability of sweeping functional changes, as a simple demonstration of the implication of this inability to anticipate: that of a land animal that walks with the aid of legs which is eventually going to achieve the ability to fly. To accomplish this, its bones need to become hollow and highly efficient with respect to weight; it has to develop the keen eyesight unique to birds that is appropriate to its mode of hunting from the air; its bone structure, particularly in its chest, needs to be arranged to be a proper scaffold for its ligaments and muscles; its arms need to assume the shape of airfoils; it needs the lightness, shape, and variability of shape of feathers for fine control over flight; its respiratory system must become suitable for the demands of flight, which involve hefty changes from the comparable functions of a land animal; its balance mechanism must be revamped to handle flight attitudes; its entire nervous system must be altered to furnish the ability to control its airfoil surfaces; and, perhaps not least, it must acquire some pretty disgusting eating habits. Each of these functional modifications involves very large numbers of changes that have to be coordinated in the proper sequence. This requirement for a large number of sequentially-supportive steps, highly-coordinated such that all are mutually compatible over a variety of different subordinate functions to the end of achieving flight, virtually demands the quality of anticipation or goal-setting which is the hallmark of a designer. As if that isn't contradictory enough of evolution, consider the implication of the large time scale evoked by most evolutionists to accomplish these changes. During the time frame over which these changes are supposedly accomplished, there will be of necessity several periods in which the unfortunate beast will be struggling with intermediate forms, such as arms that are developing into wings. In these transitional stages, the creature must continue to survive within its environment and to eat and mate. It must do so while suffering the disadvantage of limb that functions less well as an arm than it used to, and is not yet functional as a wing. At this stage, it is suited far more as a food source for some other less-advanced animal. At the other extreme, some supporters of evolution who have come to understand and appreciate just these implications of large functional changes have proposed that such changes must have occurred quite suddenly. The 'punctuated equilibrium' offshoot of Darwinian evolution, first proposed by evolutionist Stephen J. Gould[5] attempts to avoid the consequences of prolonged transition periods. The problem with this notion's supporters is that in the process of forming their opinions, they also have avoided doing the math: the odds against all these coordinated modifications occurring all at once are so astronomically huge and the numbers against even one instance of such an event having taken place are so vast that they outweigh by an enormous margin all the time available even by the most far-fetched uniformitarian assumptions of the age of the universe.

Dr. William Dembski did the math that evolutionists refrain from performing. In his book *Intelligent Design*[6], he picked a real-life example of a well-investigated biological subsystem, the bacterial flagellum that Dr. Behe had made famous, and calculated the probability of its various components having been formed and assembled together by chance to implement the function of motation. The numbers are greater by a huge ratio than what outspoken evolutionist Richard Dawkins' admitted was an upper limit for the operation of chance. As quoted by Dembski, Dawkins had written:

"We can accept a certain amount of luck in our explanations, but not too much. . .In our theory of how we came to exist, we are allowed to postulate a certain ration of luck. This ration has, as its upper limit, the number of eligible planets in the universe. . .We [therefore] have at our disposal, if we want to use it, odds of 1 in 100 billion billion as an upper limit (or 1 in however many planets we think there are) to spend in our theory of the origin of life. This is the maximum amount of luck we are allowed to postulate in our theory. Suppose we want to suggest, for instance, that life began when both DNA and its protein-based replication machinery spontaneously chanced to come into existence. We can allow ourselves the luxury of such an extravagant theory, provided that the odds against this coincidence occurring on a planet do not exceed 100 billion billion to one.[7]"

The number 100 billion billion amounts to 10^{20}. Dembski imposes a far more generous upper limit for chance, 500 bits or 10^{150}, which, as he notes, represents the number of *particles* (not planets) in the observable universe. Yet, he claims that the mere flagellum, a relatively simple subsystem within the scheme of life, is far more complex than can be embraced within 500 bits of information.[8] Furthermore, just the DNA within the cell of that simple bacterium of which the flagellum is a component contains far more than 100 thousand base pairs[9], that number representing the minimum size of DNA in the first living cell, according to evolutionists. Since each base pair position within the DNA chain can accommodate one of four base/positional states, each position is equivalent to two bits of information. All together, then, the DNA itself represents at least two hundred thousand bits of information, or four hundred times the upper limit for chance.

Dr. Michael Behe[10], in his earlier work *Darwin's Black Box*, captured the essence of this need to anticipate that is so prevalent in living systems through the term he coined 'irreducible complexity'.

A system that requires several parts all present, correctly configured for interaction, and working together to produce a specific well-defined function, to paraphrase Dr. Behe, is 'irreducibly complex'. If any of its necessary components is absent or improperly configured to make its contribution to the function, the function itself cannot be performed; all of the parts must be present and working together for the system to work at all. An irreducibly complex system, to continue to paraphrase Dr. Behe, requires so many mutually-supportive subsystems that the very existence of the top-level system without the input of anticipation is out of the question; yet the existence of such systems is so ubiquitous in living entities that such input must be acknowledged as having been present.

Dr. Behe's development of the notion of irreducible complexity is now several years old. A few years back, one of the more liberal bookstores (no longer in existence) carried more than one book that claimed, in a pro-evolution stance, to rebut Dr. Behe's notion. They did so by noting that in one of Dr. Behe's irreducibly complex systems, the flagellum that serves as the motive device of a bacterium utilizes a microbiological component that is virtually identical to the corresponding component of a completely different functional entity. "Foul!" the books cried at the perceived offense. The similarity of these components, to paraphrase the books, meant that they weren't unique to one specific function.

All but the most superficial of thought processes can see through the flaw in this line of reasoning. Dr. Behe never claimed uniqueness for the components of his irreducibly complex systems. That simply wasn't the thrust of his argument, which was to claim that all the components had to be present and working together for the system itself to work. Whether or not a component was borrowed from another system is irrelevant and misses the point; it's a shabby, logically sloppy red-herring argument that serves simply to throw the reader off-track from the real issue. We'll try to refrain from commenting further on how this kind of reasoning typifies the pro-evolutionist mindset, or the mindset of those who are taken in by their polemics.

All life possesses a non-material element: an extremely complex software code

The focus of discussion shall turn next to an example taken from molecular biology to demonstrate the failure of evolution to account for the development of life from non-life. This example considers the structure of the deoxyribonucleic acid (DNA) molecule[11], the story of mankind's understanding of its structure and function which is of itself a real scientific thriller. Only recently has man acquired an understanding of the advantages of having a generalized multipurpose machine, the computer, whose functional qualities are defined not by its physical characteristics, its hardware, but rather by the instructions that are applied to it in software code. This code may assume a number of different possible forms. There is the 8-bit ASCII code (an acronym for American Standard Code for Information Interchange), for example, wherein each group of 8-bit binary characters represents an alphanumeric symbol, such as the letter 'G' or the numeral '5'. This binary-encoded alphabet is useful for communicating among humans, but machines have a language of their own. At the lowest level of machine language, the data is encoded in a form compatible with the computer hardware, wherein groups of binary characters ('0' or '1') represents specific instructions, like telling the computer memory to accept data immediately following the code and store it in a particular location. The medium by which the code was input to the computer started out as a sequence of stiff paper cards where the information was embodied in a pattern of punched holes. The preferred medium then transitioned to tape, and after that data was stored on laser-readable discs. Beyond the disc technology, RAM (random-access memory) circuitry became so spectacularly dense that cost-effective, ultra-large capacity flash drives (memory sticks) became available .

In its most straightforward functional context, the DNA molecule represents the purest, most compact and efficient structural embodiment imaginable of a chemically-implemented storage medium for software code. It reeks of anticipation, the creation of exquisitely complex order out of chaos. Its very existence inspires the awe of someone monitoring a SETI screen, like Jodie Foster in the movie "Contact", and suddenly viewing an intelligent signal from outer space.

DNA has a skeletal backbone structure consisting of alternate sugar and phosphate molecules interconnected to form a chain of arbitrary length. The size of this chain for most animals is quite huge. Functionally it is similar to the magnetic tape medium for the storage of computer software. Embedded within two such chains is the actual software, in which each sugar-phosphate pair forms a nest for any one of four different hydrocarbon molecular pairs/positions from the following repertoire: adenine (labeled 'A'), guanine ('G'), cytosine ('C') and thymine ('T'). An essential feature of these four chemicals is that they are always coded in pairs: A to T and C to G. On the surface, these pairs seem to represent just two possibilities, but in fact their physical reversal within the sugar-phosphate matrix adds another two possibilities. The four possibilities are: A-T, T-A, C-G, and G-C. An interesting feature of these pairs is that while A is of a different size than T, and C is of a different size than G, the two pairs are virtually identical in size, so that when one end of a pair nests on one sugar-phosphate chain and the other nests into the other sugar-phosphate chain, there is no distortion of the two-chain system due to size differences. Another interesting feature of the matrix is that the system has no preferential affinity for any one pair over another and no pair has an affinity for any other pair, rendering the system completely contingent, meaning that there is no bonding preference for any particular code pattern, a necessary feature of any true software encoding medium. Another key feature of the system is that it expresses chirality[12], which means that while there are two equally-probable directions in which the sugar and phosphate molecules bond together, the life-supporting nucleotides may only be of the right-handed form. This requirement alone virtually eliminates the possibility that the first DNA string was formed by chance.

The dual-nucleotide chain, together with the specific arrangement of embedded pairs within it, form what can only be characterized as a highly-organized structure of software code. But it does more than make a machine perform a function, because first it contains the instructions to build the machine itself. As software code, theoretically one could arrange the embedded pairs to form an ASCII code, which would then be able to represent anything in the English language through this DNA string, including a complete work of Shakespeare or, better yet, the Bible. The major difference between this chemical ASCII code and its binary equivalent would be the greater transmission efficiency of the DNA over the binary code. In fact, a revised equivalent ASCII code could be formed out of just four characters instead of eight.

Scientists haven't yet decoded a single DNA string. They haven't even come close. What they have done so far, impressive as that is, is to define the entire character sequence of human DNA, in all 46 chromosomes. But they have decoded the function of only a small portion of that sequence. What they have decoded is those portions of human DNA that are gene-specific, which represent but a tiny fraction of the entire string. Genes are sections of DNA code (subroutines, if you will) that specify and direct the manufacture of proteins. Even that portion of the overall decoding task is a major accomplishment, because the process by which a cell replicates a gene-specific portion in DNA into an RNA copy (RNA stands for ribonucleic acid), and then 'reads' the RNA code into the process that assembles the corresponding amino acids into another sequence representing a specific protein, is so startlingly high-tech that if one can instantly recognize a designer behind an intricate wristwatch or an automobile, the designer recognition for the process of protein manufacture is so over-the-top that only a person blinded by a God-denying agenda can possibly fail to perceive it.

As added complicating factors, the amino acids, which also express chirality in their natural states, must all be of the left-handed variety, and only twenty out of a possible eighty amino acids are useful components of proteins.

Then there's the 'chicken-egg' problem: proteins are manufactured from software instructions, but the software reader itself is a complex assembly of proteins. This situation implies that both the first software and the first hardware had to exist simultaneously. Given the enormous complexity of both, the odds against their simultaneous creation by chance alone are beyond astronomical.

Complexity on top of complexity

On top of the enormous complexity of DNA and its interaction with RNA and the Ribosome protein to manufacture other proteins, and the chirality situation, there is another cellular mechanism beyond DNA, newly-discovered and possibly even more complex than DNA. This system, labeled the "epigenome", has been found so far to consist of three major subsystems[13]. One subsystem consists of the information embedded within the three-dimensional pattern of the microtubule structural girders that support the cell. Another subsystem is the tagging, or labeling, of various proteins, the histone spindles upon which DNA is wrapped, and selected cytosine characters within the DNA itself. The cytosine labeling is so important to the operation of the associated gene that it is sometimes referred to as "the fifth DNA letter". A third subsystem consists of the various amazing little protein machines that go around adding labels, removing labels, and reading them. It is thought that the process of adding and removing labels may be directed by segments of DNA that were once considered to be "junk", an erroneous concept that arose from evolutionary suppositions.

In the early days of developing an understanding of the protein manufacture process, some of the scientists involved were rather arrogant about the role of those portions of DNA that weren't specifically associated with proteins. Being of the evolutionary persuasion for the most part (for many of them, their grant money and even their jobs depended on their loyalty to evolution), they considered the portions of DNA for which they could find no specific use to be "junk DNA"[14], DNA that represented earlier stages of evolution and was no longer useful to and was ignored by the living system. Those who possessed this attitude were pruned back a bit by subsequent discoveries of uses that included error-correcting codes like checksum values, and sequence-control commands like punctuation marks. Further developments in the decoding of DNA await minds of sufficient genius to see more of the mechanisms in certain sections of DNA that God may have had specific uses for, like the processes associated with embryology and growth. We've often wondered whether God has put His own verbal imprint in a secluded section of code that some arrogant scientist has relegated to "junk DNA". A delightful example might be a segment in direct, in-your-face ASCII code that says "In the beginning was the Word, and. . ."

The discovery of what DNA is and does gave us an understanding of life that simply wasn't accessible to Sir Charles Darwin or his contemporaries. Actually, this one insight has only been available to us for a few short decades, and it changes everything, particularly as we can only now view its implications in the context of some other very recent technological developments, including the structure of the computer and the development of information science, the understanding of which occurred simultaneously with our understanding of DNA.

A string of DNA is nothing more nor less than software code. If we had the ability to create our own string of DNA and manipulate the coding pairs to insert them in the sugar-phosphate matrix in the sequence that we ourselves specified, we could create an ASCII-encoded version of any book we wished to. If we could then develop a machine that could accept this chemical information and read its contents, we could insert our encoded string of DNA and the machine would then print the book we had chemically encoded, or, better yet, display it on a screen like a Kindle reader. As an information storage medium, our encoded strand of DNA would be the most compact device available.

The essence of life is information

In speculating how we ourselves might employ this basic element of life, we have naturally extracted the essence of what DNA represents: pure information. Philosopher/Mathematician William Dembski came to that same conclusion several years ago, and successfully applied the principles of information science to life itself and from that synthesis developed the first principles of an exciting new mathematical discipline centered on the information-richness of life. In his book *Intelligent Design*[15], Dr. Dembski develops a theoretical model for naturalistic evolution in terms of the operation of chance on natural laws. He then develops a means of scrutinizing a living system to distinguish a naturalistic process from the input of design. He does so by means of a flowchart that he labels an explanatory filter. If, in this flowchart, a system is observed to be 'contingent', which means that it is capable of forming a variety of equally probable patterns, then its examination passes down to the next criterion; otherwise, the pattern is taken to be a predetermined necessity, like the formation of crystals, and the design hypothesis is rejected for this system. The next criterion is complexity. If the system is sufficiently complex, then its examination passes down to the third criterion; otherwise, its existence may be ascribed to chance and the design hypothesis is again rejected. The third criterion is specification. If the system exhibits the quality of specification, meaning that it serves to fulfill an identifiable and useful function, then it may be considered to have been brought into existence through design; otherwise the design hypothesis is again rejected. In all cases where the design hypothesis is rejected, the existence of the object is ascribed to a naturalistic process, either necessity or chance.

Dembski then continues to flesh out the practicality of this model by placing the complexity criterion on the firm footing of mathematical probability theory. In doing so, he transforms the expressions dealing with probabilities into information-theoretical terminology, in effect equating odds to bits of information. Having performed that translation, Dr. Dembski offers a quite generous cutoff point, as we had noted earlier, of 500 bits of information which, he assumes with considerable justification, would be acceptable to all reasonable people. A system so complex as to represent over 500 bits of information, he claims, can exist only by the aid of design. He inserts the value of 500 bits of information into his complexity criterion, thus reducing its evaluation to a straightforward and repeatable computation.

Dembski pursues the issue of complex specificity by noting that naturalistic evolution can be expressed as the operation of chance on natural laws, Dembski applies his contributions to information theory to the development of an information-theoretical proof of the inability of chance acting on laws of nature to create complex specified information. He formally states it as his Law of Conservation of Information as follows: "Natural laws are incapable of generating complex specified information[16]". He states three corollaries as immediate consequences of this law: "1) The complex specified information (CSI) in a closed system of natural causes remains constant or decreases. 2) CSI cannot be generated spontaneously, originate endogenously or organize itself . . .3) The CSI in a closed system of natural causes either has been in the system eternally or was at some point added exogenously. . .4) In particular any closed system of natural causes that is also of finite duration received whatever CSI it contains before it became a closed system."

While Dembski's Law of the Conservation of Information appears more akin to a version of the First Law of Thermodynamics (conservation of matter and energy) than the Second Law, its corollaries are actually closer to the Second Law. One controversial argument between design advocates (formerly labeled as creationists) and evolutionists was the use of the Second Law of Thermodynamics, which stated in one version that all natural processes tended to disorder. The design advocates (including us) would periodically trot out this energy-based law as a proof that the order intrinsic to life represented a reversal (and violation) of the Second Law. The evolutionists would consistently respond to this charge by declaring that the Second Law applied only to closed systems. Open systems, they claimed, permitted the input of energy (such as radiation from the sun), which negated the effect of the Second Law. While we recognized this as somewhat of a red-herring argument, we didn't come up with a refutation that clearly addressed the open system issue. The beauty of Dembski's expression of the Law of Conservation of Information is that for any attempt to evoke the possibility of an open system, the immediate implication of the external input of information is the presence of a Designer.

Dr. Dembski performs the evaluation as directed by his explanatory flowchart on actual living systems by observing whether it exhibits contingency, and if it does, then mathematically evaluating the information complexity of the system and by observing whether the quality of specificity is present. If the system passes these hoops, then he concludes that a designer was involved in its existence. He has applied this procedure to several living systems, concluding that some of them exhibit unmistakable evidence of design.

Summarizing Evolution's Basic Problems:

This very brief overview of DNA represents the tip of the iceberg regarding what scientists have discovered about the intricacy of living creatures at multiple levels from top level functions on down to machine operations at the molecular level. The references cited earlier provide much more detail, some of it of a spectacular nature. They, too, cite further references that the interested person may wish to pursue.

Many of the amazing processes associated with living systems also can be viewed via the Internet, simply by Googling on an appropriate topic, such as 'DNA', 'DNA replication', 'cell replication', 'prokaryotic cell structure', 'eukaryotic cell structure', 'RNA', 'ribosomes', 'gene transcription', and 'protein manufacture' to give just a few examples. One cannot view this information without obtaining a sense of awe at the complexity of life's most basic processes.

This appendix has addressed just a few problems out of the very many difficulties with evolution that any objective pursuit of the truth of the matter must consider. Among the ones that have been touched on here are Dr. Behe's notion of irreducible complexity, Dr. Dembski's notion of the conservation of information, the chirality obstacle, and DNA's immense complexity as well as its feature of embedded software code.

There is a rather substantial political element to the issue of the viability of evolution. This element confirms the role that "believing what we want to" plays in the acceptance or rejection of the idea of evolution. It also has led to outright deception.

Evolution's glaring frauds

Although he preferred the since-discredited Lamarckian mechanism of the inheritance of acquired characteristics over Darwin's natural selection, one of Darwin's contemporaries, the German zoologist and biologist Ernst Haeckel (1834-1919)[17], not only helped to popularize Darwin's theory in Germany, but had furnished a notion of his own that both strengthened Darwin's position and increased its popularity. This concept borrowed from Etienne Serre's earlier proposals and from Darwin's concept of homology, which, according to Darwin, was "that relation between [body] parts that results from their development from corresponding embryonic [body] parts[16]." The point here is that in seeing the same similarities between embryonic and adult body parts among various life forms, Darwin perceived embryonic development as representing a history of speciation. Haeckel picked up on this notion, formalizing it in his famous Biogenetic Law that "ontogeny recapitulates phylogeny". Stated in layman's terms, the law expresses the notion that the various stages of embryonic development (ontogeny) revisit the history of evolutionary change (phylogeny). He went so far as to create a number of drawings that expressed his law in pictorial form.

Generations of students throughout the world have been exposed to these pictures, which include a stage of human development marked by what are supposedly gill slits.

The pictures themselves long ago have been exposed as frauds, Haeckel having doctored the transcription from source object to painting to emphasize features that promoted his "law". Furthermore, his "law" has since been rejected in its entirety, modern science having exposed his "gill slits" as something else altogether and his ideas in general as oversimplifications of more complicated patterns in embryology. In Chapter 5 of *Darwin on Trial*[16], Phillip Johnson succinctly states the problem:

"Describing the facts of embryology to be 'second to none' in importance for his theory, he remarked that the early embryo is 'a picture, more or less obscured, of the progenitor, either in its adult or larval state, of all members of the same great class.' Any exceptions to this rule of early embryonic resemblance, Darwin believed, could be explained as adaptations of larval stages to differing environments. Since a larva must compete for food and survive predators, it might be modified by natural selection, even though later stages would be unaffected.

"This statement is tied to the basic logic of the Darwinian understanding of homology. If similarities inherited from an ancestral form are traceable to common developmental processes and common genes, it is logical to expect these ancestral features to be generated early in the process of embryonic development. The differing organisms in a single group (like vertebrates) should start out in life as relatively similar organisms and then form their differing features later. As with Haeckel's law, the picture is so pleasing that generations of biology students have been taught it as fact.

"Unfortunately for the theory, however, the facts do not fit so neatly into the theoretical preconception. Far from providing the simple confirmation that [modern evolutionist Dr. Douglas J.] Futuyma suggests, the embryonic patterns generate a monumental puzzle for the theory. Although it is true that vertebrates all pass through an embryonic stage at which they resemble each other, in fact they develop *to* this stage very differently (italics in the original). After a vertebrate egg is fertilized, it undergoes cell divisions and cell movements characteristic of its class: fishes follow one pattern, amphibians another, birds yet another, and mammals still another. The differences cannot be explained as larval adaptations, since these early stages occur before larvae form and thus are apparently not exposed to natural selection. Only by ignoring the early stages of development can one fit Darwin's theory to the facts of embryology, but it was precisely the early stages that Darwin claimed were the most significant!" [Exclamation in the original.]

The same fraudulent picture emerges from the evolutionary presentation of the so-called 'fossil record'. 'Evolutionary science' continues to teach our children and the public that the fossil record demonstrates the viability of evolution by confirming: first, that the 'tree' of life branches out from a single base ancestor to the many varieties that are observed today, producing many intermediate and transitional forms along the way; second, that the fossil record 'proves' the existence of many transitional forms. It does not; instead, the actual observations and facts disprove those very same claims.

The tree of life that is supposed to branch outward from a simple beginning has never been found. Nor will it ever, as what has been found instead throughout the earth is a phenomenon that is called the Cambrian Explosion[18], wherein multiple fully-formed species emerged from one stratum to the next, the previous stratum being almost entirely void of life.

The glaring discrepancy between the fossil record as Darwin envisioned it and its actual state was touched on earlier. But Darwinists have been so misleading about this issue that it deserves more of our attention. The public at large has been and continues to be subjected to periodic announcements by the pro-evolution media that a new and exciting 'find' has confirmed the existence of a transitional form, just as Darwin had predicted all along. Then, when the latest of such 'finds' has been discredited as fraudulent, a period of grace ensues wherein nothing is said either way about it. Eventually after the passage of sufficient time for the public to forget about the issue entirely, some popular magazine will scream out that a new and conclusive 'find' has proven Darwin right. Time-Life and the National Geographic Magazines are major offenders in this regard, but there are many others who are willing to follow suit.

The late Dr. Grant Jeffrey supports Phillip Johnson and others who have assessed the claims of Darwinists about the fossil record and have concluded that they are not only in error, but intentionally so. According to Dr. Jeffrey[19],

"There is no fossil evidence to support evolution. Many Christians and Jews who have been troubled by the claims of evolution will be astonished to discover that the evolutionists knew all along that there was *no* fossil evidence in support of evolution. Yet, many textbooks and teachers boldly declared that the fossils proved evolution to be true.

"After a century and a half of claims by evolutionists that just a little more time would produce the necessary fossil evidence of the missing links between species that would confirm the theory of evolution, we find there is an astonishing and *total lack of fossil evidence* to confirm any indisputable transitional forms, or 'missing links,' that must exist if the theory of evolution were actually scientifically true. However, in over one hundred and fifty years of a massive global search by scientists that has catalogued over one hundred million fossil specimens in museums and laboratories, they have failed to discover a single 'missing link' fossil. If the evolutionists were intellectually honest, they would have abandoned evolution long ago.

"In 1859, Charles Darwin acknowledged that the utter lack of fossil evidence for these missing links between one species and another provided 'an unanswerable objection' to the theory of evolution. However, Darwin assumed that the search for fossils that would establish the truth of evolution was just beginning and that, given sufficient time and effort, scientists would soon discover the millions of transitional fossils required to prove that one species gradually transformed itself by natural selection into a new species." [Italics in the original.]

Jeffrey goes on to say that "To date, though, every species discovered in the fossil record appears perfectly formed. Paleontologists have never discovered a fossil showing a partially formed species or a partially formed organ.[20]"

He furnishes detailed accounts of a number of supposed 'missing links' between ape and man, all of which were subsequently exposed as outright frauds. They are listed below.

With the help of untrained convicts, fossilized bone fragments of what came to be called Java Man were dug up in 1891 on the Indonesian island of Java. On the basis of nothing more than a fragment of a skull cap, three molar teeth and a bone fragment of a thighbone, the director of the find, Dr. Eugene Dubois, identified the fossils as belonging to *Homo erectus,* a humanoid three quarters of a million years old. Attempts to confirm his claims uncovered the following facts: the thighbone fragment was identical to that of a modern human; the skull cap was found forty-six feet away from the other fragments; there was no logical reason to associate the skull cap with the thighbone.

Piltdown Man I and II were supposedly discovered in 1912 and 1917 at the Piltdown quarry in England by amateur geologist Charles Dawson. In 1953, after over forty years of unquestioning acceptance of these findings as genuine, the skulls, after being examined by more modern techniques, were found to be intentional frauds. The skull described by Jeffrey was a composite of skull fragments of modern man and orangutan jaw. Worse, the bones had been dyed with bichromate of potash to make them appear ancient. Although evolutionists generally agree that Piltdown man was an outright fraud, they don't speak much about this incident.

Nebraska Man was found in 1922 in western Nebraska by Professor Harold Cook. His find was supported by Dr. Henry F. Osborn, head of the American Museum of History, who touted the find as finally representing the evidence linking chimpanzees, Java Man and modern man. The Java man, as noted above, was since exposed as fictitious. So was Nebraska Man, whose supposed existence was used as evidence in the famous 1925 Scopes evolution trial. The problem was that the 'evidence' amounted to a single tooth, around which very imaginative evolution-minded artists created a picture of how they wished a missing link to look. It gets worse: the tooth was later found to have belonged to an extinct pig. The same fiction applies to the Southwest Colorado Man, another 'evolutionary discovery' that also turned out to have been based on a mere tooth, this one belonging to an ancient horse.

In 1932 another supposed missing link, Ramapithecus, was found in Africa. This 'discovery' amounted to nothing more than some fossilized teeth, which were later found to belong to the modern orangutan. Here again, evolutionists generally acknowledge this 'discovery' to be false.

Dr. Jeffrey also notes that the same kind of problems attend the discovery of 'Lucy' in 1974. In this case, Professor Richard Leakey claimed that 'Lucy' was an ape-like creature who walked upright. However, the lengths of the forearm fossils found in the vicinity strongly suggest that 'Lucy' walked on all fours like any other ape-like creature. Even Dr. Leakey admitted to exercising a large amount of imagination to create a picture from a few bone fragments. What puts the lie to these excursions of the imagination is that in many, if not all, cases there is actually no logical reason to assume that the fragments belong to a single creature.

Even with such a shady history of attempting to create missing links where missing links didn't exist, the evolutionists continued to pull the wool over their own eyes as well of those of their associates and an all too-trusting public by trotting out Peking Man, Neanderthal Man, and Cro-Magnon man in a dismal and apparently desperate attempt to justify their system of belief. All three of these, it turns out, were nothing more nor less than fully human, a fact quite reluctantly admitted by the community of evolutionists.

If the history of evolutionists' attempt to find the missing link between ape and man has yielded nothing more than a sordid collection of frauds, perhaps they can fall back on the find in Australia of an archaeopteryx fossil[8], this creature supposedly representing a link between reptiles and birds.

Perhaps not. At least not in honesty. The notion that this bird represents a transitional form came from its teeth, which are unusual in a bird and more usual to a reptile. Everything else about this fossil shows absolutely nothing contradictory to what constitutes a bird. The unusual feature of teeth is not so unusual after all, considering that some reptiles have no teeth while other fossils of birds do, and other strange creatures, like the duck-billed platypus, exist that are not considered to be missing links.

But what about the dinosaur-bird so highly publicized by the National Geographic magazine, who artistically (and fictionally) portrayed a baby dinosaur with feathers and claimed that birds belong to the family of bipedal dinosaurs.

Even the community of evolutionists was taken aback by this hasty conclusion. Jeffrey quotes Professor Storrs Olson, curator of birds at the Smithsonian in the following condemnation:

"National Geographic has reached an all-time low for engaging in sensationalistic, unsubstantiated, tabloid journalism. . . It eventually became clear to me that National Geographic was not interested in anything other than the prevailing dogma that birds evolved from dinosaurs.[21]"

Irreconcilable differences between evolution and Christianity

A disagreeable problem with the theory of evolution is that it undercuts Scripture. Scripture itself, being the Word of God, is one very substantial pillar of the Christian faith. Paul (2 Timothy 3:16) and Peter (2 Peter 1:20, 21) both declared Scripture to have come from God, so a Christian takes the written Word lightly at the peril of his own soul. Nobody can deny that in claiming evolution to be compatible with Scripture, the person who does so must necessarily lose something vital to the reverence of the God who is defined by that Scripture. The creation epic and the fall of man are seen in a more distant, indirect light. *Did God really say that?* the evolutionist questions. The timing of creation is met with skepticism. *Did God really say that?* The introduction of death into God's creation with the fall of man – *well, maybe what God really meant was. . .*Man may have fallen at one time, but since then he's been evolving into something better (on his own, with the helping hand of chance).

Quite apart from a consideration of God, the dating scheme currently accepted within the secular world suffers from some profound intellectual and suppositional errors. Yet while there are glaring logical difficulties with the dating scheme, there is a possibility that even in the face of the falsehoods the assumption of a very great age of the earth and life upon it may be reconciled with Scripture by interpreting the first few verses of Genesis 1 as permitting a large time gap between a previous era in earth's history and a reconstruction into its present form. Other interpretations involving large time periods assume that each 'day' of creation was considerably longer than twenty four hours, furnishing another convenient path for reconciling Scripture with the secular paradigm of the earth's age.

On the other hand, there is no possible way that the theory of evolution can be reconciled to Christianity. Where, precisely, do evolution and Christianity clash? The specific issues presented below are but a partial listing of the most obvious areas.

As was noted above, evolution undercuts the notion that Scripture is inspired by God and inerrant. Evolution places the development of man as progressing upward, rather than downward as Scripture strongly implies, and makes light of the Genesis account of creation.

Evolution fosters a fully materialistic mindset. The theory and its numerous naturalistic offshoots place a premium on materialism, refusing to countenance the introduction of anything beyond chance and atoms in the development of life. This emphasis on the material world so intrinsic to evolution has thoroughly permeated our society, promoting hedonism and selfishness, whereas it represents the exact opposite of a major theme of Christianity, the rejection of the material world in favor of the spiritual realm. Jesus Himself said (John 18:36)

> *My kingdom is not of this world; if my kingdom were of this world, then would my servants fight, that I should not be delivered to the Jews; but now my kingdom is not from here.*

Paul continually emphasized the greater importance of the spiritual realm over the material world. A representative passage is 1 Corinthians 2:9-14:

> *But as it is written, Eye hath not seen, nor ear heart, neither have entered into the heart of man, the things which God hath prepared for them that love him. But God hath revealed them unto us by his Spirit; for the Spirit searcheth all things, yea, the deep things of God. For what man knoweth the things of a man, except that spirit of man which is in him? Even so the things of God knoweth no man, but the Spirit of God. Now we have received, no the spirit of the world, but the Spirit who is of God; that we might know the things that are freely*

given to us of God. Which things also we speak, not in the words which man's wisdom teacheth, but which the Holy Spirit teacheth, comparing spiritual things with spiritual. But the natural man receiveth not the things of the Spirit of God; for they are foolishness unto him, neither can he know them, because they are spirituall discerned.

Evolution requires more faith in the secular paradigm than in God and Scripture. The enormous complexities and interdependencies of life recently uncovered by science are so contradictory to the causal explanations of evolution that those who embrace evolution must do so on faith alone, ignoring their own intellects and common sense. Moreover, they have suspended normal standards of proof, which for evolution are nonexistent, and have disregarded the numerous outright frauds associated with the futile search for the proof of evolution. Such individuals must place more stock in current 'science' than in God, believing without reservation that if eminent people say something must be true, that it must be true. Regarding this issue of secular faith, William Dembski says it well in reminding his readers that the Intelligent Design approach to the origin of life is not only more compatible by far with Scriptural theology, but is of itself a more up-to-date and intellectually satisfying alternative to evolution:

"Unlike full-blooded Darwinists, however, the design theorists' objection to theistic evolution rests not with what the term *theistic* is doing in the phrase 'theistic evolution' but rather with what the term *evolution* is doing there. The design theorists' objection to theistic evolution is not in the end that theistic evolution retains God as an unnecessary rider in an otherwise perfectly acceptable scientific theory of life's origin and development. Rather their objection is that the scientific theory which is supposed to undergird theistic evolution, often called the neo-Darwinian synthesis, is itself problematic.

"The design theorists' critique of Darwinism begins with Darwinism's failure as an empirically adequate scientific theory, not with its supposed incompatibility with some system of religious belief. This point is vital to keep in mind in assessing intelligent design's contribution to the creation-evolution controversy.

Critiques of Darwinism by creationists have tended to conflate science and theology, making it unclear whether Darwinism fails strictly as a scientific theory or whether it must be rejected because it is theologically unacceptable. Design theorists refuse to make this a Bible-science controversy. Their critique of Darwinism is not based on any supposed incompatibility between Christian revelation and Darwinism. Instead they begin their critique by arguing that Darwinism is *on its own terms* a failed scientific research program – that it does not constitute a well-supported scientific theory, that its explanatory power is severely limited and that it fails abysmally when it tries to account for the grand sweep of natural history[22]."

Perhaps the most devastating problem of all in attempting to accommodate evolution into Christianity is a rather subtle one that doesn't outright deny the existence of God. The clash between evolution and Scripture, however, need not be in-your-face obvious; after all, satan is known to be subtle. This very real and pervasive problem is the unavoidable perception in the minds of evolutionists that the distance between God and His creation renders Him irrelevant to our daily lives. Evolution does not require the existence of God, particularly the God of Scripture. Beyond that, at best it removes God from the forefront of creation to a remote location in the very background and slaps His hands away from creative details, whereas Scripture as a whole presents God as in much more intimate connection with His creation. The kind of remoteness between God and man implicit in a belief in evolution demands an indifference of God toward us and of us toward God. Moreover, it trivializes the conscious disobedience of man that led to the entrance of sin and death into the world. Yet more, it renders insignificant the major theme of Scripture, both Old and New Testaments, that Jesus came in the flesh and died on the cross to reconcile mankind to God.

Most of the Christian world, as a matter of fact, assumes that an hour spent on Sunday getting preached to fulfills all the obligations that one might owe his God. Devoting the remainder of the week (including Sunday afternoons) to self is perfectly acceptable to those who choose to include evolution in their world view, for in doing so they aren't distancing themselves from their "God" any more than He has distanced Himself from them. How far indeed is that attitude from the commandment of Jesus in Matthew 22:37 and 38 to love the Lord our God with all our hearts, souls and minds!

How tragically remote is that attitude from even considering Jesus to be our Lord!

NOTES:

1. Dr. Michael J. Behe, *The Edge of Evolution,* Free Press Division of Simon and Schuster, 2007pp. 188-190, 233, 234

2. Dr. Phillip E. Johnson, *Darwin on Trial,* InterVarsity Press, 1993, pp. 71-100

3. Dr. Michael J. Behe, *The Edge of Evolution,* Free Press Division of Simon and Schuster, 2007pp. 188-190, 233, 234

4. Dr.Phillip Johnson, *Defeating Darwinism by Opening Minds,* InterVarsity Press, 1997, p. 15

5. Stephen Jay Gould, *Time's Arrow, Time's Cycle,* Harvard University Press, 1987

6. Dr. William A. Dembski, *Intelligent Design*, InterVarsity Press (IVP Academic), 1999

7. *ibid.,* p. 167 (quoting from Richard Dawkins, *The Blind Watchmaker,* Norton, 1987, pp. 139, 145, 146)

8. ibid., pp. 166, 178

9. Ralph O. Muncaster, *Dismantling Evolution* Harvest House Publishers, 2003, p. 131

10. Michael Behe, *Darwin's Black Box*, Free Press, 1996

11. Stephen C. Meyer, *Signature in the Cell*, HarperOne imprint of Harper Collins, 2009, pp. 240-252; Ralph O. Muncaster, *Dismantling Evolution* Harvest House Publishers, 2003, pp. 124-129

12. Meyer, *Signature in the Cell*, pp. 206, 207; Muncaster, *Dismantling Evolution*, pp. 131-136

13. Thomas E. Woodward and James P. Gills, *The Mysterious Epigenome,* Kregel Publications, 2012, p. 68

14. Meyer, *Signature in the* Cell, p. 367

15. Dembski, *Intelligent Design*

16. *ibid.*, pp. 170-174

17. Phillip Johnson, *Darwin on Trial*, pp. 71-74

18. Vance Ferrell, *The Evolution Cruncher*, Evolution Facts, Inc., 2001 pp. 420-425

19. Dr. Grant R. Jeffrey, *Creation*, Frontier Research Publications, 2003, pp. 191-212

20. *ibid.,* pp. 193

21. *ibid.,* pp. 197, 198

22. Dembski, *Intelligent Design,* pp. 109-112

PART FOUR

The Reality Behind Biblical "Myths"

Contents for Part Four

Preface to Part Four

Part Three generally addressed the distortion of truth imposed on modern man by his institutions. The focus will now turn more specifically on the particular area of natural science in this regard to illustrate how far afield from reality the rigidly secular approach to natural history, as driven by the uniformitarian mindset, may have taken us.

As anyone emerging from childhood can appreciate, science and technology have made some sweeping developments over the past half century. Even now, of course, the pace is accelerating. The natural sciences have not been immune to this change. Using new tools and techniques, man has stepped up the pace of his exploration, from the earth itself in the discovery and interpretation of archaeological finds to the outer reaches of our solar system, where the planets we view stand in naked disagreement with our simplistic assumptions of the recent past.

The picture we are finding generally contradicts the long-held uniformitarian assumption of constant, gradual change. We see evidence on Mars and the asteroid belt of more than one enormously destructive interaction of bodies within our solar system in the past that have created sudden disasters of planetary scope. We are beginning to concern ourselves with the possibility that it could happen again, and that this kind of monstrous destruction could take place right here on earth. We perceive yet dimly that such an event would not be the first to devastate our planet.

This appreciation on the part of the experts is continuing to increase. It has not yet filtered down to the public at large, who still cling to the science of the past and remain largely ignorant of the significance of this new paradigm of planet-wide catastrophe. Most importantly, Christians themselves continue to accept the secular assertion that a disconnect exists between Scripture and science, not realizing that it is science itself that is backtracking into conformity with Scripture. Indeed, some of the great Biblical events, given a literal rather than a mythical interpretation, might support our new understanding as it fleshes out a strikingly detailed picture of man's travails during times when the earth shook with violence.

1

A Mundane Account of Unexpected Importance

In the book of Genesis a list of 'begottens' is recorded. In this seemingly exhaustive presentation that goes on for page after tedious page, entries are made for the ancient patriarchs and their ages at the times when they fathered children and for the times of their deaths. Most of us have difficulty in reading these passages. We find them to be quite boring and question why a religious document would bother with such seemingly extraneous trivia. Seeing little in this presentation that furnishes insight into the nature of God or His Creation, we usually skip over the 'begottens' without a second glance.

Biblical scholar Donald Patten, however, seems to have observed something in this listing that turned the mundane into something altogether different. Applying the "begotten" data contained in Genesis to a graph of lifetimes versus generational sequence, he saw in the result a remarkable pattern. I cannot speak for the mental processes which led to Mr. Patten's hypotheses. But his writings suggest that it was from this pattern, which he included in his 1966 book *The Biblical Flood and the Ice Epoch*, that he truly began to understand the initial text of the Book of Genesis at a much deeper level than most Christians do even now, so many years later. The graph itself fit well with a constant lifetime up to the time of Noah's flood, and with an exponential decline thereafter toward the present typical lifetime of seventy years. The exponential curve is well-known among physicists and engineers, a typical example being the time-variant voltage across a capacitor as electrical current is discharged through a resistor.

The exponential nature of this graph is typical of natural processes, indicating rather strongly that one or more such processes came into play after the flood that sharply reduced the lifetimes of the earth's inhabitants. That, in turn, suggests that the events associated with the flood caused a significant change to the earth itself. Patten took up the challenge of this suggestion and investigated further. After reflecting on the possible reasons for a drastic reduction in longevity, he proposed that the antediluvian atmosphere contained significantly more water vapor than the present regime, and that there was far less wind and turbulence to cause atmospheric mixing among the various layers. Long-wave radiation from the earth would tend to be absorbed in the upper atmosphere before it reached the ozone layer, making it less effective as a decomposition agent. As a consequence, he reflected, the antediluvian regime had more ozone in the upper atmosphere and less toxic ozone at the surface. Both of these factors would have contributed to a greater longevity prior to the flood.

But there was more that came out of Patten's conjecture than an answer to the longevity question. Why, he asked, was the atmosphere so different before the flood? What mechanism, which ceased to exist after the deluge, could have produced the pre-flood climatic conditions? By the time he obtained what to him were satisfactory answers to these questions, the Bible must have literally come alive in his mind. Passages in the book of Genesis which may have appeared to make little sense before suddenly must have become strikingly clear and utterly simple of understanding. Rather than representing isolated islands of unconnected, unimportant, and fuzzy thought, they meshed together beautifully to form a precise and self-consistent picture of the climate system of the earth prior to the flood and the destruction of that regime. The picture that emerged of the flood itself described an event of planetary scope and awesome violence.

One of the first of these passages in the book of Genesis which Patten tackled in the pursuit of answers to his questions is the mysterious description of the 'firmament' in the first chapter:

> *And God said, Let there be a firmament in the midst of the waters, and let it divide the waters from the waters. . .And God said, Let the waters under the heaven be gathered together unto one place, and let the dry land appear: and it was so.*

In the context of our understanding of the world as it exists today, this passage seems to be so difficult of visualization as to be incomprehensible. This problem of visualization continues into the second chapter of Genesis, where the source of water upon the earth is said to be a mist from the ground rather than rain.

> . . .for the Lord God had not caused it to rain upon the earth, and there was not a man to till the ground. But there went up a mist from the earth, and watered the whole face of the ground.

The difficulty with a meaningful interpretation continues on through the flood of Noah, with many readers of Scripture viewing in these words a lack of sophistication on the part of the writer. Such suspicions tempt those who harbor them to dismiss as unjustified the notion that the Bible was divinely inspired. They invariably choose instead the only alternative answer that appears to makes sense: that the Biblical authors were so primitive of mind that they simply recorded myths handed down from the distant past, and garbled ones at that. The rainbow covenant of God related in the ninth chapter of Genesis is often cited as an example of Biblical myth, being considered a theatrical presentation of the mundane:

> And God said, This is the token of the covenant which I make between me and you and every living creature that is with you, for perpetual generations: I do set my bow in the cloud, and it shall be for a token of a covenant between me and the earth. And it shall come to pass, when I bring a cloud over the earth, that the bow shall be seen in the cloud: And I will remember my covenant, which is between me and you and every living creature of all flesh; and the waters shall no more become a flood to destroy all flesh.

In these passages the supposedly naïve Patten, apparently so lacking in sophistication that he failed to see the same mythical elements in this passage that everyone else did, caught a glimpse of a startling truth. From that perceived truth he formed a novel thesis. He claimed that the earth was once surrounded by a globular canopy of water vapor, in Biblical terminology the waters above the heavens. This water canopy served to moderate the temperature differential between the poles and the equator. With this canopy, our present weather mechanism did not exist before the Flood, the previous order being entirely different than what we observe today. In that order few, if any, clouds formed and very little, if any, rain fell. The atmospheric pressure was higher then than it is now, supporting the existence of flying creatures whose fossils suggest, to the consternation of modern scientists, that they were too large to fly in our present atmosphere.

With the canopy gone, clouds formed for the first time, produced by the much larger temperature differential that prevailed in the absence of the canopy. The familiar rainbow became possible with the advent of rain. It would be seen from that time forward because the canopy no longer existed. The 'mythical' statement, discarded by generations of scholars to be virtually extraneous to the subject, turned out to be a clue to understanding the entire first chapter of Genesis with a clarity that must have been entirely unexpected.

There are other Christian researchers who have also failed to be outsmarted by their own presumed sophistication. These have been so bold instead as to consider these passages in Genesis to have scientific validity. Henry Morris, for example, collaborated with John Whitcomb in writing *The Genesis Flood*, an extensively researched account of that event. In that book, the concepts and techniques of modern science are carefully applied to the examination of evidence that the flood, as presented in the Bible, actually occurred and was of planetary scale.

Taking a more secular approach to world history, geographer Charles Hapgood found evidence in old maps of a high level of technical sophistication of ancient societies. He marveled at the remarkable information embedded in obscure pre-renaissance maritime charts, some of which accurately depicted the Antarctic continent as if it was free of the ice sheet which currently obscures the shoreline. In the course of his research into the source of these ancient maps, he came to a similar appreciation of great catastrophes of planetary scope which destroyed and buried entire civilizations. He devoted an enormous amount of time and effort in the pursuit of his own theory that the earth's poles had shifted frequently in the past, with devastating effects on the earth and its civilizations. In addition to the widespread destruction, this movement of the poles and the consequent change in the alignment of the Earth's ecliptic to its orbital path may also have contributed to a more extreme post-flood differential between the temperature of the poles and the equator. Hapgood was able to obtain the interest of Einstein in his books on the subject, as well as from the public at large. But the attention span of the public was fleeting. It was an interesting topic for a while, but since it didn't fit in well with the standard party line, it was soon forgotten.

Much more recently, the father-son team of Luis and Walter Alvarez succeeded in the 1990s in scientifically linking the extinction of the dinosaurs with an event that occurred suddenly and was worldwide in its effects. This connection created repercussions within the scientific community which, although not yet appreciated outside that community, are leading to drastic revisions of scholarly understanding of natural history.

In this same time frame, a number of astronomers and archaeologists have been gathering increasingly irrefutable evidence in support of several major catastrophic events that have been visited on earth in the recent past, one of which appears to have caused an end to the latest ice age a mere ten thousand years ago, even by secular reckoning. An increasing number of these scientists have come to at least privately reject the uniformitarian scheme so loudly proclaimed by their more vocal and less intelligent colleagues. According to author Graham Hancock, the ranks of those who have perceived the profound influence of catastrophes on the recent history of Earth include Sir Fred Hoyle, Professor Chandra Wickramasinghe, and Drs. Napier and Clube, all of whom are eminent in the field of astronomy.

Patten and the others noted above were not the first of the modern catastrophists. The main thrusts of their theses followed those of the Russian-born physician Immanuel Velikovsky, who was the real pioneer of this new paradigm. Around the mid-twentieth century, Velikovsky created an uproar within the scientific community with his carefully-researched account of recent and recurring catastrophes on earth that involved not only the flood, but great periodic upheavals which followed that event. The name-calling and general verbal mayhem that accompanied his books rivaled the violence of which he wrote. Einstein thought his old associate should have seen more humor in the situation: it was difficult to see which was more epic, the catastrophes or the mud-slinging among the uniformitarian-based scientists, who conducted such an unseemly inquisition of Velikovsky. Their tactics had the intellectual honesty and maturity of restraint of a third-grade playground. People are still writing about the episode, trying to explain in quasi-scientific terms how supposedly rational professionals could allow themselves to degenerate into animals.

The cause of this consternation was Velikovsky's assertion that enormous upheavals recurred at various times throughout ancient times from the flood until about the eighth century B.C or even later. The continuous freedom from Earth-wide catastrophe which the world has enjoyed since that time has permitted mankind to forget the terrible destruction that prevailed earlier and the pervasive fear which accompanied it. Perhaps even more troubling to the secular scientists was Velikovsky's use of the Bible in reconstructing the events of which he wrote. As can be noted by the flavor of their arguments, the scientists very definitely didn't want God to get His foot in the door of their discipline.

2

Some Mechanisms Postulated for Past Catastrophes of Planetary Scale

What possibly could have caused such monstrous upheavals of our planet? Until very recently, science has denied that the possibility of events of such magnitude could occur at all, since no mechanism of sufficient strength can be observed today. In line with the uniformitarian presupposition, that rules out the possibility of any such mechanism operating in the past. Consequently, for the past few centuries the earth sciences have insisted, sometimes with tantrum-like behavior, that the earth has been stable for multiple thousands, if not millions, of years. Yet evidence continues to mount that such events did indeed take place. Some of this evidence, moreover, points to events which occurred within the memory of man.

Christian scholars John Whitcomb and Henry Morris describe the great flood of Noah in terms of just such a titanic catastrophe that befell the earth when civilizations were upon the land. In chapter six of their book *The Genesis Flood: The Biblical Record and Its Scientific Implications* is found one of many capsule summaries of the disaster and its effects:

"The picture then is of awesome proportions. The vast 'waters above the firmament' poured forth through what are graphically represented in the Scriptures as the 'floodgates of heaven,' swelling the rivers and waterways and initiating the erosion and transportation of vast inland sediments. At the same time, waters and probably magmas were bursting up through the fractured fountains of the great subterranean deep. In the seas, these 'fountains' not only belched forth their waters and volcanic materials, but the corresponding earth displacements must have been continually generating powerful tsunamis.

"This tremendous complex of forces, diastrophic and hydrodynamic, must beyond any question have profoundly altered the antediluvian topography and geology of the earth's crust. Powerful currents, of all directions and magnitudes and periods, must have been generated and made to function as agents of immense eroding, transporting, and depositional potency. Under the action of this combination of effects, almost any sort of deposit or depositional sequence becomes possible and plausible. An immense variety of sediments must finally have been the result, after the Flood had run its course.

"And yet, in spite of the complexity of physical agencies involved and the resulting variety of formations and sediments, certain general semblances of order might be anticipated in the deposits when the waters abated. The creatures of the deep sea bottoms would universally be overwhelmed by the toxicity and violence of the volcanic emanations and the bottom currents generated thereby and would in general be mixed with the inorganic materials simultaneously dislodged from the bed, transported and eventually re-deposited on the bed.

"In similar fashion, the fish and other organisms living nearer the surface would subsequently be entrapped by either materials washing down from the land surface or the shallow coastal sea bottoms or by materials upwelling from the depths. Again these sediments would be transported and re-deposited either on the sea bottom or occasionally on top of other sediments already laid down.

"On the land, the raging rivers would carry great quantities of detritus seaward, occasionally entombing animals or reptiles, together with great rafts of vegetation. These would normally be deposited finally in some more or less quiescent reach of stream or finally in the sea on top of other deposits or perhaps on the exposed bottom itself.

"As far as land animals and man were concerned, their greater mobility would have enabled most of them to escape temporarily to higher ground as the waters rose, only occasional individuals being swept away and entombed in the sediments. Eventually, of course, the floodwaters overtook even those who had fled to the highest elevations, but in most cases these men and animals would not be buried but simply drowned and then carried about by the waters on or near the surface until finally decomposed by the elements. Certain spectacular exceptions to this rule might occur when groups of animals, huddled together in a cave on some hillside or on a summit, were swept away by a sudden, sediment-laden wave of water to be buried en masse at another place.

"Even after the first forty days, when the greatest of the rains and upheavals diminished, the Scriptures say that the waters 'prevailed' upon the earth for one hundred and ten days longer. This statement - together with what one might infer from the prevalent unique meteorological conditions during that period, with a universal ocean still reacting to the great dynamic imbalance so recently imposed on the earth - would certainly imply that extensive hydraulic and sedimentary activity continued for a long time, with many earlier flood deposits perhaps re-eroded and reworked. Some sediments may well have been transported and deposited several times before reaching their final resting-place."

In other words, according to Whitcomb or Velikovsky or any of the other writers of that persuasion, stark, unremitting terror must have forced itself upon every living creature on earth that had sufficient intelligence to perceive the magnitude of the devastation. It was an agony that was mitigated only by the rapidity by which their lives were terminated.

How could that kind of damage be accepted as actually having occurred if no appropriate mechanism can be found on earth? Patten supplies one possible and logically reasonable answer in a source outside our planet. As we have noted, he postulated that the earth prior to the Flood possessed a canopy of water vapor which moderated the temperature differential between the equator and the poles. At the time of the flood, according to him, the earth suffered a close encounter with a comet, bringing the water of the canopy crashing down upon the earth and forever changing the atmospheric regime.

This canopy was shattered by the visitation upon earth of a comet which, as it destroyed the canopy, created a gravitational instability that resulted in the sudden and violent release of earthbound waters. Patten's mechanism of violence was not a small, fast object that collided with the earth. Like Velikovsky before him, Patten saw a large mass which was captured temporarily by the earth's gravity, wreaking destruction on earth through the influence of gravitational and possibly electromagnetic coupling forces. The interaction between this unwelcome visitor and earth not only destroyed the canopy of water surrounding the earth, but also caused great tectonic disturbances, one effect of which was the breaking up of the fountains of the deep. A probable contribution to the massive earthquakes that must have shaken the earth at that time may have been the closeness of the cosmic visitor's approach to earth, possibly intruding into Roche's Limit, causing the gravitational turmoil that broke up the fountains of the deep.

In support of his thesis of the close approach to Earth of a massive object, Patten supplies an interesting observation regarding the earth's two primary systems of mountain ranges, the Alpine-Himalayan and the Circum-Pacific. He notes that each of these ranges consists of a linear series of arcs, the centers of which follow a great circle path along the surface of the earth. This pattern is precisely what would be expected from coupling stresses, either gravitational or electromagnetic, or possibly both, arising from a large object orbiting closely about our planet.

Patten notes further that the earth is not a perfect sphere: due to the centrifugal force of the earth's rotation, the polar regions are flattened by tens of miles with respect to the equatorial regions. The great rift valley in Africa exhibits properties that are consistent with an expansion of ground due to an increased diameter over its location caused by a continental movement from a polar toward an equatorial location. Similarly, a continental movement in the opposite direction, or from equatorial to polar, would cause a wrinkling of the earth's crust, evidenced by mountain ranges, due to a decreased diameter of the earth over that location. This process of diametrical adjustment must have taken years, perhaps centuries, after the polar shift occurred, and may have been the cause of the dividing of the earth in the days of Peleg in the fifth generation after Noah.

Having penetrated Earth's gravitational field sufficiently close to Roche's Limit to cause a fragmentation of its icy cloak, Patten's comet shed pieces which fell to the earth toward the polar regions under the influence of the earth's magnetic field. Patten sees as one effect of this event the disruption of the pre-existing atmospheric system, which with his suspected canopy of water vapor, included a much larger proportion of atmospheric water than the present regime. His interpretation borrows from the hitherto difficult-to-understand Genesis account of the creation, wherein God divided the waters of heaven from the waters of the earth.

If the ice age itself was suddenly initiated by the mechanism that caused the flood, transient effects would be expected. The levels of the oceans would undergo an adjustment due to the melting of ice. Evidence generally acknowledged as firm exists throughout the world that the oceans once were hundreds of feet lower than at the present time. The same may be said of our atmosphere, which may have been significantly cooler immediately following the flood and steadily rose in temperature toward a new equilibrium. That equilibrium may not yet have been reached even today, giving us a false impression that global warming is coming from other causes. The reach for stability from the Flood event may still be significant: lakes continue to dry in the American Southwest; the Sahara Desert continues to encroach upon land that was fertile and productive; the Antarctic Ice continues to melt. The earthquakes we experience may indicate that our contents are still being subjected to diametric adjustment following an initial rapid shift either toward or away from the equator. Perhaps also our continental plates are continuing a long process of deceleration, reaching toward an eventual stability that has not yet been achieved. After all, to feed the uniformitarians a little dose of their own medicine, a duration of a few millennia is supposedly a drop in the bucket in the grand scheme of things. In that context, we, living a cosmic instant after the cause, may still be observing its effects.

Other investigators support this notion that the ice age began with the flood, and while they also assume a primordial canopy that encompassed the globe, theirs is of ice rather than water vapor. They, too, see the initial cause of this catastrophe as an unwelcome visitor from space that sent the waters from heaven crashing upon the polar regions of the earth under the influence of its magnetic field. Some of those who have taken this view have speculated on how the atmosphere must have appeared to those who lived before the flood. They supply vivid images of Adam gazing up at a rose-colored sky of surpassing beauty, and of Eve watching crystalline sunsets of spectacular colors. If they are correct, the world then was of an entirely different order of perfection.

The gradualist would be tempted to summarily dismiss the canopy scenario, pointing to recently developed or improved techniques which earth scientists have been employing to ascertain, from historical data, probable mechanisms to explain our currently accelerating global warming process. Among these techniques are pollen and ice-core sampling. Ice cores have been taken from the Greenland Ice Cap, for example, which supposedly extend back 100,000 years. If Greenland was continually covered in ice all the way back then, both the canopy thesis and the notion of very recent catastrophes lose some (but not necessarily all) of their credibility. But there is a possible problem with the interpretation of the data to date: even as it demonstrates sudden changes in line with potential catastrophic causes, the data, and especially its timing, is almost certainly based on uniformitarian assumptions. Do the layers actually represent yearly depositions, especially back beyond a few thousand years, or does each layer represent the deposition over a much shorter time interval? Are links made between thickness and time of the layers on the basis of uniformitarian expectations of yearly accretions, ignoring the possibility that under catastrophic circumstances they may demonstrate the ebb and flow of troubled waters? The cores may present a very different picture of events and their timing if all such uniformitarian assumptions were stripped of their *a priori* status at the very beginning of the investigation.

Immanuel Velikovsky preceded Patten in claiming, with a wealth of Scriptural and legendary evidence to support his assertion, that the earth suffered multiple episodes of planetary-scale destructive events, one of which occurred during the time of the Exodus. Looking beyond the plethora of mythical and trivialized explanations for the traditions of peoples around the world, Velikovsky applied common sense and basic mechanics to the details of these so-called myths, coming to the pioneering understanding that the earth experienced repeated encounters with objects beyond the Earth between the fifteenth and eighth centuries B.C. Unfortunately, his pioneering work is still discredited among modern naturalists for its development out of 'legends' rather than hard scientific data. One modern scholar, in noting the source of Velikovsky's thesis, dismisses it as 'unscientific nonsense'. The predictive utility alone of this thesis automatically elevates it above the purely nonsensical. This same scholar proposes a different scenario of cosmic violence which may perhaps be closer to describing actual events than Velikovsky's thesis. Ironically, however, the scenario remains catastrophic. In that feature alone the scholar necessarily borrowed from the initial work performed by Velikovsky, whether he chooses to acknowledge that fact or not. Despite a common disdain for the words of ancient peoples, the initial impetus for *all* modern catastrophic research, regardless of whether it is performed by Christians, Buddhists, or agnostics, came from Judeo-Christian Scripture.

In the context of life as we know it today, the chronicle of the Exodus in Scripture is full of enigmas. Even under the duress of natural but infrequent events, the kinds of things such as volcanoes, earthquakes, high winds and floods that we can observe today, the Exodus account is often mysterious. In the thirty-second chapter of Exodus, for example, there is an account of trouble during the wandering of the Israelites in the wilderness. To the modern mind, the behavior of the Israelis in this passage seems strange, even inappropriate:

> *And when the people saw that Moses delayed to come down out of the mount, the people gathered themselves together unto Aaron, and said unto him, Up, make us gods, which shall go before us: for as for this Moses, the man that brought us up out of the land of Egypt, we wot not what is become of him. And Aaron said unto them, Break off the golden earrings, which are in the ears of your wives, of your sons, and of your daughters, and bring them unto me.*

> *And all the people brake of the golden earrings which were in their ears, and brought them unto Aaron. And he received them at their hand, and fashioned it with a graving tool, after he had made it a molten calf: and they said, These be thy gods, O Israel, which brought thee up out of the land of Egypt.*

Why were they so quick to fall away, and why indeed was the object of their worship a calf? In the context of life as we experience it, it doesn't make sense, even for members of a primitive, superstitious society. But what if it was because they were in the thrall of terror from an apparition in the sky above whose gravitational disruptions made its presence felt upon the earth as trembling and quaking? They must have seen in that sky a great object that loomed above them, accompanied by shakings of the earth and mountains on fire. It was possibly the same body that led them as a cloud by day and a pillar of fire by night, turning more threatening as it came closer, its coma, through gravitational and electromagnetic forces, becoming a horned apparition. To the Israelites and those who lived in the Indus Valley, the horns must have resembled those of a calf. To the Chinese and American peoples, the apparition must have appeared to be a dragon or a serpent. That may explain why, to this day, the cow is so sacred in India that its very dung is considered holy. Consider the eighteenth Psalm of David:

> *In my distress I called upon the lord, and cried unto my God: he heard my voice out of his temple, and my cry came before him, even into his ears.*

> *Then the earth shook and trembled; the foundations also of the hills moved and were shaken, because he was wroth. There went up a smoke out of his nostrils, and fire out of his mouth devoured: coals were kindled by it. He bowed the heavens also, and came down: and darkness was under his feet. And he rode upon a cherub, and did fly: yea, he did fly upon the wings of the wind. He made darkness his secret place; his pavilion round about him was dark waters and thick clouds of the skies. At the brightness that was before him his thick clouds passed, hail stones and coals of fire. The Lord also thundered in the heavens, and Highest gave his voice; hail stones and coals of fire. Yea, he sent out his arrows, and scattered them; and he shot out lightnings, and discomfited them. Then the channels of waters were seen, and the foundations of the world were discovered at thy rebuke, O Lord, at the blast of the breath of thy nostrils.*

When we apply the notion of cosmic disturbance to the wandering Israelis, they no longer seem remote and mythical. They become real, people like us except for the terror they had to endure. They come to life in the Bible, and we are moved to feel compassion for their lot.

Immanuel Velikovsky fleshes out his account of the Exodus catastrophe in Chapter 3 of his book *Worlds in Collision*:

"The swift shifting of the atmosphere under the impact of the gaseous parts of the comet, the drift of air attracted by the body of the comet, and the rush of the atmosphere resulting from inertia when the earth stopped rotating or shifted its poles, all contributed to produce hurricanes of enormous velocity and force and of world-wide dimensions.

"*Manuscript Troano*" and other documents of the Mayas describe a cosmic catastrophe during which the ocean fell on the continent, and a terrible hurricane swept the earth. The hurricane broke up and carried away all towns and all forests. Exploding volcanoes, tides sweeping over mountains, and impetuous winds threatened to annihilate humankind, and actually did annihilate many species of animals. The face of the earth changed, mountains collapsed, other mountains grew and rose over the onrushing cataract of water driven from oceanic spaces, numberless rivers lost their beds, and a wild tornado moved through the debris descending from the sky. The end of the world age was caused by Hurakan, the physical agent that brought darkness and swept away houses and trees and even rocks and mounds of earth. From this name is derived "hurricane", the word we use for a strong wind. Hurakan destroyed the major part of the human race. In the darkness swept by wind, resinous stuff fell from the sky and participated with fire and water in the destruction of the world. For five days, save for the burning naphtha and burning volcanoes, the world was dark, since the sun did not appear.

"The theme of a cosmic hurricane is reiterated time and again in the Hindu *Vedas* and in the Persian *Avesta*, and *diluvium venti*, the deluge of wind, is a term known from many ancient authors. In the Section, 'The Darkness', I quoted rabbinical sources on the 'exceedingly strong west wind' that endured for seven days when the land was enveloped in darkness, and the hieroglyphic inscription from el-Arish about 'nine days of upheaval' when 'there was such a tempest' that nobody could leave the palace or see the faces of those beside him, and the eleventh tablet of the *Epic of Gilgamesh* which says that 'Six days and a night. . .the hurricane, deluge, and tempest continued sweeping the land', and mankind perished almost altogether. In the battle of the planet-god Marduk with Tiamat, 'he

[Marduk] created the evil wind, and the tempest, and the hurricane, and the fourfold wind, and the sevenfold wind, and the whirlwind, and the wind which had no equal.'"

"The Maoris narrate that amid a stupendous catastrophe 'the mighty winds, the fierce squalls, the clouds, dense, dark, fiery, wildly drifting, wildly bursting', rushed on creation, in their midst Tawhiri-ma-tea, father of winds and storms, and swept away giant forests and lashed the waters into billows whose crests rose high like mountains. The earth groaned terribly, and the ocean fled.

"'The earth was submerged in the ocean but was drawn by Tefaafanau', relate the aborigines of Paumotu in Polynesia. The new isles 'were bated by a star.' In the month of March the Polynesians celebrate a god, Taafanua. In Arabic, Tyfoon is a whirlwind and Tufan is the Deluge; and the same word occurs in Chinese as Ty-fong. It appears as though the noise of the hurricane was overtoned by a sound not unlike the name Typhon, as if the storm were calling him by name."

Velikovsky continues with a catastrophic interpretation of the parting of the Red Sea during the Exodus drama:

"The cosmic upheaval proceeded with a 'mighty strong west wind', but before the climax, in the simple words of the Scriptures, 'the Lord caused the sea to go back by a strong east wind all that night, and made the sea dry land, and the waters were divided.'"

Both Patten and Velikovsky draw from Biblical accounts much of the material by which they have pieced together their scenarios of past events. As we have noted, the Bible alludes to multiple catastrophic events often and in rich detail. In the context of these events, Biblical passages considered to be unrelated come together with magnificent consistency. But the Bible is not the only source of such information. In addition to the Bible, every society on earth refers to great catastrophes that occurred within the memory of man. From a purely secular perspective, furthermore, these same events resolve a great many scientifically baffling paradoxes and enigmas on Earth and our planetary neighbors that are unexplainable in the context of a dogmatic belief in the mythical or allegorical nature of the Bible. Joshua's long day, during which the sun stood still in the sky for an inordinately long time, followed by forty years the Exodus catastrophe that befell the Egyptians and their Israelite captives. Its cause, according to Velikovsky and others, was a periodic return of the comet into a close orbital proximity with the Earth. Serious research has revealed a corresponding long night on the other side of the world, as recorded in the traditions of the ancient Americans.

Lake Titicaca and nearby Tiahuanaco exhibit evidence that a seaport existed there, with shipbuilding and oceangoing commerce. The problem with that historical fact is that these villages reside in the Andes Mountains at an altitude of over ten thousand feet. The Earth abounds with numerous other equally enigmatic features. Ancient maps accurately describe the boundaries and mountain ranges of Antarctica, boundaries and ranges that today are buried beneath the ice. The remains of beached whales have been found in Ohio. The very existence of these real anomalies contradicts the uniformitarian assumptions which have been long cherished by orthodox science and demand that we take a fresh look at some of our other wonders such as the Grand Coulee in Washington and the Grand Canyon in Arizona and question whether, instead of having been formed over vast stretches of time by glacial action, they may have been created over the span of perhaps a month or even a week by raging waters moving over troubled lands.

With a more accurate view of our own history and of the terrible forces that may well have reshaped our earth in the memory of man it is appropriate to return to the Word of God with a deeper understanding of the reality of great Biblical events, seeing in passages such as the following from 2 Samuel chapter 22 not myth, but the precise truth:

> *In my distress I called upon the LORD, and cried to my God: and he did hear my voice out of his temple, and my cry did enter unto his ears. Then the earth shook and trembled; the foundations of heaven moved and shook, because he was wroth. There went up a smoke out of his nostrils, and fire out of his mouth devoured: coals were kindled by it. He bowed the heavens also, and came down; and darkness was under his feet. And he rode upon a cherub, and did fly: and he was seen upon the wings of the wind. And he made darkness pavilions round about him, dark waters, and thick clouds of the*

skies. Through the brightness before him were coals of fire kindled. The LORD thundered from heaven, and the most High uttered his voice. And he sent out arrows, and scattered them; lightning, and discomfited them. And the channels of the sea appeared, the foundations of the world were discovered, at the rebuking of the LORD, at the blast of the breath of his nostrils.

Those of us who in the knowledge of the Bible have come to love God see in Scripture such a remarkable self-consistency, prophetic record, and purity of love that it testifies of itself to its supernatural origins. Nevertheless, the cataclysmic events of the past may have created such fear in the heart of man that in them were the beginnings of some religions. Overwhelmed with terror, stark, naked and unrelenting, its cause great turmoil and upheaval upon the earth, mankind may have held on to a thread of sanity by inventing forms of worship. In the midst of thunder, hail and flood, mountains melting like wax to be replaced by yet larger collossi, he may well have bowed the knee in anguish. Watching in horror as transgressing sea clashed with bursting rock in titanic battle, the tiny and insignificant fragment of mankind that remained alive may have indeed witnessed helplessly as his shivering body polluted itself with adrenalin.

Terrified, man may have glimpsed the source of this horror through dark and oily clouds that rushed past on the screeching wind as the intruder from the sky, in refusing to leave earth alone, loomed ever larger. The source may have been cursed as evil or worshiped as a god, a frightening apparition in the sky whose coma was twisted into fantastic shapes that to some frightened watchers looked like a cow and to others like a calf, and to still others yet like a woman on a broomstick. The appearance of this apparition to all beings on earth who had the ability to see it must have been unrelentlessly terrifying.

Even that well-known passage in Isaiah 14, where the prophet mocks the fall of Satan, may have another meaning as well:

How art thou fallen from heaven, O Lucifer, son of the morning! How art thou cut down to the ground, which didst weaken the nations! For thou hast said in thine heart, I will ascend into heaven, I will exalt my throne

316

above the stars of God: I will sit also upon the mount of the congregation, in the sides of the north: I will ascend above the heights of the clouds; I will be like the Most High.

Yet thou shalt be brought down to hell, to the sides of the pit. They that see thee shall narrowly look upon thee, and consider thee, saying, Is this the man that made the earth to tremble, that did shake kingdoms; That made the world as a wilderness, and destroyed the cities thereof; that opened not the house of his prisoners?

Isaiah lived in one of the troubling times of which Velikovsky spoke. As Dr. Velikovsky surmised, he may have been describing the fall of Satan in terms of the relief and satisfaction of every person on earth of the taming of a terrifying comet into a stable and benign planetary orbit.

3

A Conflict in Biblical Interpretation

Patten, Morris, Whitcomb and others had acquired from God's gift to mankind of the rainbow a remarkable insight into the nature of the world before the Flood, one that integrates the various difficulties in Genesis into a single, self-consistent, and information-rich body of text. These investigators may differ in their view of the mechanism behind the disasters, but on the major point they are in full agreement: these events actually happened and their enormity reached the scale of planetary disaster. The Flood occurred when mankind was upon the earth, it was universal, and it was of such a catastrophic nature that it changed the regime under which the climate was influenced.

Patten's book did not enjoy the same wide public following as did Velikovsky's books. Even to a largely Christian audience it contradicted the standard secularly-induced interpretation of Genesis, regardless of how shallow and information-poor that interpretation is. Perhaps many Christians were merely indifferent to the entire subject. For a time the more secular-minded Velikovsky, unlike Patten, did enjoy a broader audience for his best-seller books. But what he really wanted was scientific recognition on the order of his peers and sometime associates Einstein and Freud. This he failed to achieve. His popularity was short-lived, having been squelched by those of his scientific peers who clung to the uniformitarian mindset which insisted that the features of the world had been shaped by infinitesimal changes occurring over vast durations of time. He died a disillusioned man, realizing that in the absence of scientific acceptance of what to him was the obvious truth, his fickle public had returned to what he considered to be false beliefs.

Velikovsky, Patten, and the other modern catastrophists were by no means the first to see a pattern of sudden and violent upheaval in the evidence of soil, rock, mountain and bones. They were preceded by an impressive array of geologists, physicists, and philosophers whose speculations on the enormity of the events that shaped the surface of our planet extended back in time from at least 30 A.D. and continued on until the end of the eighteenth century. Unfortunately, except perhaps for William Whiston and Isaac Newton, virtually all of these scholars were preoccupied with the effects rather than the cause. In failing to look to the sky for answers as to how these things might have taken place, they left the door open for the uniformitarians which followed them to claim that the catastrophes could not have happened at all. The more closed-minded uniformitarians were not interested in finding mechanisms for disasters. They had their own godless agenda, and it was in sharp conflict with any notion of catastrophe.

Perhaps that is one reason why little is known outside of a few Christian circles of the contributions of these pioneers to the field of natural history. Their works have instead been dismissed without real thought by mainstream science, which greatly prefers to view Scripture as mythical, in conflict with science, and consequently irrelevant to the daily order of our lives. When a scholar such as Patten comes along with a reasonable interpretation based on an assumption of Biblical truth, he is casually rejected. Because of this rejection many Christians, in glossing over the Genesis text or applying an allegorical interpretation to Scripture, have also turned away both from a viable understanding of the book of Genesis and an intuitive acceptance of the truth of Scripture.

What is so significant about the rejection by the scientific community of these scholars' contributions is not that their notions or their development violated established scientific principles. It was not that at all, for these concepts dovetail remarkably well with known facts regarding geology and the other earth sciences. The larger reason for our ignorance of these writers is that their concepts violated the current belief system within the ranks of the scientific establishment. That is the most important reason why the catastrophic authors' heartfelt contributions fell on deaf ears. They violated what we perceive as the constant order of nature, which as we insist has remained unchanged since mankind inhabited the earth. God anticipated this mindset, equating it with a system of false beliefs based on a self-serving, sinful nature, for we read in II Peter 3:3-7 that:

Knowing this first, that there shall come in the last days scoffers, walking after their own lusts, and saying, Where is the promise of his coming? For since the fathers fell asleep, all things continue as they were from the beginning of the creation. For this they willingly are ignorant of, that by the word of God the heavens were of old, and the earth standing out of the water and in the water: Whereby the world that then was, being overflowed with water, perished: But the heavens and the earth, which are now, by the same word are kept in store, reserved unto fire against the day of judgment and perdition of ungodly men.

As Peter clearly implies in this remarkable forecast of modern man's belief system, central to uniformitarian thought is the dogmatic notion that God does not exist. When and how did this uniformitarian notion come into the minds of men?

Quite arbitrarily and with no logical or observational basis whatsoever, uniformitarianism demands that observations of the earth's features and geological history be interpreted exclusively in terms of processes that can be observed in the present. By the beginning of the nineteenth century the application of the uniformitarian notion to geology, having been presented in 1795 by James Hutton, was expanded upon by Charles Lyell. Neither of these gentlemen had the benefit of formal training in the physical sciences, large domains of which themselves were in their infancy. Nevertheless, their views eventually came to be accepted as axiomatic within the earth sciences with precious little justification.

Unfortunately, most of us do not realize how intellectually shaky are the foundations of the commonly accepted view of the earth's geological history. Nor do we appreciate that these foundations are now in the process of collapsing, unable to bear the weight of new evidence acquired through modern scientific techniques and engineering marvels.

Throughout the nineteenth century and all but a decade of the twentieth, the uniformitarian paradigm was accepted without question within the mainstream scientific community. The politic of success required those of its members who hoped to achieve a measure of stature within that community to thoroughly embrace the uniformitarian principle. Their unquestioning adherence to this doctrine successfully shut out the free discourse of catastrophism for the better part of two centuries. Increasingly throughout the latter half of the twentieth century, however, our rapidly-developing technology was furnishing information from both earth and space that surprised rather than confirmed, clashing rather dramatically in each instance with the uniformitarian paradigm. By the decade of the 1990s, the notion of strict uniformitarianism had succumbed, albeit without grace, to the more reasonable admission that catastrophe indeed had a hand in shaping the features of our planet. Among the first to rip apart the uniformitarian curtain were the Alvarez team, who, in linking the extinction of the large reptiles with a worldwide layer of iridium ash, iridium being rare on Earth but abundant in comets, eventually found the cause in the enormous crater off the Yucatan peninsula. Now, as we look to Venus and Mars and the asteroids and Jupiter and our own moon, we find further evidence, and that in abundance, of the contributions of catastrophic events to the present state of the planets in our solar system.

Even well into the twenty-first century, moreover, most mainstream researchers yield most grudgingly to the acceptance of catastrophic events in the past, still insisting without justification upon the scheme of dating established at the beginning of the modern era of the natural sciences and based upon the uniformitarian mindset. In this dogged resistance that denies the scientific spirit, they misuse the dating tools with which our technology has provided them. Mainstream science continues to claim, utterly without logical justification, that all such catastrophes took place in the remote past, being separated from our own time by millions of years. But the surface of our moon does not support this presumption of great antiquity. Nor does Venus, nor Mars, nor the several thousand known earth-crossing asteroids that are catalogued to date. Nor does our own atmosphere, with its present weather system.

The heat engine that drives the earth's weather system is sufficiently well-understood by modern science that weather forecasting, supported by computer technology, has become an increasingly successful engineering art. Fuelled by the enormous temperature differential between equator and poles, this engine creates the clouds, wind and rain that cycle fresh water about the earth. In none of the scientific principles that explain our weather can be found a mechanism to produce such a drastic systemic change as the Bible indicates. This lack of a currently observable mechanism, coupled with the uniformitarian mindset, has been a significant driving force behind the current widespread treatment of the Flood as largely mythical. Those who adhere to the mythical stance regarding the Bible fail to appreciate that it is not the lack of a mechanism that would have prohibited the Flood from having occurred, but rather their own lack of either interest or comprehension. In their stubborn, myopic, and rather unscientific refusal to look beyond the existing regime in their search for a cause, they excluded without justification several readily understandable potential physical causes of the Flood, including those presented by Velikovsky, Patten, Morris and other credible researchers.

A half century has passed since the uniformitarian scientists summarily dismissed Immanuel Velikovsky. Their rebuttals, which in their tantrum-like behavior offered precious little in the way of logic, invariably failed to address the contradictions to their paradigm that his facts represented. They ignored, for example, the odd circumstances surrounding the demise of the mammoths. Entire islands in Siberia are formed of the battered and flash-frozen remains of the extinct wooly mammoth, the flesh of which could still be eaten within the past century. These unfortunate animals died in the midst of violence so sudden and profound that the food in their stomachs, food that is inappropriate to the latitude at which they were found, remained preserved without decay. They disregarded the odd situation in eastern Washington State, where in the past century ice has been found sandwiched between layers of igneous rock. They failed to explain the origin of Halley's Comet, its youth manifest in its rate of disintegration. They remained mute to the public in explaining the surface of Mars, with its rifts and craters and evidence of past water that now is nowhere to be found except in tiny underground pockets. They failed to tell us why our own moon is pocked with craters of such recent origin that its surface lacks the expected dust.

Significantly, Velikovsky made several predictions which necessarily followed from his catastrophic thesis. Among these predictions, which contradicted the scientific wisdom of the day, were statements about the temperature of Venus and its retrograde orbit, the devastation of the surface of Mars, remanent magnetism on the moon, and the importance of electromagnetic effects in planets and interplanetary space. All of these predictions turned out to be correct, and they represented surprises, even shock, to the scientists who learned of their truth. It must be remembered that it was after Velikovsky challenged the scientific community with his predictions that space probes established the very hot surface temperature of Venus, its retrograde rotation, the Van Allen Radiation Belt surrounding the earth, the intense electromagnetic activity of Jupiter, the past violence on the surface of Mars, the remanent magnetism of moon rocks, and many other facts regarding our solar system, such as Martian water, about which the experts failed to anticipate.

When the Venera probe first radioed back the Venusian temperature, the scientists were so surprised at its magnitude that they passed it off as a failed temperature sensor. When other probes confirmed the values, the experts belatedly came up with the greenhouse explanation, which has since been found to be thoroughly inadequate in light of the fact that the planet radiates more heat than it receives from the sun.

The weight of our rapidly-expanding knowledge continues to impose an increasingly heavy burden on the uniformitarian belief system. In the years since Velikovsky first published his books *Worlds in Collision* and *Earth in Upheaval*, the information obtained from our technological achievements has constantly surprised mainstream scientists, inexorably forcing them toward a reconsideration of his thesis. They move in that direction with great reluctance, failing quite frequently to disseminate their changing views to the world at large, and consistently failing to acknowledge the original source of their new viewpoints when they grudgingly offer them to the public. Consequently, while our natural sciences are just now starting to turn back to their catastrophic roots, their new perspective has not yet filtered down to the man on the street. The common person continues to accept the notions of stability and slow, continuous change that were so loudly insisted upon as recently as a few short decades ago. It is to Immanuel Velikovsky's credit that he persisted with his views in the face of a massed onslaught by contemporary mainstream science. And it is probably the embarrassment of the Velikovsky episode that spanned two of those decades that is causing our modern science to backtrack with such furtive silence.

Backtracking it is indeed. The increasingly popular focus, stimulated by the impact of comet Shoemaker-Levy 9 on Jupiter in 1994 and the recognition of numerous impact craters on earth previously thought to be of volcanic origin, is of asteroid collisions with Earth and the consequences of such events on our history and future. Graham Hancock provides an excellent overview of this new catastrophism in *The Mars Mystery*, clearly tracing a hypothesis, gleaned from a variety of sources, of how our world (and our planetary neighbors) came to find itself in such unhappy circumstances. According to a this hypothesis, presented very briefly here, our solar system passed through a portion of the galaxy that disturbed the Oort Cloud of cometary bodies. About five million years ago this disturbance caused a very large object to slip out of a stable orbit, slowly heading toward the inner planets. By fifty thousand years ago, this object had come sufficiently close to our region that it was influenced by Jupiter's gravity, which thrust it into an elliptical orbit between Jupiter and the Sun. The orbit itself made it a potential threat to Earth and its neighbors, but with the single object, large as it apparently was, the odds were against a collision event. However, under gravitational stresses induced by Jupiter and the Sun, it began to break up, greatly increasing the chance of a planet coming into contact with one of the pieces. According to Hancock, this did happen eventually, possibly as recently as ten thousand years ago. The event caused severe impact events on Earth as well as on Mars and the Moon. Mars appears to have fared the worst, having been stripped of a large portion of not only its atmosphere but its surface in the cataclysm. The Tharsis Bulge, in fact, may represent a distortion caused by the impact of a massive asteroid-like object into the opposing side. The Taurid meteor stream is an apparent remnant of the original object. Ominously, recent investigations of this stream furnish some evidence that it represents a significant future danger to Earth, as the continuous precession of their point of collision may bring our planet into contact with larger elements of the meteor stream.

The hypothesis generally ignores Velikovsky and his pioneering thesis of a comet originating in Jupiter. It also ignores the Biblical time frame, including Noah's Flood. While all three accounts ultimately result in the same order of effects with the two extra-Biblical accounts easily fitting into the Biblical time frame, the two differ in some important respects. Hancock's asteroid thesis presumes a relatively small object, on the order of five to ten kilometers, traveling at a very high velocity relative to earth, directly impacting the surface like a massive bullet. Velikovsky's comet, on the other hand, is of planetary size but approaches quite near and perhaps even orbits briefly or partially under the influence of both gravitational and electrical forces without actually colliding with the earth. An asteroid approaching from the dayside would be visible for perhaps a minute or less before the collision event; it is difficult to reconcile this brevity of view with underlying folklore describing terrifying apparitions in the sky that take on recognizable forms. It is equally difficult to imagine an asteroid impact as the source of the kind of disturbance to the earth's rotation that led to Joshua's long day and the long night in the Americas. On the other hand, it is just as difficult to explain the numerous and supposedly recent impact craters on Earth, Mars, and the Moon in terms of Velikovsky's comet.

Perhaps the implication of the surprisingly dramatic effect on the impact of the Shoemaker-Levy 9 fragments on Jupiter should be reexamined. It is possible that this relatively minor event actually furnishes corroboration for Velikovsky's thesis while reconciling it to its asteroid contender. What if the asteroid hypothesis was correct, but its primary target was Jupiter itself, in addition to the smaller terran planets? If a truly enormous asteroid impacted this giant planet at great speed, could it not involve sufficient energy to cause more than a Tharsis-like bulge on the other side of Jupiter, and to actually initiate the ejection of a hot, planet-sized mass from the mother planet? Could not this secondary object, birthed out of a high-energy asteroid impact, then proceed through the inner planets as the very comet of which Velikovsky spoke? This is mere conjecture, but it is worth investigating further, for it would certainly reconcile the differing views into a cohesive picture that is consistent with both what we observe today and the folklore of yesterday.

Even the newer asteroid view, however, remains essentially private to the scientific world. Of this particular fact there is little doubt. Our institutions, both secular and Christian, continue to push the old uniformitarian view.

Graham Hancock, among others, has expressed his deep concern over the failure of the scientific community to give public voice to the emerging catastrophic paradigm. But if the secular community has suffered an intellectual impoverishment at the hands of the uniformitarians, Christians have fared even worse. The havoc wrought against them by this false science has turned their system of faith into a chaotic mess. Secularly-oriented theologians continue to insist to the public that God's domain is of such limited scope as to rule out the possibility of a universal flood. Timid pastors, swayed by their outspoken onslaught, either refuse to address the issue or parrot the secular beliefs. But even as they speak, the science that they claim for the justification of their stance, as we have noted, is quietly backtracking in betrayal: slinking away, under cover of public silence, to a position that supports the ubiquitous catastrophe. As long as the Christian public continues to receive its information from such shallow sources as television and the daily newspapers and timid pastors, it will continue to be misled regarding the so-called clash between religion and science. Worse, that public will continue to misunderstand the real nature of miracles and their interplay with perfectly natural events.

Instead of conflicting with our modern science, as the secular-minded and confused Christians among us presuppose, the properly-interpreted Word of God fully supports the shift in viewpoint that our science is currently undergoing. But this Word is capable not only of setting the record straight, but of extending our science to new frontiers. Considering that our God also created the universe with its physical laws governing its electromagnetic and gravitational interactions, we may also find in Scripture a deeper meaning to these fundamental relationships, and of the marvel of life itself, than we can achieve out of our secular-based science, the "soft" elements of which are themselves riddled with myths.

Ironically, the scientific community's earlier refusal to accept catastrophism now may be the cause of its present consternation. Surprised and somewhat alarmed by the impact of Comet Shoemaker-Levy 9 into Jupiter, they were further unsettled by the Alvarez team's linkage of the extinction of the dinosaurs with the impact of an extraterrestrial object. Roused into action by such events, some respected members of the scientific community have fielded a search for other impact craters around the earth. They have found them in numbers sufficient to generate an additional measure of concern. Now that they have turned around to embrace the notion of our catastrophic history, they are shifting their attention to the cosmos, looking for possible new threats. Their efforts have attracted government interest just within the last couple of decades, its delay in response due primarily to its past uniformitarian bias, preventing it from considering as real the potential of imminent catastrophe from space.

The Appendices to this section present admittedly partial lists of facts which are in serious conflict with the mythical paradigm that remains in current favor with the public. Specifically, Appendices 4-1 and 4-2 summarize in outline form the primary information and arguments presented by a number of prominent modern authors in (A) support of their catastrophist theses and (B) rebuttal of the uniformitarian dogma.

Extensive as they are, the fact that these lists only scratch the surface indicates how far astray we have been led by the desire to remove our God from the bounds of objective reality. The references listed in those appendices are highly recommended for persons who wish to obtain some in-depth understanding of the controversy over the past several decades between the uniformitarianism which most of us have been taught in school and the thesis of recent catastrophism. As the serious reader of these books will quickly appreciate, their primary focus is secular rather than religious. Nevertheless, their viewpoints have a great potential impact on the Christian individual's appreciation of the truth of Scripture.

There is a strong possibility that those who insist on a mythical interpretation of Scripture are themselves the victims of an enormous irony in accepting as truth certain scientific notions that are in reality nothing but myths. Paul writes of this possibility in his Second letter to the Thessalonians:

For the mystery of iniquity doth already work: only he who now letteth will let, until he be taken out of the way. And then shall that Wicked be revealed, whom the Lord shall consume with the spirit of his mouth, and shall destroy with the brightness of his coming: Even him, whose coming is after the working of Satan with all power and signs and lying wonders, And with all deceivableness of unrighteousness in them that perish; because they received not the love of truth, that they might be saved.

And for this cause God shall send them strong delusion, that they should believe a lie: That they all might be damned who believed not the truth, but had pleasure in unrighteousness.

Appendix 4-1
Condensed Outline of Items Supporting Thesis of Historical Catastrophes Beyond the Present Scale

Bibliography key for outline:

BF - Donald W. Patten, *The Biblical Flood and the Ice Epoch,* Pacific Meridian Publishing Company (1968)

CS - Charles Ginenthal, *Carl Sagan & Immanuel Velikovsky,* New Falcon Publications (1995)

EU - Immanuel Velikovsky, *Earth in Upheaval,* Dell Publishing Company (Laurel Edition) (1968)

GF - John C. Whitcomb and Henry M. Morris, *The Genesis Flood,* The Presbyterian and Reformed Publishing Company (1989)

JR - John R. Gribbin and Stephen H. Plagemann, *The Jupiter Effect Reconsidered,* Vintage Books (Random House) (1982)

MK - Charles H. Hapgood, *Maps of the Ancient Sea Kings,* E. P. Dutton (1979)

PP - Charles H. Hapgood, *The Path of the Pole,* Adventures Unlimited Press (1999)

SG - Ed. Dale Ann Pearlman, *Stephen J. Gould and Immanuel Velikovsky,* Ivy Press Books (1996)

TR - Walter Alvarez, *T. Rex and the Crater of Doom,* Princeton University Press (1997)

VOR - Robert M. Schoch, *Voices of the Rocks,* Harmony Books (Random House) (1999)

VR - Ed. Stephen L. Talbott, *Velikovsky Reconsidered,* Warner Books (1966)

WC - Immanuel Velikovsky, *Worlds in Collision,* Pocket Books (Simon & Schuster) (1977)

Note 1: Hapgood postulates a cause within the earth rather than an object from space for his catastrophic pole shifts. Nevertheless, some of the evidence he produces to demonstrate that one or more catastrophes did indeed occur can apply equally well to a space-oriented thesis regarding the cause. A more serious potential problem with Hapgood's work is his acceptance of uniformitarian assumptions in the application of the relatively new technical methods of geomagnetic mapping and isotope dating. For example, his dating sequence of geomagnetic samples follows that proposed over a century ago (with very little justification and even less scientific knowledge) for the locations of the samples within the standard geologic column. In fact, different elements of this standard column may represent little more than the pattern of nearly-simultaneous deposition arising from the same catastrophic event. The interpretation of his results should take into consideration the possibility that the uniformitarian bias will lead to significant errors, not only with regard to dates, but of the number and assumed location of polar positions. The works of Alvarez and Schoch should also be treated carefully. Despite his claims regarding the paradigm shift away from uniformitarianism that his science of geology is presently undergoing, Schoch quite frequently displays a uniformitarian bias, including his unquestioning acceptance of the dating of meteorite ALH84001 and its subsequent journey to earth. The same may be said of the Alvarez' dating of the extinction of the dinosaurs. Both

Alvarez and Schoch provide interesting insights into the politics of science and of how the mentor may pass his mindset to his student along with facts and techniques.

Note 2: The notation '(P)' preceding an item in the outline below indicates that the item was predicted on the basis of the thesis of recent catastrophism, usually in opposition to the generally accepted theories at the time of prediction, prior to its confirmation through the recent acquisition of scientific data via the Apollo missions, space probes, and other technological advances.

Earth

Geological

Surface features

> Ubiquity of enormous lava beds of recent origin, e.g. Alaska, Canada, Washington/Oregon States, Deccan Plateau of India, Argentina, Brazil, South Africa, strongly indicates recent volcanic activity orders of magnitude greater than occurs at present; in many cases, this lava is intermixed with sedimentary rock, requiring that its origin be more recent than the supposed sedimentation process that usually is associated with great age - GF126,127,137-139; VOR28,29

> Recent *and ongoing* changes in significant geological features. These changes may point to a continuing adjustment to the last catastrophic episode rather than to a recent or current change in the weather pattern or other modern factors.

> Desertification of the Sahara - EU94-98; GF314

> Drying up of lakes; recency of some lakebeds - EU94-98, 169, 170, 265; GF313-318

> Recent extinction of many volcanoes and reduction in earthquake intensity (some investigators argue that earthquake frequency is currently increasing, but present activity is less than that recorded for 7th and 8th centuries B.C.) - EU142-147, 182, 183, 186-189; VOR134

Youth of earth's crust

Crustal volume insufficient, in terms of current rates of lava emission from volcanic activity alone, to support commonly accepted geological dating of several billion years - GF389-391

Extreme youth of water-created features on land

Coulees in Eastern Washington State and elsewhere. The enormity of the coulee system of the Columbia Plateau in Washington State has led to a general agreement that its cause was a huge flood. However, the prevailing theory of a breached ice dam has been discarded by some as highly improbable due to the mechanics of ice. This has led to a rival hypothesis of a tidal wave from the Pacific Ocean or the Gulf of Mexico. This newer theory is supported by the existence of erratic boulders and the skeletons of beached whales elsewhere; the boulders are of enormous size and were not deposited by glacial action, since their deposition followed the melting of the ice sheets. The height of the tidal wave has been estimated at around 5,000 feet. - CS186-188; GF149; VOR140-142

Youth and brevity of existing glaciers - EU156, 157, 190, 265, WC44; GF292-330

Youth of riverbeds and falls (Niagara, Mississippi, others) as determined from erosion rates vs. erosion distance from known beginning point - EU154-156, 158, 159, 181, 190, 265

Major rivers lie within channels much larger than they are presently capable of cutting; given the many different hypotheses presented to explain this discrepancy, logic favors the existence of temporary flows arising from catastrophe. Arizona's Grand Canyon, for example, shows evidence of having been rapidly carved out by hydraulic action (rapidly moving water) on a scale far beyond what is possible with mechanisms observable at present (as determined by engineering model tests) - GF153,154, 224-227

Extreme youth, short duration of lakes - EU149, 151-154, 162-164, 190, 191, 195; WC44, 45; GF313-318

Sudden formation of Greenland ice cap 3-4,000 years ago - SG431

Patterns, distribution of water-related features on land

Pattern of polar ice: lack of ice in northern Greenland, Alaska, Siberia - EU50, 106; WC40

Large-scale, recent tilting of lakebeds - EU 169, 170, 265

Massive peneplains (areas eroded flat beneath strata) formed by processes not evident today - GF148,149

Evident extensive water-distributed flat surfaces so recent as to be virtually untouched by erosion (Great Plains of U.S., from Rockies to the Mississippi, Kansas, Texas, New Mexico; Tibetan plateaus) could have been formed only by water movement of a magnitude that must necessarily have been catastrophic. Many such plateaus exhibit horizontal strata of marine (fossil) deposition of enormous thickness at great heights (e.g. vicinity of Arizona's Grand Canyon) - GF149-153

Mountains

Great circle patterns of earth's major mountain ranges and rifts, height similarity with ranges on moon indicates source was gravitational stress from an external body - EU91; WC6; BF75-90

Extreme youth (postglacial) of mountain building, on enormous scale, in Alps, Rockies, Himalayas, Andes: in some cases, contemporary with modern man; metamorphic rocks attest to enormous stresses after deposition of sediments; no satisfactory explanation exists in uniformitarian context - EU74, 88, 89, 266; GF127, 128, 139-142; GF312

Combination of mountain ranges, upthrust patterns and rifts indicates displacement of geographical poles, and corresponding expansive, compressive stresses involving equatorial bulge (27 mile diametric difference between poles and equator) - EU114, 122-125; PP220-224 [see Note 1]

Formation of many prominent mountain ranges indicates recent lateral overthrust of many miles, far too much for radial shrinkage to be the major factor - EU74-76, 132-134, 145, 146; WC36

Strata, soil, rocks

Upthrusting of strata containing paleolithic fossils - WC36, 37

Twisting of strata indicates massive violence - EU75, 78, 132-134

Numerous instances of alternating strata of terrestrial, freshwater, and marine fossils - EU23

Strata of fossilized fish found at extreme altitudes on tops of high mountains, including Himalayas - WC35

Beds of marble, sandstone, limestone exhibit compaction to such a degree as to mystify investigators with regard to possible source - EU25

Recent mixing of ice with igneous rock during formation of rock as found in ice caves of Eastern Washington State. Presence of ice in caves is very recent (ice was used to preserve food in 19th century) or ice still exists - BF120-124

Erratic boulders displaced by hundreds of miles from origins - EU21-23, 38, 39, 67, 135-138

Meteor Impacts

Lakes and craters on the sea floor have been found earthwide: Carolinas, Mexico, Labrador, Arabia, Northern Alaska, Yukon Territory, Caribbean Sea, North Sea, Kalahari Desert, Southwestern Australia, Northeastern Bolivia. These depressions have common features of groupings in large numbers at each site (most have numbers ranging from thousands to hundreds of thousands), ellipticity, parallelism, and extreme youth (less than 5000 years age, as indicated by lack of erosion, filling in of depressions) - EU98, 99, 266, 267; CS181-186

(P) Meteorite found in Antarctic has signature of Martian atmosphere; generally acknowledged as having a Martian source - CS380; VOR117,118 [see Note 1]

Barringer Crater in Arizona - CS185,186

Ice Age Indicators

Enormous extent of past glaciation (as proposed by uniformitarian geology) is incompatible with uniformitarian mechanisms - GF142-144

(P) Indications of youth, sudden onset, sudden termination of ice ages - SG37, EU107-125, 148-164, 267; PP45-59

Modern human remains in direct association with ice age animals, many of which are extinct - EU159-162, 193-196; WC43, 44

Combination of Ice age and surface features points to pole shift, as does geographical shape, eccentric locations of ice encroachment and recession (in some cases, from equator toward poles; lack of ice in northern Alaska, Siberia, Greenland) - EU116, 122-125, WC40, 329; BF117-120; PP45-59

Closer proximity of polar ice mass to magnetic than geographic pole (which has subsequently undergone an extensive migration) suggests polar accumulation of ice from space, concentrated along paths of highest magnetic flux - BF117-120; PP47-49

Glacial moraines - corroborate above, in that anomalous directions indicate melting from higher toward lower latitudes; tropical locations of some supposed glaciers as well as the numbers, sizes and locations of erratic boulders supposedly carried by ice creates difficulties with uniformitarian assumptions - EU 45-48, 135-138

Excess dust in bottom layers of glacial ice - SG431

Onset of ice age requires catastrophic sequence: excessive heating initially, suddenly followed by excessive cooling. Neither excessive cooling alone, nor excessive heating alone, will produce observed encroachment of ice, much of which can only be obtained by partial evaporation of sea beyond current level. EU127-130; WC39, 40

(P) Magnetic torque causing pole shift has been postulated - anticipated results of this event represent excellent fit with observed characteristics of ice age. EU107-115, 129-134, 140

Rifts

Systems of rifts and lineaments - indicate tangential tension, loss of earth's angular momentum (rotation velocity) at some time, and/or pole shifts, and/or shifting of earth's crust with respect to flattened poles, equatorial bulge - SG102,103; VR37; EU91-93

Great circle patterns of midocean rifts - EU93; BF75-90

Seabed lineament patterns are indicative of rapid change of earth's angular momentum - SG102,103

Shoreline features

Strand lines - indicate sudden uniform, simultaneous sea level drop of 18-20 feet on global scale 3-4,000 years ago - SG427; EU59, 85, 87, 88, 171-174, 191, 192, 264; GF294, 324-326; BF73; PP227-232; CS189, 190

Hudson River bottom extends out into Atlantic past continental shelf, indicating large-scale submergence of land area - EU102-104; GF125, 126

Change in level of Mediterranean Sea - VOR55

Non-volcanic seamounts over a mile below the sea furnish evidence of having been above the surface - GF125

Sea, Seabed features

Quantity of ocean water insufficient, in terms of current geological dating, for conservatively-estimated input rates of juvenile water from volcanic activity - GF387-389

Composition of saltwater

Source of saltwater chemistry, composition a mystery (including source of chlorine) - WC33,383

Quantity of salt in sea insufficient, in terms of current geological dating, for known rates of river transport of sodium and chlorine - GF385-387

Nonuniform patterns of submergence - VR76

Sediments and bottom

Inexplicably thin sedimentation, unexpected distribution - VR77; EU101, 102, 209, 210, 264

Sediments - core samples disagree with uniformitation presuppositions - EU103

Beach sand found midocean - EU100

Submerged forests of young age found on bed of North Sea along with human artifacts - EU165, 174-177, 265

White ash found in oceanic sedimentation indicates major meteor-related events - VR134, 207; EU101-105, 264; WC6

Reddish clay in Pacific seabed is similar to that found on land in China (which is alien to that area) and is associated with meteors via nickel deposits - EU67, 68, 104, 105

Underground features

Lava of Northwest/Washington State and Deccan Trap of India represent enormous lava floods - up to a mile thick over hundreds of thousands of square miles (all ctive volcanoes of world combined would be unable to produce a fraction of this volume); human artifact (figurine of baked clay) embedded within lava a considerable distance (320 ft.) from surface - EU89, 90, 143; CS223

Maximum of volcanic activity (quantity and size of volcanoes) dated coincident with last ice age at about 3400 years ago (also coincident with Exodus); this activity included Thera explosion - CS157,158; VOR89

Quantity of earth's internal heat, its location and its non uniform distribution suggests friction heating by rapid, large-scale movement of crust over mantle - PP224-227

Petroleum

(P) Petroleum deposits - youth (< 4200 years) per radiocarbon dating, likelihood of extraterrestrial origin of at least some deposits; irrelevance of oil sources to historical geology and inability of geology to account for formation - SG247; VR134, 135; EU267; GF429-437; CS247,250

Petroleum is found in association with helium. Helium is not a product of biological processes. This weakens uniformitarian argument regarding origin of petroleum. - CS248

(P) Recent discovery of petroleum and natural gas beneath meteor crater in Sweden may establish direct link of petroleum with comets - CS250

High pressure of natural gas deposits indicates very recent formation - CS250

Embedded Biological masses

Enormous areas in continental U.S., Alaska, South America, Italy, China, Burma, India, Germany containing compacted masses of crushed and dismembered remains of extinct and surviving plant and animal species. The remains show evidence of both recency and extreme violence. Human artifacts have been found in the midst of some beds. At some locations, unnatural signs of coexistence of carnivores with herbivores has been found (as would be found in panic situations), as well as unnatural ratios of these two types. EU13-20, 26, 28-31, 56-61, 64-73, 81-83, 191, 192, 211-213, 261, 262

Nature of coal seams is more consistent with water deposition under catastrophic circumstances than uniformitarian processes - GF277-279

General composition of strata

Large areas of alternating strata of petrified wood, ice, petrified ash, and sand - EU18, 19

Atmospheric

Presence of free oxygen (not all combined with iron in earth's atmosphere) contradicts uniformitarian sequences postulated for formation of planet - WC33

Excess of Tritium 3 in atmosphere supports hypothetical water canopy in past, as well as differing levels of atmospheric radiocarbon prior to flood, making past C14 dating suspect - GF375

Quantity of helium in atmosphere insufficient, in terms of current geological dating, for known quantities in rocks and rate of escape into air - GF384,385

(P) Atmospheric components suggest atmospheric exchange with Mars, Venus - CS286,287, 298, 379-383

Evidence of climate change

Pollen density, type as function of stratum indicates recent abrupt climate changes concurrent with violent geological events - EU166, 170, 171, 265; GF304-311

Tree ring counts indicate that no living tree is older than Exodus disaster (ca 1500B.C.); tree ring variations indicate sudden climate changes concurrent with ends of dynasties, civilizations. Tree-ring dating of Sequoia

Gigantea and Bristlecone Pines yields maximum ages of 3300 and 4600 years, respectively. These are oldest dates of any living matter on earth, and indicate an abrupt end of life at about the time corresponding to those ages. - EU167, 168; GF391-393

Ancient floral and faunal types and their state of preservation in Siberia and Alaska indicates sudden climate change; some (but not all) isotope dates are compatible with Noah's Flood, Exodus - PP258-279; CS172-174

Evidence of drastic climate change in Middle East - VOR40

Chemical, radioactive dating analyses of arctic, antarctic sea-floor samples and discovery of coal, wood and fossils indicates that the climates in these areas was recently temperate - PP61-67, 106,107; CS151-153; VOR101

Core sample studies indicate that in one recent ice-age interstadial event, the rate of temperature change was as high as 14 degrees Fahrenheit over a 15-year period - VOR147,197

Climate zone chemical analyses indicate pole shifts in support of geomagnetic findings - PP42-79

Climate zone fossil coral analyses support chemical analyses re extensive pole shifts - PP79-87

Ancient maps (from pre-Columbian sources), e.g. the Oronteus Finaeus map of Antarctica, display what could be interpreted as an ice-free Antarctica (as well as demonstrating a puzzling sophistication) - MK69-95; VOR98-100

Electromagnetic Features

(P) Extensive magnetic region above atmosphere (Van Allen Radiation Belt) unknown prior to Velikovsky's prediction - VR68,77,82; EU272, 273; WC6; GF353,354; CS93

(P) Recent reversals of earth's magnetic field (some independently dated coincident with Exodus, Amos time frames) - VR72,73,78, 135; EU138-142, 263; WC6; WC126-128; CS145,146,159-161

Geomagnetic mapping points to a number of rapid, extensive shifts in the location of the magnetic poles with respect to the surface geography. Under the common assumption that the magnetic poles remain in proximity to the axis of the earth's rotation, this indicates an extensive shifting of the geographic surface with respect to the axis. This shifting is not explainable in terms of continental drift - PP4-39 [see Note 1]

Magnetic disturbances linked to Tunguska explosion - VOR186

(see also Ice Age under Geological re magnetic torque)

Biological

(P) Recent corals display signs of 360-day year, as predicted by Velikovsky - SG104

(P) Fossil vines, shells - samples from both northern and southern hemispheres display reversals in direction of twist - VR73,78

Mass fossil graveyards of fauna on scale and diversity (in many cases species from around earth concentrated in single formations) for which present processes are utterly inadequate to explain, suggest a global event - GF156-161; PP280-294

Location (e.g. caves), condition of fossil remains commonly found throughout world, and degree of preservation (in many cases soft parts of animals, including insects, and clorophyll of plants) indicate a suddenness and violence for which accepted geological processes cannot account - GF158-161

Strata and large erratic boulders interbedded with coal seams indicates violent hydraulic deposition - GF165

Preservation of footprints (e.g. in Texas, where dinosaur and human footprints are seen together) indicates recent catastrophic event, and contradicts accepted dating of either humans or dinosaurs - GF166-168, 172-175

Extinctions

Sudden worldwide extinction of dinosaurs, accompanied by layer of iridium ash - GF279-281

Sudden extinction of mammoths and other animals; very recent or present edible state of some remains - EU15-18, 164, 192, 214, 215; WC40-43; BF104-109; PP249-279

Simultaneous mass extinctions of large varieties of animals in diverse locations; at some locations human remains found violently intermixed with those of extinct animals, e.g. saber-toothed tigers; some mass extinctions in S. America dated simultaneous with 13,500 ft. rise of Cordilleras above sea level - EU213-218; CS191,192, 208-211

Study of heat transfer vs. decomposition rate of mammoth's internal organs yield sudden temperature change down to minus 150 degrees Fahrenheit, found nowhere on earth at present - CS199

Misplaced flora, fauna -

Misplaced latitudes: remains of mammoths, buttercups in Siberia; food in mammoths' stomachs alien to latitudes where remains found; accepted theories unable to account for extent of frozen fauna; deaths attributed to suffocation under violent circumstances indicating recency and water transportation; elephant, rhinocerus, hippopotomus bones in England (1450 ft. elevation); reindeer remains in France; corals in Spitzbergen; coal beds in Antarctica and other regions of excess cold and little or no food - EU16-20, 51-53, 61-67, 73, 95, 134, 261, 262; WC37, 40-43; WC330-332, 383,384, GF156,162, 288-291; CS200

Incompatible terrain: remains of whales, marine deposits found inland at high elevations at diverse locations around world; remains of tortoises on hills too steep for travel - EU53-55; CS161-172

Kinematic

Synchronicity of earth's rotation with those of Mars and Venus as w ould be expected from Velikovsky's scenario. The length of the Martian day is about a half hour more than earth's; Venus' rotation is linked to earth's by synchronicity at inferior conjunction) - WC365; CS 135,136

Alignment of earth's ecliptic with that of Mars (Mars' angle of obliquity is 24 degrees vs. earth's of 23 ½ degrees, although the range of earth's tilt {21.6 to 24.5 degrees} brackets that of Mars' current value) - WC23, 24, 365; EU126,127

Close conjunction of Mars, Earth in 15-year intervals (interval is the same as the period between major catastrophes in the 7th and 8th centuries B.C. and agrees with Biblical events in the Book of Amos) - SG328

(P) Earth's rotational rate changes with sunspot activity, supporting Velikovsky's thesis that electromagnetic forces play an important role in planetary, cometary motions - VR176-194; JR81-95

Chandler wobble indicates past catastrophic perturbation; decay rate of wobble indicates recency - VR95, 96; EU113; CS225

Possibility of celestial reorientation of axis by gyroscopic precession - fits survivability of earth under Velikovsky's catastrophic condition, including energy input but with minimal heating - VR172-176

Archaeological

No trace of civilization past about fourth millenium B.C. (some archaeologists date the beginning of civilization beyond this time, but their dating methods use uniformitarian assumptions and are therefore suspect) - GF393-396

Habitation of Pacific islands placed no earlier than 3500 years ago - CS191

Synchronicity of destruction of civilizations indicates common, immense catastrophe: Israeli, Egyptian, Minoan (Crete), European lake dwellings, Thera, Troy, Ugarit - EU168-171, 178-192; VOR56

Nature of digs throughout entire middle east and other diverse locations indicate multiple, extensive cataclysmic destructions and burials in historical times - SG38,418; EU178-192, 256; WC37; CS386

Weathering of Sphinx attributable either to drastic climate change, flood, or both (if flood was the cause, lower portions could have been differentially preserved by *partial* coverage in sand) - VOR42,47,48

Tiahuanacu - composition, sudden tilting and lowering of nearby Lake Titicaca (Peru and Bolivia), artifacts indicate sudden rise in historic time from sea level to well over 10,000 feet. This indication is corroborated by evidence of population too large for support by current means, agricultural terraces too high for plant growth (up to 18,400 ft.); studies indicate that economy suddenly changed from fishing to agriculture - EU83-89; PP280-286; CS167-172

Ollantaytambo (Peru): built in presently uninhabitable region, constructed of blocks for which present terrain does not support transport - EU87

Caves in Alps, Himalayas with human artifacts in midst of glaciers at high elevations indicates drastic increase in elevation during man's habitation - EU76, 77; CS161-167

Art, sculptural representations of elephants in America - CS205-208

Recent discovery of ancient villages and human activity (Yakutsk, Ipiutak, Spitzbergen) in arctic locations too cold to support evident lifestyle - EU259-261; WC239, 330-332; CS202

Location of ancient sundials and waterclocks at latitudes incompatible with designs, operation - SG100; EU255; WC324-328

Otherwise competent calendric and astronomical data of Egyptians, Babylonians do not agree with present order (uniformitarian assumption is sloppy observation- a more reasonable assumption, given the known accuracy of other observations by same civilizations is that the observations were indeed correct); widespread occurrence elsewhere of calendars which do not correspond to current length of month or year; equally universal instances of calendric changes; Ancient Hindu, Greek, Chinese astronomical data do not agree with present order or latitude of observations -SG81;VR97; EU255; WC317-321

C14 dating of Tutankhamon's burial objects contradict common dating of Egyptian dynasties - SG29; EU258, 259

Star chart in Senmut's tomb shows Orion following Sirius, indicating reversal of earth's direction of rotation - SG98, WC316,317

Brahman sky chart indicates movement of location of poles - WC329

Hindu tablets and Babylonian Ninsianna (Venus) tablets (Ammisaduqa) show orbits of earth and Venus that do not correspond to current order. Orbital calculations using Ammisaduqa data shows support of Velikovsky's historical reconstruction - SG84-87, VR94, 110-124; WC205-207, 317-321; CS364-368

Babylonian, Hindi planetary records with Venus missing – VR preface, WC170-173

Dated earthquake records from Babylon ca. 600-700 B.C. indicate a frequency and duration well beyond modern experience. These earthquakes are associated with Mars - corroborated with evidence at numerous places in the Mideast of massive destruction by earthquake where earthquakes are now rare, including Troy and Jericho; records of earthquakes in Rome ca. 200 B.C. (57 in a year) support thought that earthquake activity was greater in past at that location - WC279,282

Altered orientation of temple foundations; ancient temples and obelisks no longer face east, as would be expected from otherwise precise construction - VR97; EU255; WC321-324

Orientation of Pyramid of Gizeh 4 minutes of arc to the west of its original alignment with true north suggests geographical movement of earth with respect to axis in historical times. Shift was hypothesized by Sir Flinders Petrie in 1940 - CS398,399

Otherwise enigmatic motivation behind construction of Stonehenge and other ancient observatories, temples, and obelisks is readily explainable in terms of catastrophic change in orbits of earth and potentially threatening objects; corroborated by apparent astronomical purpose but lack of correlation between construction and present astronomical order - VR99, 101; WC321-324

Possible correspondence of 56 hole-pattern at Stonehenge with the 'sacred to Typhon' nature of the number 56 per Pythagorean secret teaching - VR108

Repeated revisions of Stonehenge (built five times with differing layouts in each case) indicates recurring changes to astronomical order - VR101

Possible astronomical function of Nabta, Gizeh artifacts similar to Stonehenge - VOR57,58,77

(P) Revision of current Egyptian historical sequence - WC382

Widespread population shifts, abandonment of civilizations around late 12th century A. D. in Asia, Polynesia, and Central and South America recently linked to impact of bolides - VOR211-217

Anthropological

Enigmatic brevity of man's recorded history is readily explainable in catastrophic context, unexplainable otherwise - WC22; GF393-396

Conservative extrapolation from population statistics (numbers vs. dates and rates of population growth) indicates initialization of human population in fourth millenium B.C. - GF396-398

Repeated extensive cultural destructions in Middle East, China, and Americas, apparently attended by catastrophe. Numerous indications that common notion of linear progression of societies may be wrong; early civilizations may have been sophisticated and beaten into stone-age existence by catastrophic events - SG419ff; EU256-260; VOR35,52 [this is a misstatement of Christian teaching],55,58,60128-130

Biblical longevities and post-flood declines are supportive of different pre-Flood atmospheric regime - GF399-405; BF194-224

Common theme of ages ending in violence, dominating agency variously water, fire, earthquake, wind; common traditions of flood and other catastrophic events (As Velikovsky noted, stories have the same elements in very different settings): Etrurians, Greeks, Tibetans, Hindu Indians, Persians, Chinese, Incas, Aztecs, Mayas, Polynesians, Icelanders, Hebrews, Armenians, Arabs, American Indians - WC46-50, WC195-201, 263, 303-315; BF164-193; VOR139

Common theme of new sun (implying reappearance after protracted darkness on different orbital path) following violent end of age; coupled with widespread references to sun rising, setting in reversed direction of rotation, corroborated by star charts (also see Archaeological) - WC50-52,WC166-169

Widespread references to 360-day year, with later changes made as tack-ons; virtually all ancient civilizations in both hemispheres had 360-day years and 30-day months, including those civilizations with the capability of handling fractions and demonstrated precision and sophistication in the employment of math - WC333-361; CS50-56

Common theme of recalculating seasons after period of darkness; recalculation sometimes associated with Venus; importance of Venus in calendrics - WC166-168, WC202-205, WC217-219, 333-361

Israeli, Babylonian dismay at irregularity of Venus sightings - WC207-211

Common theme of cometary apparition, sometimes head in battle with tail (coma, as disturbed by gravity, electromagnetic interaction); widespread worship of cow or bull; widespread theme of planetary battles in ancient art and literature - Vishnu & crooked serpent (Hindi), Zeus & Typhon (Greek), dragons (China,), feathered serpent (Mexico), Isis & Set (Egyptian); pillar of fire, column of smoke (Bible - Israel) - Vrpreface;WC95-99,284; CS75-78; VOR14,57,59,62-65

Foreknowledge of Mars' satellites - number, size, orbital speed - WC283,284; BF184-187; CS372-377

Astronomical discrepancies (greater than accepted accuracy of observations) in ancient recordings of solar eclipses - SG88,89

Alignment of Biblical (Israeli) and Egyptian histories with corresponding accounts of identical catastrophes - SG255; EU256-260

Correspondence of Joshua's long day (Biblical - middle east) with long night in America (opposite side of earth) in same year, as described in Mayan records;

synchronization of start of new time in Israel with Mexico ca. -747 (Mars); - SG97, WC55-62; WC218,219

Correspondence of Exodus plagues with similarly-described events in Mayan, Greek, Egyptian, Babylonian, Iranian, Finnish records - WC63-81

Correspondence of Exodus post-plague events with similarly-described events elsewhere - WC82-211

Accompaniment of Joshua's static sun (and later with Amos' and Hezekiah's moving sun) with earthquakes and meteorite activity - WC58-60,239-243

Ubiquitous (Babylonian, Chinese, Indic, American) association of Venus with cometary attributes, comet-like glyph - SG74,75,455; WC173-176

Widespread worship of Venus (and later with Mars), as well as cows, dragons, other apparitions has possible roots in bizarre patterns of coma, distorted by mechanical (and possibly electrical) interaction with earth's atmosphere; Hebrew worship (or veneration, at least) by association of archangels with planets (Venus=Michael, Mars=Gabriel); - WC91-95, WC183-195, WC244-249,258-260,266-273, 295-301, 307

Widespread theme of interplay among planets, earth and moon - WC251-259,363; BF166-193

Theme shared by Israelis and Greeks of sun moving forward or back before it should, and of changes in positions/paths of constellations, associated with great violence upon the earth in 8th,7th centuries B.C. (including destruction of Sennacherib's army, also shared by Chinese, who described unnatural movement/position of sun similar to Joshua account) - WC223-227,239-244, 298, 311, 315; BF45,46

Inexplicable importance of astrologers, stargazers, and prognosticators in ancient civilizations; equally inexplicable fixation on Venus, use of superlatives in description in many societies - SG74,75; VOR73

Babylonian reference to sighting Venus at or near zenith, an impossibility in current order - SG74

Common theme of transformation, or birth, of Venus from comet, and of change from four-planet to five-planet system - WC166-173,WC177-180,247

(P) Verification (1953) of Velikovsky's prediction, based on catastrophic interpretation of history, that Minoan B script would be found to be early form of Greek - SG38; EU258

Periodic nature of some catastrophic events (e.g. 50-53 year interval between Exodus and Joshua) agrees with dynamics of object in near-collision orbit with earth - WC63, WC163-166, WC216,219,220, 225

Nature of Biblical prophecies ca. -747 indicates enormous catastrophes of periodic nature (15 years-WCp.220) - WC215-223, 225

Widespread association of Mars with fear and destruction - WC244-274

Association of meteorites with planets - WC293,294

Relationship between 52-year period of fear and the planet Venus - WC164-166

Both the nature and sequence of recorded events (e.g. the plagues of the Exodus) pertaining to some catastrophes agrees with progressive interaction between object and earth as the distance between them diminishes - WC 63-108

Greek and South American references to time when man lived on earth before the appearance of the moon - VR124-128

Association of exceptional physical activity with destructive events: superhurricane - WC82-85; tsunamis and flooding - WC85-91, WC114-117, 159-162; apparitions in sky - WC91-95; parting of Red Sea with exceptional electromagnetic activity - WC100-103; low clouds, darkness - WC103,104,138-145; boiling earth and sea - WC105-110; super-earthquake - WC110-114; altered rotation, orbit of earth - WC118-137;

Explanation of manna as hydrocarbon derivative from coma of Venus - WC145-151

Association of hailstones suspended in air from Exodus events with Joshua, later events from prophets - WC152-156, 285-298

Venus was replaced by Mars in eighth century B.C. as a source of fear and worship (Israel, Greece, Rome, Troy, Mexico, China, India, Babylon). Velikovsky conjectures that Venus nearly collided with Mars, putting it in its stable planetary orbit and throwing Mars into a near-collision orbit with Earth. Velikovsky sees in Homer's *Iliad* an accurate and detailed picture of this event, reflected in earthwide violence and conflict between Greeks and Trojans, as well as Toltecs and Aztecs. Elements of this cosmic conflict have similar descriptions in Mexican, Chinese, Hindu, and Israeli, and Babylonian records - WC 250-265,270-274

Ancient literature describes how two planets (or comets) behave when they are very close to each other, including interplanetary discharges and including violence when one of the planets is Earth - WC274-278

Plato suggests a large change in Mideast climate - VOR122-125

Moon

Geological

Recency of heating catastrophes in presence of magnetic field as indicated by remanent magnetism (see electromagnetic section)

(P) Recency of heating catastrophes (est. about 10,000

years) as indicated by thermoluminescence studies - VR266, 267, 271; CS178-180

(P) Craters - impact, surface melting (bubbling) as indicated by massive craters (much larger than earth's) and unbroken bubbles, extensive surface glazing and extensive 'rays'; volcanic action, lava flows; current volcanic activity - VR86-88, 255, 256, 262, 264; EU144, 145, 269; WC362-364; CS227

Persisting bulge and mascons on moon indicate recent catastrophe, as do relatively high readings of radioactive materials in Imbrium Basin - CS228,229

Non uniform distribution of craters, favoring one hemisphere over the other; this phenomenon, which is also seen on Mars and Mercury, indicates the influence of an external object - CS39,40

(P) Rocks rich in oxygen, iron, chlorine, sulphur - VR89

(P) Recency of geological features. The lack of surface dust was a surprise during the moon landings, for which the lander was designed for several feet of dust - VR85; CS175,176; CS175-178

(P) Vestiges of water - VR256, 257

(P) Petroleum derivatives - VR74,88, 262

(P) Thermal gradient, interior to surface - VR89, 255, 256, 262; CS229

(P) Argon 36, 40, Neon of external origin - SG540,541; VR90, 23, 264

(P) Carbides - SG540,541

Lineaments (straight stress cracks) indicate loss of angular momentum - SG123

The pattern and height of lunar mountains is similar to that of earth and indicates gravitational stresses; maria and mountains on moon exhibit great circle pattern of distribution; maria are of recent origin as indicated by lack of dust, radioactivity level - BF46-48; CS225,226

(P) Frequent moonquakes; moonquakes exhibit pattern of two belts extending 2000 km across surface of moon, indicating subsurface rupture - VR257; CS226

(P) Escaping gases - VR256; WC6

Depletion of volatile elements in moon rocks compared to those on earth - VR264

Electromagnetic

(P) Coherent remanent magnetism, indicating global influence from external source - SG38,373,374, VR87,88, 256, 271, 273-275; CS93,94, 210

(P) Localized radioactivity near Aristarchus crater - predicted on presumption of interplanetary discharges - SG540,541, VR73,86-88, 255-257, 262, 263

(P) Rocking of moon as it traverses earth's magnetosphere - VR256

Kinematic

Moon exhibits wobble similar to Chandler Wobble on earth; caused by some catastrophic perturbation less than 20,000 years ago - CS224; VOR213 (also see Kinematic - earth)

Venus

Geological

(P) Inordinately hot surface; radiating more heat than absorbed from sun, which cannot be accounted for by Greenhouse theory - SG37,371,375,395,425, Vrintro,20,21,69, 133, 211-213, 215-217, 255, 777; WC6, 7,371-373; CS93, 300-321

(P) Decrease in temperature over observation time indicates recency of existence as planet and again contradicts the Greenhouse theory - VR83, 208, 217, 276-278

(P) Extremely low surface erosion, lack of soil - SG375,383; CS337-339

(P) Extensive cratering, vulcanism - SG134,389; VR214; CS327-333

(P) Higher surface features than sustainable for long durations, given estimated plasticity; Youth of elevated regions (less than expected relaxation time) - VR208,214; SG396; CS333-336

(P) relative abundance of primordial Argon 36, dearth of Argon 40 indicate extreme youth of planet - SG375,380; CS124; CS309

(P) Hydrocarbons in atmosphere - VR202-208, 217-230, 232-252; WC370,371

Discovery of water, more extensive in past – recent observation

(P) Iron, sulfur in atmosphere - VR246, 247

(P) Massive atmosphere (high surface pressure) - VR203, 211-213, 232, 255; WC6-8

Chemical composition of atmosphere (sulfuric acid, carbon dioxide) indicates youth of planet - CS292-294

Electromagnetic

(P) Net electrical charge of planet - VR83

Kinematic

(P) Retrograde rotation - SG37,375, VR41,44; WC8; CS336,337

Vestigial tail per Mariner 2 - SG463

(Almost) precise synchronicity of Venus' rotation with earth's orbit at inferior conjunction - SG213, VR41, 214, 255; CS135,136

(P) Very low eccentricity (.007) of Venus' present orbit supports Velikovsky's surmise of hot (very plastic) mantle; the circularization was noted by Velikovsky as having other precedents in our solar system - VR171, 172, 255; WC384; CS346-363

Differential rotational velocity of atmosphere and surface - VR207

Axis of rotation is perpendicular to ecliptic rather than plane of orbit - VR207 (also see Kinematic - earth)

Mars

Geological

(P) Impact craters, nonuniform hemispherical distribution, mascons - WC369; CS39,40; CS265,266

Enormous rifts, including crack over ¼ to 1/3 of surface; system of lineaments (straight cracks) indicate deceleration of angular momentum - SG117; VR139; WC365, 366, 369; CS267

Enormous volcano - largest in solar system - SG103; VR134

(P) Juvenile argon 36 - VR83; CS379-383

(P) Relative abundance of Neon and Argon - VR90,91; WC366-368; CS296

Atmospheric carbon dioxide, nitrogen-15 indicate recent change in atmosphere - CS295

Surface scars, sharpness of surface features vs. predicted erosion rates and observed erosion at some locations indicate youth of formation, catastrophe, as does evidence of past water and recent loss - SG117; VR134; CS258-273

Tarsus bulge indicates impact of enormous object on opposite side of planet - CS272

(P) Presence of organic molecules - VR83

Thermal imbalance - emits more heat than insolation allows - WCWC369

Electromagnetic

(P) Localized radioactivity indicates past interplanetary electrical discharge - VR73,86,87

Kinematic

Orbital speed of Phobos is greater than rotation of primary (Mars); contradicts accepted theory of satellite formation - WC29

Angular momentum conflicts with uniformitarian theory of planetary formation, orbital stability; indicates deceleration at some time in the past - VR134, 135, 139, 255

Rotational period of slightly over 24 hours is nearly synchronous with that of earth; inclination to ecliptic is also strikingly similar - VR139; WC23, 365

Period of favorable (minimum distance) opposition to earth of fifteen years agrees dramatically with fifteen-year periods of devastation on earth associated with Mars - WC364 (vs. WC215-223, 225) (also see Kinematic - earth)

Jupiter

Geological

Internal heat (surface temp > 1000 F), turbulence, explosions supports Velikovsky's theory that Jupiter birthed Venus - VR41

(P) Iron and Sulphur in vicinity of Red Spot - VR84, 248

Electromagnetic

(P) Intense electrical energy, including strong radio emissions, provides further support of activity capable of birthing Venus - SG259,375, VR68, 255; EU276; WC6; CS91,92

(P) Influence of magnetic field on bending of stellar light - VR85

Kinematic

(P) Shoemaker-Levy 9 Comet impacts surface, giving astronomers their first full appreciation that Jupiter is influential in events within our solar system; there have been multiple observed interaction of comets with Jupiter, involving orbital changes - EU270; VR141

Solar System and beyond

Geological

(P) Presence of Chlorine, water on Saturn - VR247, 248

Observed decay rate of comets indicates extreme youth of comets or their present orbits - VR134; EU146, 147, 269, 270; WC32; GF382,383; CS123,124

Discovery of hydrocarbons in comet tails - EU267; VOR190,191

Origin of Zodiacal Light has been found to be dust particles in orbit of Venus (another dust ring has been found between orbits of Mars and Jupiter, and another between earth and Venus, defining probable path of Venus away from earth; the Earth-Venus dust has been estimated at less than 10k years old) - EU268; CS125, 180,181

Nonuniform distribution of craters on Mercury, as well as on our moon and Mars - CS39,40

Electromagnetic

(P) Discovery of electromagnetic activity in stars - EU273, 274; WC5

(P) Charge, Magnetic coupling, earth to moon and solar system to planets as indicated by changes in rotational velocity and radio transmission - VR41, 77, 82, 83; EU274, 275

(P) Large electrical charges of sun and planets - VR81-84, 181-185; WC6

(P) Evidence of electrical nature of sun, e.g. sunspots, corona of sun involve enormous electrical energy and violate purely gravitational mechanics - VR186-191, 255; EU272, 273

(P) Solar winds, plasma characteristics of interplanetary space - SG37, 375; VR176-178, 255

(P) Magnetic field of Uranus - VR84

(P) Electromagnetic influence of Neptune/Pluto interaction - VR84

(P) Emission of low-energy cosmic rays from Saturn - VR84

Kinematic

Variations from common of rotations (e.g. Venus), inclinations of ecliptics, and other kinematic nonuniformities contradict accepted theories of formation of bodies within our solar system - BF285,286

(P) Rotation rate of Saturn's rings exceeds that of primary (Saturn) - VR84

Retrocalculations of comets' and asteroids' orbits indicates collision events in recent times, origin of comets at a common point between Jupiter and Mars - EU268; CS127

Number, location and motions of comets are inconsistent with prevailing theories of capture - CS109-118

Location of asteroids in vacant orbit according to Bode's Law, number of bodies, and their distribution in belts at distances in harmonic relation to Jupiter's orbit suggest that asteroids are fragments of a planet which suffered destruction from a collision; astronomer Fred Whipple placed the disturbance in time as recently as 1500 to 4700 years ago, in excellent agreement with Velikovsky's time frame - BF43-46

Characteristics of comets, including extraordinary recency as established by observed rates of decomposition, support Vsehkvyatskiy's theory of Jupiter's fission, origin of comets on or near surface of Jupiter, in agreement with Velikovsky's scenario - VR132; BF48

Consistency of calculated orbits of Venus, Earth, Mars with physical laws per Velikovsky's scenario before, during, and after near-collisions; proposed orbits are also compatible with 50-52-year Exodus cycle and 15-year Amos cycle - VR139-146, 147-170

Location of Saturn's rings within Roche's Limit suggests near collision of external body with Saturn and consequent fragmentization - BF39-43

Apparent displacement of Uranus, Neptune, Pluto into present orbits by near collisions, e.g. Pluto's orbit crosses inside Neptune's once every 250 years - VR132, BF35-37

Neptune's satellites Triton and Nereid as well as all comets in Neptune family possess retrograde orbits; Neptune is only planet in solar system to have that feature, supporting thesis of interference between Neptune and Pluto or loss of Pluto as satellite of Neptune; Nereid's orbit also has pronounced eccentricity of .749 - BF38,39

Appendix 4-2
Summary Rebuttals to Gradualism As Applied to Historical Geology

Note 1: References are identical to those noted in Appendix 4-1

Dating errors

Sources of inaccuracy

Atomic dating accuracy is subject to: the assumption of constant decay rates, which could have differed under the pre-Flood atmospheric regime, or varied during the transition of regimes from pre-Flood to post-Flood or varied under the influence of a near-collision of the earth with another body; the presupposition without justification of initial ratios of elements; contamination; selective leaching; and evaluation error, in which bias plays an important part. These errors may apply universally among the tests, making them suspect even when consistency is obtained among two or more atomic test procedures. Some methods (e.g. radiocarbon) are valid for a limited time in the past. In practice, the dating procedure allows the introduction of bias. Where dating is subject to independent verification, errors of huge magnitudes have been observed. The difficulties are tacitly acknowledged by practitioners who routinely discard results that may actually be correct but indicate unacceptable recency - GF43,44, 334-378; CS192-195

Known dating inconsistencies

Age estimates of tektites do not agree with presumed ages of strata in which they are embedded - GF381,382

Fossil-based errors in dating/dating sequence:

The entire strata dating system is based on circular reasoning: the foundational dating system keys off strata, identified by its fossil content. The underlying assumption in dating fossils is evolution, generally from simple life forms to more complex. Yet the sequence of strata identified via this guideline is the very data used to demonstrate the viability of evolution. The dating itself was essentially accomplished in mid-nineteenth century, based on limited observations and a strong uniformitarian bias rather than hard supporting facts. Subsequent modifications have generally been made to accommodate anomalous (out-of-sequence) fossil finds. The occurrence of missing and out-of-sequence strata is common. Arbitrary, complex, logically untenable, and even bizarre explanations have been made in attempts to accommodate these numerous exceptions. The concept of overthrusting, for example, to account for the placement of layers of 'older' strata atop the 'newer' is highly speculative and may represent a gross violation of engineering principles, especially in light of the enormous masses involved (thousands of square miles, hundreds of feet thick), and the great transport distances (tens to hundreds of miles). This is compounded by the frequent inability to determine the source location (placement of the out-of-sequence layers prior to overthrusting), and the lack of evidence that the boundaries (contact lines) were subjected to the enormous stresses that would have been involved. Significantly, such explanations of themselves necessarily violate the uniformitarian principles upon which the entire system is based - GF136, 180-211

The 'standard geologic column' is based on virtually nothing other than index fossils, which in turn are dated under the *a priori* assumption of biological evolution, which itself violates the Second Law of Thermodynamics. The 'standard geologic column' exists in its entirety nowhere in the world and may, indeed, be fictitious - GF 131-136, 169, 170, 205-207, 224-227, 271

The nature (and supposed relative sophistication) of fossils embedded within various layers of strata, and commonly used to establish relative dates per an evolutionary bias, may instead merely reflect hydrodynamic sorting factors (size, shape, and density) during (possibly sudden) deposition process; in addition, the location of higher forms in supposedly more recent strata may reflect avoidance mobility factors (postponement of entrapment) as well as characteristics noted above impacting settling velocities - GF273-277, 281,283

Politically-motivated mindset, often sloppy-minded, untrue or lacking justification, and contradictory to principles and theories the investigator attempts to promote elsewhere. The real danger with this kind of thinking is that it usually displays an inconsistency of thought that may well carry over from personal commentary into an inconsistent or overly narrow or overly emotional application of facts and theories to the subject the investigator is attempting to address- SG1-69,257-351[typical];   CS15-41,102-130[typical]; TR50,51, VOR25, 50,51,155,156

Sterility with respect to utility in practical application of theories (information-poor, irrelevant) - GF118,119, 429-438

Keying geological sequences to the fossil record assumes *a priori* both uniformitarianism and evolution; stratigraphic deposition on basis of size, density, and shape is an equally valid assumption but in direct opposition to gradualism. - GF131-137

Difficulties with presently-accepted geology

Inconsistencies and lack of explanatory power

Cannot account for major geologic features, e.g. orogenesis, glaciation, sedimentation/fossilization. At the theoretical level, success limited to classifying effects of sediment deposition rather than understanding hydrodynamic causes (e.g. geosynclines). Even proposed classification schemes intrinsically violate uniformitarian principles - GF144-169

Use of foraminafera as index fossils has recently become suspect due to discovery that all species are capable of assuming form factors previously attributed to time (and evolution) - GF282

No satisfactory uniformitarian-only explanation exists for the recent Ice Ages, given that the immense amount of snowfall involved required energy input to (i.e. heating) of the oceans, coupled with locally cold conditions. (e.g., the conjecture that the earth entered a cosmic dust cloud is insufficient as it does not supply the required energy input; it also does not explain the pattern of cooling noted on the surface.) A better explanation, in terms of observations, is that much of what has been attributed to glacial action was actually hydraulic (i.e. immense water currents); but what can indeed be attributed to ice (the existence of an ice age is not in doubt, due to evidence of a much lower sea level in the recent past, coupled with definite indicators of a rapid warming, such as rapid increase in silting of river deltas and increase in ocean surface temperatures) may have been caused by atmospheric cooling due to volcanic activity, accompanied by heating of the earth due to stresses caused by near-collision or pole shift (the same stresses which caused the volcanic activity); that polar shifts were at least peripherally involved is indicated by the observed patterns of ice boundaries (moraines, limits of striation); the possibility of multiple separate ice ages (as presently accepted) may indeed indicate the involvement of multiple catastrophes, of which the Flood, the Exodus catastrophe, and the Amos catastrophe are possible contributors (note: these individual catastrophes may well be periodic manifestations of the same basic cause, e.g. close approaches of a foreign body). Sudden rise in sea level may be attributed to the relative size of the first (post-Flood) glaciation compared with the subsequent glaciations linked to polar shifts; rise may thus be due to first polar shift subsequent to that which may have caused the Flood - GF294-305

Scientific acceptance in 1990s of impact of comet or asteroid as cause of mass dinosaur extinction demonstrates how dogmatic, biased, and ultimately wrong the scientific community was in objecting to catastrophic theories. The recent admission of catastrophic events in earth's history not only required a much more reasonable mechanism to account for observed effects than the prevailing notions, but virtually irrefutable proof in the form of the worldwide iridium layer associated with the K-T boundary. Even that wasn't sufficient - the Alvarez team also had to find the crater. Given the almost universal acceptance of the catastrophic theory regarding dinosaur extinction, many of the similar arguments against the Flood and Exodus scenarios should be recognized by the same community as no longer valid. Having accepted the probability of occurrence of an enormous catastrophe, however, the community should also recognize the logical inconsistency of attempting to maintain its rigid adherence to the uniformitarian system of dating. The various components of the geological column, for example, should now be seen not so much as various ages but as more probably representing sequences of deposition based on location and hydrodynamic properties following the turbulence of a violent event. This is not to say that boundaries such as the K-T may not represent the same time at various locations, but rather the sequence among boundaries and how much time is represented from one boundary to another. In this dinosaur extinction event, science for the first time recognized the possibility of a tsunami approaching a mile in height - TR31,34,35,37,42,50-58,68,69,75-77,83,86,87,106,117-120, 124,125,139-143 [see Note 1]; VOR28 [Schoch does not clearly state Alvarez here: the iridium was determined to have originated from bolide rather than volcanic activity on basis of iridium/ ruthenium/rhodium ratio.]

In the face of the overwhelming evidence in support of geographic movement, much of it from paleomagnetic data which has enjoyed widespread acceptance, the uniformitarian community is at least tacitly endorsing novel theories which attempt to explain the observations. The proposed mechanisms appear to be reasonable and supportive of the observed data. Although some of the theories remain uniformitarian in nature, they can also be placed into a catastrophic framework. The Plate Tectonic theory, for example, describes an essentially uniformitarian process. Its utility in accounting for detailed facts supports its correctness, at least with regard to the basics of the mechanism, although the plates may have been initially set in motion by catastrophic causes as well as or instead of by convective motion within the mantle. Kirschvink's theory of 'True Polar Wander', as described by Schoch, defines another apparently reasonable process, the movement of the solid part of the earth about the liquid core, which maintains its original spin axis. Thus, while the axis of the earth's rotation remains fixed with respect to the stars, geographic locations (latitude and longitude of specific points on the surface of the earth) will change. The proposed driving mechanism behind this movement is the well-known kinematic tendency of an unbalanced rotating object to align its spin with its maximum moment of inertia. The source of the unbalance may be catastrophic, as in the impact of a large object upon the earth. In this regard, Schoch cites the Tharsis volcano on Mars and its associated gravity anomaly (unbalance). Schoch claims that its location at the equator is not a coincidence; for this location, the unbalance presents the maximum moment of inertia. The earth may have experienced a number of rotational reorientations via this mechanism subsequent to catastrophic events. Schoch also cites Barbiero's gyroscopic mechanism for the shifting of the earth's axis of spin. According to Schoch, Barbiero claims that if it struck in the right direction, a colliding bolide of a diameter of only 1100 yards could exert sufficient torque to cause a shift. While these mechanisms actually support the claims of catastrophists, the community continues to avoid any endorsement of those individuals who pioneered this new and vastly more realistic view of historical geology; in many cases they still stubbornly insist on applying uniformitarian dating schemes to the events they describe; in other instances they repeat the work of the pioneers, presenting their own work as novel. - VOR169-174, 220; SG433-436

Superior consistency and explanatory utility of Flood-based dating

The Biblical flood account is an information-rich explanation of a catastrophic event; it is self-consistent, consistent with Scripture and capable of explaining some Scriptural and current geological enigmas.

Self-consistency of Genesis account with respect to anthropologically and geographically universal flood - GF1-35

Canopy encircling globe (water, water vapor, or ice) is a consistent unifying concept for the following:

Genesis account: division of waters from waters, separated by firmament - GF76,77

Genesis account: mist rather than rain prior to the Flood; possible different atmospheric composition (e.g. % oxygen, ozone); strong indication of much greater temperature uniformity, less winds, clouds - GF241,242

Genesis account: rainbow for first time, guarantee of no similar future flood event - GF216

Collapse of canopy as source of enormous quantity of water, sudden freezing (ice age, quick-freezing of mammoths) - GF240-258

Curve of lifetimes vs. generation is consistent with and loosely supports natural cause of drastic reduction in longevity associated with collapse of canopy - BF215

Majority of fossilized strata (including Permian, with non-glacial interpretation of striation, tillites) indicates mild climate uniform throughout world, readily explainable only in terms of a different pre-flood climate regime in which some mechanism such as global water-vapor canopy provided more evenly-distributed temperatures throughout world. - GF245-250, 253-258

Arguments against universal flood not supportable:

Ark capable of accommodating world's animals - 'designed in' hibernation/estivation capability, structural adaptability of various genera, in which varieties represent (designed variability, as opposed to evolution) adaptations to specific environmental conditions - GF63-75

Some arguments against universal flood presuppose non-universal flood (e.g. worldwide pre-flood distribution of flora and fauna), creating circular reasoning - GF64

Universal flood traditions throughout mankind support rather than refute universal flood - WC46-50, WC195-201, 263, 303-315; GF48-54

Standard geological arguments against a short geological time scale are based on uniformitarian assumptions; these same arguments disappear in catastrophic context and in many cases support catastrophism over uniformitarianism. They include the following: thicknesses of sedimentary rock beds; coral reefs; deep-sea sediments; evaporites, such as salt domes; formation of stalactites; buried forests; varves; great depth of stratified shale; - GF405-429

Attempts to downplay catastrophic causes for observed effects lead to hastily-constructed alternate scenarios which are inconsistent with all the facts. An example is a common treatment of the mammoth carcasses frozen *in situ* in Siberia and Alaska. Of these carcasses, the edibility is often downplayed, but edible is edible. Alternate scenarios often have the mammoths drowned in icy streams, caught in blizzards, or stumbling into glacial crevasses. All such scenarios miss the essential point: mammoths are huge animals with correspondingly large daily diets. The lushness of vegetation required to support herds of these animals is simply not found in areas with icy streams, blizzards, and glacial crevasses. - VOR158

Inability to properly integrate field observation, e.g. out-of-sequence strata (missing periods and strata of 'reversed' order), fossils of one geologic period embedded in strata of another period, and to explain the tuatara. The tuatara is a lizard-like reptile from the 'extinct' order of beakheads, for which the geological record stops at the cretaceous period. Despite the lack of fossils in strata 'newer' than the cretaceous, these creatures have been seen sunning themselves on rocks. A similar situation exists with the coelacanth, a supposedly extinct fish which was recently caught by a fisherman, and the presence of coal in the form of a perfectly-shaped human skull in the midst of an ancient coal seam, and with mollusks supposedly extinct for 280 million years. See also the anomalies noted in earth geology - GF119; VOR4,6,12,13

Richness of fossil record vs. special geological conditions required for formation and lack of expected transitional forms ('missing links') - GF128-130, 154,155

PART FIVE

A Riddle and a Sign

Contents for Part Five

Preface to Part Five

This essay addresses what I consider to be a prophetic element associated with the activity of Jesus in His feeding of the multitudes. If this interpretation is correct, the Biblical accounts of the feeding events may be comparable to other numerically-oriented prophetic Biblical passages such as the prophecy of Daniel regarding the initial coming of Messiah. Moreover, the treatment illustrates the remarkable depth of Scripture, underscoring the necessity for treating it with more than casual regard. It is only by viewing Scripture as divinely inspired and fully consistent among its various books that one can conceive such richness of information as being available within its words. Certainly the trivial Bible perceived by those who place its origin as having come from man alone would be incapable of furnishing such depth of corroboration of Jesus' mission on earth.

Like the essay of Part One, this work is not necessarily uniquely modern. As much as I can discern, however, the topic has never been approached before. Furthermore, given the casual manner in which Scripture is currently treated, and the disdain with which some Bible expositors treat the apparent lack of sophistication of its contributors, it is timely to remind the Christian public of the great depth of Wisdom embodied in Scripture, and of its supernatural roots.

Most importantly, the information developed here speaks clearly about how God intended us to treat Scripture. If we are to worship God, it is not to enshrine His Scripture on a pedestal, offering meaningless praise to its holy quality. It is an inexhaustible treasure chest of knowledge, given to us to increase our wisdom. We are to study it, diligently and thoroughly, so that we might come to a better understanding of the intrinsic nature of God and the remarkable thoroughness with which He defined Himself to us. Simply put, if we want to find God, we should actively look for Him in the one place He gave us where we can reliably find Him.

1
Introduction to the Analysis

Over the past few decades the discoveries associated with Christian research have provided information beyond the level of the text itself by which the divine inspiration of Scripture may be authenticated to the satisfaction of all but the most hardened skeptic. Perhaps God intended that the discovery of these nontextual relationships would be made at a time when the veracity of the Bible has been attacked as never before. In Daniel Chapter 12, Daniel was told to seal the book until the time of the end, when 'many shall run to and fro, and knowledge shall be increased'. I believe that this is that time spoken by Daniel and that over the next few years wisdom hidden within Scripture will continue to be revealed, to the astonishment of many and the consternation of those who attempt to belittle its contents.

In that context there is an element of mystery, of information hidden beneath the surface, that accompanies the Gospel accounts of Jesus' feeding of the multitudes. On the face of the accounts, they speak of His authority over the affairs of man, of His compassion in providing for our needs. They support His credentials as God.

But the Gospel accounts of the feeding events may go deeper than this level in addition to and without negating the significance of the basic spiritual message. They may also speak of Jesus' destiny, of the mission that He came to earth to perform.

Jesus spoke of having ears to hear and eyes to see, linking these faculties of perception to the more fundamental prerequisite of faith. In the eighth chapter of Mark's Gospel, Jesus made a pointed and direct association of faith with understanding as he spoke with His disciples after feeding four thousand people with seven loaves and a few fish. Significantly, just prior to that incident as recorded in Mark He had encountered the Pharisees, who had sought some confirmation from heaven regarding Jesus' credentials.

And he sighed deeply in his spirit, and saith, Why doth this generation seek after a sign? verily I say unto you, There shall no sign be given unto this generation.

As the account in Mark 8 continues, Jesus recalls to His disciples the events in which He fed the multitudes, as if the details represented something of great importance.

And he left them, and entering into the ship again departed to the other side.

Now the disciples had forgotten to take bread, neither had they in the ship with them more than one loaf.

And he charged them, saying, Take heed, beware of the leaven of the Pharisees, and of the leaven of Herod.

And they reasoned among themselves, saying, It is because we have no bread.

And when Jesus knew it, he saith unto them, Why reason ye, because ye have no bread? perceive ye not yet, neither understand? have ye your heart yet hardened?

Having eyes, see ye not? and having ears, hear ye not? and do ye not remember?

When I brake the five loaves among five thousand, how many baskets full of fragments took ye up? They say unto him, Twelve.

And when the seven among four thousand, how many baskets full of fragments took ye up? And they said, Seven.

And he said unto them, How is it that ye do not understand?

In this account, Jesus confronts his disciples with their lack of understanding. In a commentary that appears at the first reading to be somewhat cryptic, He recalls the feeding of the five thousand and the four thousand. In this recollection, Jesus emphasizes numbers: the number of people fed, along with the number of baskets that contained the fragments that remained. Having recalled the specific numbers associated with these feeding events, Jesus makes the odd demand: *"How is it that ye do not understand?"*

It is tempting, in a first reading of this and the surrounding verses, to think of Mark as lacking in sophistication. He seems to mix numbers inappropriately into the basic message, and too many details are left unanswered. Why, for example, did Jesus emphasize the numbers associated with the feedings, as if these values were somehow related to their faith? Jesus painstakingly recalls to His disciples the number of individuals fed and the number of remaining baskets, but fails to complete the picture. How many fragments did each basket contain? Of what importance was the number of baskets of leftovers to the event itself, or to the disciples' faith? How can the number of baskets of leftovers have such theological significance that Jesus placed so much emphasis upon it in the recollection of the feeding events to His disciples? Why were 5,000 fed with five loaves, whereas seven loaves were required to feed the 4,000?

What if Mark, as guided by the Holy Spirit and therefore far from being unsophisticated of word, was actually presenting a truth of great depth? In this light, the passage literally pleads for a deeper understanding of the feeding of the people. When Jesus spoke about the specifics of the feedings to His disciples, it was as if he was presenting the future reader with a riddle and commanding him to solve it.

As this essay shall endeavor to show, the feeding of the multitudes contained the rudiments of such a sign as the Pharisees had requested of Jesus. But the completion of its components had to await the Pentecost. The Gospels also had to be written first, in the unique manner in which they presented the elements for later examination. Next, the Gospels had to be integrated into Scripture and thus become available for open review. Finally, a generation had to emerge whose perspective was conditioned to view Scripture beyond that which is immediately apparent. This may be the generation to whom the sign embodied in the feedings is addressed.

A number of basic assumptions are made in the following development. They will be addressed before proceeding further. One might readily see from the nature of these assumptions and the arguments made for their justification that a symbolic interpretation of the feeding events is on firmer ground than a dogmatic assertion that the feeding took place exactly as the development might imply. Although the development might reflect the nature of the actual events as they took place, one cannot be certain of this on the basis of the information which we have been given. We can be more sure, on the basis of the information which we do have and the manner in which it dovetails together so well, that Scripture intended to provide the reader of the feeding accounts with a symbolic imagery beyond the plain text, a picture that transcends the material realm. This symbolism gives us both a beautiful picture rich with meaning and a demonstration of the unbounded depth of Scripture.

The first assumption made herein is that the feeding may be described as an ordered one, that the assembly of people may be characterized in terms of rectangular arrays having structured rows and columns. This view departs from the historic one in which the people are imagined to have congregated in a haphazard, amorphous fashion. It may be argued that there is no Scriptural justification whatsoever to impose such order on the assemblies. Yet Scripture itself hints of order in noting the commandment to sit down in companies. If indeed the actual assemblies did not assume rectangular appearances, this reference alone is sufficient to justify at least that symbolic appearance to the reader of Scripture.

The second assumption is that a miracle actually took place, but that its occurrence was also an ordered one and simple to understand. Specifically, the assumed miracle is that during the distribution each loaf of bread became whole after it was broken and passed from one participant to another. In this process, the breaking of the bread quite openly symbolizes Jesus' act on the cross, and its restoration, being of God rather than leaven, speaks of His regenerative power. The process also follows closely the propagation of the Word of God, the most important food offered by Jesus.

The third assumption is that the congregations consisted of precisely the number of people noted in the Scriptural accounts. Indeed, the word 'about' was sometimes used in describing these numbers. Furthermore, there is at least the suggestion that the numbers should be taken as only approximate in the reference to 'besides women and children'. I would suggest, on the other hand, that these references actually support the significance of the numbers as given, directing the reader to consider the 'core' group defined by the numbers to represent some truth of at least symbolic importance.

The fourth assumption is that the baskets of leftovers all contain the same number of fragments. It is certainly not a necessity, nor does Scripture specifically note that the remaining fragments were equally distributed among the baskets. This is just one representative case of a more general assumption that has been made throughout the development. In several instances the development applies the well-known principle of Ocham's Razor, the basic validity of which is recognized by many, but certainly not all, members of the scientific community. This principle simply states that if a number of answers to a problem are possible, the simplest one is the most likely. Those who view the application of this principle with suspicion may object to the elevation of a mere convenience to the status of a law. They state with logical certainty that the assumption of simplicity does not carry the weight of truth. As a matter of fact, I wholeheartedly agree with such detractors, having presented this argument a number of times myself in another context. But in this case, I feel entirely justified in applying this principle on the basis of my perception that the intent of Scripture is to supply the diligent reader with the most straightforward answer, rather than to mislead him with unnecessary complications. Actually, the sizes of the baskets differ between the feeding of the five thousand and the feeding of the four thousand. This issue has been addressed in Chapter 3 as well as in Appendix 5-3, with the observation that this initial assumption remains correct.

The fifth assumption is that in addition to the three events where the 100, 5,000 and the 4,000 were actually fed with physical bread there was another, strictly symbolic event, as noted in Scripture, where 3,000 were fed with by Peter with the Word of God. This incident taken from the Acts has been integrated into the others to complete the symbolic image. The Scriptural link between bread and the Word is so emphatic in the Gospels that it requires no further explanation. When Jesus, whom John specifically describes as the Word, particularly in John 1 and 6, both feeds the multitudes and claims that "I am the Bread of Life" He makes the obvious connection Himself. When, in John 21, Jesus commands Peter to "Feed my sheep", and repeats this command three times, can one fail to see some prophetic significance to His words? When we as Christians partake of the Sacrament in honor of the Incarnate Word, do we not make that link? Perhaps one cannot expect the multitudes who were fed with physical bread to have appreciated the image they were forming, nor to have linked that bread with the Word.

But the symbolic picture that is presented herein was not intended for them. It was intended for the reader of New Testament Scripture who came after all of the events which were described at that time.

It is left to the reader of this essay to determine for himself whether these assumptions are reasonable and proper in the context of a perceived intent of Scripture to provide the diligent reader with a reward for his effort to understand it.

The search into a deeper meaning behind the passage in Mark Chapter 8 begins with Mark's presentation of the two feeding accounts to which Jesus referred. The first, which may be found in all the Gospels, is in Mark Chapter 6:

> *And Jesus, when he came out, saw much people, and was moved with compassion toward them, because they were as sheep not having a shepherd: and he began to teach them many things. And when the day was far spent, his disciples came unto him, and said, This is a desert place, and now the time is far passed: Send them away that they may go into the country round about, and into the villages, and buy themselves bread: for they have nothing to eat.*
>
> *He answered and said unto them, Give ye them to eat. And they say unto him, Shall we go and buy two hundred pennyworth of bread, and give them to eat?*
>
> *He saith unto them, How many loaves have ye? go and see. And when they knew, they say, Five, and two fishes. And he commanded them to make all sit down by companies upon the green grass. And they sat down in ranks, by hundreds, and by fifties.*
>
> *And when he had taken the five loaves and the two fishes, he looked up to heaven, and blessed, and brake the loaves, and gave them to his disciples to set before them; and the two fishes divided he among them all.*
>
> *And they did eat, and were filled. And they took up twelve baskets full of the fragments, and of the fishes. And they that did eat of the loaves were about five thousand.*

The second account of Jesus' providing bread to the multitudes is related in Mark Chapter 8:

In those days the multitude being very great, and having nothing to eat, Jesus called his disciples unto him, and saith unto them, I have compassion on the multitude, because they have now been with me three days, and have nothing to eat: And if I send them away fasting to their own houses, they will faint by the way: for divers of them came from far.

And his disciples answered him, From whence can a man satisfy these men with bread here in the wilderness?

And he asked them, How many loaves have ye? And they said, Seven. And he commanded the people to sit down on the ground: and he took the seven loaves, and gave thanks, and brake, and gave to his disciples to set before them; and they did set them before the people. And they had a few small fishes: and he blessed, and commanded to set them also before them.

So they did eat, and were filled: and they took up of the broken meat that was left seven baskets. And they that had eaten were about four thousand: and he sent them away.

The two Gospel accounts of Jesus' feeding of the multitudes are not the only accounts of the process given in the Bible. This situation is quite fortunate, for as well as corroborating the significance of the numbers, it furnishes just that necessary additional numerical information regarding the feedings to permit a meaningful analysis. In Second Kings Chapter 4 there is a precursor account in which Elisha feeds a company of one hundred with twenty loaves. Also, the twenty-first chapter of John's Gospel records that Jesus demanded of Peter three times that he feed His sheep. The fulfillment of this prophecy is noted in the second chapter of the Acts of the Apostles, where by preaching the word of God Peter brings three thousand souls to the salvation of Jesus Christ. It may not be significant, but it is at least interesting to note that, with the addition of the three thousand fed by Peter, the three events recounted in the New Testament amount to the feeding of twelve thousand souls.

The inclusion of Peter's event in the feedings is justified by the association of bread with the Word of God, a notion which is firmly implanted in the Bible. In chapter 4 of Matthew's Gospel, for example,

Then was Jesus led up of the spirit into the wilderness to be tempted of the devil. And when he had fasted forty days and forty nights, he was afterward an hungred. And when the tempter came to him, he said, If thou be the Son of God, command that these stones be made bread.

But he answered and said, It is written, Man shall not live by bread alone, but by every word that proceedeth out of the mouth of God.

Later, Jesus was more direct in symbolically equating the Word with bread. As He instructed his disciples at the Last Supper,

And he took bread, and gave thanks, and brake it, and gave unto them, saying This is my body which is given for you: this do in remembrance of me.

As John's Gospel goes to painstaking lengths to emphasize, Jesus Christ Himself is the Personification of the Word of God:

In the beginning was the Word, and the Word was with God, and the Word was God. . .And the Word was made flesh, and dwelt among us, (and we beheld his glory, the glory as of the only begotten of the Father,) full of grace and truth. . .For the law was given by Moses, but grace and truth came by Jesus Christ.

These passages clearly demonstrate an intimate connection between the consecrated bread and the Word of God. It is this equivalence that permitted the Word that Peter fed the people to be equivalent to the bread that Jesus fed the multitudes.

The linkage of bread with the Word of God in feeding the people is further established in the sixth chapter of John's Gospel. There Jesus not only claims Himself as the source of the manna that fed the Israelites for forty years in the wilderness, but defines Himself, the Living Word, as the true bread. Significantly, His claims are made almost in the same breath as the recollection of the feeding of the multitudes:

Jesus answered them and said, Verily, verily, I say unto you, Ye seek me, not because ye saw the miracles, but because ye did eat of the loaves, and were filled.

Labour not for the meat which perisheth, but for that

meat which endureth unto everlasting life, which the Son of man shall give unto you: for him hath God the Father sealed.

Then said they unto him, What shall we do, that we might work the works of God?

Jesus answered and said unto them, This is the work of God, that ye believe on him whom he hath sent.

They said therefore unto him, What sign shewest thou then, that we may see, and believe thee? what dost thou work? Our fathers did eat manna in the desert; as it is written, He gave them bread from heaven to eat.

Then Jesus said unto them, Verily, verily, I say unto you, Moses gave you not that bread from heaven; but my Father giveth you the true bread from heaven. For the bread of God is he which cometh down from heaven, and giveth life unto the world.

Then said they unto him, Lord, evermore give us this bread.

And Jesus said unto them, I am the bread of life: he that cometh to me shall never hunger; and he that believeth on me shall never thirst.

Thus, the Living Word of God also claims to be the bread of life, furnishing a profoundly intimate linkage between the bread of his feedings and the symbolic bread of Peter's message to the multitudes.

In all, then, there were at least four feeding events for which numerical values were presented: the one wherein Elisha fed the group of a hundred, the two where Jesus fed the multitudes, and the one where Peter fed the three thousand.

In generating an abundance of food out of paltry beginnings, the feeding of the multitudes did indeed involve the miraculous. However, since they originate from the Source of our physical laws, miracles themselves may be expected to exhibit some degree of mechanical logic. This expectation is even greater for miracles that are intended to demonstrate a point. Rather than dismissing the feeding accounts as simple parables, it shall be assumed that the miracle took a specific form as fleshed out below.

2

Description of the General Feeding Process

The first task of the analysis which follows shall be to describe the general mechanics of the feeding process in a manner that will be amenable to a detailed analytic treatment.

The analysis begins by considering the nature of leaven, which Jesus had firmly associated with these events. Leaven expands by dividing and growing back to its pre-division size. Consequently, the miracle that happened during the feeding may simply have been in the breaking of the bread, where each half subsequently returned to wholeness. More importantly, this miracle also replicates in the physical realm the propagation without loss of the Word of God, the spiritual food. When Jesus first blessed the loaves, the blessing extended to the entire crowd so that every time a whole remnant was broken by anyone in the group one half was retained and eaten as a whole loaf, while the other half was passed by the receiver as a whole loaf to the next person in line.

Because of the emphasis that Jesus placed on the number of baskets remaining, it appears that the specific arrangement of people was highly significant. Mark, in Chapter 6 of his gospel, notes that there was order in the manner in which the multitudes were arranged. As it is written there,

> *And He commanded them to make all sit down by companies upon the green grass. And they sat down in ranks, by hundreds, and by fifties.*

Suppose there was an orderly arrangement of the people into rows and columns. If a single loaf were given to feed the entire group, the first row of individuals (except the individual at the end of the row) would perform the breaking and passing operation twice, as shown on Figure 1: first to the individual next in line along the same row, and second to the individual next in line along the same column. The individuals residing in the second and following rows would only perform the operation once, passing the loaves along the same column.

Figure 1: Basic Pattern of Feeding

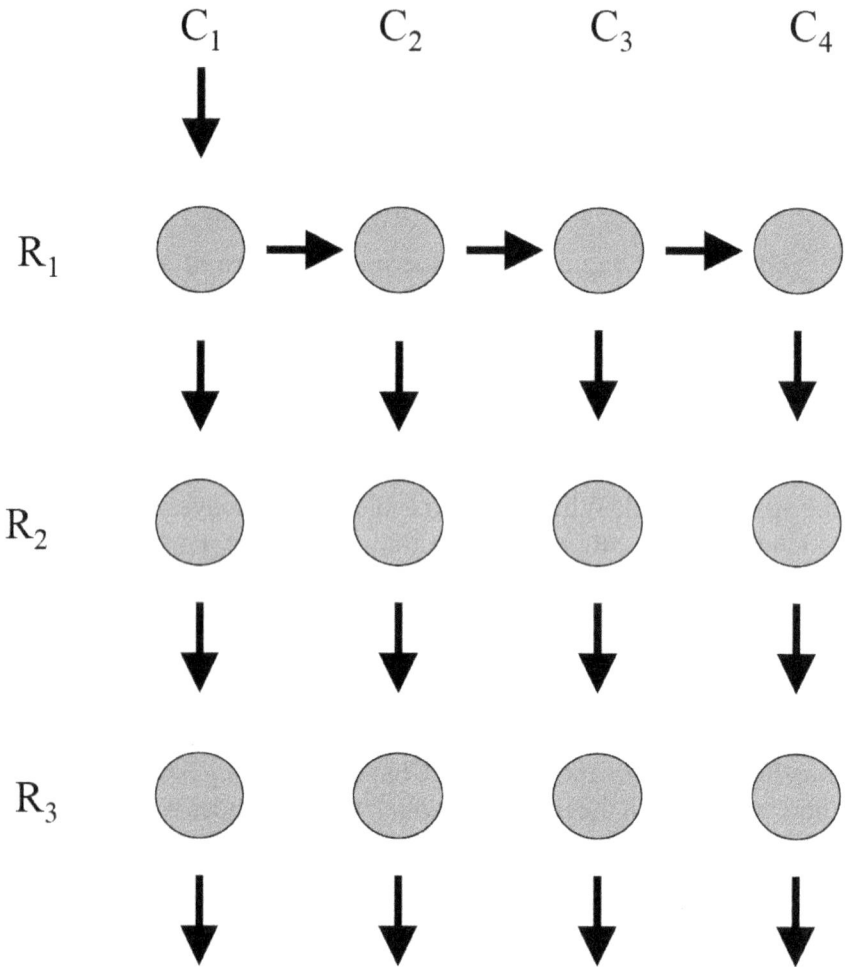

According to this procedure there would have been one remaining loaf from each column. Thus the number of remaining loaves, as the number of starting loaves, is determined entirely by the geometry of the assembled group. The number of companies in the first row would establish the required number of starting loaves, being equivalent to that value. Similarly, the entire number of loaves remaining after the feeding would be equal to the total number of columns. An interesting facet of this process is that the number of remaining fish, which were noted as being a part of the feeding of both the five thousand and of the four thousand, would be exactly the same as the number of remaining loaves; the numbers of both are entirely pattern-dependent.

In Mark's account of the five thousand fed, mention is made of companies of hundreds and fifties, indicating that the people are arranged by rows and columns of companies during the distribution. Consistent with the arrangement by companies, a loaf may be handed to the captain of a company, who, by successively breaking it, hands a loaf to the head of each column. The loaf makes its way down the column, returning to a whole loaf with each breaking, feeding each of the persons that breaks it and passes it along. When it reaches the end, the last person in each column hands the loaf, as a remainder, to others who collect the remainder into baskets.

A brief digression will be made here to furnish some justification for the basic process described above. The nature of the miracle involved in the feeding may have been hinted at in Mark 4:8 and 4:20. In Mark 4:20, Jesus, in explaining His parable of the sower to His disciples, comments on the seed which grows to bear fruit, linking it to the Word of God:

> And these are they which are sown on good ground; such as hear the word, and receive it, and bring forth fruit, some thirtyfold, some sixty, and some an hundred.

In His use of these numbers, Jesus was apparently making a supplementary observation of the kingdom of God, in that the important factor is bearing fruit, not in its quantity nor in the amount labor involved. Rather, these elements, like the work itself and the motivating power behind it, are strictly in God's Hands. Jesus explicitly presents that same theme in His parable of the laborers in the vineyard, as recorded in Matthew Chapter 20.

But why did Jesus use those three specific numbers in Mark 4 to describe the increase? They don't seem to relate to each other in a linear fashion or by any other apparent logic, as one might expect. If the numbers in this parable of Jesus are indeed related to what might be considered a riddle associated with the feeding of the multitudes, an arrangement of individuals may be proposed such that those numbers emerge naturally in a context similar to that proposed for the feeding process.

Figure 2: Linear Arrangement in Support of Mark 4

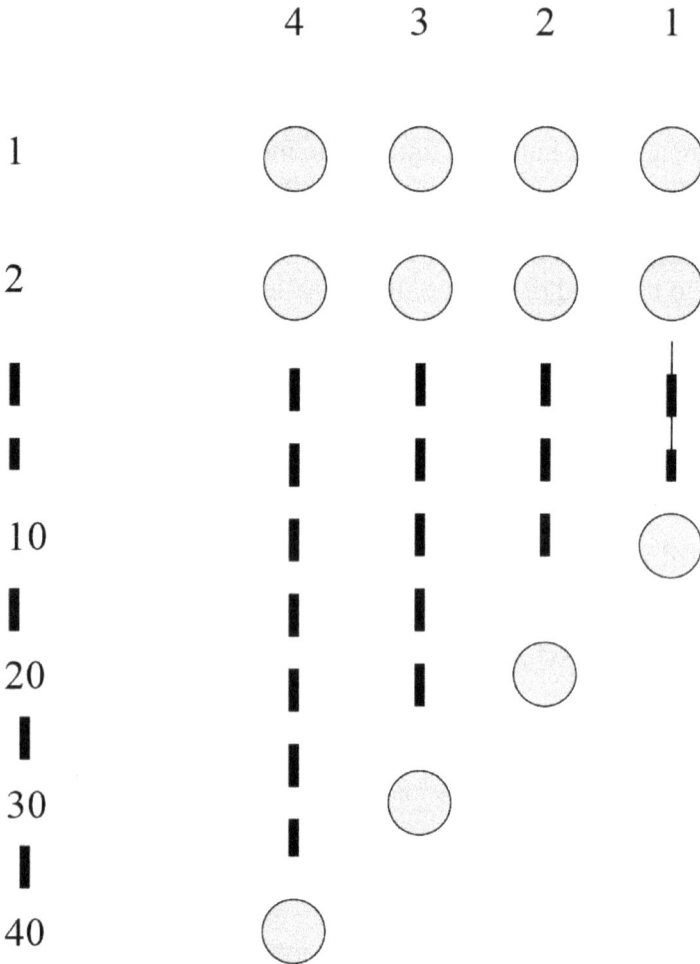

One such grouping would be the simple arrangement shown in Figure 2, where the first column would consist of ten individuals, and each successive column would increase by ten individuals. Beginning with the individual at the first row, and at the column next to the end, all individuals on the same row would perform exactly the same operation. (The person on the end, in the column of ten, would perform a different operation than the others in that row. Consequently, it is logical that he be omitted from inclusion in the parable.) But the first of these individuals performing identical operations would feed (10 + 20), or thirty of his companions, including himself, whereas the next would feed (10 + 20 + 30), or sixty people, and the next would feed (10 + 20 + 30 + 40), or a hundred individuals.

It may be stretching matters a bit to claim, on the basis of such a tenuous matching of numerical patterns, that the parable furnishes proof of the method by which the multitudes were fed. Yet the process does indeed provide an otherwise difficult link between what might be considered a random selection of numbers with a logically simple linear arithmetic progression. In doing so it may give us cause to consider the numbers chosen by Jesus as representing at least a clue to the process by which manyfold increases are accomplished. We note in that context that we, in digesting the Word of God, do not actually consume it unless we refuse to share. But in the process of accurately speaking it to others, we call it forth as a whole entity, regardless of the number of times we share it. And if those to whom we speak it also share this Word, then our own initial sharing may have a manyfold increase without our further participation. Furthermore, if such was the process to which Jesus was actually referring in the parable, it makes of the miracle a simple, logical, and easily-understood principle whose application permits us not only to understand in considerable depth the exact nature of the feeding process, but to appreciate, in our awe of the depth of Mark's Gospel, the working of the Holy Spirit upon his writing. That is the greater miracle by far.

Having made that digression, this work shall return to an analysis of the actual feeding events. The approach to this topic shall be to treat the desired information algebraically as a set of unknowns that are solvable as a system of simultaneous equations. Since the number of unknowns in the Gospel accounts exceeded the number of direct equations, additional information is supplied in the form of reasonable assumptions such as consistency of some parameters among the events, and the necessity for the use of integer values in expressing numbers of parameters such as people.

A rigorous mathematical development of the event's relevant properties, under the basic assumptions noted above, is made prior to delving into specific numbers. The mathematical characterization and detailed evaluation are presented in Appendix 5-1. A simpler, less formal version of this same evaluation is given in Appendix 5-2. The reader who would prefer to skip over the detailed math is nevertheless encouraged to review the figures in the appendix, especially the patterns for the separate feeding events as shown on Figures 7 through 10 (Figures 6 through 9 in the alternate version) therein. Appendix 5-3 provides a purely visual confirmation of the mathematical analyses given in Appendices 5-1 and 5-2.

3
Conclusions

As established in Appendix 5-1 (alternatively, the simpler version presented in Appendix 5-2), the primary objective was satisfied. A unique numerical value of 5 was found for the number of loaves in each basket collected as remainder, and solutions were found that furnished specific arrangements of individuals for each of the feeding cases. These arrangements were compatible with all the values explicitly noted in Scripture. As far as has been determined, this compatibility is unique to the arrangements presented herein. Although this uniqueness has not been proven, i.e. all possible row by column shapes of companies of 50 and 100 have not been exhaustively analyzed, experience suggests that the possibility is remote of obtaining alternate arrangements that simultaneously satisfy the numerical values presented in Scripture. Of most significance is the reconciliation of the initial loaves with the number fed and the remainder baskets (and loaves) for the two cases where these three parameters were spelled out. A further feature established in this analysis is that the process allows the number of loaves to be reconciled with the number of fish.

Moreover, there was a remarkable consistency of unspecified parameters as well as process among the four events. The solutions emerged under the imposition of a number of consistency-driven constraints: the consistency of process; the limitation of company sizes to the two which were overtly mentioned in Scripture; the consistency of company shape (10 x 5 and 20 x 5); the consistency of the distribution of initial (specified) loaves one to a frontmost company; the requirement that the company rows and columns align with each other, coupled with the requirement that each column furnish one and only one remainder loaf; and the consistency of the number of remainder loaves per basket.

An interesting feature of the analysis is that once the feeding patterns were established, the math was no longer required – the patterns

387

themselves were self-explanatory regarding their consistency with the Scriptural accounts, including the numbers involved. Appendix 5-3, originally presented as Appendix 2 to *Marching to a Worthy Drummer,* provides this post-analysis overview of the feedings.

The algebraic treatment described in appendices 5-1 and 5-2 initially was important in that it established the symbolic patterns for the feeding events. After the patterns have been derived, however, a simple visual examination of them is sufficient to understand and verify that they indeed produce the means by which 5000 men can be fed with 5 loaves (and two fish) and generate precisely 12 baskets of leftovers with 5 loaves per basket, and 4000 men can be fed with 7 loaves and generate precisely 7 baskets of leftovers with 5 loaves per basket.

It is important to recognize that although the size of baskets for these two events differ, they each contain a core number of 5 loaves that applies to the feeding of the men. The smaller baskets used in the feeding of the 5000 contained just the leftovers from the men, which is consistent with the predominantly Jewish nature of the 5000 event, as indicated by not only the symbolism of the number 12 but also by the location of that event (Bethsaida). The feeding of the 4000 is consistent with the predominantly Gentile nature of that event, as indicated by the symbolism of the number 7 as well as the different location of that event (Decapolis). The result is that the remainders from the feeding of the 4000 included the leftovers from the women and children as well as for the core number of 5 for the men, supporting the more inclusive nature of the predominantly Gentile Church, hence the larger baskets for that event.

Next, one simply refers to the patterns of the following figures, visualizing the distribution patterns of Figures 4 and 5 of Appendix 5-1, noting that the actual miracle involved the restoration of each portion of a loaf to wholeness after it was broken as shown in Figures 7 through 10. As for the integration into the pattern of the cross, note that Elisha's feeding of 100 dovetails into the missing 100 of the 5000 event to create a perfect rectangle, and the feeding of the 4000 creates two distinct rectangles, one of 3850 and the other of 150, the smaller of which represents the titulus which was written in three languages, Hebrew, Latin and Greek.

Another interesting aspect of the analysis is that it finds corroboration in the twenty-first chapter of John's Gospel. The total

value of the remainder from all four events, under the assumption of
the integration of the first event into the second as suggested below,
is 155. This number represents the remainder of either bread or fish
because the strict pattern-dependency of these numbers requires
the remainders in either case to have the same values. When this
number is compared with the number of fish described in John 21,
the result provides an additional confirmation of this interpretation
of the feeding. For if the 153 fish that the disciples caught is added
to the apparent two fish that Jesus had on the fire, the total number
of fish noted in John 21 is also 155.

There were, however, two exceptions to the general consistency
of pattern. The analysis actually produced far more information than
anticipated, and this information came out of these exceptions.

The first exception was the orientation parameter u, which was
not consistent among the cases, differing in Case 3 from the other
three. Among the initial assumptions of consistency for the event in
which Jesus fed the four thousand was that it, like the other events,
would have a vertical orientation to the direction of feeding. But for
this event a vertical pattern (long side, or column, extending outward
from Jesus with the feeding taking place from front to rear) refused
to yield numerical values that fit in with the other events. Eventually,
a horizontal pattern was considered for this case, which led to the
inclusion of the parameter u in the analysis. With a horizontal pattern,
the bread and fish were passed on in a direction at right angles to the
spatial orientation of the congregation. This pattern fit surprisingly
well, and it fit only for the event of the four thousand. In regard
to this parameter it is noted that there was one and only one valid
orientation for each case, hinting that the exception itself favors the
probability of design over chance in the differing orientations.

The second exception revealed that the individual patterns of Cases
2 and 3 did not result in the establishment of perfect rectangles as
initially expected. However, the patterns of Cases 1 and 2 combined
to form the perfect complete rectangle initially assumed for each
case, and the pattern of Case 3 produced two perfect rectangles, one
of which was large and the other of which was much smaller.

These anomalies in the patterns, rather than indicating flaws in
the Gospel accounts, suggest that their sequential linkage might
combine into a composite pattern. This suggestion is given further

credence in noting that the width of the pattern of Case 4 is identical to the width for Case 2.

When the operation of combining patterns, as suggested by these characteristics, was performed in the same sequence as the presentation of the events in the Bible, a composite pattern was

Figure 4: Rearrangement of Composite Figure to Represent the Tau Cross

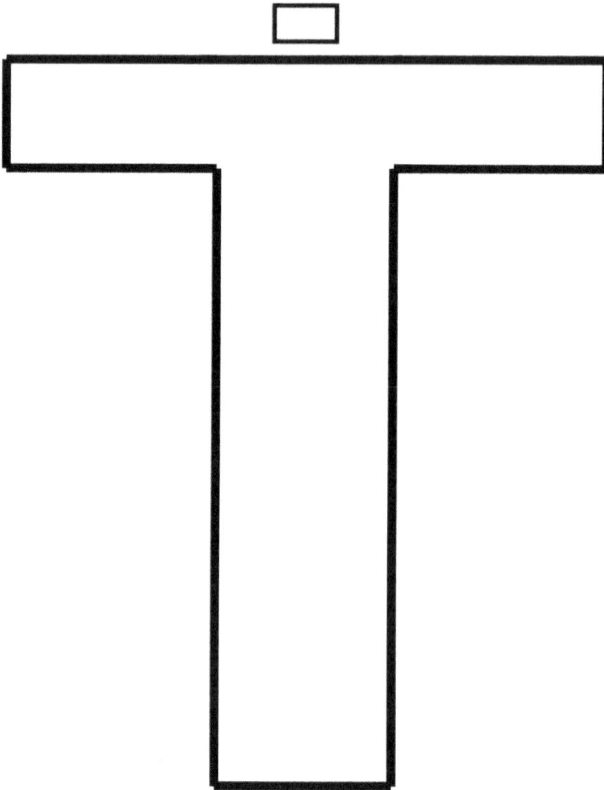

indeed formed. That such a pattern existed was not an original objective, nor was it expected. It was found with astonishment that the exceptions described above were indispensible features of just such a composite pattern whose significance was immediately discernable. In retrospect, this integrating pattern seems to have been hinted at by Jesus in Mark 8.

The resulting pattern is that shown in Figure 3. The significance of the pattern in this figure is immediately apparent, revealing at once why the parameter u is not a constant over the events and why the rectangles had the precise shapes defined in the analysis.

As shown on Figure 3, this combined pattern forms the figure of a cross. The upper limb of this cross is furnished by Peter's three thousand; the lower limb is provided by Jesus' five thousand, and the crosspiece (patibulum) is represented by the horizontal bar of Jesus' four thousand. Although a variety of shapes have been suggested for the actual cross upon which Jesus was slain, the shape as depicted on the figure is the one which is most commonly associated with the event of His Passion.

The small rectangle formed from the extra three companies in Case 3 is interpreted as representing the sign, called the titulus, inscribed with the subject's name and supposed crime, which was attached to the cross along with the victim at the time of crucifixion. Jesus' titulus read "Jesus of Nazareth, King of the Jews".

Figure 3: Composite Figure for Cases 1 Through 4

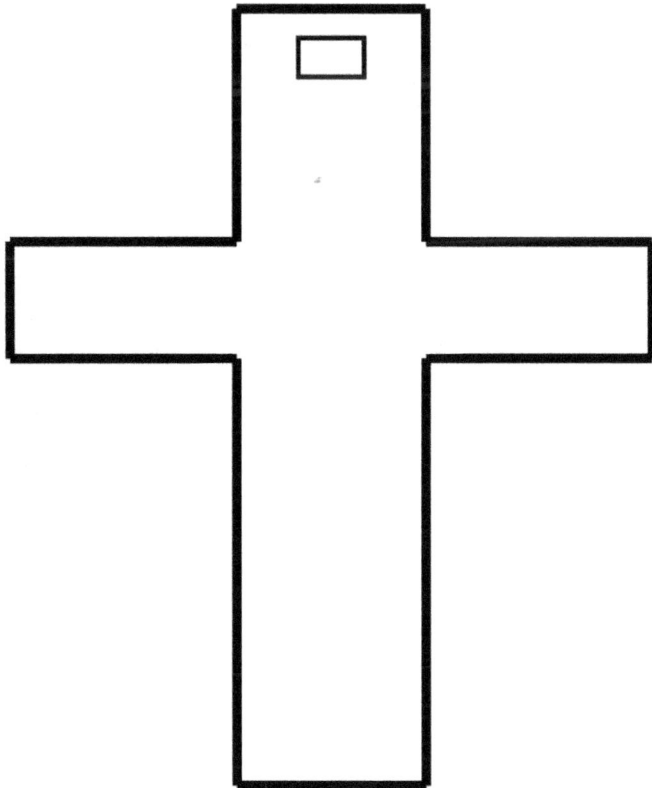

It is fascinating to note that if indeed Jesus' cross had been a Tau cross, as was commonly used by Romans at the time of Christ, then the simple rearrangement of the composite pattern, as shown on Figure 4, would furnish the associated representation. (See, for example, the article entitled "On the Physical Death of Jesus Christ" by William D. Edwards, MD, et al in the March 21, 1986 issue of JAMA.) For that period of time, the crosspiece (patibulum) was usually 5 to 6 feet in length, and the vertical post (stipes) was 6 to 8 feet in height. The average length ratio of patibulum to stipes for these ranges is $(5/8+1)/2$, or about 0.8 (.814). The length ratio of these members as shown in Figure 4 is nearly identical to this average, being approximately 0.8 (.8125).

The pattern of the cross clearly indicates the significance of the feeding events as representing a sign. As noted in the gospels, this sign would not be given to the generation that asked for one. It required, for its recognition, the fulfillment of Jesus' mission and beyond that the completion provided by Peter in feeding three thousand souls with the Word of God.

It is appropriate that the cross should have been associated with the feeding. A symbol of weakness and shame to the unsaved, the cross is the most powerful implement that the earth has ever seen for turning death into life, for reconciling man to his God, and with this link created out of the feeding of the multitudes, for representing the Living Word which is also the Bread of Life.

The significance of the feeding process may go beyond the sign of the cross. In the link established between Jesus' feeding events and Peter's feeding of the word may found a prophetic representation of the growth of the Church.

Appendix 5-1 Mathematical Solution to the Feeding Pattern

Note: for a simplified mathematical development, please refer to Appendix 5-2; for a visual non-mathematical development, please refer to Appendix 5-3

Section 1: Mathematical Characterization of the Feeding

A congregation being fed may be considered to have two basic types of attributes: spatial and procedural. The congregation's spatial attributes define its size, shape, and orientation with respect to some reference. Its procedural attributes characterize the manner in which the initial food is distributed, how it is then passed from individual to individual, and how the remainder enters the area from which it is collected into baskets.

Figures 1 and 2 present detailed illustrations of the congregation's spatial attributes. Figure 1 shows the attributes associated with a single company, and Figure 2 depicts the congregation as a whole with the company as the basic unit. Similarly, the procedural attributes are shown on Figures 3 through 5. Figure 3 addresses the intra-company procedures for a congregation as a whole, where the congregation is organized into companies for feeding. Figures 4 and 5 illustrate the feeding procedures at the more detailed level internal to the companies. Figure 4 shows the procedure for a typical forward company, which receives an initial loaf. Figure 5 shows the procedure for a typical company situated behind the forward companies.

As shown on Figure 1, a company consists of a two-dimensional array of individuals, each of whom is oriented in a specific direction. The size of the company is determined by the total number of individuals of which it is comprised and the space occupied by each individual. Its shape is specified by the ratio of the lengths of the sides, which in turn is dependent on the relative numbers of rows and columns of individuals and the shape factor associated with the individuals' orientation. The orientation of the company (as opposed to the orientation of the individuals within it) is defined in terms of the actual numbers of rows and columns within the company as would be seen by a hypothetical observer, and is independent of the orientation of the individuals. This company-level orientation is assumed to be a constant for each company of a particular size for all such companies within a congregation and for all congregations over the range of feeding events. The orientation of the individuals within the companies and the congregation is assumed to be a constant for all individuals participating in a particular feeding.

Figure 1: Spatial Properties of a Company

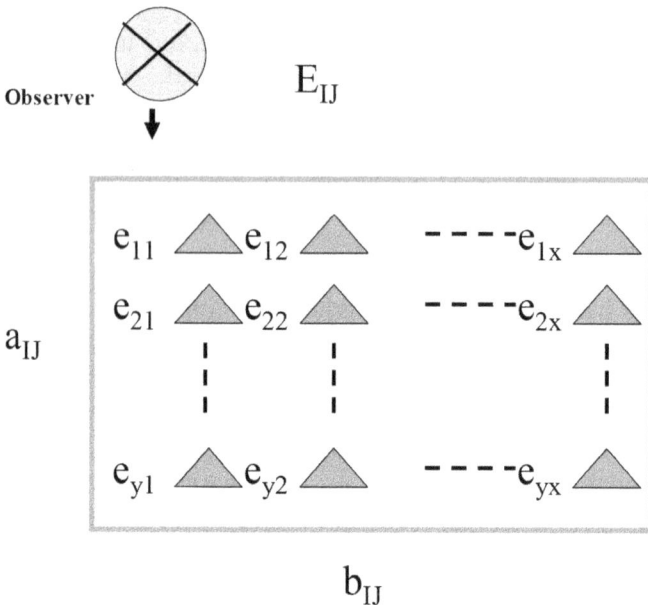

The size, shape, and orientation of the entire congregation is dependent on the factors shown on Figure 2, where the companies are assumed to be situated adjacent to each other with no separation space between them. The congregation size is determined by the number of companies of which it is comprised and the space occupied by each company. The shape is a factor of its composite proportions as determined by the shape of the component companies and the ratio of the lengths of the sides, which in turn is dependent on the relative number of rows and columns of companies and the shape factor associated with the companies' orientation. The orientation of the congregation is specified in terms of the number of rows and columns of companies of which it is comprised, where the rows at the company level have the same orientation as the rows within the companies.

Figure 2: Spatial Properties of Nth Congregation

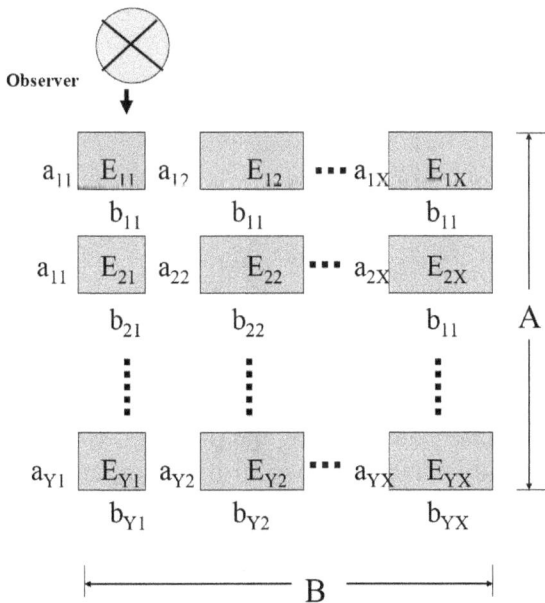

The assumed feeding procedure for the entire congregation is shown on Figure 3. As shown, each company in the most forward line of companies is provided with one initial loaf. Here the forwardmost position is that line which is first to receive the food and is determined by the individuals' orientation rather than the location of the companies within the array. The loaves are broken and passed on within the companies, exiting in parallel streams from the rear. From there they enter the next companies directly to their rear, maintaining the parallel streams or, if the previous companies occupied the rearmost positions, the remainder is taken up in the collection baskets.

Figure 3: Feeding Procedure Within a Congregation

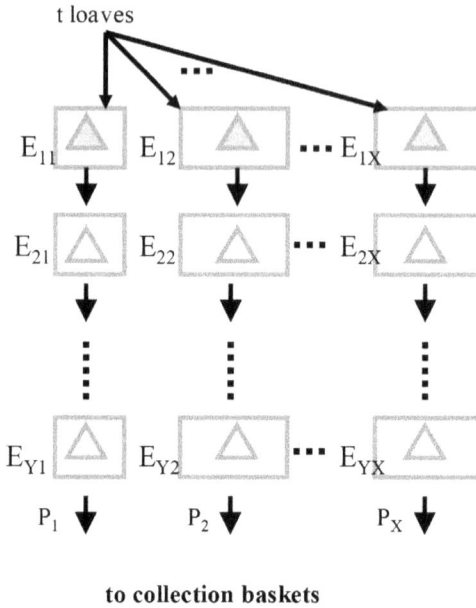

to collection baskets

The feeding procedure as described above differs between the most forward companies and those to their rear. Figure 4 illustrates the factors involved as the feeding proceeds within a forward company. As shown on the figure, the procedure is dependent on the orientation of the individuals within the company. Although there is more than one way in which the feeding may be accomplished, the alternatives produce equivalent results with respect to the flow of food into and out of the company. The following procedure is assumed: the initial loaf is given to the individual in the forward left corner as determined by his orientation rather than his position. If his orientation is as shown on Figure 4, this initial individual will be the one located in the upper left corner as shown. If his orientation is pointing to the right, on the other hand, the individual will be located in the upper right corner. In either case, the initial individual breaks it and hands half to the individual to his immediate right.

Then the same individual breaks the remainder (which is whole again) once more and hands half to the individual behind him. Individuals behind the most forward row within the company, as well as the rightmost individual in the most forward row, will only break their received loaves once and hand the remainder to the individuals behind them. As described, the loaves will propagate to the right along the single most forward row (or column, depending on the individuals' orientation), and toward the rear of the company in a stream of parallel paths. For the orientation shown in figure 4, the number of parallel rearward paths is equal to the number of columns. For a transverse orientation, the number of paths is equal to the number of rows. The remaining loaves in each company pass out the rear of the company as determined by the orientation of the individuals rather than their position.

Figure 4: Feeding Procedure Within a Forward Companyp

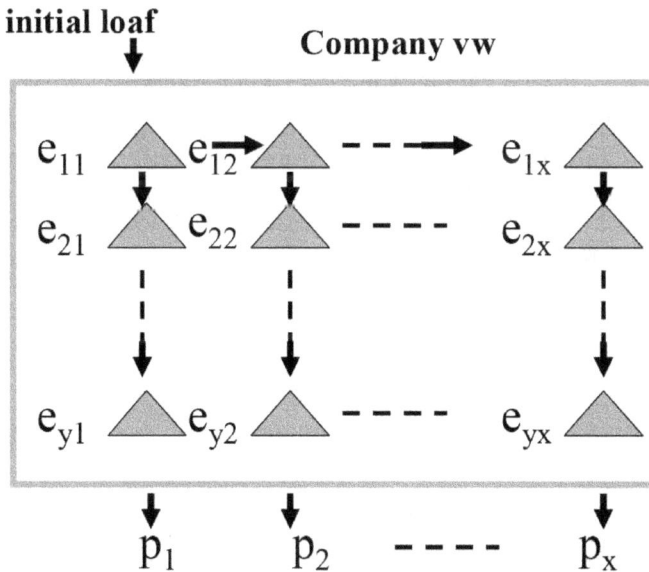

to next company or collection baskets

The feeding procedure within companies not in forward positions is shown on Figure 5. As shown, the loaves are broken and passed to the rear only, maintaining the parallel stream in receiving the loaves and propagating them rearward.

Figure 5: Feeding Procedure Within a Nonforward Company

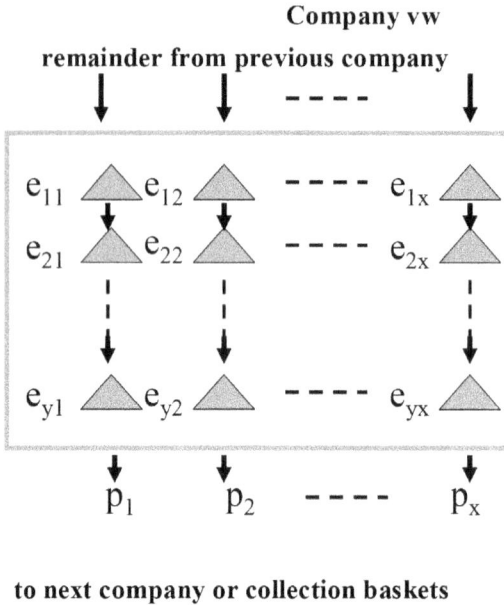

General mathematical representations shall now be developed to express the physical and procedural properties associated with the feeding events. These general representations are not specific to the actual events, but instead furnish a background that will permit a systematic exploration of those events with a minimum of ambiguity. The following development is derived from the verbal description given above.

The notation will follow these general guidelines:

Symbols representing parameters and variables are italicized

Company-level symbols are generally lower case; congregation-level symbols are generally upper case

Symbols followed by brackets { } are interpreted as varying as 'a function of' the symbols that the brackets enclose

Subscripts are sometimes omitted if their inclusion would add unnecessary clutter and the interpretation is clear

The spatial and procedural attribute types will be addressed separately below. The spatial attributes will be considered first because they furnish the mathematical setting for the expression of the procedural attributes. Each attribute type will furnish numerical relationships that must be simultaneously satisfied in the evaluation of the feeding events. The approach to be taken herein toward the characterization of attributes will be to furnish a reasonably complete characterization regardless of whether all items are of immediate relevance to the current application.

A. Spatial Attributes:

1) Company-level:

The spatial characteristics of a company include numerical attributes such as the number of rows and columns, and dimensional attributes such as its height and length. The numerical attributes shall be addressed first.

For each case (i.e. the feeding of 5000, etc.), the congregation is assembled in companies. As shown on Figure 1, each company E_{IJ} consists of an array of n_{IJ} elements e_{ij}, where lower-case subscript i denotes the ith (horizontal) row, and lower-case subscript j denotes the jth (vertical) column. The organization of rows and columns is independent of the orientation of the constituent individuals. Instead, the spatial organization references a fixed hypothetical observer (see Figure 3), where the first row forms a line closest to the observer and perpendicular to his line of sight to the array.

If subscript i of element e_{ij} in company E_{IJ} ranges from 1 to y_{IJ}, and subscript j ranges from 1 to x_{IJ}, then the number of rows r_{IJ} and columns c_{IJ} in E_{IJ} are:

$$r_{IJ} = y_{IJ} \qquad\qquad\qquad <1>$$

$$c_{IJ} = x_{IJ}$$

The number n_{IJ} of elements in E_{IJ} is the product of rows and columns of individuals. From <1>, this product is:

$$n_{IJ} = r_{IJ}c_{IJ} = x_{IJ}y_{IJ} \qquad\qquad <2>$$

Equations <1> and <2> define the primary numerical attributes. The dimensional attributes of a company shall be considered next.

The elements e_{ij} within a company are assumed to be adjacent to each other, each occupying a space that may be sensitive to the orientation of individuals. An individual space/orientation factor, denoted u, is defined to specify the orientation. The complement to u, denoted as u', is defined such that its value is the opposite of the value associated with u. A variable q is also defined, to account for the effect of the individual's orientation on the space he occupies. Figure 6 describes the properties of variables u and q.

Figure 6: Orientation Factors u and q

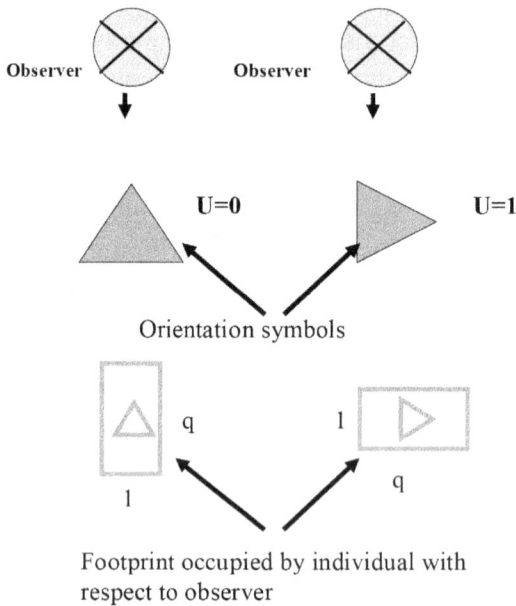

Orientation symbols

Footprint occupied by individual with respect to observer

$u = 0$ for individual facing observer   **<3>**

$u = 1$ for individual at right angles to observer

$u' = 1$ for individual facing observer

$u' = 0$ for individual at right angles to observer

width of ground occupied by individual $= 1$

length of space on ground of individual $= q$

Since u can only assume the values of 0 and 1, it serves as a logical, as opposed to numerical, operator. The use of this operator is a convenience, permitting the inclusion of alternative conditions in a single expression. As noted elsewhere in this paper, the orientation factor u was found to be an important factor in the original development.

The space factor q is not a crucial parameter, but its inclusion leads to more aesthetically appealing results. Initially included only for that reason, it is thought to provide important supplementary information regarding specifics of the feedings. As defined above, q can assume a different value for a standing individual than for a sitting one.

Company E_{IJ} occupies a rectangular space whose height a_{IJ} is the product of the space/orientation factor and the number of rows r_{IJ}, and whose length b_{IJ} is the product of the space/orientation factor and the number of columns c_{IJ}. Applying the above to <1>,

$$a_{IJ} = y_{IJ}(q+[1-q]u) \qquad\qquad\qquad \text{<4>}$$

$$b_{IJ} = x_{IJ}(q+[1-q]u')$$

where $u = 0$ or 1

$u' = 1$ or 0

Equations <3> and <4> describe the essential dimensional attributes of a company.

2) Congregational level:

The numerical attributes of the congregation are addressed first, as was done for the company-level characterization.

The mth congregation G_m, for case m, comprises N_m individuals who are recorded as being fed. As shown on Figure 4, these individuals are organized in rows and columns of companies, where the companies are directly adjacent to each other.

The congregation is generally a rectangular array having company elements E_{IJ}, where subscript I denotes the Ith row, and subscript J denotes the Jth column. The evaluation of a congregation will initially assume the closest fit of a perfectly rectangular array to the approximate parameters of the case under consideration. Companies will then be added or removed from the resulting array to render the parameters exact. The addition or removal will be made in multiples of whole companies.

If subscript I of company element E_{IJ} in congregation G_m ranges from 1 to Y, and if X is the range of subscript J, then the number D_m of companies in G_m is:

$$D_m = \sum_{I=1}^{Y} X \{I\} \qquad \text{<5>}$$

Furthermore, the number of rows R_J in the Jth column of G_m is:

$$R_J = \sum_{I=1}^{Y} y_{IJ} \qquad \text{<6>}$$

Similarly,

$$C_I = \sum_{J=1}^{X} x_{IJ} \qquad \text{<7>}$$

where C_I represents the number of columns in the Ith row of G_m.

In line with the assumption of general rectangularity and the maintenance of the parallel feeding streams from company to company, all elements E_{IJ} having common row subscript I are constrained to have the same number of rows within a company. Similarly, all elements having common column subscript J are assumed to have the same number of columns within a company.

Applying the commentary above regarding common row and column subscripts to <1>,

$$y_{IJ} = y_I \text{ for all } J = 1 \ldots X \qquad \text{<8>}$$

$$x_{IJ} = x_J \text{ for all } I = 1 \ldots Y$$

From <6>, <7>, and <8>,

$$R_J\{m\} = R_m = \sum_{I=1}^{Y} y_I \qquad \text{<9>}$$

$$C_I\{m\} = C_m = \sum_{J=1}^{X} x_J$$

The congregation G_m as a whole will contain a number N_m individual elements e_{IJ} in the product of its total number of rows and columns. Therefore, from <9>,

$$N_m = R_m C_m \qquad \text{<10>}$$

Alternatively, from <5>,

$$N_m = \sum^D n_{IJ} = \sum^Y_{I=1} \left(\sum^X_{J=1} n_{IJ} \right) \qquad \text{<11>}$$

Equations <5>, <8>, <9>, <10>, and <11> comprise the primary numerical characterization at the congregational level. The dimensional characterization follows.

The congregation G_m will occupy a rectangular space whose height A_m is the summation of the company heights over the number Y_m of rows, and whose length B_m is the summation of the company lengths over the number X_m of columns.

Applying <8> to <4>,

$$a_{IJ} = a_I \text{ for all } J = 1 \ldots X \qquad \text{<12>}$$

$$b_{IJ} = b_J \text{ for all } I = 1 \ldots Y$$

Applying <12> to the commentary above defining A_m and B_m,

$$A_m = \sum^Y_{I=1} a_I \qquad \text{<13>}$$

$$B_m = \sum^X_{J=1} b_J$$

The further constraint shall be made that the orientation of individuals is the same throughout at least the entire congregation:

$$u_{ij}\{m\} = u_m \qquad \text{<14>}$$

Applying <8> and <14> to <4> in <13>,

$$A_m = (q+[1-q]u)\sum^Y_{I=1} y_I \qquad \text{<15>}$$

$$B_m = (q+[1-q]u') \sum^X_{J=1} x_J$$

Alternatively, applying <9> to <15>,

$$A_m = (q+[1-q]u)R_m \qquad \text{<16>}$$

$$B_m = (q+[1-q]u')C_m$$

Equations <14> through <16> describe the primary dimensional attributes of a congregation.

B. Procedural Attributes:

1) Company-level:

As noted in the discussion of feeding procedures and illustrated on Figure 4, the feeding within a frontmost company follows a number of parallel paths from the frontmost to the rearmost individuals.

Let p_{IJ} represent this number of parallel feeding paths generated within a company E_{IJ}. In general, if the individuals in the company are facing the observer ($u = 0$), the number of paths is equivalent to the number of columns. Similarly, if $u = 1$, the number of paths is equivalent to the number of rows in the company:

$$p_{IJ} = x_{IJ} + [y_{IJ} - x_{IJ}]u \qquad <17>$$

Applying <8> to <17>,

$$p_{IJ} = x_J + [y_I - x_J]u \qquad <18>$$

If company E_{IJ} is a rearmost company as shown on Figure 5, then its output p_{IJ} will represent that company's portion of the congregation's remainder to be collected into baskets. The topic of remainders will be treated in detail at the congregational level.

Let g represent the number of loaves input into a company, and p the number of loaves output from a company. Also let E_{IJ} represent a non-forward company, and E'_{IJ} a forward (frontmost) company. It was assumed in the previous description that each forward company receives one initial loaf and outputs a parallel stream of loaves in the front-to-rear direction, and each non-front company inputs a parallel stream of loaves from the previous company and outputs the same parallel stream. From these assumptions,

$$g\{E_{IJ}\} = p_{IJ} \qquad <19>$$

$$g\{E'_{IJ}\} = 1$$

2) Congregational level:

As noted above, each company within a congregation G_m consists of an array of elements e_{ij}, one element representing each individual. All individuals are assumed to be oriented in the same direction, and their orientation defines the frontmost companies in the congregation. As shown on Figure 3, the frontmost companies receive the initial loaves, the number of which, for the mth case, is implied in <19> to be the number L_m of initial loaves. The number F_m of frontmost companies, then, is constrained to be equivalent to L_m:

$$F_m = L_m \qquad <20>$$

But the number of frontmost companies is also either X_m or Y_m depending on the orientation factor u:

$$F_m = X_m + [Y_m - X_m]u \qquad <21>$$

From <20> and <21>,

$$L_m = X_m + [Y_m - X_m]u \qquad <22>$$

If P_m represents the number of loaves collected into baskets as the remainder from congregation G_m, then P_m will be the sum of paths p_{IJ} from all the rearmost companies. Depending on the individuals' orientation, this sum will be either the total number of rows R_m or columns C_m in the congregation, as defined in <9>. Applying the orientation factor to <9> in a manner similar to the development of <17> and <18>,

$$P_m = C_m + [R_m - C_m]u \qquad <23>$$

Let h represent the number of loaves contained in each basket of remaining loaves. Then the number of baskets Z_m produced by congregation G_m will be

$$Z_m = P_m/h \qquad <24>$$

An interesting facet to the development so far is that the loaves of bread are assumed to have been initially distributed whole, such that one loaf was given to each frontmost company. If the initial fish were divided such that they matched and were handed out along with the initial distribution of loaves, the pattern-dependency of the process from that point would ensure that in every case the numbers of fish would be identical to those associated with the loaves.

C. Additional Assumptions associated with the characterization

In addition to the organization assumed for the arrangement and feeding process, the following initial assumptions are made. They reflect the expectation of consistency among the several events of important unspecified parameters:

(1) There were in all cases companies of 50 and 100

(2) All variables and constants must be integers; a fraction of a person, for example, is not permitted

(3) The number h of remainder loaves in each basket is assumed to be a constant for all feeding events.

(4) Unless otherwise noted as exceptions, all individuals were seated; in the seated position, the individual's shape factor is 2:1 in the direction of orientation.

Minor additional assumptions are made in the development below as indicated by logic, simplicity of development, or specific supporting data.

Assumption 1) requires that the sum of companies of 50 and 100 in a congregation for each case furnish the total number of individuals for that case. If d_m represents the number of companies of 50 in $G_{m'}$ then from <11>,

$$N_m = \sum^d (50) + \sum^{D-d} (100) = 50d + 100(D-d) \qquad <25>$$

Also, <2> takes the specific values

$$n_{IJ} = 50 \text{ or } 100 \qquad\qquad <26>$$

A logical operator v and its complement v', similar in function to u and u', are defined to accommodate the either-or type of expressions as <26> which involve either the 50-element company or the 100-element company.

$v = 0$ for a company of 100   <27>

$v = 1$ for a company of 50

$v' = 1$ for a company of 100

$v' = 0$ for a company of 50

Applying <27> to <26>,

$$n_{IJ} = 50v + 100v' \qquad \qquad <28>$$

From assumption 4), the orientation factor q is a constant of value 2:

$$q = 2 \qquad \qquad <29>$$

At this point, two further simplifying assumptions shall be made, constraining a company of 100 to have the specific shape of 5 rows by 20 columns, and a company of 50 to have 5 rows by 10 columns. Although these assumptions will ultimately be justified by producing results which are consistent with the numerical data furnished in the Gospels, some initial justification is obtained by looking ahead to the single company involved in Elisha's feeding event. In that event, the hundred individuals were fed from an initial quantity of 20 loaves of barley. For this case, an assumption of a nonforward company (inputting and outputting 20 loaves), and with individuals having an orientation toward the hypothetical observer ($u = 0$), while representing a reasonable estimate, also greatly simplifies the mathematical analysis.

As noted in the development of <5>, the term $X\{I\}$ defines the number of companies in the Ith row of a congregation. As noted previously, the initial assumption will be that the congregation will be a perfectly rectangular array producing the total number of elements closest to the number in the congregation. The array will then be adjusted from that initial estimate to produce an exact match. Given that approach,

$$X\{I\} = X \qquad \qquad <30>$$

Where X is a constant for all rows throughout a congregation.

A term X' is now defined as a simplifying factor, given the assumption that there are only two unique company sizes, to represent the number of companies of size 50 in a particular row. Then, from <30>, the number of companies of size 100 in a particular row will be ($X - X'$). Applying this simplification to <7>, noting the assumption made above regarding the number of columns in the companies of 50 and 100, results in

$$C_m = 10\,X_m' + 20\,(X_m - X_m') \qquad\qquad\qquad \text{<31>}$$

An alternate form of <25> shall be utilized in the analysis of the specific Cases. If the approach to solving for data, as noted above, is to first assume a perfectly rectangular grouping for the closest fit to the approximate number of individuals involved in the feeding and then to adjust as required for an exact fit, <5> may be expressed as:

$$D_m = X_m Y_m \qquad\qquad\qquad\qquad\qquad \text{<32>}$$

In the same manner, the variable d may be expressed as:

$$d_m = X_m' Y_m \qquad\qquad\qquad\qquad\qquad \text{<33>}$$

Applying <32> and <33> to <25>,

$$N_m = Y_m(50\,X_m' + 100(X_m - X_m')) \qquad\qquad \text{<34>}$$

The simplifications presented in this section result in a straightforward modification to the equations derived above. Their application to the company-level relationships are given in <35> below.

$$a_{IJ} = a_m = 5(2-u) \qquad\qquad\qquad\qquad \text{<35>}$$

$$b_{IJ} = (10v + 20v')(2-u')$$

$$r_{IJ} = 5$$

$$c_{IJ} = x_{IJ} = 10v + 20v'$$

$$n_{IJ} = 50v + 100v'$$

$$p_{IJ} = v(10 - 5u) + v'(20 - 15u)$$

The values in <35>, as applied to the congregational-level relationships developed previously, produce the relationships presented below as <36> and <37>. The summary relationships grouped under <36> provide the working equations for the specific case-by-case analyses; the relationships of <37> are then applied to the solutions to furnish dimensional and other supporting information.

Summary of Relevant Relationships:

$$R_m = 5Y_m \qquad\qquad\qquad <36>$$

$$C_m = 10\, X_m' + 20\, (X_m - X_m')$$

$$N_m = R_m C_m = Y_m (50\, X_m' + 100(X_m - X_m'))$$

$$L_m = F_m = X_m + [Y_m - X_m]u$$

$$P_m = C_m + [R_m - C_m]u$$

$$Z_m = P_m/h$$

$$A_m = 5Y(2-u) \qquad\qquad\qquad <37>$$

$$B_m = (2 - u')\, [10\, X'_m + 20(X_m - X'_m)]$$

$$D_m = X_m Y_m$$

$$d_m = X'_m Y_m$$

where

D_m is the number of companies in a congregation

d_m is the number of companies of size 50 in a congregation

Y_m is the number of rows of companies in a congregation

X_m is the number of columns of companies in a congregation

X_m' is the number of companies of 50 in a row

R_m is the total number of rows in a congregation

C_m is the total number of columns in a congregation

N_m is the total number of individuals in a congregation

A_m is the height of the congregation

B_m is the length of the congregation

p_{IJ} is the number of feeding paths in a company

F_m **is the number of frontmost (receiving) companies in a congregation**

L_m **is the initial number of loaves for a congregation**

P_m **is the number of remainder loaves collected into baskets**

h **is the number of remainder loaves per basket**

Z_m **is the number of remainder baskets for a congregation**

Section 2: Evaluation of Structural Details Associated with Feeding Events

A. Specification of Cases

Four feeding events are assumed, which are labeled as Cases in this analysis: the two performed by Jesus (5000 and 4000); the precursor case performed by Elisha that enabled Jesus as the Son of man to perform his own feeding, and the case prophesied by Jesus in John 21 and fulfilled in Acts 2 of Peter feeding three thousand souls with the Word of God.

Case 1: Reference Second Kings Chapter 4; Elisha feeds a company of one hundred with twenty loaves.

Case 2: Reference Matthew 14, Mark 6, Mark 8, Luke 9, John 6; Jesus feeds 5000 individuals with 5 loaves, leaving a remainder of 12 baskets. They were all commanded to sit during the feeding, in ranks (companies) of 50 and 100.

Case 3: Reference Matthew 15, Mark 8 (twice); Jesus feeds 4000 individuals with 7 loaves, leaving a remainder of 7 baskets. The multitude was commanded to sit during the feeding. It is a matter of interpretation as to whether 'the multitude' means 'all'.

Case 4: Reference John 21, Acts 2; Peter feeds 3000 individuals with the Word of God. A symbolic remainder of 12 baskets (one for each Apostle) is assumed. Note in regard to this event that in the twenty-first chapter of John's Gospel, Jesus demanded of Peter three times that he feed His sheep, a prophesy the fulfillment of which is noted in the referenced event. The thrice-stated command to feed is taken to correspond to three symbolic initial loaves.

B. Detailed evaluation

The validity of the assumptions made to this point will be assessed below for each of the four cases noted above, and for each of the two orientations for each case. If a valid solution cannot be found for at least one orientation in every case, the assumptions will be revisited. Where a valid solution can be found, the specific congregational pattern and size will be established.

1A. Case 1, $u = 0$

The following values are taken directly from the information provided in Scripture for this case:

$$N_1 = 100 \hspace{7cm} \text{<38>}$$

$$L_1 = 20$$

$$Z_1 = \text{unknown } (P_m \text{ is assumed to be 20})$$

As noted in the previous section, case 1 ($m = 1$) involves only one company of one hundred people and was used to establish the spatial pattern of 20 x 5 for a company of one hundred, which will be regarded as a constant value over all the events. The pattern for a company of 50 was assumed as having half the longest dimension of the company of 100, and will also be regarded as a constant value.

From case 1 of Elisha the hundred individuals were fed from an initial quantity of 20 loaves of barley. For this case, the company is taken to be a nonforward company (inputting and outputting 20 loaves), and with individuals having an orientation toward the hypothetical observer ($u = 0$). Therefore, the assumed feeding process as depicted on Figure 7 requires a company of 100 to have a width of 20, in which all of the front participants each receive a loaf; otherwise, the initial distribution is awkward and unnecessarily complex. A company of 50 is taken as half that width, or of 10. These values require both company types to have a single, constant depth (row size) of 5.

Figure 7: Feeding Pattern for Case 1 (Elisha's Feeding of 100)

One company of 100:

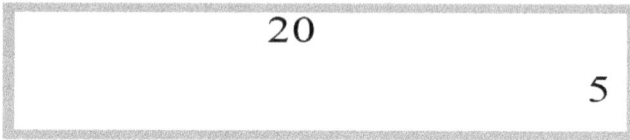

20	
	5

Applying the values applicable to Case 1 as noted in <38> to summary relations <36> noting that X_1 and Y_1 are both 1 and the assumed company size is 100:

$$R_1 = 5Y_1 = 5 \qquad\qquad\qquad <39>$$

$$C_1 = 10\,X_1' + 20\,(X_1 - X_1') = 20$$

$$N_1 = Y_1(50\,X_1' + 100(X_1 - X_1') = 100$$

$$L_1 = 20 \text{ (non-frontmost company assumed for this case)}$$

$$P_1 = C_1 + [R_1 - C_1]u = 20$$

$$Z_1 = P_1/h = 20/h$$

As specified in equations <39>, Case 1 with u=0 represents a single company of 100 individuals consisting of 5 rows and 20 columns and having a (normalized) height of 10 units and a (normalized) length of 20 units. The feeding was initiated and proceeded along 20 paths.

The ambiguity of Z_1 may be partially resolved by listing the possible values for Z_1 vs. h in tabular form, with the intent, as justified by <14>, of reducing the possible values of h in the analysis of subsequent cases.

The following table of possible values for h is derived from the relation for Z_1 in <39>, imposing the requirement that both Z_1 and h must be integers:

TABLE 1

h	$Z_1 = 20/h$
1	20
2	10
3	- (not an integer)
4	5
5	4
6-9	-
10	2
11-19	-
20	1

1B. Case 1, $u = 1$

Since case 1 involves a single company both receiving and outputting 20 loaves, an orientation transverse to the observer is inconsistent with the current assumption of a company of 100 having only 5 rows. Changing the company shape to provide 20 rows would simply redefine u and either render the result for Case 1, $u = 0$ invalid or require that the shape of a basic company to be case-dependent, violating the guiding principle that the simplest solution is the preferred one. Therefore, Case 1, $u = 1$ is considered to be invalid.

2A. Case 2, $u = 0$

The following values are taken directly from the information provided in Scripture for this case:

$N_2 = 5000$ <40>

$L_2 = 5$

$Z_2 = 12$

Applying the parameter values of <40> to the relevant equations out of the summary set <36> produces the following values:

$$R_2 = 5Y_2 \qquad \text{<41>}$$

$$C_2 = 10\,X_2' + 20\,(X_2 - X_2')$$

$$N_2 = Y_2(50\,X_2' + 100(X_2 - X_2')) = 5000$$

$$L_2 = X_2 + [Y_2 - X_2]u = 5$$

$$P_2 = C_2 + [R_2 - C_2]u$$

$$Z_2 = P_2/h = 12$$

L_2 is first solved for $u = 0$ to establish that

$$X_2 = 5 \qquad \text{<42>}$$

It is next noted from <41> that

$$C_2 = P_2 \qquad \text{<43>}$$

The evaluation will seek next to establish a value for h by reducing the possible values given in Table 1. To that end, Table 2 below presents the values of P_2 , and consequently of C_2 ,associated with the valid values of h as generated from Table 1:

TABLE 2

h	$C_2 = 12h$
1	12
2	24
4	48
5	60
10	120
20	240

Next, it is noted from the relation $X_2 = 5$ in <42> that X'_2 may assume only whole number values from 0 through 5. From the expression for C_2 in <41> the following relationship is obtained:

$$X'_2 = 10 - C_2/10 \qquad \text{<44>}$$

Table 3 below defines the possible values of C_2 corresponding to this range:

TABLE 3

H	X'_2
1	Not an integer
2	Not an integer
4	Not an integer
5	4
10	Negative value
20	Negative value

A comparison of Tables 2 and 3 establishes the only possible valid value of X_2 is 4, with a corresponding value of h as:

$$h = 5 \tag{45}$$

Substituting <42> through <45> into <41> yields

$$R_2 = 5Y_2 \tag{46}$$

$$C_2 = 60$$

$$Y_2(300) = 5000$$

$$L_2 = X_2 = 5$$

$$P_2 = 60$$

$$Z_2 = 12$$

$$X'_2 = 4$$

In the establishment of the specific data associated with case 2, a perfectly rectangular array consisting of 5100 elements was evaluated, via solving for Y_2, as the best first approximation for 5000 elements. One whole company of 100 individuals was then removed from the array to arrive at an exact correspondence to the 5000 individuals. The resulting value for Y_2 is

$$Y_2 = 17 \tag{47}$$

Finally, <46> and <47> were applied to summary relations <37> to give:

$$A_2 = 170 \tag{48}$$

$B_2 = 60$

$d_2 = 68$

$D_2 = 85$ (reduced to 84 by deleting one company as discussed below)

The associated array is shown on Figure 8, and consists of 17 rows by 5 columns, 1 of which consists of companies of 100 and 4 of which consist of companies of 50. One company of 100 is missing from this array, having the center column consist of 16 rows instead of 17.

Figure 8: Feeding Pattern for Case 2 (Jesus' Feeding of 5000)

68 companies of 50 and 16 companies of 100 arranged in companies of 50 in 2 columns of 17 rows on each side of companies of 100 in center column of 16 rows :

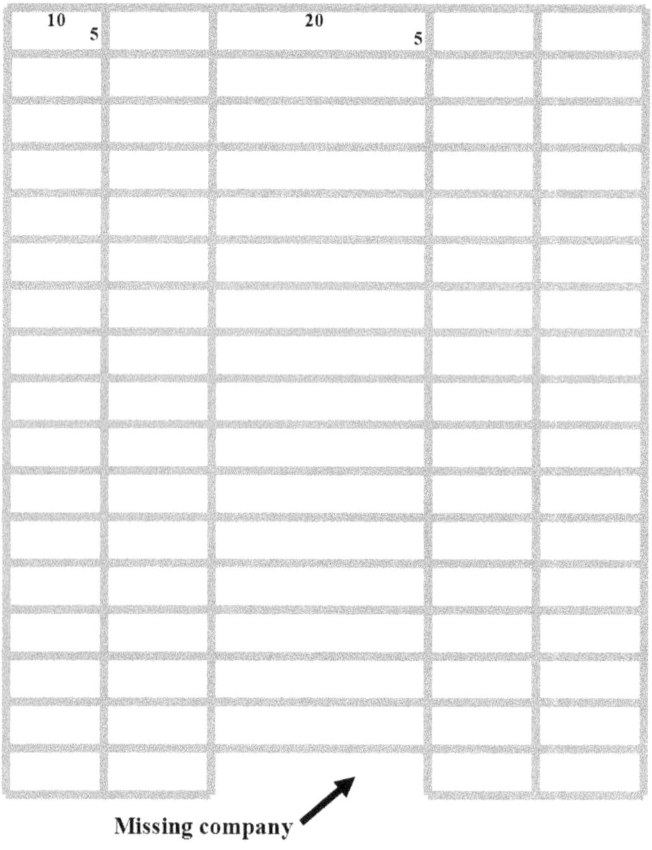

Missing company

2B. Case 2, $u = 1$

Applying the parameter values of <40> to the relevant equations out of the summary set <36> with $m = 2$ and $u = 1$ produces the following values:

$$R_2 = 5Y_2 \tag{49}$$

$$C_2 = 10\,X_2' + 20\,(X_2 - X_2')$$

$$N_2 = R_2 C_2 = Y_2(50\,X_2' + 100(X_2 - X_2')) = 5000$$

$$L_2 = F_2 = X_2 + [Y_2 - X_2]u = Y_2 = 5$$

$$P_2 = C_2 + [R_2 - C_2]u = R_2$$

$$Z_2 = P_2/h = 12$$

The following are derived from the values given in <49> above:

$$Y_2 = 12h/5 \tag{50}$$

$$Y_2 = 5$$

Which require that $h = 25/12$, invalid because it violates the requirement that h be an integer. Therefore, Case 2, $u = 1$ is considered to be invalid.

3A. Case 3, $u = 0$

The following values are taken directly from the information provided in Scripture for this case:

$$N_3 = 4000 \tag{51}$$

$$L_3 = 7$$

$$Z_3 = 7$$

Applying the parameter values of <51> with $u = 0$ to the relevant equations out of the summary set <36>, and including <45>, produces the following values:

$$R_3 = 5Y_3 \tag{52}$$

$$C_3 = 10\,X_3' + 20\,(X_3 - X_3')$$

$$N_3 = R_3 C_3 = Y_3(50\ X_3' + 100(X_3 - X_3')) = 4000$$

$$L_3 = F_3 = X_3 + [Y_3 - X_3]u = X_3 = 7$$

$$P_3 = C_3 + [R_3 - C_3]u = C_3$$

$$Z_3 = P_3/h = 7$$

$$h = 5$$

The following is derived from the values given above:

$$35 = 10\ X_3' + 20\ (7 - X_3') \tag{53}$$

Which reduces to $X_3' = 105/10$, invalid because it is a nonzero value that violates the requirement that X_3' be an integer. Therefore, Case 3, $u = 0$ is considered to be invalid.

3B. Case 3, $u = 1$

Applying the parameter values of <51> to the relevant equations out of the summary set <36> with $m = 3$ and $u = 1$ (and including <45>) produces the following values:

$$R_3 = 5Y_3 \tag{54}$$

$$C_3 = 10\ X_3' + 20\ (X_3 - X_3')$$

$$N_3 = R_3 C_3 = Y_3(50\ X_3' + 100(X_3 - X_3')) = 4000$$

$$L_3 = F_3 = X_3 + [Y_3 - X_3]u = Y_3 = 7$$

$$P_3 = C_3 + [R_3 - C_3]u = R_3$$

$$Z_3 = P_3/h = 7$$

$$h = 5$$

These parameters produce the following relationships:

$$C_3 = 800/7 \tag{55}$$

$$X'_3 = 2X_3 - C_3/10$$

For which the nearest integer values corresponding to the assumption of a perfectly rectangular array are

$C_3 = 110$ <56>

$X'_3 = 2X_3 - 11$

Equation <56> is satisfied for variable X'_3 over the range of odd numbers from 1 through 11. In actuality, the number selected will have no influence on the shape or size of the resulting rectangle. A value of 11 is selected for simplicity, such that all companies in the congregation will have a size of 50 individuals:

$X'_3 = X_3 = 11$ <57>

$X_3 - X'_3 = 0$ (no companies of 100)

Applying <57> into <54> while temporarily avoiding the utilization of the congregation size of 4000 furnishes the following values:

$R_3 = 35$ <58>

$C_3 = 110$

$N_3 = R_3 C_3 = 7(550) = 3850$

$L_3 = Y_3 = 7$

$P_3 = R_3 = 35$

$Z_3 = 7$

$h = 5$

Results <58> are next applied to summary relations <37> to give

$A_3 = R_3 = 35$ <59>

$B_3 = 220$

$d_3 = 77 \ (80)$

$D_3 = 77$ (increased to 80 by adding three companies of 50
        as discussed below)

The following specific data is associated with case 3. In the establishment of this data, a perfectly rectangular array consisting of 3850 elements was evaluated as the best first approximation for 4000 elements. Three whole companies of 50 individuals were then added to the array to arrive at an exact correspondence to the 4000 individuals. These companies may be added in any combination to end companies of the basic 3850-element rectangular congregation without disturbing the feeding process.

The associated array is shown on Figure 9, and consists of 7 rows by 11 columns, all of which consists of companies of 50. An additional three-company (of 50 elements each) array is attached to this array.

Figure 9: Feeding Pattern for Case 3 (Jesus' Feeding of 4000)

77 companies of 50 arranged in 11 columns of 7 rows, plus 3 additional companies of 50:

three additional companies of 50, not necessarily arranged as shown

4A. Case 4, $u = 0$

The following values are taken directly from the information provided in Scripture for this case:

$$N_4 = 3000 \qquad\qquad <60>$$

$L_4 = 3$

$Z_4 = 12$

Applying the parameter values of <60> to the relevant equations out of the summary set <36> with $m = 4$ and $u = 0$ (and including <45>) produces the following values:

$R_4 = 5Y_4$ <61>

$C_4 = 10 X_4' + 20 (X_4 - X_4')$

$N_4 = R_4 C_4 = Y_4 (50 X_4' + 100(X_4 - X_4')) = 3000$

$L_4 = F_4 = X_4 + [Y_4 - X_4]u = X_4 = 3$

$P_4 = C_4 + [R_4 - C_4]u = C_4$

$Z_4 = P_4/h = 12$

$h = 5$

These parameters produce the following relationships:

$C_4 = 60$ <62>

$X_4' = 2X_4 - 6 = 2(3) - 6 = 0$

$X_4 = 3$

$Y_4 C_4 = 600$

$Y_4 = 10$

which correspond to a perfectly rectangular 3 X 10 array of companies of 100.

Results <62> are next applied to summary relations <37> to provide dimensional data. In the establishment of this data, a perfectly rectangular array consisting of 3000 elements was confirmed as the actual value for the 3000 elements. The array consists entirely of companies of 100 individuals.

$A_4 = 5Y_4(2-u) = 10Y_4 = 100$ <63>

$B_4 = (2 - u') [10 X_4' + 20(X_4 - X_4')] = 60$

$$d_4 = X'_4Y_4 = 0$$
$$D_4 = X_4Y_4 = 30$$

The associated array is shown on Figure 10, and consists of 10 rows by 3 columns, all of which consists of companies of 100. No companies are missing from or extra to this array.

Figure 10: Feeding Pattern for Case 4
(Peter's Feeding of 3000 with Word)

30 companies of 100 arranged in 3 columns of 10 rows:

4B. Case 4, $u = 1$

Applying the parameter values of <60> to the relevant equations out of the summary set <36> with $m = 4$ and $u = 1$ produces the following values:

$$R_4 = 5Y_4 \qquad\qquad\qquad \text{<64>}$$
$$C_4 = 10\,X'_4 + 20\,(X_4 - X'_4)$$

$$N_4 = R_4 C_4 = Y_4(50\ X_4' + 100(X_4 - X_4')) = 3000$$

$$L_4 = F_4 = X_4 + [Y_4 - X_4]u = Y_4 = 3$$

$$P_4 = C_4 + [R_4 - C_4]u = R_4$$

$$Z_4 = P_4/h = 12$$

$$h = 5$$

These relationships, in turn, produce the following data:

$$R_4 = 5Y_4 = 15 \hspace{4cm} <65>$$

$$R_4 = P_4 = 60$$

Which forces the numerical relationship $15 = 60$, a nonvalid equivalence. Therefore, Case 4, $u = 1$ is considered to be invalid; consequently $u = 0$ is the only valid orientation for Case 4.

Appendix 5-2
Alternate (Simplified) Mathematical Solution to the Feeding Pattern

SECTION 1 (ALTERNATE): MATHEMATICAL CHARACTERIZATION OF THE FEEDING:

A congregation being fed may be considered to have two basic types of attributes: spatial and procedural. The congregation's spatial attributes define its size and shape. Its procedural attributes characterize the manner in which the initial food is distributed, how it is then passed from individual to individual, and how the remainder enters the area from which it is collected into baskets.

Figures 1 and 2 present detailed illustrations of the congregation's spatial attributes. Figure 1 shows the attributes associated with a single company, and Figure 2 depicts the congregation as a whole with the company as the basic unit. Similarly, the procedural attributes are shown on Figures 3 through 5. Figure 3 addresses the intra-company procedures for a congregation as a whole, where the congregation is organized into companies for feeding. Figures 4 and 5 illustrate the feeding procedures at the more detailed level internal to the companies. Figure 4 shows the procedure for a typical forward company, which receives an initial loaf. Figure 5 shows the procedure for a typical company situated behind the forward companies.

As shown on Figure 1, a company consists of a two-dimensional array of individuals. The size of the company is determined by the total number of individuals of which it is comprised and the space occupied by each individual. Its shape is specified by the ratio of the lengths of the sides, which in turn is dependent on the relative numbers of rows and columns of individuals.

Figure 1: Spatial Properties of a Company

$$E_{IJ}$$

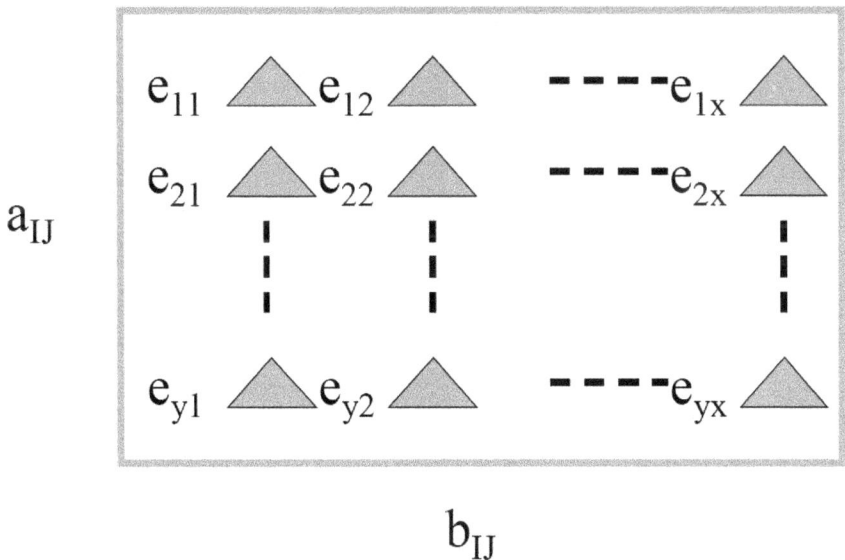

$$a_{IJ}$$

$$b_{IJ}$$

The size and shape of the entire congregation is dependent on the factors shown on Figure 2, where the companies are assumed to be situated adjacent to each other with no separation space between them. The congregation size is determined by the number of companies of which it is comprised and the space occupied by each company. The shape is a factor of its composite proportions as determined by the shape of the component companies and the ratio of the lengths of the sides, which in turn is dependent on the relative number of rows and columns of companies.

Figure 2: Spatial Properties of Nth Congregation

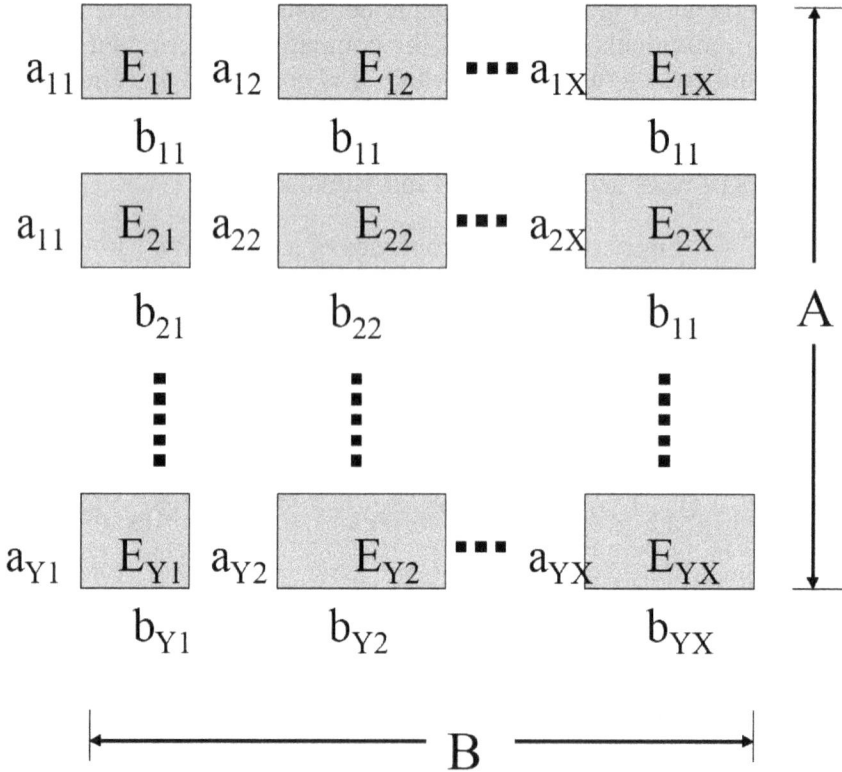

The assumed feeding procedure for the entire congregation is shown on Figure 3. As shown, each company in the most forward line of companies is provided with one initial loaf. Here the forwardmost position is that line which is first to receive the food. The initial assumption will be that this line is comprised of the first (frontmost) row. The loaves are broken and passed on within the companies, exiting in parallel streams from the rear. From there they enter the next companies directly to their rear, maintaining the parallel streams or, if the previous companies occupied the rearmost positions, the remainder is taken up in the collection baskets.

Figure 3: Feeding Procedure Within a Congregation

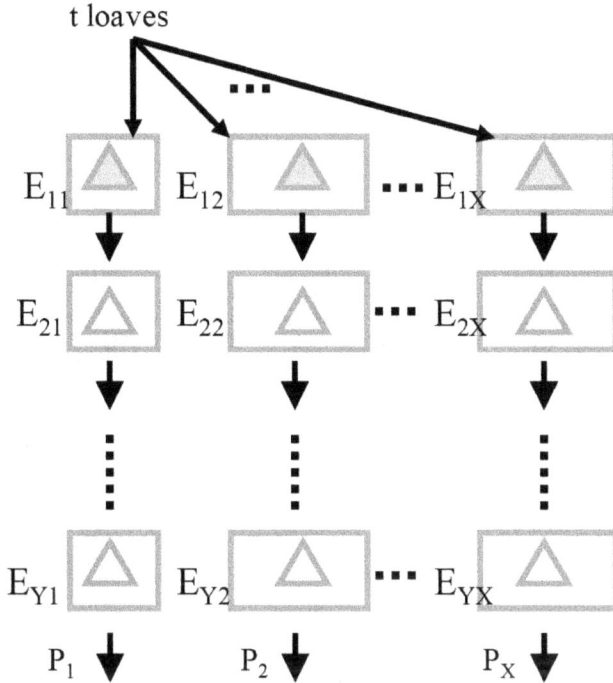

t loaves

to collection baskets

The feeding procedure as described above differs between the most forward companies and those to their rear. Figure 4 illustrates the factors involved as the feeding proceeds within a forward company. Although there is more than one way in which the feeding may be accomplished, the alternatives produce equivalent results with respect to the flow of food into and out of the company. The following procedure is assumed: the initial loaf is given to the individual in the forward left corner. Correspondingly, this initial individual will be the one located in the upper left corner as shown. This individual breaks it and hands half to the individual to his immediate right. Then the same individual breaks the remainder (which is whole again) once more and hands half to the individual behind him. Individuals behind the most forward row within the company, as well as the rightmost individual in the most forward row, will only break their received loaves once and hand the remainder to the individuals behind them. As described, the loaves will propagate to the right along the single most forward row, and toward the rear of the company in a stream of parallel paths. The number of parallel rearward paths is thus equal to the number of columns. The remaining loaves in each company pass out the rear of the company.

Figure 4: Feeding Procedure Within a Forward Company

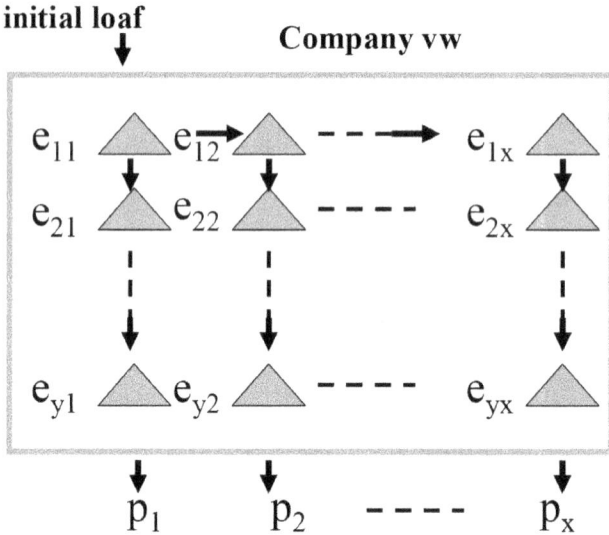

to next company or collection baskets

The feeding procedure within companies not in forward positions is shown on Figure 5. As shown, the loaves are broken and passed to the rear only, maintaining the parallel stream in receiving the loaves and propagating them rearward.

General mathematical representations shall now be developed to express the physical and procedural properties associated with the feeding events. These general representations are not specific to the actual events, but instead furnish a background that will permit a systematic exploration of those events with a minimum of ambiguity. The following development is derived from the verbal description given above.

Figure 5: Feeding Procedure Within a Nonforward Company

Company vw

remainder from previous company

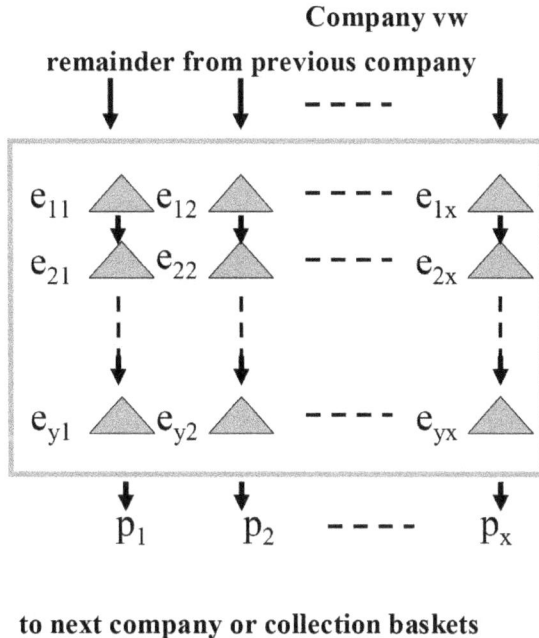

to next company or collection baskets

The notation will follow these general guidelines:

Symbols representing parameters and variables are italicized

Company-level symbols are generally lower case; congregation-level symbols are generally upper case

Symbols followed by brackets { } are interpreted as varying as 'a function of' the symbols that the brackets enclose

Subscripts are sometimes omitted if their inclusion would add unnecessary clutter and the interpretation is clear

The spatial and procedural attribute types will be addressed separately below. The spatial attributes will be considered first because they furnish the mathematical setting for the expression of the procedural attributes. Each attribute type will furnish numerical relationships that must be simultaneously satisfied in the evaluation of the feeding events. The approach to be taken herein toward the characterization of attributes will be to furnish a reasonably complete characterization regardless of whether all items are of immediate relevance to the current application.

A. Spatial Attributes:

1) Company-level:

The spatial characteristics of a company include numerical attributes such as the number of rows and columns, and dimensional attributes such as its height and length. The numerical attributes shall be addressed first.

For each case (i.e. the feeding of 5000, etc.), the congregation is assembled in companies. As shown on Figure 1, each Company E_{IJ} consists of an array of n_{IJ} elements arranged in A$\{I,J\}$ horizontal rows and B$\{I,J\}$ vertical columns.

The number of elements n_{IJ} in E_{IJ} is simply the product of the number of rows and columns:

$$n_{IJ} = \text{A}\{I,J\}\ \text{B}\{I,J\} \qquad\qquad \text{<1>}$$

The space which the company occupies will be proportional to the number of elements (individuals) within it and the space occupied by each individual. Scripture indicates that in at least some cases the individuals were sitting down. In that position they occupy a rectangle of proportions about 2:1, facing the shorter side. This factor will be addressed later.

Setting aside for now the space factor of the individual, Equation <1> defines the primary spatial attributes of a company.

2) Congregational level:

The congregation G for a feeding event comprises N individuals who are recorded as being fed. As shown on Figure 4, these individuals are organized in rows and columns of companies, where the companies are directly adjacent to each other.

The congregation, like the companies of which it is comprised, is generally a rectangular array having company elements E_{IJ}, where subscript I denotes the Ith row, and subscript J denotes the Jth column of the company within the congregation.

At this point a simplifying assumption shall be applied to the pattern, constraining all companies within a particular row of companies to have the same number of rows internally to them, and all companies within a particular column of companies to have the same number of columns internal to them. The more formal analysis of Appendix 5-1 does not make this assumption at the outset; the tradeoff is the greater complexity of subscripts in that analysis.

Given the simplifying constraint noted above, the number D of companies E_{IJ} in the congregation G is simply the product of the number of rows Y over which row subscript J ranges and the number of columns X over which column subscript I ranges:

$$D = XY \qquad\qquad\qquad <2>$$

If all the companies in a congregation were assumed to be of the same size, the congregation G as a whole would contain a number N individual elements which would simply be the product of the number of elements within each company and the number of companies within the congregation. But since Scripture indicates that companies were of different sizes (50 and 100 individuals), we cannot make that assumption. Instead, the total number of rows in the congregation is taken to be the summation of the number of rows in each company over the range Y of companies in a column. Applying the definition of the number of rows within a company, this amounts to:

$$\mathbf{R} = \sum_{I=1}^{Y} \mathbf{A}\{I,J\} \qquad\qquad\qquad <3>$$

Similarly, the number of columns C in the congregation is:

$$\mathbf{C} = \sum_{J=1}^{X} \mathbf{B}\{I,J\} \qquad\qquad\qquad <4>$$

The number N of individual elements is taken to be the summation of the number n_{IJ} within each company over the ranges Y and X of the congregation. Applying <1>,

$$N = \sum^{D} n_{IJ} = \sum_{I=1}^{Y} \left(\sum_{J=1}^{X} \mathbf{A}\{I,J\}\, \mathbf{B}\{I,J\} \right) \qquad <5>$$

Equations <1> through <5> comprise the primary numerical/spatial characterization of the congregation.

The evaluation of a congregation will initially assume the closest fit of a perfectly rectangular array to the approximate parameters of the case under consideration. Companies will then be added or removed from the resulting array to render the parameters exact. The addition or removal will be made in multiples of whole companies.

The procedural characterization follows.

B. Procedural Attributes:

1) Company-level:

As noted in the discussion of feeding procedures and illustrated on Figure 4, the feeding within a frontmost company follows a number of parallel paths from the frontmost to the rearmost individuals.

Let p_{IJ} represent this number of parallel feeding paths generated within a company E_{IJ}. In general, if the individuals in the company are facing the observer as we have assumed, the number of paths is equivalent to the number of columns within the company.

$$p_{IJ} = B\{I,J\} \qquad\qquad <6>$$

If company E_{IJ} is a rearmost company as shown on Figure 5, then its output p_{IJ} will represent that company's portion of the congregation's remainder to be collected into baskets. The topic of remainders will be treated in detail at the congregational level.

Let g represent the number of loaves input into a company, and p the number of loaves output from a company. Also let E_{IJ} represent a non-forward company, and E'_{IJ} a forward (frontmost) company. It was assumed in the previous description that each forward company receives one initial loaf and outputs a parallel stream of loaves in the front-to-rear direction, and each non-front company inputs a parallel stream of loaves from the previous company and outputs the same parallel stream. From these assumptions,

$$g\{E_{IJ}\} = p_{IJ} = B\{I,J\} \qquad\qquad <7>$$
$$g\{E'_{IJ}\} = 1$$

2) Congregational level:

As noted above, each company within a congregation G consists of an array of elements, one element representing each individual. All individuals are assumed to be oriented in the same direction (toward the front), and that orientation defines the number of frontmost companies in the congregation. As shown on Figure 3, the frontmost companies receive the initial loaves, the number of which is L. The number of frontmost companies, then, is constrained to be equivalent to L. But since the number of frontmost companies is also the number of columns X,

$$L = X \qquad\qquad\qquad\qquad\qquad\qquad <8>$$

If P represents the number of loaves collected into baskets as the remainder from congregation G, then P will be the sum of paths p_{IJ} from all the rearmost companies. Given the assumed orientation of the individuals as facing the front, this sum will be the total number of columns C in the congregation, as defined in <5>.

$$P = C = \sum_{J=1}^{X} B\{I,J\} \qquad\qquad\qquad\qquad <9>$$

Let h represent the number of loaves contained in each basket of remaining loaves. Then the number of baskets Z produced by congregation G will be

$$Z = P/h \qquad\qquad\qquad\qquad\qquad\qquad <10>$$

An interesting facet to the development so far is that the loaves of bread are assumed to have been initially distributed whole, such that one loaf was given to each frontmost company. If the initial fish were divided such that they matched and were handed out along with the initial distribution of loaves, the pattern-dependency of the process from that point would ensure that in every case the numbers of fish would be identical to those associated with the loaves.

C. Additional Assumptions associated with the characterization

In addition to the organization assumed for the arrangement and feeding process, the following initial assumptions are made. They reflect the expectation of consistency among the several events of important unspecified parameters:

(1) There were in all cases companies of 50 and 100

(2) All variables and constants must be integers; a fraction of a person, for example, is not permitted

(3) The number h of remainder loaves in each basket is assumed to be a constant for all feeding events.

(4) Unless otherwise noted as exceptions, all individuals were seated; in the seated position, the individual's shape factor is 2:1 in the direction of orientation.

Minor additional assumptions are made in the development below as indicated by logic, simplicity of development, or specific supporting data.

Assumption 1) requires that the sum of companies of 50 and 100 in a congregation for each case furnish the total number of individuals for that case. If d represents the number of companies of 50 in G, then from <11>,

$$N = \sum^{d} (50) + \sum^{D-d} (100) = 50d + 100(D-d) \qquad <11>$$

Also, <1> takes the specific values

$$n_{IJ} = A\{I,J\}\ B\{I,J\} = 50 \text{ or } 100 \qquad <12>$$

At this point, two further simplifying assumptions shall be made, constraining a company of 100 to have the specific shape of 5 rows by 20 columns, and a company of 50 to have 5 rows by 10 columns. Although these assumptions will ultimately be justified by producing results which are consistent with the numerical data furnished in the Gospels, some initial justification is obtained by looking ahead to the single company involved in Elisha's feeding event. In that event, the hundred individuals were fed from an initial quantity of 20 loaves of barley. For this case, an assumption of a nonforward company (inputting and outputting 20 loaves), and with individuals having an orientation toward the hypothetical observer, while representing a reasonable estimate, also greatly simplifies the mathematical analysis. It will be noted from this constraint that the number of rows I in a company is a constant number of 5 throughout the congregation. Applying $J = 10$ or 20 to <5>, <8>, and <9>,

$$C = P = (10 \text{ or } 20)L \qquad \text{<13>}$$

A term X' is now defined, given the assumption that there are only two unique company sizes, to represent the number of companies of size 50 in a particular row. From this assumption, the number of companies of size 100 in a particular row will be $(L - X')$. Applying this definition to <13> results in

$$C = P = 10\,X' + 20\,(L - X') \qquad \text{<14>}$$

Applying the specifics noted above to <3> through <5> and <12>,

$$A\{I,J\} = 5 \qquad \text{<15>}$$

$$B\{I,J\} = 10 \text{ or } 20 \qquad \text{<16>}$$

$$n_{IJ} = 5\, B\{I,J\} = 50 \text{ or } 100 \qquad \text{<17>}$$

$$R = 5Y \qquad \text{<18>}$$

As noted previously, the initial assumption will be that the congregation will be a perfectly rectangular array producing the total number of elements closest to the number in the congregation. The array will then be adjusted from that initial estimate to produce an exact match.

The variable d may be expressed in terms of the product of the number of companies of size 50 in a particular row and the number of rows of companies comprising the congregation:

$$d = X'Y \qquad \text{<19>}$$

Applying <19> to <11>,

$$N = Y(50\,X' + 100(L - X')) \qquad \text{<20>}$$

Summary of Relevant Relationships

$$R = 5Y \qquad \text{<21>}$$

$$C = P = 10\,X' + 20\,(X - X')$$

$$N = RC = Y(50\,X' + 100(X - X'))$$

$$L = X$$

$$d = X'Y$$

$$D = LY$$

$$Z = P/h$$

Where

X is the number of columns of companies in a congregation

X' is the number of columns of companies of size 50 in a congregation

Y is the number of rows of companies in a congregation

R is the total number of rows in a congregation

C is the total number of columns in a congregation

L is the initial number of loaves for a congregation

P is the number of remainder loaves collected into baskets

D is the number of companies in a congregation

Z is the number of remainder baskets for a congregation

h is the number of remainder loaves per basket

d is the number of companies of size 50 in a congregation

N is the total number of individuals in a congregation

Section 2 (alternate): Evaluation of Structural Details Associated with Feeding Events

A. Specification of Cases

Four feeding events are assumed, which are labeled as Cases in this analysis: the two performed by Jesus (5000 and 4000); the precursor case performed by Elisha that enabled Jesus as the Son of man to perform his own feeding, and the case prophesied by

Jesus in John 21 and fulfilled in Acts 2 of Peter feeding three thousand souls with the Word of God.

Case 1: Reference Second Kings Chapter 4; Elisha feeds a company of one hundred with twenty loaves.

Case 2: Reference Matthew 14, Mark 6, Mark 8, Luke 9, John 6; Jesus feeds 5000 individuals with 5 loaves, leaving a remainder of 12 baskets. They were all commanded to sit during the feeding, in ranks (companies) of 50 and 100.

Case 3: Reference Matthew 15, Mark 8 (twice); Jesus feeds 4000 individuals with 7 loaves, leaving a remainder of 7 baskets. The multitude was commanded to sit during the feeding. It is a matter of interpretation as to whether 'the multitude' means 'all'.

Case 4: Reference John 21, Acts 2; Peter feeds 3000 individuals with the Word of God. A symbolic remainder of 12 baskets (one for each Apostle) is assumed. Note in regard to this event that in the twenty-first chapter of John's Gospel, Jesus demanded of Peter three times that he feed His sheep, a prophesy the fulfillment of which is noted in the referenced event. The thrice-stated command to feed is taken to correspond to three symbolic initial loaves.

B. Detailed evaluation

The validity of the assumptions made to this point will be assessed below for each of the four cases noted above. If a valid solution cannot be found for the assumed orientation in every case, this assumptions will be revisited. Where a valid solution can be found, the specific congregational pattern and size will be established.

1. Case 1:

The following values are taken directly from the information provided in Scripture for this case:

$N = 100$ <22>

$L = 20$

Z = unknown (P is assumed to be 20)

As noted in the previous section, case 1 involves only one company of one hundred people and was used to establish the spatial pattern of 20 x 5 for a company of 100, which will be regarded as a constant value over all the events for a company of size 100. The pattern for a company of 50 was assumed as having half the longest dimension of the company of 100, or of 10 x 5, and will also be regarded as a constant value for companies of 50. These values require both company types to have a single, constant depth (row size) of 5.

From case 1 of Elisha the hundred individuals were fed from an initial quantity of 20 loaves of barley. For this case, the company is taken to be a nonforward company (inputting and outputting 20 loaves). Therefore, the assumed feeding process as depicted on Figure 6 requires a company of 100 to have a width of 20, in which all of the front participants each receive a loaf; otherwise, the initial distribution is awkward and unnecessarily complex.

Applying the values applicable to Case 1 as noted in <22> to summary relations <21> noting that X and Y are both 1 and the assumed company size is 100:

Figure 6: Feeding Pattern for Case 1 (Elisha'sFeeding of 100)

One company of 100:

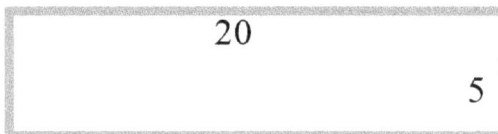

$R = 5 Y=5$ <23>

$C= 10\ X'+ 20\ (X - X') = 20$

$$N = Y(50\ X' + 100(X - X')) = 100$$

$$L = X = 20 \text{ (non-frontmost company assumed for this case)}$$

$$P = C = 20$$

$$Z = P/h = 20/h$$

As specified in equations <23>, Case 1 represents a single company of 100 individuals consisting of 5 rows and 20 columns and having a (normalized) height of 10 units and a (normalized) length of 20 units. The feeding was initiated and proceeded along 20 paths.

The ambiguity of Z now may be partially resolved by listing the possible values for Z vs. h in tabular form, with the intent, as justified by <10>, of reducing the possible values of h in the analysis of subsequent cases.

The following table of possible values for h is derived from the relation for Z in <23>, imposing the requirement that both Z and h must be integers:

TABLE 1

h	$Z = 20/h$
1	20
2	10
3	- (not an integer)
4	5
5	4
6-9	-
10	2
11-19	-
20	1

2. Case 2:

The following values are taken directly from the information

provided in Scripture for this case:

$$N = 5000 \qquad\qquad\qquad <24>$$

$L = 5$

$Z = 12$

Applying the parameter values of <24> to the relevant equations out of the summary set <21> produces the following values:

$R = 5Y$ <25>

$C = P = 10\,X' + 20\,(X - X')$

$N = Y(50\,X' + 100(X-X')) = 5000$

$L = X = 5$

$Z = P/h = 12$

$d = X'Y$

The evaluation will seek next to establish a value for h by reducing the possible values given in Table 1. To that end, Table 2 below presents the values of P, and consequently of C associated with the valid values of h as generated from Table 1.

TABLE 2

h	$C = 12h$
1	12
2	24
4	48
5	60
10	120
20	240

Next, it is noted from the relation $X = 5$ in <25> that X' may assume only whole number values from 0 through 5. From the expression for C in <25> the following relationship is obtained:

$X' = 10 - C/10$ <26>

Table 3 below defines the possible values of C corresponding to this range:

TABLE 3

h	X'
1	Not an integer
2	Not an integer
4	Not an integer
5	4
10	Negative value
20	Negative value

A comparison of Tables 2 and 3 establishes the only possible valid value of X as 4, with a corresponding value of h as:

$$h = 5 \qquad\qquad <27>$$

Substituting <26> and <27> into <25> yields

$$R = 5Y \qquad\qquad <28>$$

$$C = 60$$

$$Y(300) = 5000$$

$$L = X = 5$$

$$P = 60$$

$$Z = 12$$

$$X' = 4$$

$$D = 5Y$$

$$d = X'Y$$

In the establishment of the specific data associated with case 2, a perfectly rectangular array consisting of 5100 elements was evaluated, via solving for Y, as the best first approximation for 5000 elements. One whole company of 100 individuals was then removed from the array to arrive at an exact correspondence to the 5000 individuals. The resulting values for the variables of interest associated with case 2 are:

$R = 85$ <29>

$C = 60$

$Y = 17$

$L = X = 5$

$P = 60$

$Z = 12$

$X' = 4$

$D = 85$ (reduced to 84 by deleting one company as discussed below)

$d = 68$

Figure 7: Feeding Pattern for Case 2 (Jesus' Feeding of 5000)

68 companies of 50 and 16 companies of 100 arranged in companies of 50 in 2 columns of 17 rows on each side of companies of 100 in center column of 16 rows :

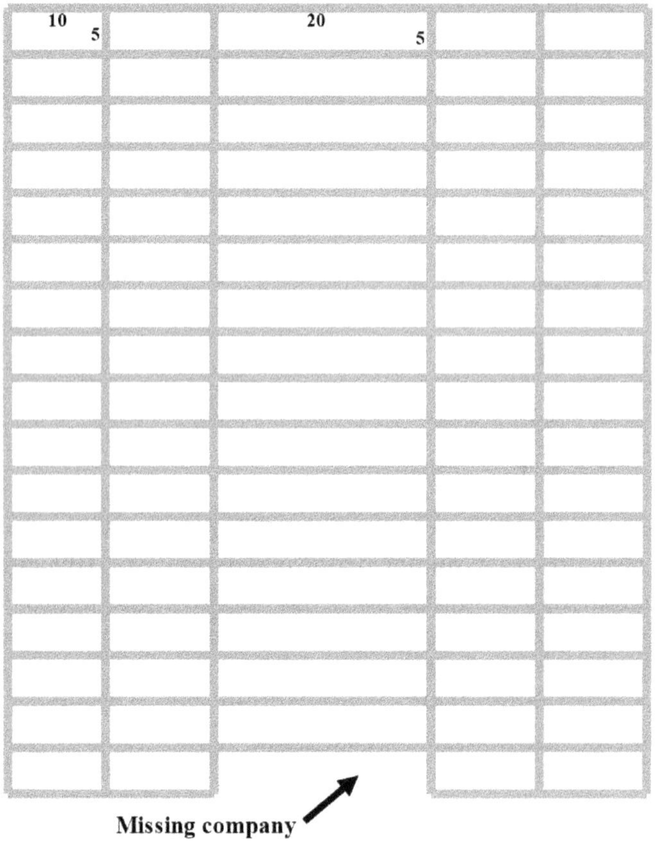

Missing company

The associated array is shown on Figure 7, and consists of 17 rows by 5 columns of companies, one column of which consists of companies of 100 and four columns of which consist of companies of 50. One company of 100 is missing from this array, having the center column consist of 16 rows instead of 17.

3. Case 3:

The following values are taken directly from the information provided in Scripture for this case:

$$N = 4000 \qquad\qquad\qquad <30>$$

$$L = 7$$

$$Z = 7$$

Applying the parameter values of <30> to the relevant equations out of the summary set <21>, and including <27>, produces the following values:

$$R = 5Y \qquad\qquad\qquad <31>$$

$$C = 10\,X' + 20\,(X - X')$$

$$N = RC = Y(50\,X' + 100(X - X')) = 4000$$

$$L = X = 7$$

$$P = C$$

$$Z = P/h = 7$$

$$h = 5$$

The following is derived from the values given above:

$$35 = 10\,X' + 20\,(7 - X') \qquad\qquad <32>$$

Which reduces to $X' = 105/10$, invalid because it is a nonzero value that violates the requirement that X' be an integer. The lack of a valid solution for this case demands that the initial assumptions be reexamined. It turns out that a solution is not possible under the assumption that $L = X$, meaning that for this particular case, the initial loaves were not distributed from the front. But if the loaves are distributed and collected from the side instead for this case, such that $L=Y$, (and making $P=R$), the following alternate results are obtained while maintaining the same company sizes and orientations as in the other cases:

$$R = 5Y \qquad\qquad \text{<31A>}$$

$$C = 10\ X' + 20\ (X - X')$$

$$N = RC = Y(50\ X' + 100 - X')) = 4000$$

$$L = Y = 7$$

$$P = R$$

$$Z = P/h = 7$$

$$h = 5$$

Reapplying the parameter values of <30> to alternate relations <31A> produces the following values:

$$C = 800/7 \qquad\qquad \text{<32A>}$$

$$X' = 2X - C/10$$

For which the nearest integer values corresponding to the assumption of a perfectly rectangular array are

$$C = 110 \qquad\qquad \text{<33A>}$$

$$X' = 2X - 11$$

Equation <33A> is satisfied for variable X' over the range of odd numbers from 1 through 11. In actuality, the number selected will have no influence on the shape or size of the resulting rectangle. A value of 11 is selected for simplicity, such that all companies in the congregation will have a size of 50 individuals:

$$X' = X = 11 \qquad\qquad \text{<34A>}$$

$$X - X' = 0 \textbf{ (no companies of 100)}$$

Applying <34A> into <31A> through <33A> while allowing the congregation size to have an approximate value near 4000 furnishes the following values:

$R = 35$ <35A>

$C = 110$

$N = RC = 7(550) = 3850$

$L = Y = 7$

$P = R = 35$

$Z = 7$

$d_3 = 77\ (80)$

$D_3 = 77$ **(increased to 80 by adding three companies of 50 as discussed below)**

$h = 5$

An interesting fact regarding these values is that they produce a rectangular array for which the long side is rotated 90 degrees from that of the other cases. This seemingly minor point will be seen to be of exceptional importance later when the cases are integrated together. The following specific data is associated with case 3. In the establishment of this data, a perfectly rectangular array consisting of 3850 elements was evaluated as the best first approximation for 4000 elements. Three whole companies of 50 individuals were then added to the array to arrive at an exact correspondence to the 4000 individuals. These companies may be added in any combination to end companies of the basic 3850-element rectangular congregation without disturbing the feeding process.

The associated array is shown on Figure 8, and consists of 7 rows by 11 columns, all of which consists of companies of 50. An additional three-company (of 50 elements each) array is attached to this array.

Figure 8: Feeding Pattern for Case 3 (Jesus' Feeding of 4000)

77 companies of 50 arranged in 11 columns of 7 rows, plus 3 additional companies of 50:

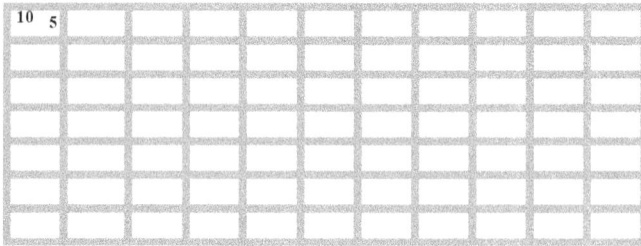

three additional companies of 50, not necessarily arranged as shown

4. Case 4:

The following values are taken directly from the information provided in Scripture for this case:

$$N_4 = 3000 \qquad\qquad <36>$$
$$L_4 = 3$$
$$Z_4 = 12$$

Applying the parameter values of <36> to the relevant equations out of the summary set <21> and returning to the original assumption that $L = X$ (and including <27>) produces the following values:

$$R = 5Y \qquad\qquad <37>$$
$$C = 10\,X' + 20\,(X - X')$$
$$N = RC = Y(50\,X' + 100(X - X')) = 3000$$
$$L = X = 3$$
$$P = C = C$$
$$Z = P/h = 12$$
$$h = 5$$

These parameters produce the following relationships:

$$C = 60 \qquad\qquad\qquad\qquad <38>$$
$$X' = 2X - 6 = 2(3) - 6 = 0$$
$$X = 3$$
$$YC = 600$$
$$Y = 10$$
$$d = X'Y = 0$$
$$D = XY = 30$$

which correspond to a perfectly rectangular 3 X 10 array of companies of 100. The associated array is shown on Figure 9, and consists of 10 rows by 3 columns, all of which consists of companies of 100. No companies are missing from or extra to this array.

Two points are noted in concluding this development. The first is that all cases were reevaluated under the revised assumption that the loaves would be distributed to and collected from the sides as was applied to Case 3. This revised assumption produced valid results for Case 3 alone. The second point is that a space factor of 2:1 corresponding to sitting individuals was applied to the rectangles developed above prior to integrating them together.

Figure 9: Feeding Pattern for Case 4
(Peter's Feeding of 3000 with Word)
30 companies of 100 arranged in 3 columns of 10 rows

Appendix 5-3
Jesus' Feeding of the Multitudes

*A pictorial, non-mathematical presentation of Jesus' feedings,
compatible with the associated numbers given in Scripture*

Introduction

The Bible contains many mysteries. God appears to have purposed it that way in order that man would find from a diligent search the truth in the Word of God, and from that truth, come to know and love his God with the fervor of Jesus' Great Commandment in Matthew 22:37 and 38:

> *Jesus said unto him, Thou shalt love the Lord, thy God, with all thy heart, and with all thy soul, and with all thy mind. This is the first and great commandment.*

As with other things that we treasure the most, the solving of many of the mysteries of God require patience and hard work. God Himself said as much in Proverbs 25:2:

> *It is the glory of God to conceal a thing, but the honor of kings is to search out a matter.*

Not all mysteries of God are intended to be understood as soon as they are voiced or set down in Scripture. Many mysteries are intended to be revealed at a certain period of history, perhaps, as suggested in Daniel 12:4, at the end of the age of man's government on earth.

> *But thou, O Daniel, shut up the words, and seal the book, even to the time of the end; many shall run to and fro, and knowledge shall be increased.*

Jesus' feeding of the multitudes is an enigma that has eluded a solution for many centuries. Only recently was it found to be amenable to a mathematical solution, suggesting that the solution to the puzzle was intended for our present age. The proof of the mystery is an amazing image, a sign denied to the generation in which Jesus lived on earth, but now available to all to know that the Lord Jesus Christ is indeed the true Messiah sought by the Jews over centuries of hardship and persecution.

Scripture, in recounting Jesus' feeding of the multitudes, furnishes information regarding those events that extend quite deeply beyond the surface of the narrative. The mathematical solution to the feeding of the multitudes requires a complex analysis that draws upon different passages of the Bible, both the Old and the New Testaments, and is comprised of different meanings for the word 'feedings.' There are two very distinct definitions for 'feedings' that must be used together to solve the puzzle. One definition of feedings is nourishment found in food. The other definition of feedings is the nourishment found in the Word; one for sustenance of the body, the other for the sustenance of the soul, as Jesus Himself suggested in Matthew 4:4:

> But [Jesus] answered [the devil] and said, It is written, Man shall not live by bread alone, but by every word that proceedeth out of the mouth of God.

Considering the spiritual feedings to be the one most important to God and dovetailing it into the physical feedings leads to the solution of the mystery.

The integration of these feedings into a meaningful pattern is found in the following essay and is meant to bless mankind with the beautiful nature of the Word of God and its inherent truth down to the smallest detail, including a prophetic element of importance to the people of today.

The Mystery

There is an element of mystery, of information hidden beneath the surface, that accompanies the Gospel accounts of Jesus' feeding of the multitudes. In the eighth chapter of Mark's Gospel, Jesus made a pointed and direct association of faith with understanding as he spoke with His disciples after feeding four thousand people with seven loaves and a few fish. Significantly, just prior to that incident as recorded in Mark He had encountered the Pharisees, who had sought some confirmation from heaven regarding Jesus' credentials.

*And he sighed deeply in his spirit, and saith, Why doth
this generation seek after a sign? verily I say unto you,
There shall no sign be given unto this generation.*

As the account in Mark 8 continues, Jesus recalls to His disciples
the events in which He fed the multitudes, as if the details represented
something of great importance.

*And he left them, and entering into the ship again
departed to the other side.*

*Now the disciples had forgotten to take bread, neither
had they in the ship with them more than one loaf.*

*And he charged them, saying, Take heed, beware of the
leaven of the Pharisees, and of the leaven of Herod.*

*And they reasoned among themselves, saying, It is
because we have no bread.*

*And when Jesus knew it, he saith unto them, Why reason
ye, because ye have no bread? perceive ye not yet, neither
understand? have ye your heart yet hardened?*

*Having eyes, see ye not? and having ears, hear ye not?
and do ye not remember?*

*When I brake the five loaves among five thousand, how
many baskets full of fragments took ye up? They say unto
him, Twelve.*

*And when the seven among four thousand, how many
baskets full of fragments took ye up? And they said,
Seven.*

*And he said unto them, How is it that ye do not
understand?*

In this account, Jesus confronts his disciples with their lack of
understanding. In a commentary that appears at the first reading to
be somewhat cryptic, He recalls the feeding of the five thousand and
the four thousand. In this recollection, Jesus emphasizes numbers:
the number of people fed, along with the number of baskets that
contained the fragments that remained. Having recalled the specific
numbers associated with these feeding events, Jesus makes the odd
demand: *"How is it that ye do not understand?"*

It is tempting, in a first reading of this and the surrounding
verses, to think of Mark as lacking in sophistication. He seems to

mix numbers inappropriately into the basic message, and too many details are left unanswered. Why, for example, did Jesus emphasize the numbers associated with the feedings, as if these values were somehow related to their faith? Jesus painstakingly recalls to His disciples the number of individuals fed and the number of remaining baskets, but fails to complete the picture. How many fragments did each basket contain? Of what importance was the number of baskets of leftovers to the event itself, or to the disciples' faith? How can the number of baskets of leftovers have such theological significance that Jesus placed so much emphasis upon it in the recollection of the feeding events to His disciples? Why were 5,000 fed with five loaves, whereas seven loaves were required to feed the 4,000?

What if Mark, as guided by the Holy Spirit and therefore far from being unsophisticated of word, was actually presenting a truth of great depth? In this light, the passage literally pleads for a deeper understanding of the feeding of the people. When Jesus spoke about the specifics of the feedings to His disciples, it was as if he was presenting the future reader with a riddle and commanding him to solve it.

As this essay shall endeavor to show, the feeding of the multitudes contained the rudiments of such a sign as the Pharisees had requested of Jesus. But the completion of its components had to await the Pentecost. The Gospels also had to be written first, in the unique manner in which they presented the elements for later examination. Next, the Gospels had to be integrated into Scripture and thus become available for open review. Finally, a generation had to emerge whose perspective was conditioned to view Scripture beyond that which is immediately apparent.

The Significance of Jesus' Feedings

The physical bread represented only a part of the feeding events. In fact, it wasn't even the most significant part. The bread was only symbolic of a much greater spiritual Bread, the Word of God.

There are several proofs of this. First, there is the spiritual representation of Jesus in John 1:1 and 14 as the Word of God:

> *In the beginning was the Word, and the Word was with God, and the Word was God - - - And the Word became flesh, and dwelt among us.*

Jesus, in fact, considered the material world, including physical bread, to be of little value. According to John 18:36a:

Jesus answered, My kingdom is not of this world.

But even before He made that statement, He was more direct in John 6 regarding the relative importance of bread and His Word:

Jesus answered them, and said, Verily, verily, I say unto you, Ye seek me, not because ye saw the miracles, but because ye did eat of the loaves, and were filled. Labor not for the food which perisheth, but for that food which endureth unto everlasting life, which the Son of man shall give unto you; for him hath God the Father sealed.

Then said they unto him, What shall we do, that we might work the works of God? Jesus answered, and said unto them, This is the work of God, that ye believe on him whom he hath sent. They said, therefore, unto him, What sign showest thou, then, that we may see, and believe thee? What dost thou work? Our fathers did eat manna in the desert; as it is written, He gave them bread from heaven to eat.

Then Jesus said unto them, Verily, verily, I say unto you, Moses gave you not that bread from heaven; but my Father giveth you the true bread from heaven. For the bread of God is he who cometh down from heaven and giveth life unto the world. Then said they unto him, Lord, evermore give us this bread. And Jesus said unto them, I am the bread of life; he that cometh to me shall never hunger, and he that believeth on me shall never thirst.

The Miraculous Element of the Feedings

The element of the feedings that is the simplest to grasp is the miracle itself, as it simply mimics the process of the Word's propagation from ear to mouth without loss. After having been blessed by Jesus, the bread returned to wholeness every time it was broken. That's all there is to it. The rest of the process involves the mechanics of the distribution.

The leaven of the Pharisees that Jesus warned His disciples to beware of referred to the distortion of the Word and its consequent corruption as it was propagated by the religious leadership.

Preliminary Facts About the Feeding Process

Not having access to detailed eyewitness accounts of the feeding events, we can't be certain how the feedings actually took place. But enough information can be gleaned from Scripture to suggest that the process was an orderly one, at least in the spiritual domain regarding the feeding of the Word.

According to Mark 6:39 and 40, the men being fed were grouped into companies, where the size of each company was either 50 or 100 men.

> *And [Jesus] commanded them to make all sit down by companies upon the green grass. And they sat down in ranks, by hundreds, and by fifties.*

Given that information, a typical company of 100 might be arranged in the 20 by 5 configuration shown in Figure 1 below, and a company of 50 might be half that size, or 10 by 5. These particular arrangements will be justified through Scripture later.

Figure 1: Typical Company of 100

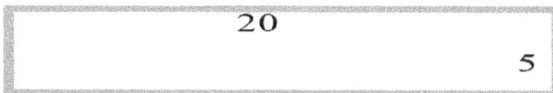

20
5

According to Matthew 14:19, the feeding was initiated first by Jesus, who blessed the bread, and second by His disciples, who then gave the loaves to the multitudes:

> *And [Jesus] commanded the multitude to sit down on the grass, and took the five loaves, and the two fishes, and looking up to heaven, he blessed, and broke, and gave the loaves to His disciples, and the disciples gave them to the multitudes.*

It will be assumed here that when Jesus broke the loaves, the two halves remained attached to each other as He handed them to His disciples. Each disciple, in turn, handed a loaf to one member (perhaps the captain) of the group of fifty or one hundred nearest him. This group will be called the frontmost group. As there were five loaves in the feeding of the five thousand, five disciples were involved. But there also were seven loaves associated with the later feeding of four thousand, which involved the remaining seven disciples, such that each of the twelve disciples (apostles) was involved once in the two feeding events.

A mathematical analysis was performed on the information in Scripture regarding the feedings. A reproduction of the analysis is beyond the scope of this essay (refer to Appendices 5-1 and 5-2) and involves Scriptural information beyond that which has been presented to this point. Nevertheless, useful as it was toward the development of an understanding of the feeding process, it is not necessary for the reader to refer to it to acquire his own understanding, as such may be achieved merely by inspecting the pattern. One item of that analysis is helpful, however: if the number of fragments from the feeding of the menfolk is constrained to be the same for both the feeding of the five thousand and the four thousand, then the analysis demands that the number must necessarily be five. Therefore, it will be assumed that there were five fragments of leftover loaves due to the menfolk in each basket.

The Mechanics of the Distribution

The loaves can be visualized, with the aid of Figure 2 below, as being distributed one to each frontmost company by each disciple, to whom Jesus gave the initial loaves, to the first man in the front of the company, which, to the disciple would be the individual at the right end of the row as he faces him. The individual does three things: first he breaks the loaf and gives it to the next man to his right, who does the same to the man on his right, and so on, until each of the men in the frontmost row of the company have received a loaf; second, the men in the frontmost row break the half-loaves that they retained, which in the meantime have become whole again according to the nature of the miracle, and give half to the men directly behind them; finally, these men eat the loaves remaining in their hands. Now all the men behind the frontmost row will just break the loaves that they receive from the men in front of them, pass a loaf to the men to their rear and eat the loaves that remain. In this way, the bread propagates to the rear of the columns, where the rearmost fragments from each column are collected in baskets.

As the process is described, it will be noted that, regarding each company adjacent to the others in the same row, what happens within a frontmost company stays in that company, the residue going to the company behind it but not to the sides. In other words, the distribution proceeds along the companies in each column, the process being independent from one column to another. It also can be seen that as many companies as desired may be stacked behind each frontmost company without altering the final number of fragments collected in the baskets.

Another point to consider from the fact that one loaf is given to each of the twelve apostles over Jesus' two feeding events is that there will be exactly as many frontmost companies as the number of initial loaves: five for the feeding of the five thousand, and seven for the feeding of the four thousand.

Figure 2: Basic Pattern of Feeding

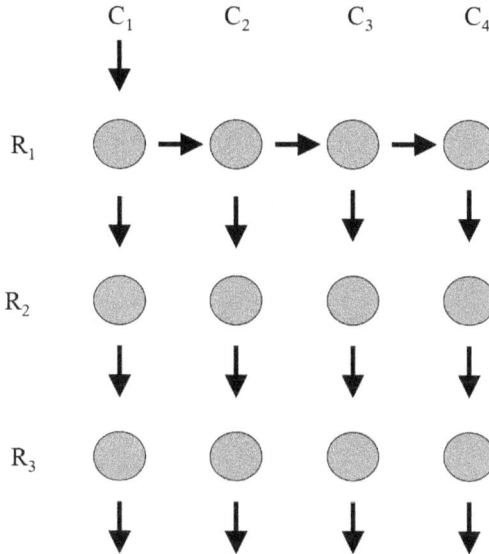

The pattern of stacking is summarized in Figure 3 below, which emphasizes the numerical constraints of each particular feeding event, which are the number of starting loaves and the number of remainder loaves that are collected in the baskets. If there are N loaves at the beginning of the feedings, where N is 5 for the feeding of the 5000 and 7 for the feeding of the 4000, then there will be N frontmost companies. This is the first constraint. Therefore, for the feeding of the 5000, there will be 5 frontmost companies, and for the feeding of the 4000, there will be 7 frontmost companies. There will be the same number of companies at the rear for the collection. The size of each of the rearmost companies, which must be the same as the size of each of the frontmost companies, is established by the number of baskets of remainders and the number of remainders in each basket.

The number of remainders in each basket was established from the arithmetic analysis as 5, as noted earlier. The size of each company is constrained at either 50 or 100. Thus the number of columns of individuals in a company of 50 is either 5 or 10, depending on the side (width or length) representing the columns, and the number of columns of individuals in a company of 100 is either 5 or 20, again depending on the side representing the columns. This is the second constraint.

The number of columns of individuals associated with each feeding event also is constrained to be 5 times the number of baskets of remainders, which, for the feeding of the 5000 is 12 times 5 or 60, and for the feeding of the 4000 is 7 times 5 or 35. This is the third constraint.

The number of frontmost companies of size 50 and the number of frontmost companies of size 100 is established by simultaneously satisfying the first, second and third constraints noted above. After establishing these numbers, the pattern is filled in with the number of companies of the sizes previously established to arrive at the total number of menfolk fed, noting that the number of companies involved in the rearward propagation of the loaves from frontmost to rearmost does not affect the number of starting loaves or the number of remaining loaves. While perfect rectangles are preferred, they are not necessary at this stage of the development.

Figure 3: Association of Loaves with Frontmost
Companies and Remainders with Columns of Individuals

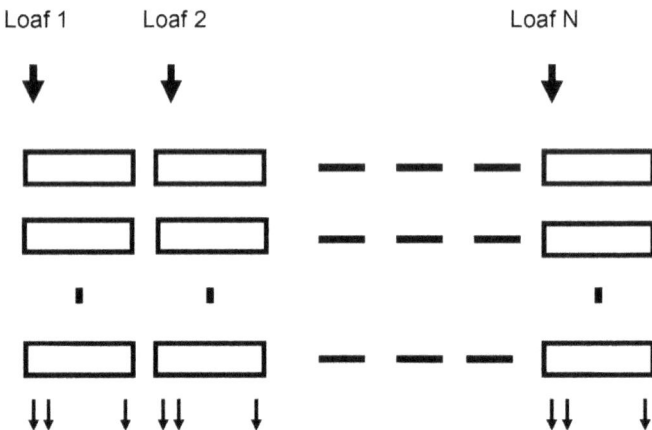

Individual Columns to Collection Baskets

Specifics of the Feeding of the Five Thousand

As noted earlier, the specifics of the feeding of the five thousand were given by Jesus Himself in Mark 8:

> *When I brake the five loaves among five thousand, how many baskets full of fragments took ye up? They say unto him, Twelve.*

As the process has been developed to this point, the five initial loaves involves five frontmost companies. The twelve baskets of leftovers from the menfolk requires, at twelve baskets and five loaves per basket, 12 x 5 = 60 columns of people. A unique pattern of companies of 50 and 100 may be constructed from this information, keeping in mind that as many companies as required to come up to five thousand may be stacked behind the frontmost companies without altering the numbers of frontmost companies or of the number of remainder loaves. This pattern is shown on Figure 4 below.

As shown on the figure, the pattern involves four frontmost companies of 50 and one frontmost company of 100, for a total of five frontmost companies, which agrees with the number five of initial loaves. The number of columns of menfolk furnishing leftovers is 4 x 10 + 1 x 20 = 60, which, at 5 loaves per basket, yields 12 baskets.

There are 17 x 4 rows of companies of 50 and 16 x 1 rows of companics of 100, producing 17 x 50 + 16 x 100 = 5000 menfolk exactly, which agrees with the number given in the Gospel accounts of that feeding event. The fact that the resulting figure is not a perfect rectangle is somewhat awkward, but that issue will be addressed later.

Specifics of the Feeding of the Four Thousand

As in the case of the feeding of the five thousand, Jesus Himself, as recorded in Mark 8, described the specifics of His feeding of the four thousand.

> *"And when the seven among four thousand, how many baskets full of fragments took ye up? And they said, Seven."*

As before, the seven initial loaves involves seven frontmost companies. The seven baskets of leftovers from the menfolk requires, at seven baskets and five loaves per basket, 7 x 5 = 35 columns of people. A unique pattern of companies of 50 and 100 cannot be constructed from this information as in the case of the feeding of the five thousand. In order to come up with a workable pattern, it is necessary to rotate the process 90 degrees from vertical to horizontal such that, preserving the orientation of the companies themselves as in the feeding of the 5000, the frontmost companies are now to the right and the process of propagating the loaves from one company to the next is to the left instead of rearward. The remainders are also gathered in baskets at the left. This apparent inconsistency between the two feedings was initially somewhat disturbing, but was found to have much significance, as will be brought out later. The resulting pattern for the feeding of the four thousand is shown on Figure 5 below.

Figure 4: Pattern for Jesus' Feeding of 5000

68 companies of 50 and 16 companies of 100 arranged in companies of 50 in 2 columns of 17 rows on each side of companies of 100 in center column of 16 rows :

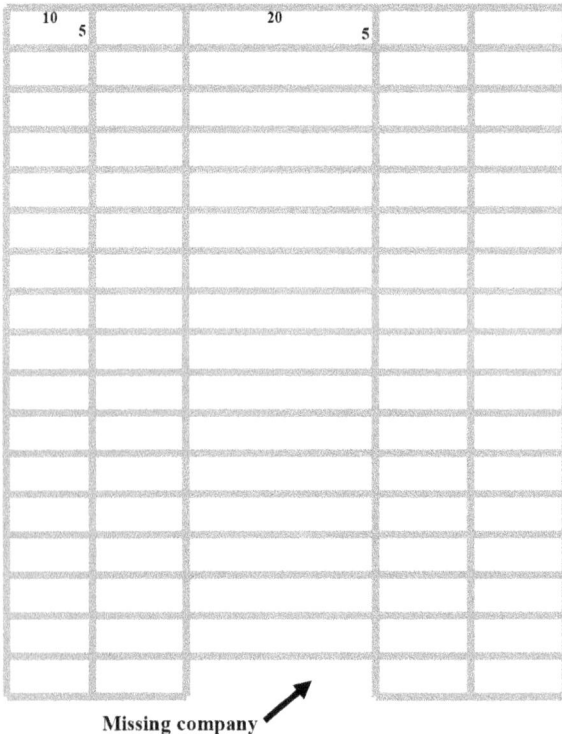

Missing company

As shown on the figure, the pattern involves seven frontmost (rightmost) companies of 50 for a total of seven frontmost companies, which agrees with the number seven of initial loaves. The number of columns of menfolk furnishing leftovers is 7 x 5 = 35, which, at 5 loaves per basket, yields 7 baskets.

There are 11 columns x 6 rows of companies of 50 and 14 columns x 1 row of companies of 50, producing 11 x 6 x 50 + 14 x 50 = 4000 menfolk exactly, which agrees with the number given in the Gospel accounts of that feeding event. The figure shows the removal of 3 companies of 50 from one group of companies, resulting in two perfect rectangles, one of 3850 menfolk and the other of 150 menfolk. As in the case of the feeding of the 5000, the resolution of imperfect rectangles into combinations of perfect rectangles associated with both cases will be addressed later.

It should be noted that the three additional companies of 50 could have been tacked onto the end of the rectangle of 3850 menfolk in a variety of ways that don't alter the arithmetic, including one in which four rows consisted of 11 columns and the remaining three rows consisted of 12 columns each.

Figure 5: Pattern for Jesus' Feeding of 4000

77 companies of 50 arranged in 11 columns of 7 rows, plus 3 additional companies of 50:

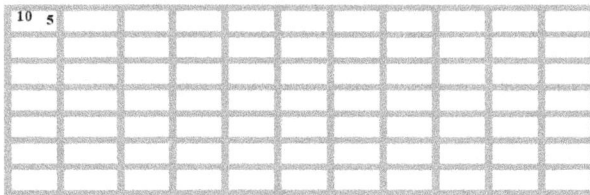

three additional companies of 50, not necessarily arranged as shown

To this point, patterns have been developed for Jesus' feedings of the 5000 and the 4000 menfolk that show precisely how 5000 menfolk can be fed with 5 loaves and yield 12 baskets of remainders, and 4000 menfolk can be fed with 7 loaves and yield 7 baskets of remainders. This information answers the questions that Jesus asked of His disciples in Mark 8, linking their response to their faith. The answer also reveals something of the incredible depth and accuracy of Scripture.

But there's more to the story of the feedings. Jesus implied that while there was no sign to be given to the generation in which He came to earth, perhaps there might be one given to a future generation, maybe even ours. It is to the end of uncovering this sign that we proceed further, driven at first by our discomfort at the imperfection of the rectangles.

Elisha as a Precursor to Jesus in Feeding Many

As was the case with many other acts that Jesus performed, Jesus' feeding of the multitudes was not the first such incident to have occurred. God had permitted the prophet Elisha to prefigure Jesus in the feedings. The account is given in 2 Kings 4:

> And there came a man from Baalshalisha, and brought the man of God [Elisha] bread of the first fruits, twenty loaves of barley, and full ears of corn in its husk. And he said, Give unto the people, that they may eat. And his servant said, What, should I set this before a hundred men? He said again, Give the people, that they may eat; for thus saith the Lord, They shall eat, and shall have some left. So he set it before them, and they did eat, and left some, according to the word of the Lord.

The process described above is remarkably similar to the accounts of Jesus' feeding of the multitudes. In fact, the numbers involved point to a configuration of 20 x 5 men, which furnishes a prototype of the configuration of a company of 100 men as shown on Figure 1 above, and justifies the assumption made in the preceding discussion of Jesus' feedings that a company of 100 is arranged 20 x 5.

It does more than that. If Elisha's feeding of 100 is combined with Jesus' feeding of the 5000, it supplies the missing company of 100 for that account, creating in the combination a perfect rectangle of 5100 menfolk. This property, in turn, strongly suggests that all of the feeding incidents, including the feeding of the 4000, with its two perfect rectangles of 3850 and 150, may be combined in some meaningful way out of perfect rectangles.

Before that is attempted, there is another feeding incident to investigate.

Jesus' Feedings as Precursor Events to Peter's Feeding of 3000

In John 14:12, Jesus said:

> *Verily, verily, I say unto you, He that believeth on me, the works that I do shall he do also; and greater works than these shall he do, because I go unto my Father.*

It was noted earlier that the primary significance of Jesus' feedings was regarding His Word rather than physical bread. Peter may not have fed multitudes with bread, but he certainly did so with the Word of God. Furthermore, in doing so, he was simply obeying the commandment of Jesus as recorded in John 21. When, in John 21, Jesus commands Peter to "Feed my sheep", and repeats this command three times, can one fail to see some prophetic significance to His words? The first fulfillment of that command is given in Acts 2:41:

> *Then they that gladly received [Peter's] word were baptized; and the same day there were added unto them about three thousand souls.*

Figure 6 on the next page shows an arrangement that satisfies the feeding of three thousand people with the Word of God. It consists of three columns of companies of 100 stacked 10 rows deep to yield three thousand people. Note that the total width of this pattern exactly matches the width of the pattern associated with Jesus' feeding of the five thousand men. This feature further suggests that all the figures associated with the four feeding events can be integrated into a composite figure.

The Integration of the Four Feeding Events into a Composite Figure

The four feeding events produce the five rectangular objects shown in Figure 7. As shown in the figure, four of the five objects are perfect rectangles, while the one associated with Jesus' feeding of the 5000, is not. However, this very imperfection in that one object urges the observer to dovetail Elisha's feeding of 100 into the larger object of Jesus' feeding of the 5000, making it a perfect rectangle.

461

This development, in turn, encourages the observer to combine all the objects into a single composite figure.

Figure 6: Pattern for Peter's Feeding of 3000 With the Word of God

30 companies of 100 arranged in 3 columns of 10 rows:

If the four feeding events are combined into a composite while preserving the vertical orientation of Jesus' feeding of the 5000 (combined with Elisha's feeding of 100) and Peter's feeding of the 3000, and the horizontal orientation of Jesus' feeding of the 4000, the following two alternate figures (Figures 8 and 9) result:

Figure 7: Five Elements of the Feeding Events

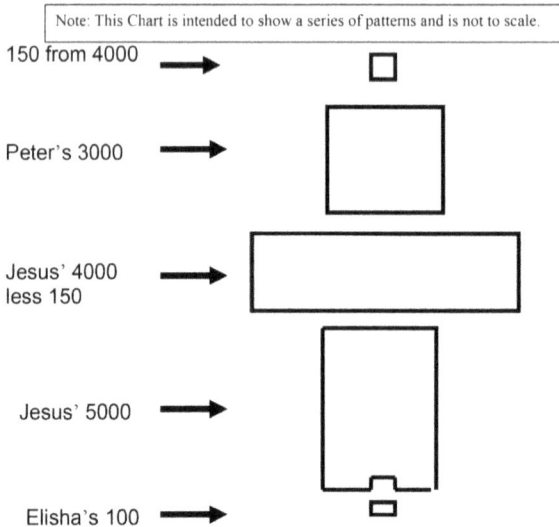

Figure 8: Composite of Four Feeding Events

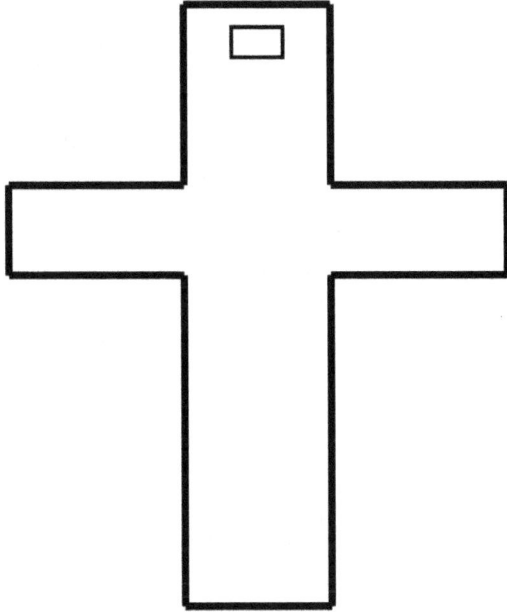

Figure 9: Alternate Rearrangement of
Composite Figure into Tau Cross

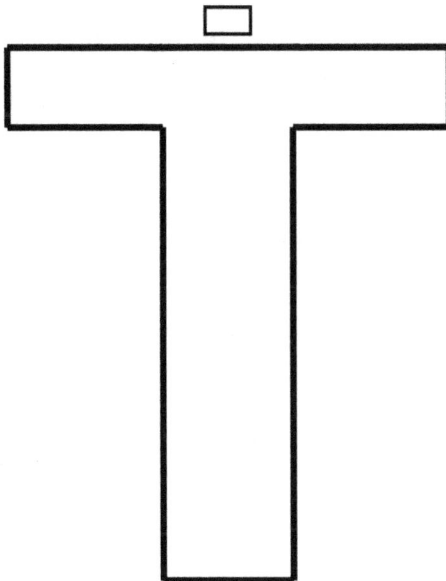

These figures are self-explanatory. They represent a sign indeed, but one which wasn't available until Scripture was completed. The proportions shown on the figure reflect a 2:1 ratio for individuals in the sitting position, as noted in Scripture. As shown in the figures, the three companies of 50 that were left over from the perfect rectangle of 3850 in Jesus' feeding of the 4000 represent the Titulus, the inscription placed on the cross which, interestingly, was presented in three languages according to Luke 23:38.

It is fascinating to note that if indeed Jesus' cross had been a Tau cross, as was commonly used by Romans at the time of Christ, then the simple rearrangement of the composite pattern, as shown on the latter figure, would furnish the associated representation. (See, for example, the article entitled "On the Physical Death of Jesus Christ" by William D. Edwards, MD, et al in the March 21, 1986 issue of JAMA.) For that period of time, the crosspiece (patibulum) was usually 5 to 6 feet in length, and the vertical post (stipes) was 6 to 8 feet in height. The average length ratio of patibulum to stipes for these ranges is (5/8+1)/2, or about 0.8 (.814). The length ratio of these members as shown in the figure above is nearly identical to this average, being approximately 0.8 (.8125).

A Word About the Baskets of Leftover Loaves

The assumption was made in the mathematical analysis and in the above development that each basket of leftover loaves contained the same number of loaves for both the feeding of the 5000 and the 4000.

This was probably not the case, as the original Scripture notes that the baskets used for the feeding of the 5000 was a small handbasket, for which 5 loaves would be appropriate, while the baskets used for collecting the remainder loaves in the feeding of the 4000 was a larger basket. It was for that reason that the development above was careful in attributing the 5 loaves per basket to the menfolk only.

In actuality, there were women and children in addition to the menfolk in both feeding events. According to Mark 7:31 the four thousand were fed near Decapolis on the south shore of the Sea of Galilee, while, according to Luke 9:10, the five thousand were fed near Bethsaida on the north shore, the implication being that the four thousand were mostly Gentile, while the five thousand were primarily Jewish. Further weight is given to this difference by the fact that the seven baskets of the four thousand correspond to the seven representative Churches that Jesus addressed in Revelation 1:20, while the twelve baskets of the five thousand match the twelve tribes of Israel."

The makeup of the audience is relevant to the size of the baskets in that the practice of the Jewish faith is patriarchal in nature, with the menfolk almost exclusively being involved in the ceremonial ritual. Also, the faith was exclusive in another sense, being restricted to Jews. Given the symbolic nature of the feedings, then, the sizes of the baskets, which represented the growth of the faith, were exceedingly important. The Jewish women and children were certainly fed along with the men, but it was the menfolk to whom the Word of God was primarily directed, it being their responsibility to interpret and direct this Word to their womenfolk. This changed radically with the birth of the Church at the Pentecost following Jesus' resurrection. For the first time, women and even children were to be directly involved in the spread of the Christian faith. This difference is borne out in Acts 2:16 - 18, wherein the Christian women as well as the men not only were involved in the gift of the indwelling Holy Spirit, but were expected to actively use that gift:

But this is that which was spoken through the prophet, Joel: And it shall come to pass in the last days, saith God, I will pour out my Spirit upon all flesh; and your sons and your daughters shall prophesy, and your young men shall see visions, and your old men shall dream dreams; and on my servants and on my handmaidens I will pour out in those days of my Spirit, and they shall prophesy: . . .

The bottom line is that the menfolk of both the four and the five thousand contributed five loaves to each basket. But the women and children of the Gentile four thousand added their share into the baskets of remainders, while only the menfolk of the five thousand contributed to their baskets of remainders.

www.ingramcontent.com/pod-product-compliance
Lightning Source LLC
Chambersburg PA
CBHW071402090426
42737CB00011B/1312